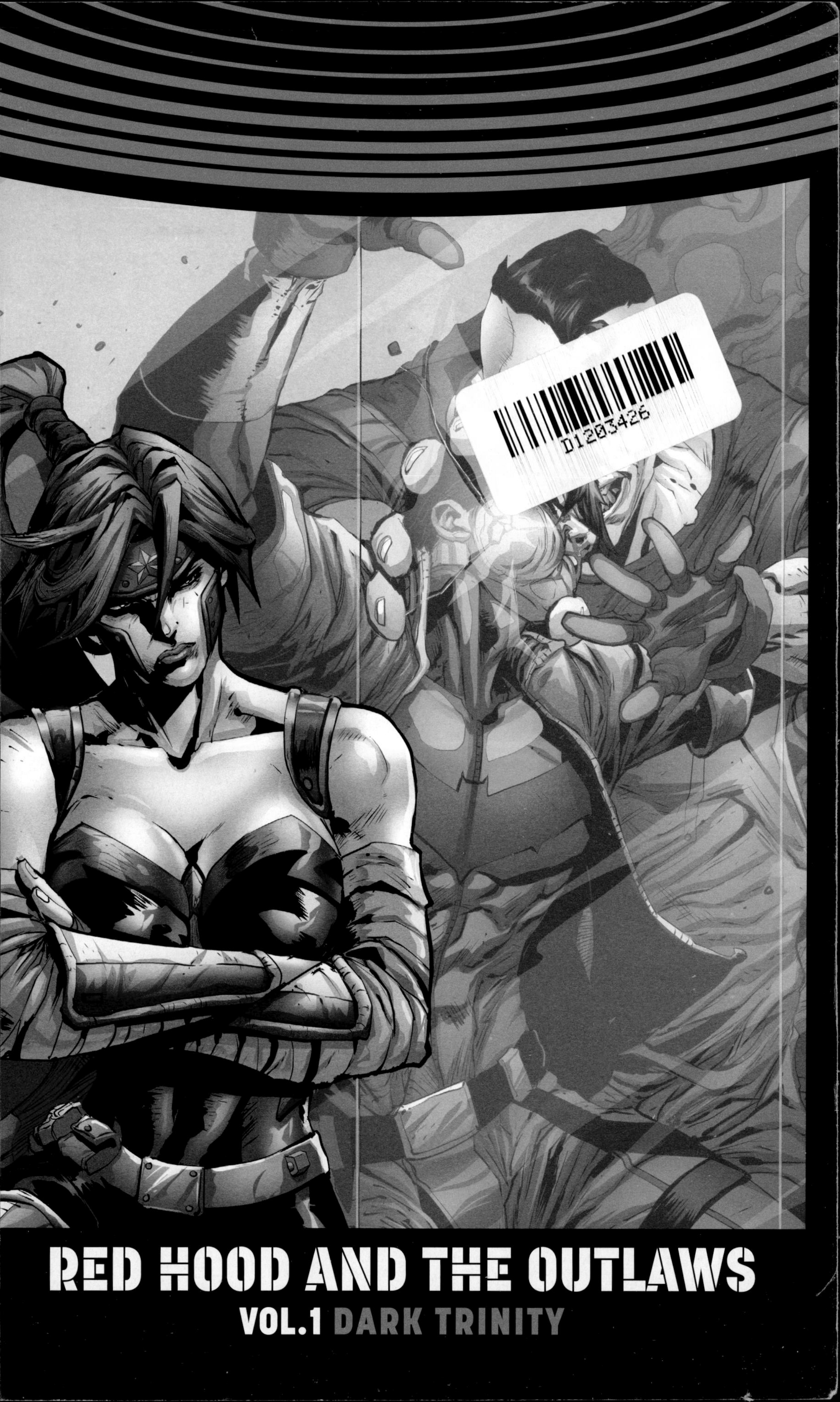

RED HOOD AND THE OUTLAWS

VOL.1 DARK TRINITY

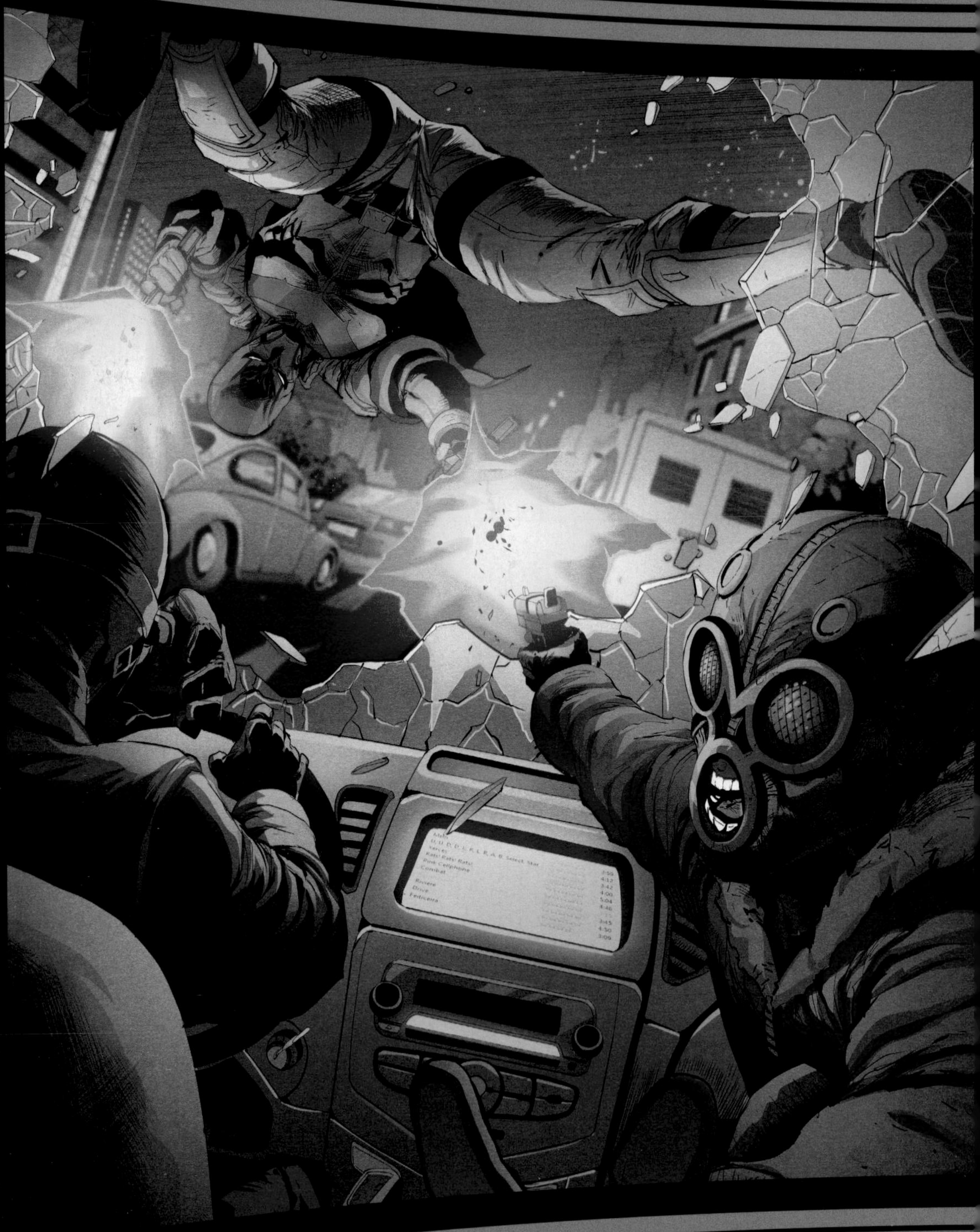

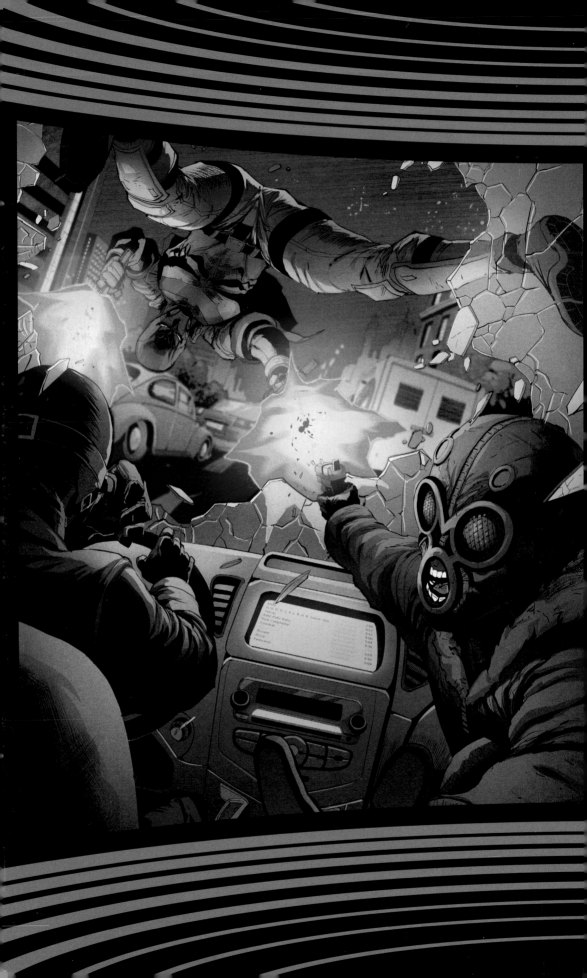

RED HOOD AND THE OUTLAWS
VOL.1 DARK TRINITY

SCOTT LOBDELL
writer

DEXTER SOY
artist

VERONICA GANDINI
colorist

TAYLOR ESPOSITO
letterer

GIUSEPPE CAMUNCOLI with CAM SMITH & DEAN WHITE
series and collection cover artists

SUPERMAN created by Jerry Siegel and Joe Shuster
By special arrangement with the Jerry Siegel family

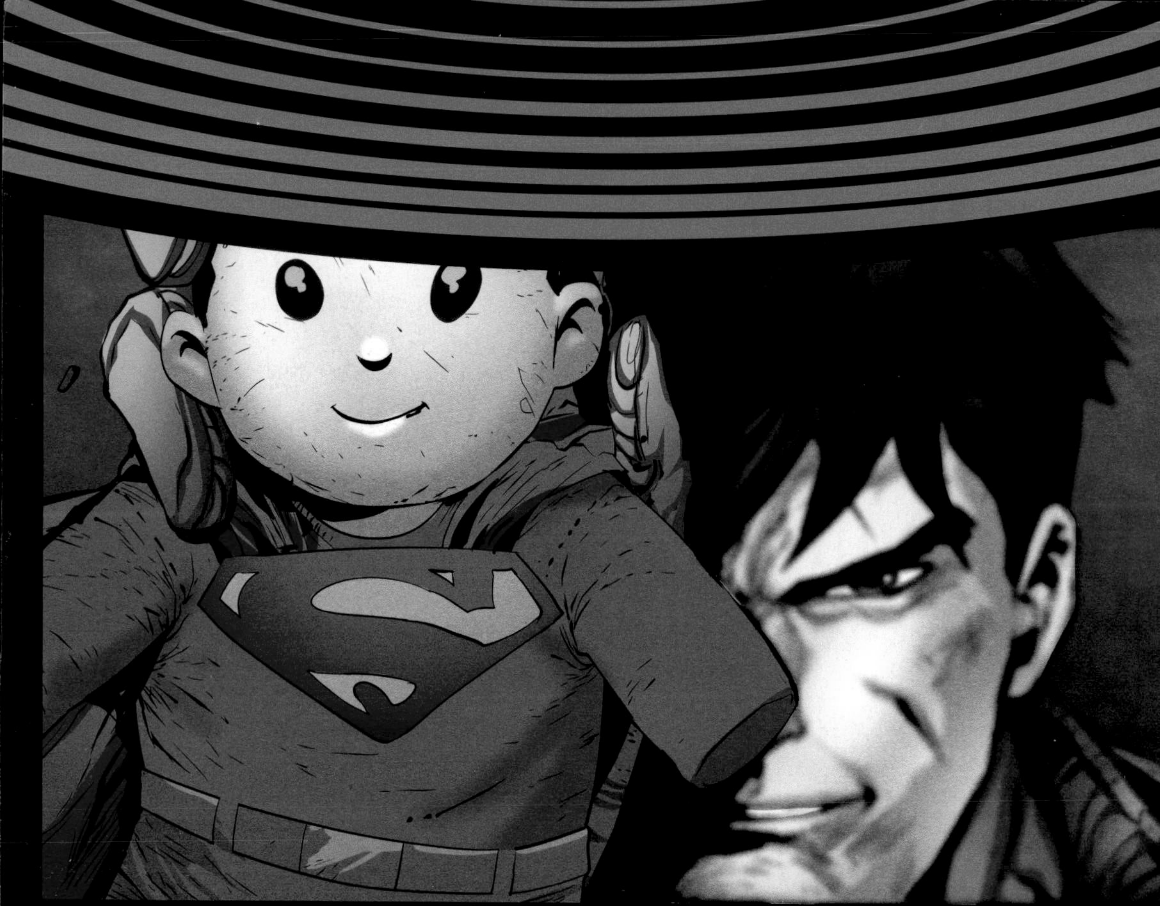

ALEX ANTONE Editor - Original Series * **BRITTANY HOLZHERR** Assistant Editor - Original Series
JEB WOODARD Group Editor - Collected Editions * **LIZ ERICKSON** Editor - Collected Edition
STEVE COOK Design Director - Books * **MONIQUE GRUSPE** Publication Design

BOB HARRAS Senior VP - Editor-in-Chief, DC Comics

DIANE NELSON President * **DAN DiDIO** Publisher * **JIM LEE** Publisher * **GEOFF JOHNS** President & Chief Creative Officer
AMIT DESAI Executive VP - Business & Marketing Strategy, Direct to Consumer & Global Franchise Management * **SAM ADES** Senior VP - Direct to Consumer
BOBBIE CHASE VP - Talent Development * **MARK CHIARELLO** Senior VP - Art, Design & Collected Editions
JOHN CUNNINGHAM Senior VP - Sales & Trade Marketing * **ANNE DePIES** Senior VP - Business Strategy, Finance & Administration
DON FALLETTI VP - Manufacturing Operations * **LAWRENCE GANEM** VP - Editorial Administration & Talent Relations
ALISON GILL Senior VP - Manufacturing & Operations * **HANK KANALZ** Senior VP - Editorial Strategy & Administration
JAY KOGAN VP - Legal Affairs * **THOMAS LOFTUS** VP - Business Affairs
JACK MAHAN VP - Business Affairs * **NICK J. NAPOLITANO** VP - Manufacturing Administration
EDDIE SCANNELL VP - Consumer Marketing * **COURTNEY SIMMONS** Senior VP - Publicity & Communications
JIM (SKI) SOKOLOWSKI VP - Comic Book Specialty Sales & Trade Marketing * **NANCY SPEARS** VP - Mass, Book, Digital Sales & Trade Marketing

RED HOOD AND THE OUTLAWS VOL. 1: DARK TRINITY

DC Comics, 2900 West Alameda Ave., Burbank, CA 91505. Printed by LSC Communications, Salem, VA, USA. 3/24/17.
First Printing. ISBN: 978-1-4012-6875-6

Library of Congress Cataloging-in-Publication Data is available.

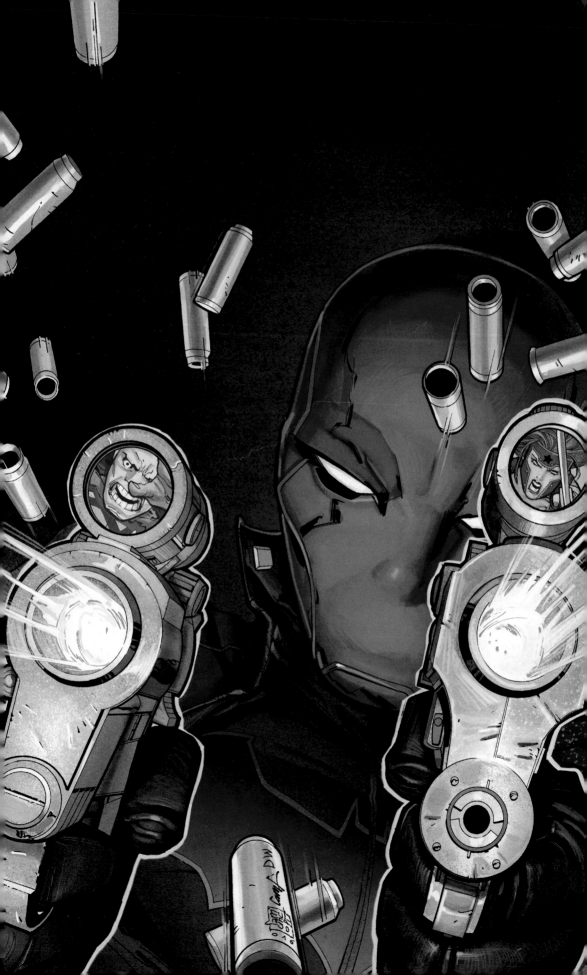

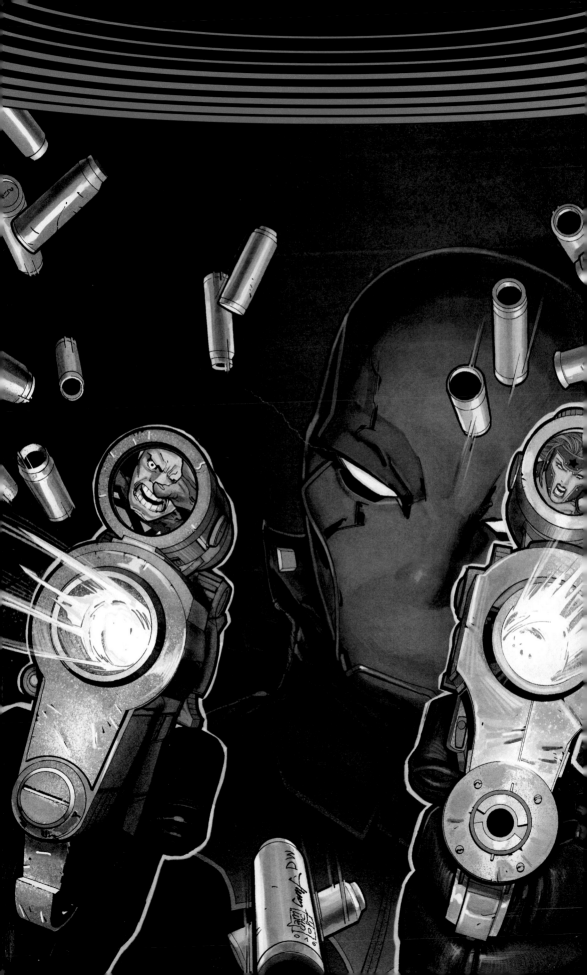

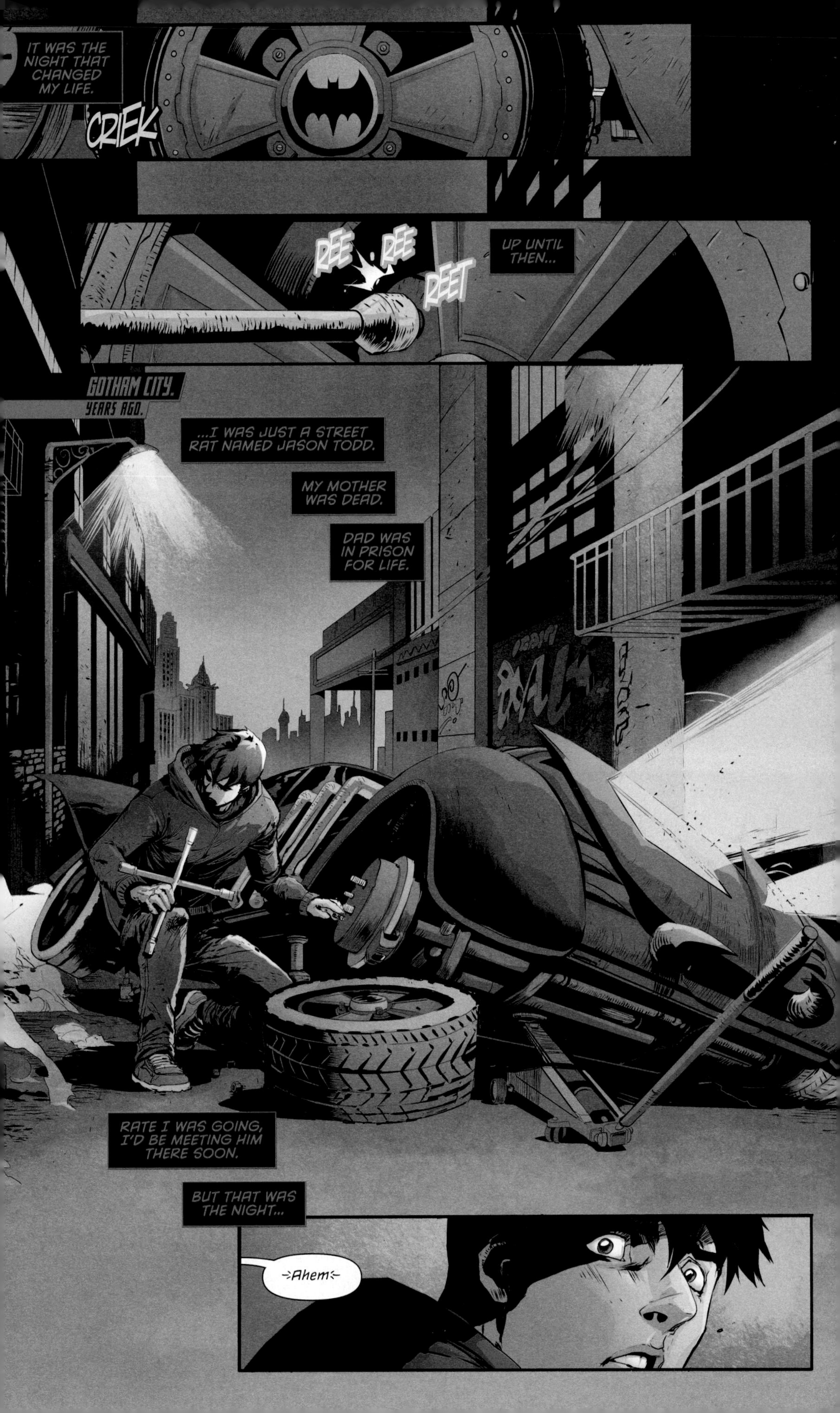

IT WAS THE NIGHT THAT CHANGED MY LIFE.
CRIEK
REE REE REET
UP UNTIL THEN...
GOTHAM CITY.
YEARS AGO.
...I WAS JUST A STREET RAT NAMED JASON TODD.
MY MOTHER WAS DEAD.
DAD WAS IN PRISON FOR LIFE.
RATE I WAS GOING, I'D BE MEETING HIM THERE SOON.
BUT THAT WAS THE NIGHT...
Ahem

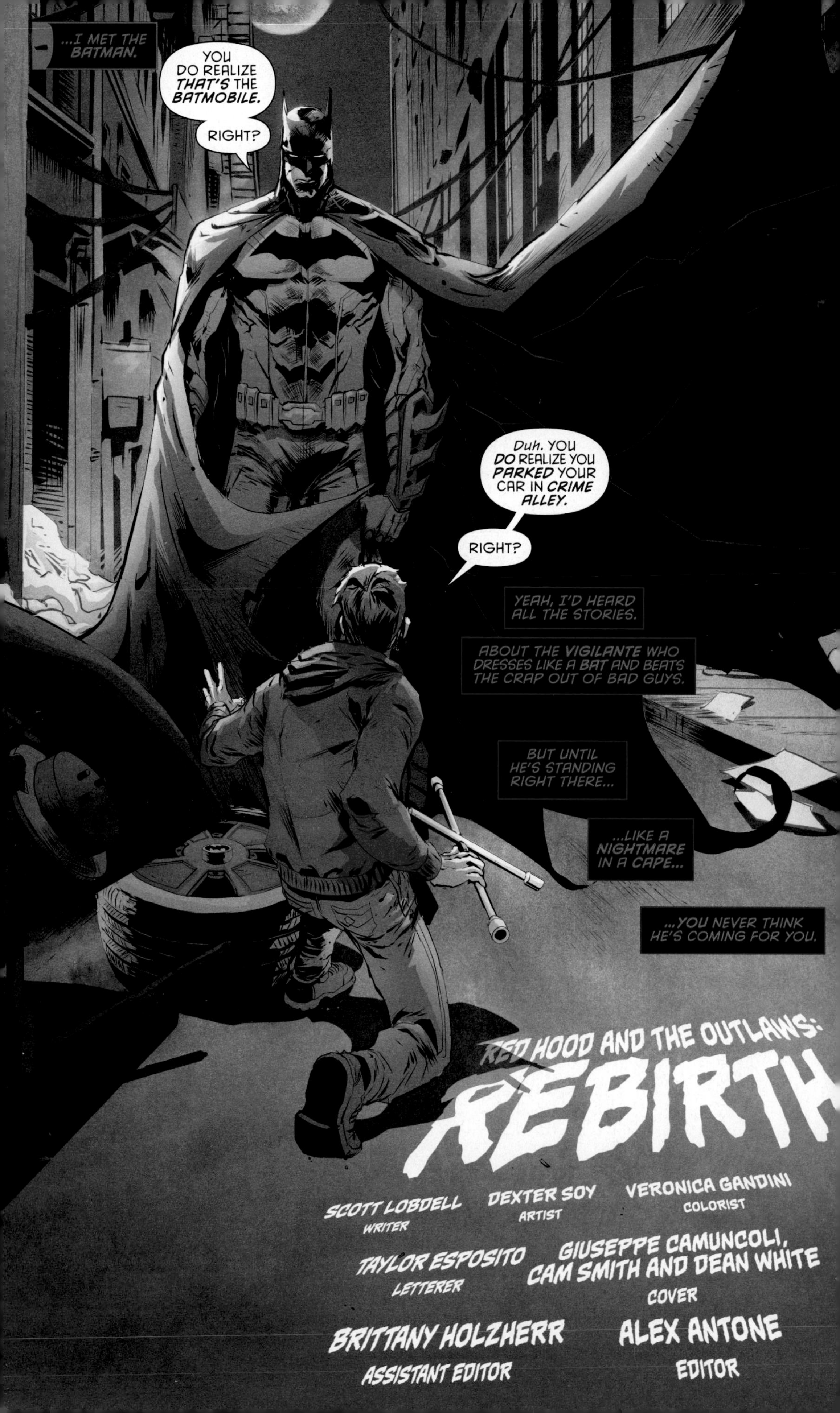
...I MET THE BATMAN.
YOU DO REALIZE THAT'S THE BATMOBILE.
RIGHT?
Duh. YOU DO REALIZE YOU PARKED YOUR CAR IN CRIME ALLEY.
RIGHT?
YEAH, I'D HEARD ALL THE STORIES.
ABOUT THE VIGILANTE WHO DRESSES LIKE A BAT AND BEATS THE CRAP OUT OF BAD GUYS.
BUT UNTIL HE'S STANDING RIGHT THERE...
...LIKE A NIGHTMARE IN A CAPE...
...YOU NEVER THINK HE'S COMING FOR YOU.
RED HOOD AND THE OUTLAWS: REBIRTH
SCOTT LOBDELL WRITER
DEXTER SOY ARTIST
VERONICA GANDINI COLORIST
TAYLOR ESPOSITO LETTERER
GIUSEPPE CAMUNCOLI, CAM SMITH AND DEAN WHITE COVER
BRITTANY HOLZHERR ASSISTANT EDITOR
ALEX ANTONE EDITOR

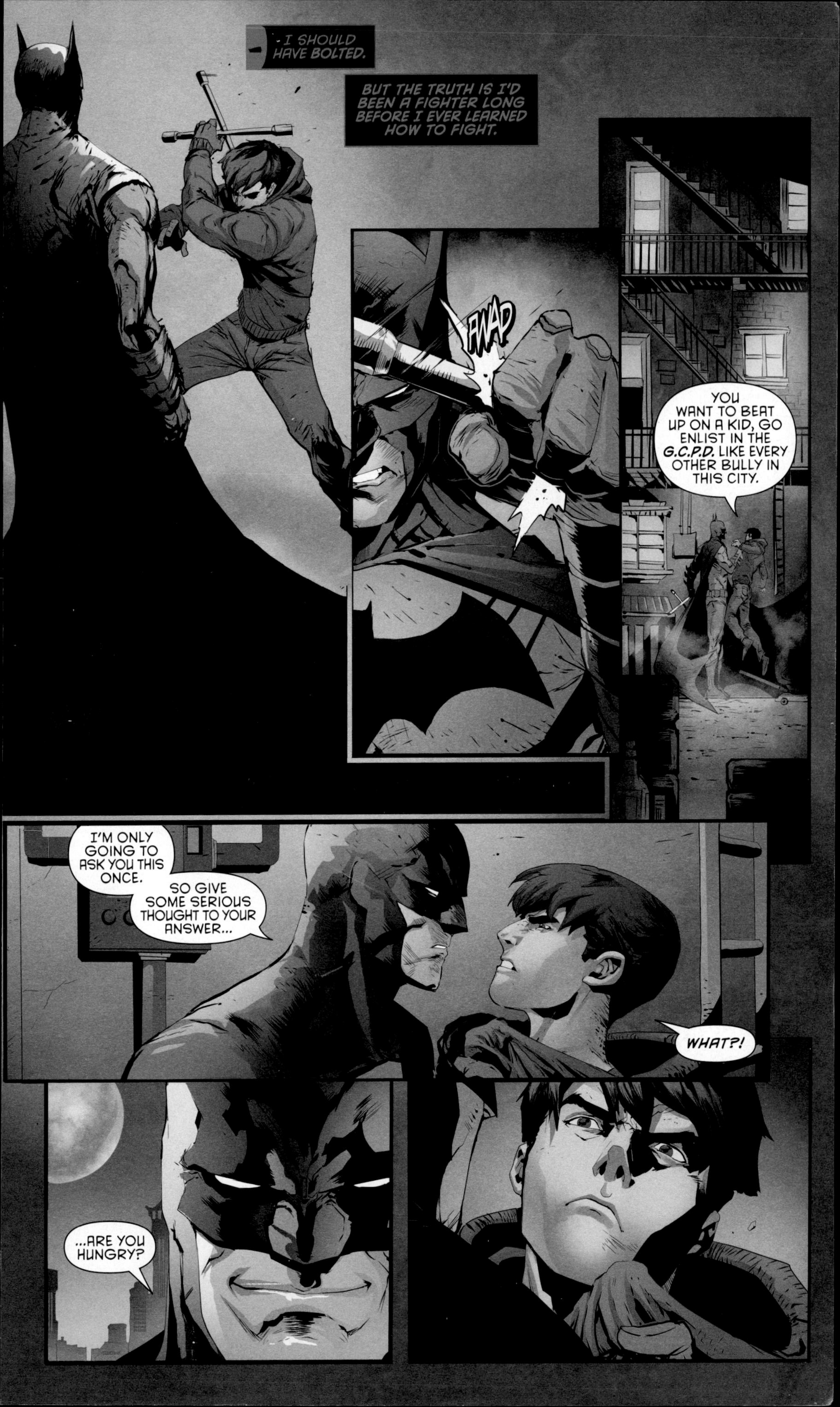
-I SHOULD HAVE BOLTED.
BUT THE TRUTH IS I'D BEEN A FIGHTER LONG BEFORE I EVER LEARNED HOW TO FIGHT.
FWAP
YOU WANT TO BEAT UP ON A KID, GO ENLIST IN THE G.C.P.D. LIKE EVERY OTHER BULLY IN THIS CITY.
I'M ONLY GOING TO ASK YOU THIS ONCE.
SO GIVE SOME SERIOUS THOUGHT TO YOUR ANSWER...
WHAT?!
...ARE YOU HUNGRY?

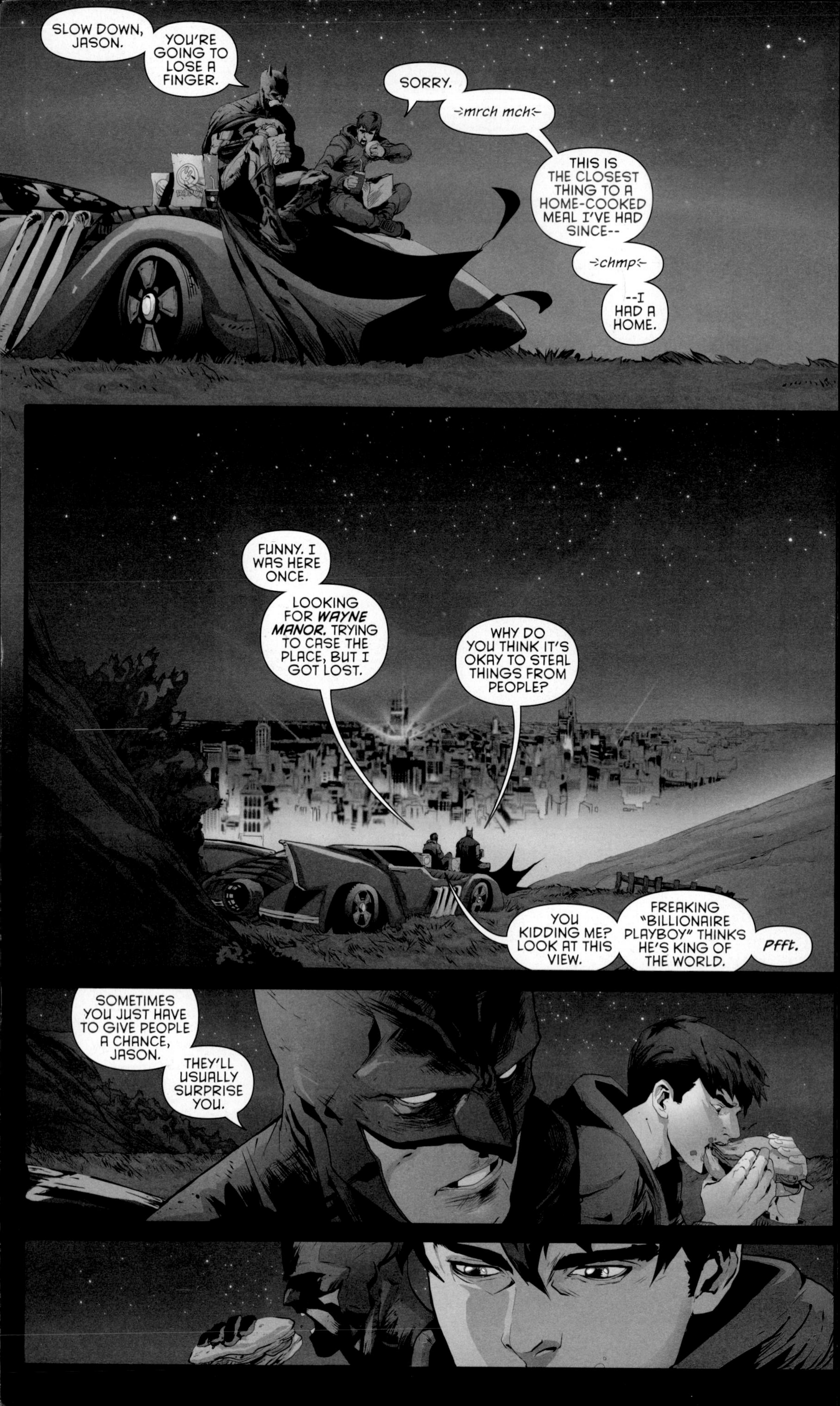

SLOW DOWN, JASON.
YOU'RE GOING TO LOSE A FINGER.
SORRY.
mrch mch
THIS IS THE CLOSEST THING TO A HOME-COOKED MEAL I'VE HAD SINCE--
chmp
--I HAD A HOME.
FUNNY. I WAS HERE ONCE.
LOOKING FOR WAYNE MANOR. TRYING TO CASE THE PLACE, BUT I GOT LOST.
WHY DO YOU THINK IT'S OKAY TO STEAL THINGS FROM PEOPLE?
YOU KIDDING ME? LOOK AT THIS VIEW.
FREAKING "BILLIONAIRE PLAYBOY" THINKS HE'S KING OF THE WORLD.
Pfft.
SOMETIMES YOU JUST HAVE TO GIVE PEOPLE A CHANCE, JASON.
THEY'LL USUALLY SURPRISE YOU.

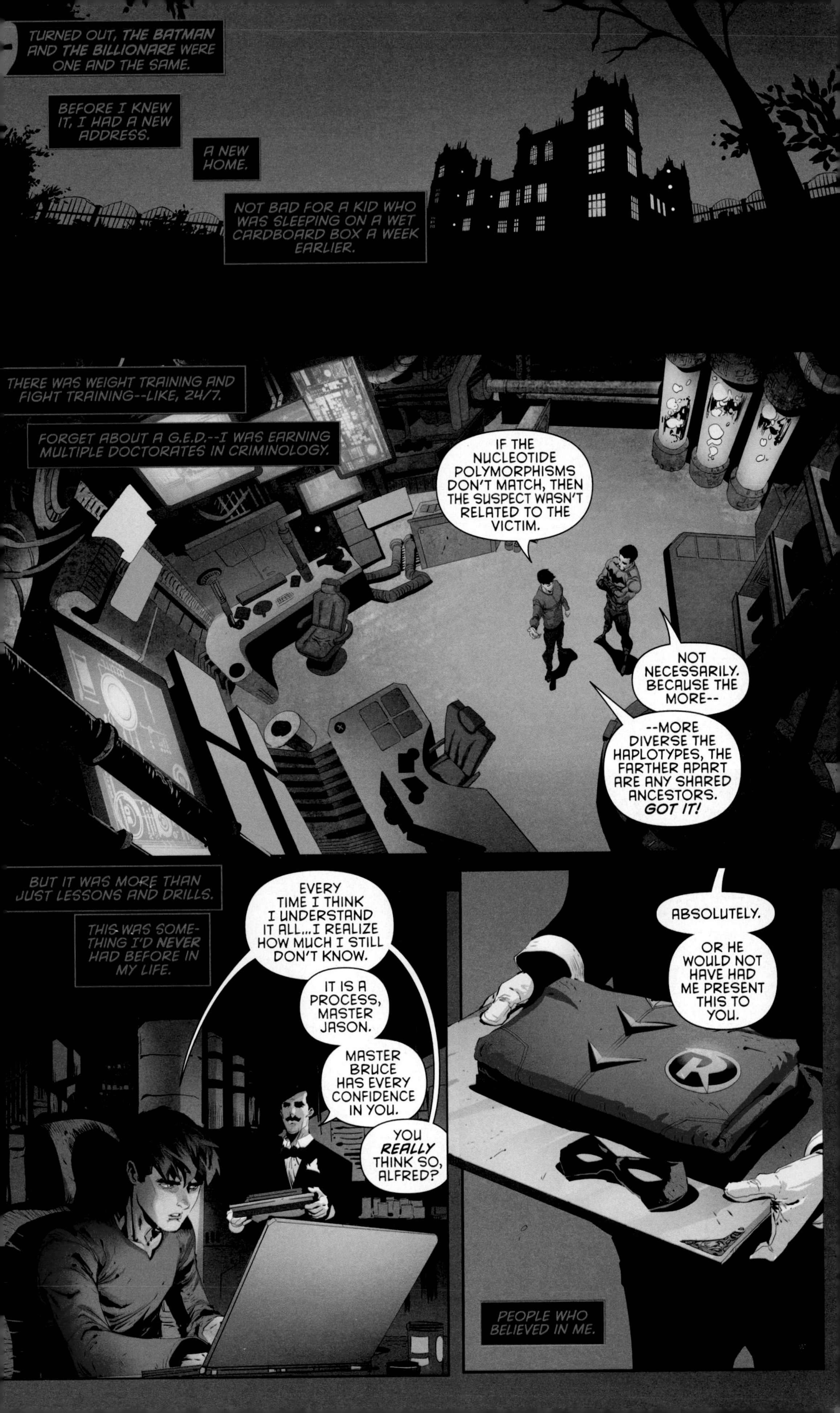
TURNED OUT, THE BATMAN AND THE BILLIONAIRE WERE ONE AND THE SAME.
BEFORE I KNEW IT, I HAD A NEW ADDRESS.
A NEW HOME.
NOT BAD FOR A KID WHO WAS SLEEPING ON A WET CARDBOARD BOX A WEEK EARLIER.
THERE WAS WEIGHT TRAINING AND FIGHT TRAINING--LIKE, 24/7.
FORGET ABOUT A G.E.D.--I WAS EARNING MULTIPLE DOCTORATES IN CRIMINOLOGY.
IF THE NUCLEOTIDE POLYMORPHISMS DON'T MATCH, THEN THE SUSPECT WASN'T RELATED TO THE VICTIM.
NOT NECESSARILY. BECAUSE THE MORE--
--MORE DIVERSE THE HAPLOTYPES, THE FARTHER APART ARE ANY SHARED ANCESTORS. GOT IT!
BUT IT WAS MORE THAN JUST LESSONS AND DRILLS.
THIS WAS SOMETHING I'D NEVER HAD BEFORE IN MY LIFE.
EVERY TIME I THINK I UNDERSTAND IT ALL...I REALIZE HOW MUCH I STILL DON'T KNOW.
IT IS A PROCESS, MASTER JASON.
MASTER BRUCE HAS EVERY CONFIDENCE IN YOU.
YOU REALLY THINK SO, ALFRED?
ABSOLUTELY.
OR HE WOULD NOT HAVE HAD ME PRESENT THIS TO YOU.
PEOPLE WHO BELIEVED IN ME.

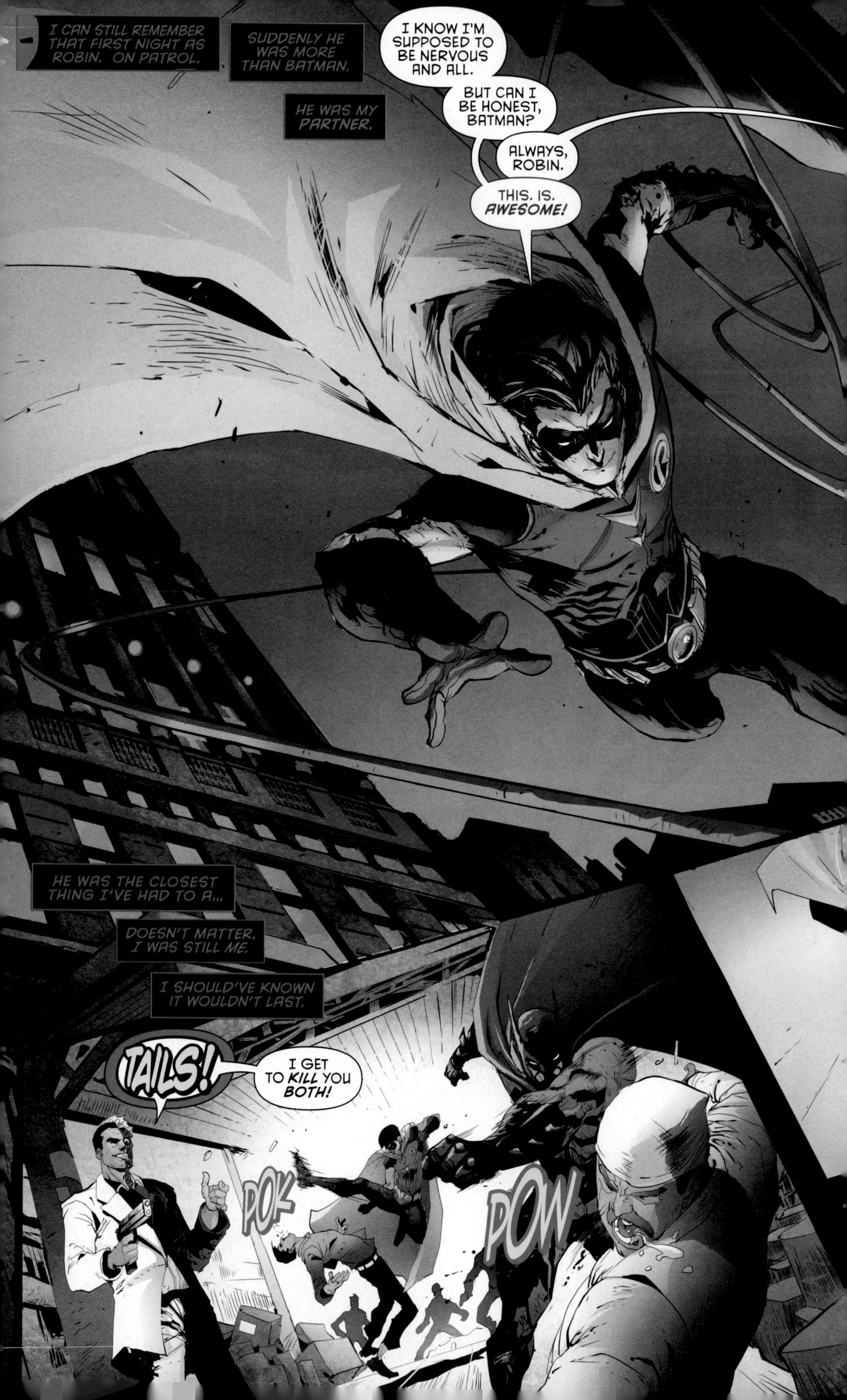

I CAN STILL REMEMBER THAT FIRST NIGHT AS ROBIN. ON PATROL.
SUDDENLY HE WAS MORE THAN BATMAN.
HE WAS MY PARTNER.
I KNOW I'M SUPPOSED TO BE NERVOUS AND ALL.
BUT CAN I BE HONEST, BATMAN?
ALWAYS, ROBIN.
THIS. IS. AWESOME!
HE WAS THE CLOSEST THING I'VE HAD TO A...
DOESN'T MATTER. I WAS STILL ME.
I SHOULD'VE KNOWN IT WOULDN'T LAST.
TAILS!
I GET TO KILL YOU BOTH!
POK
POW

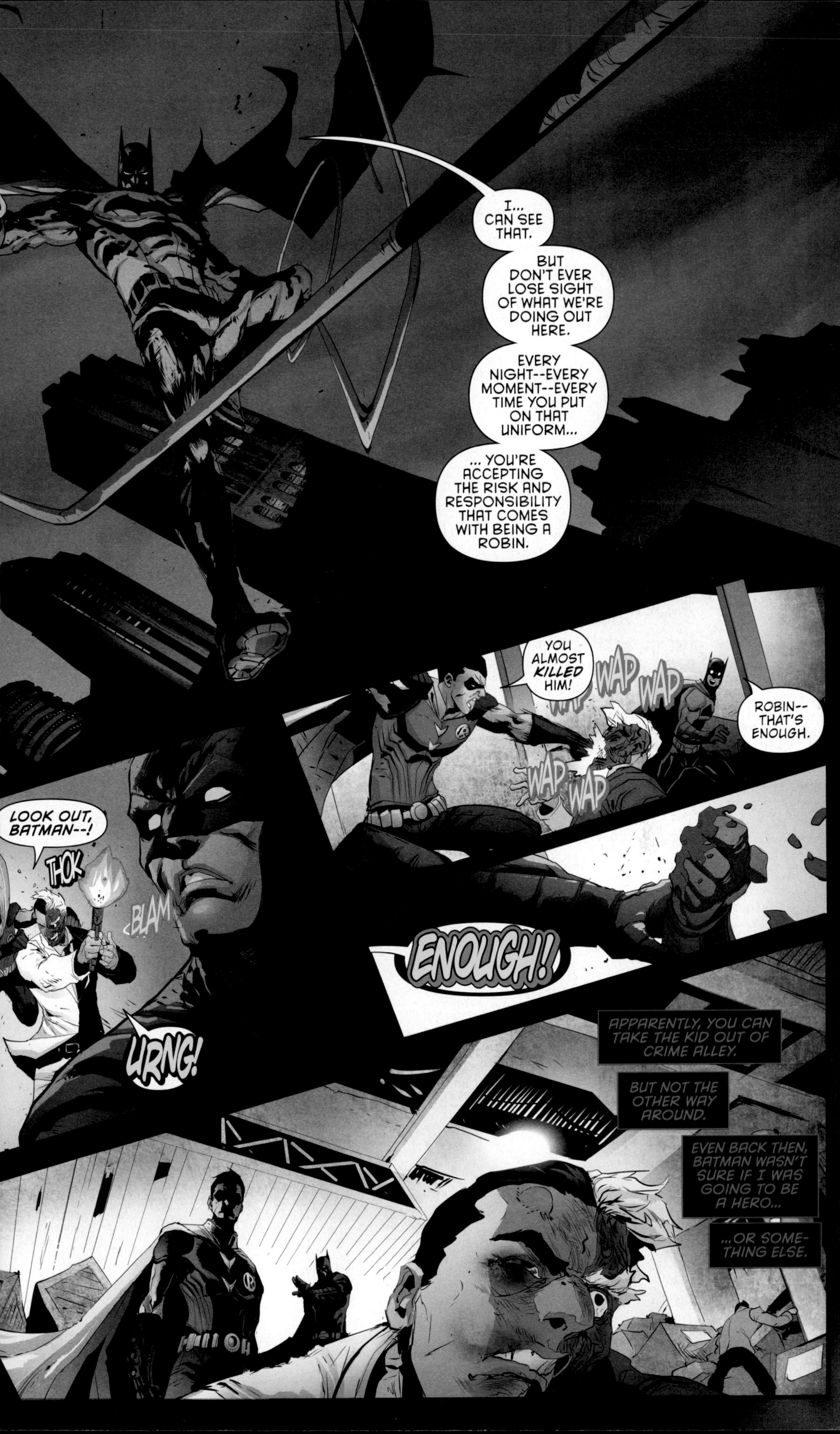
I... CAN SEE THAT.
BUT DON'T EVER LOSE SIGHT OF WHAT WE'RE DOING OUT HERE.
EVERY NIGHT--EVERY MOMENT--EVERY TIME YOU PUT ON THAT UNIFORM...
... YOU'RE ACCEPTING THE RISK AND RESPONSIBILITY THAT COMES WITH BEING A ROBIN.
YOU ALMOST *KILLED* HIM!
WAP
WAP
WAP
WAP
ROBIN-- THAT'S ENOUGH.
LOOK OUT, BATMAN--!
THOK
BLAM
ENOUGH!
URNG!
APPARENTLY, YOU CAN TAKE THE KID OUT OF CRIME ALLEY.
BUT NOT THE OTHER WAY AROUND.
EVEN BACK THEN, BATMAN WASN'T SURE IF I WAS GOING TO BE A HERO...
...OR SOMETHING ELSE.

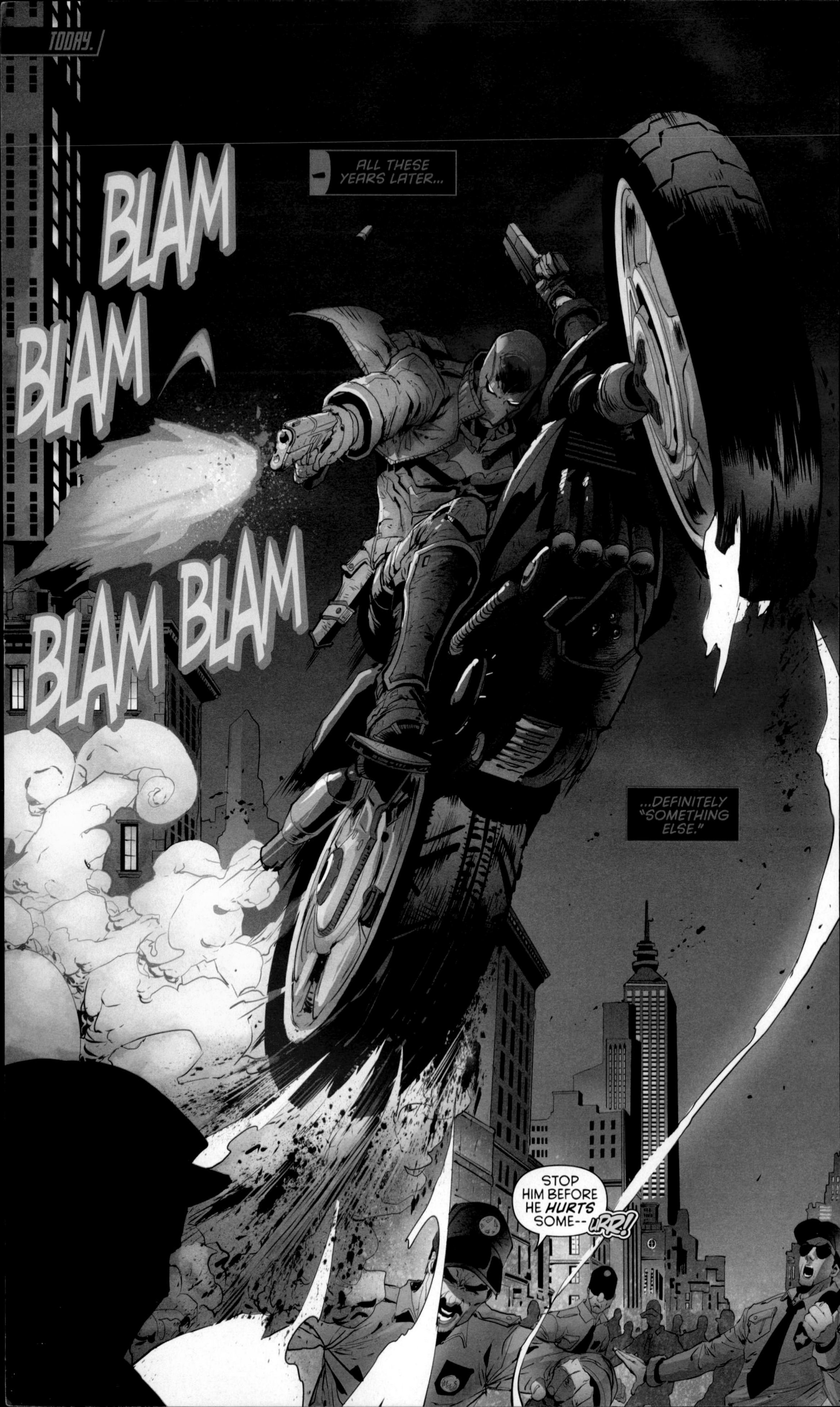
TODAY.
ALL THESE YEARS LATER...
BLAM
BLAM
BLAM BLAM
...DEFINITELY "SOMETHING ELSE."
STOP HIM BEFORE HE HURTS SOME--URR!

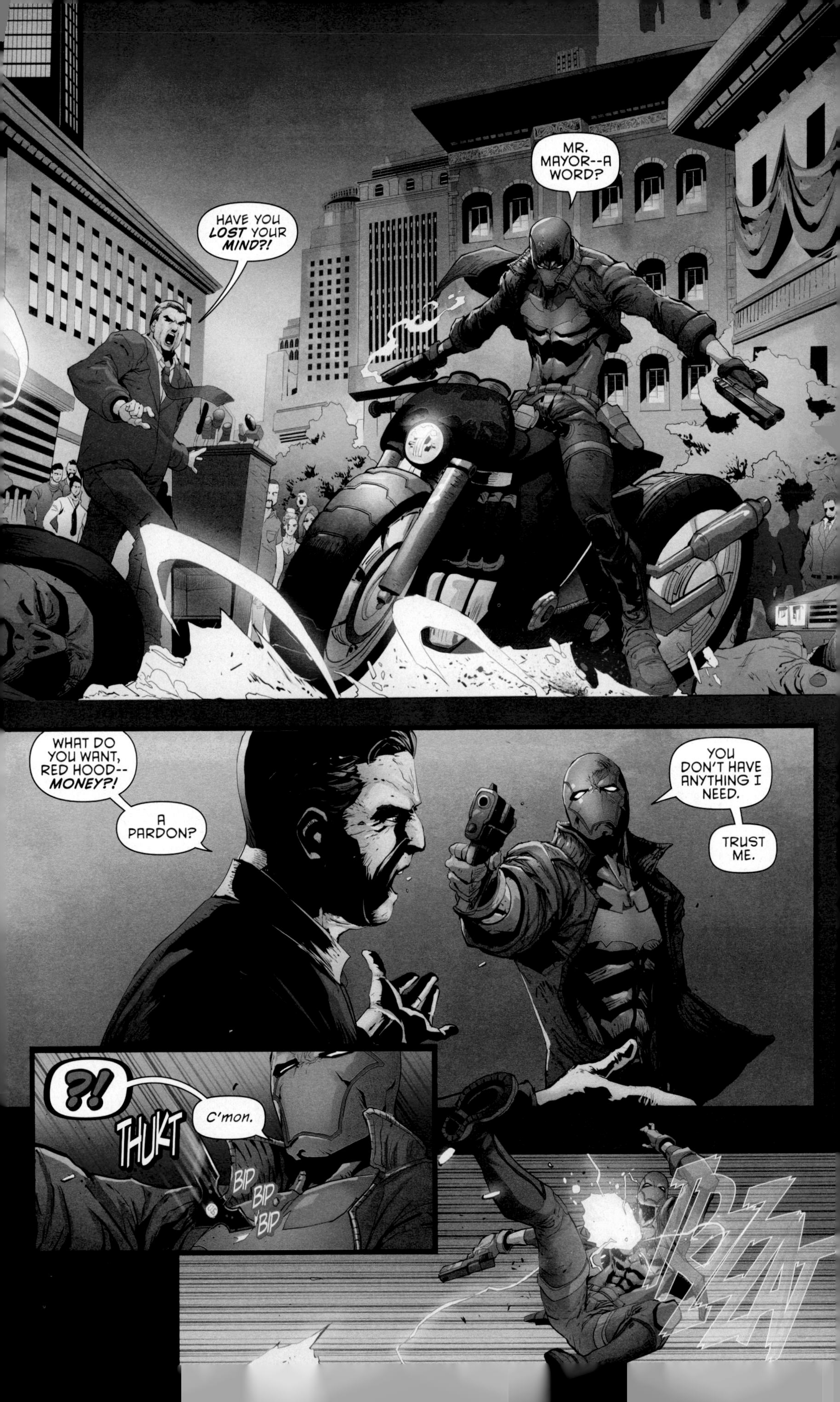
HAVE YOU *LOST* YOUR *MIND?!*
MR. MAYOR--A WORD?
WHAT DO YOU WANT, RED HOOD-- *MONEY?!*
A PARDON?
YOU DON'T HAVE ANYTHING I NEED.
TRUST ME.
?!
THUKT
C'mon.
BIP BIP BIP
BZZAT

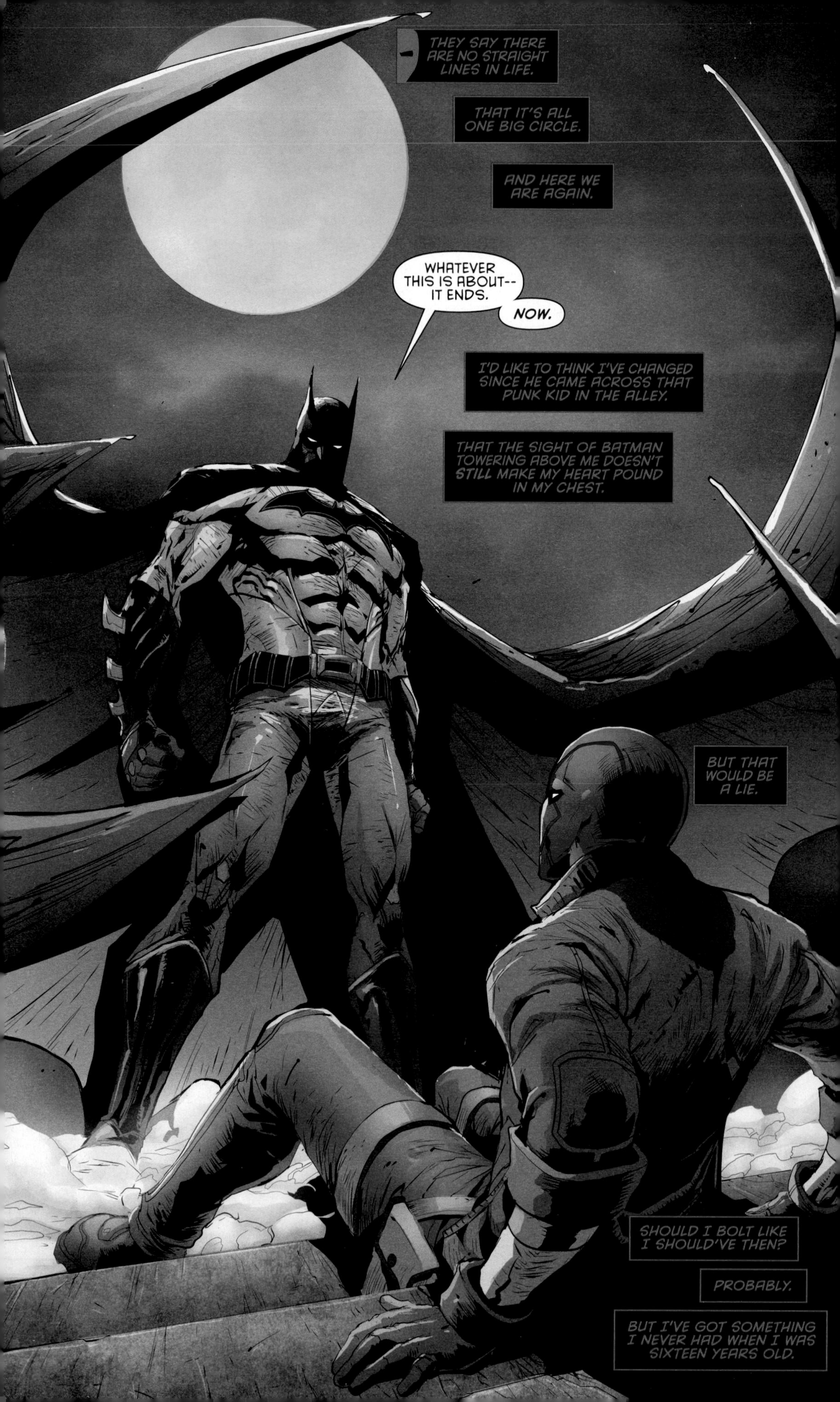
THEY SAY THERE ARE NO STRAIGHT LINES IN LIFE.
THAT IT'S ALL ONE BIG CIRCLE.
AND HERE WE ARE AGAIN.
WHATEVER THIS IS ABOUT-- IT ENDS.
NOW.
I'D LIKE TO THINK I'VE CHANGED SINCE HE CAME ACROSS THAT PUNK KID IN THE ALLEY.
THAT THE SIGHT OF BATMAN TOWERING ABOVE ME DOESN'T STILL MAKE MY HEART POUND IN MY CHEST.
BUT THAT WOULD BE A LIE.
SHOULD I BOLT LIKE I SHOULD'VE THEN?
PROBABLY.
BUT I'VE GOT SOMETHING I NEVER HAD WHEN I WAS SIXTEEN YEARS OLD.

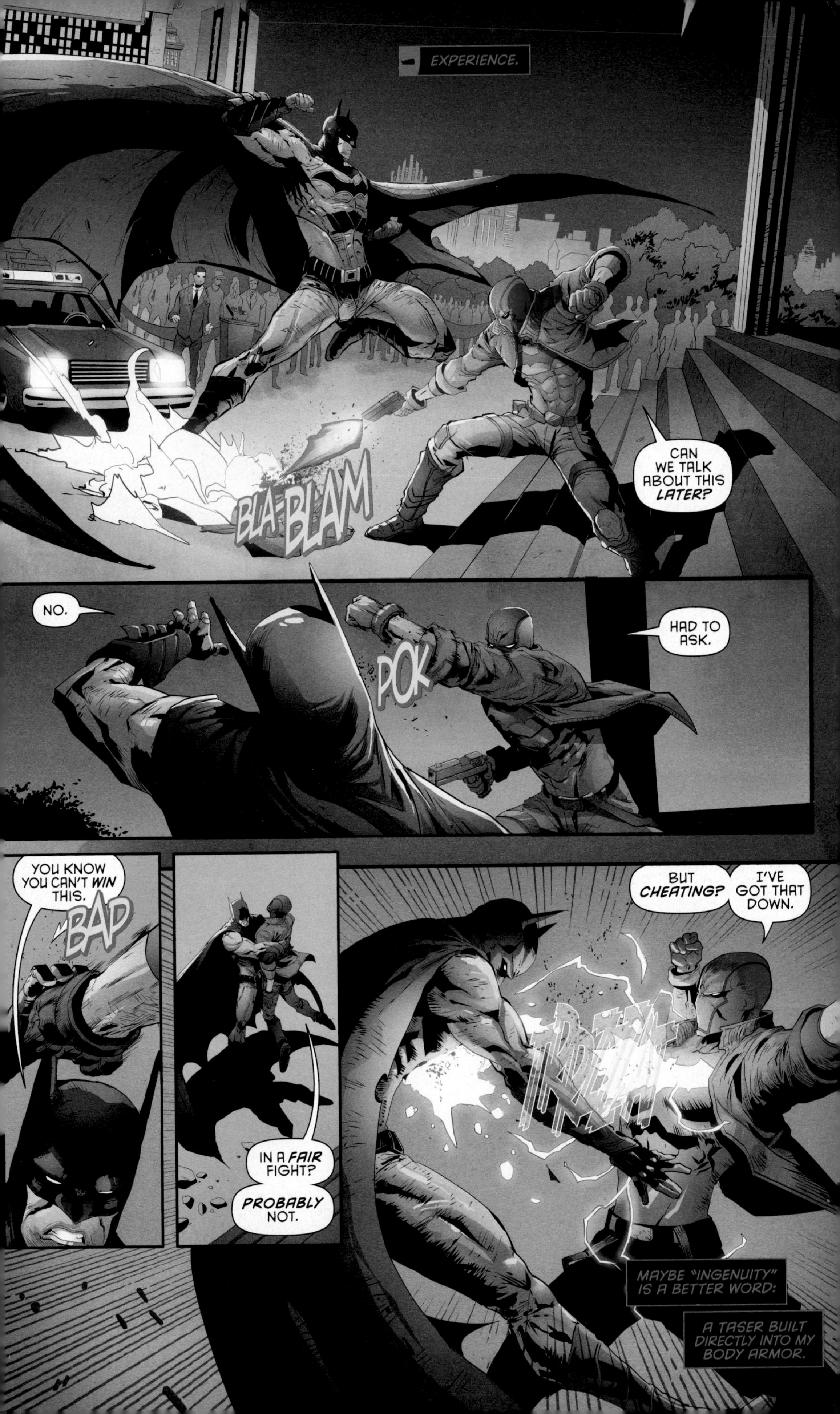

EXPERIENCE.
CAN WE TALK ABOUT THIS *LATER?*
BLA-BLAM
NO.
POK
HAD TO ASK.
YOU KNOW YOU CAN'T *WIN* THIS.
BAP
IN A *FAIR* FIGHT?
PROBABLY NOT.
BUT *CHEATING?*
I'VE GOT THAT DOWN.
MAYBE "INGENUITY" IS A BETTER WORD:
A TASER BUILT DIRECTLY INTO MY BODY ARMOR.

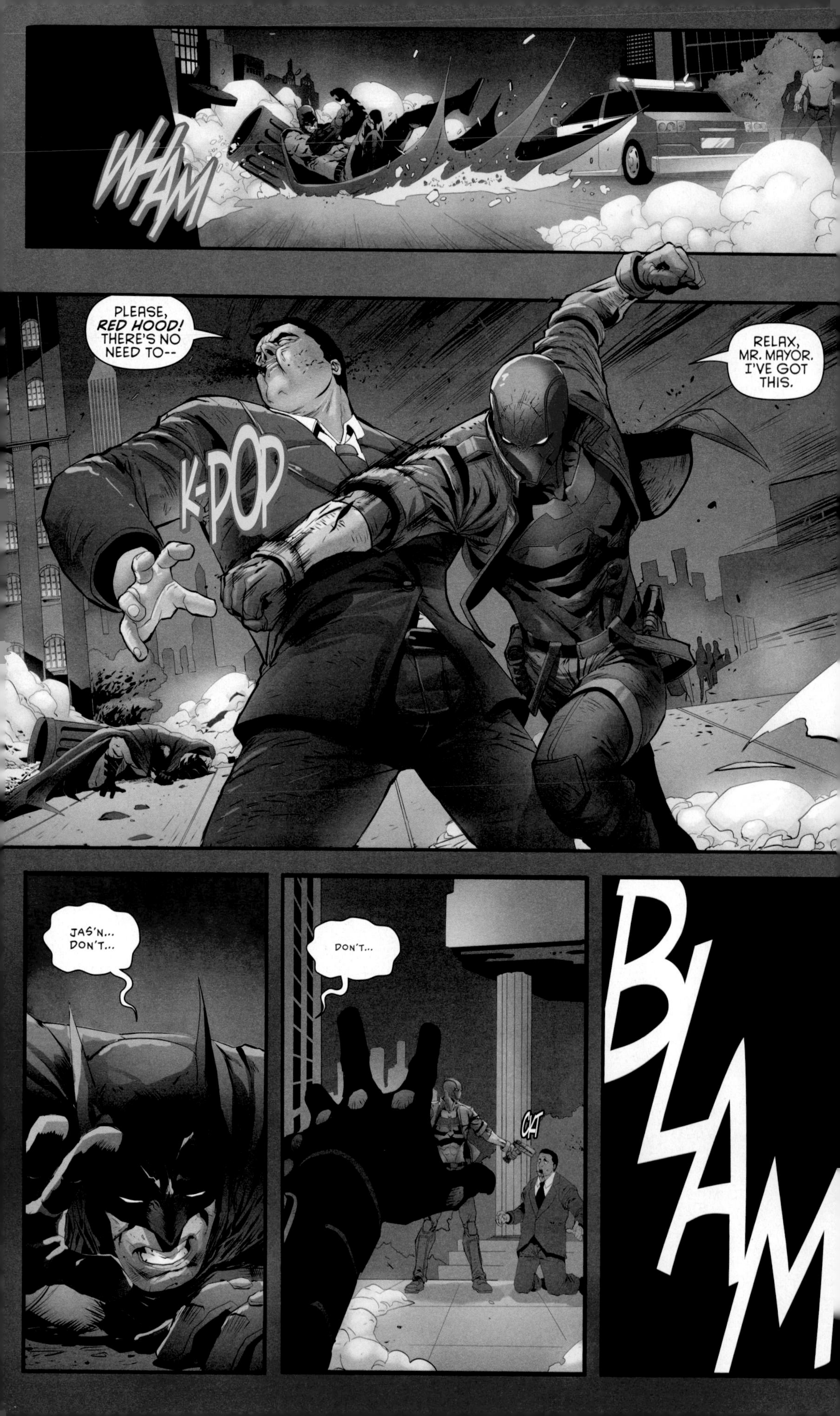

WHAM
PLEASE, RED HOOD! THERE'S NO NEED TO--
RELAX, MR. MAYOR. I'VE GOT THIS.
K-POP
JAS'N... DON'T...
DON'T...
CLAT
BLAM

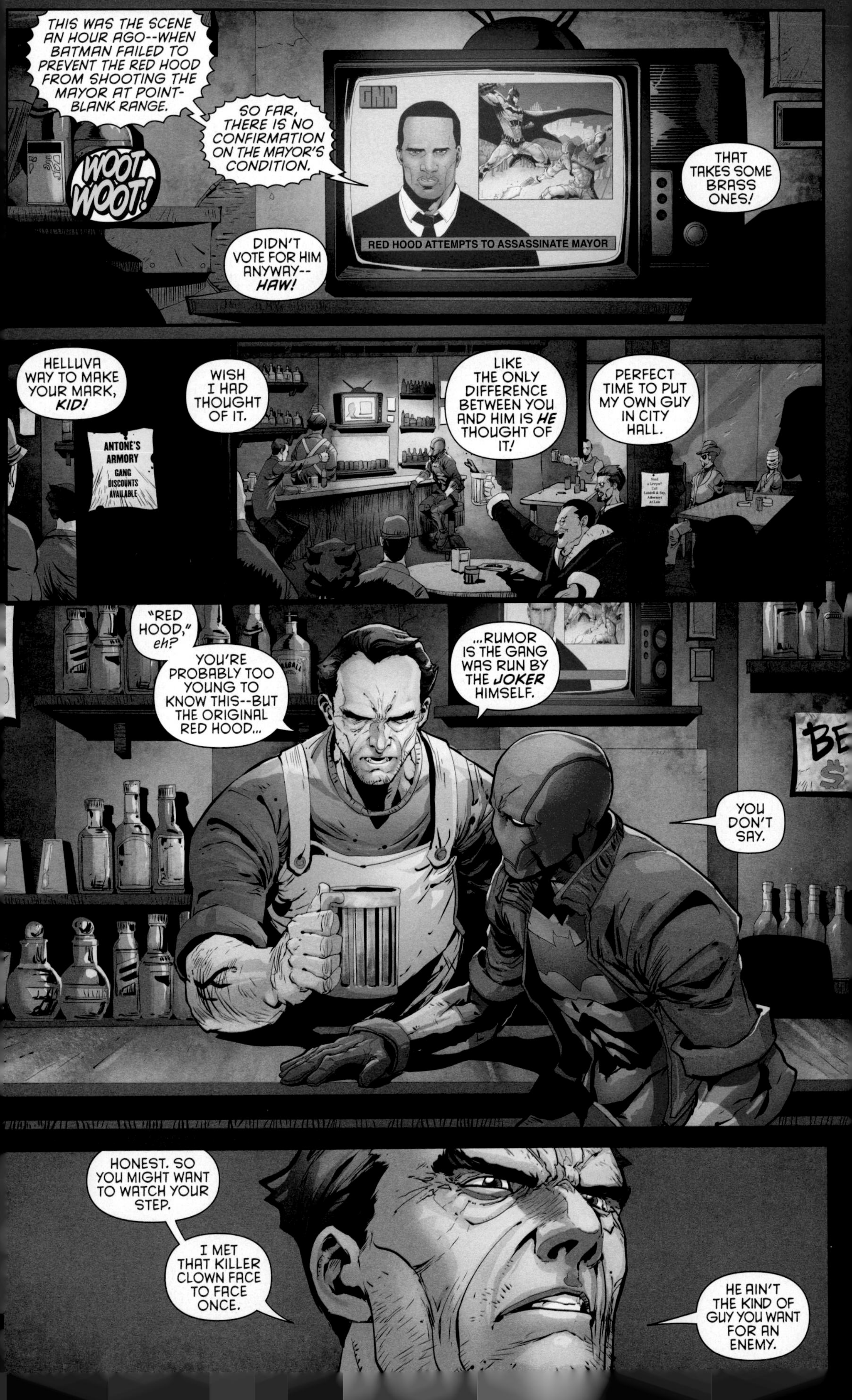
THIS WAS THE SCENE AN HOUR AGO--WHEN BATMAN FAILED TO PREVENT THE RED HOOD FROM SHOOTING THE MAYOR AT POINT-BLANK RANGE.
SO FAR, THERE IS NO CONFIRMATION ON THE MAYOR'S CONDITION.
GNN
RED HOOD ATTEMPTS TO ASSASSINATE MAYOR
WOOT WOOT!
DIDN'T VOTE FOR HIM ANYWAY--HAW!
THAT TAKES SOME BRASS ONES!
HELLUVA WAY TO MAKE YOUR MARK, KID!
ANTONE'S ARMORY GANG DISCOUNTS AVAILABLE
WISH I HAD THOUGHT OF IT.
LIKE THE ONLY DIFFERENCE BETWEEN YOU AND HIM IS HE THOUGHT OF IT!
PERFECT TIME TO PUT MY OWN GUY IN CITY HALL.
"RED HOOD," eh?
YOU'RE PROBABLY TOO YOUNG TO KNOW THIS--BUT THE ORIGINAL RED HOOD...
...RUMOR IS THE GANG WAS RUN BY THE JOKER HIMSELF.
YOU DON'T SAY.
HONEST. SO YOU MIGHT WANT TO WATCH YOUR STEP.
I MET THAT KILLER CLOWN FACE TO FACE ONCE.
HE AIN'T THE KIND OF GUY YOU WANT FOR AN ENEMY.

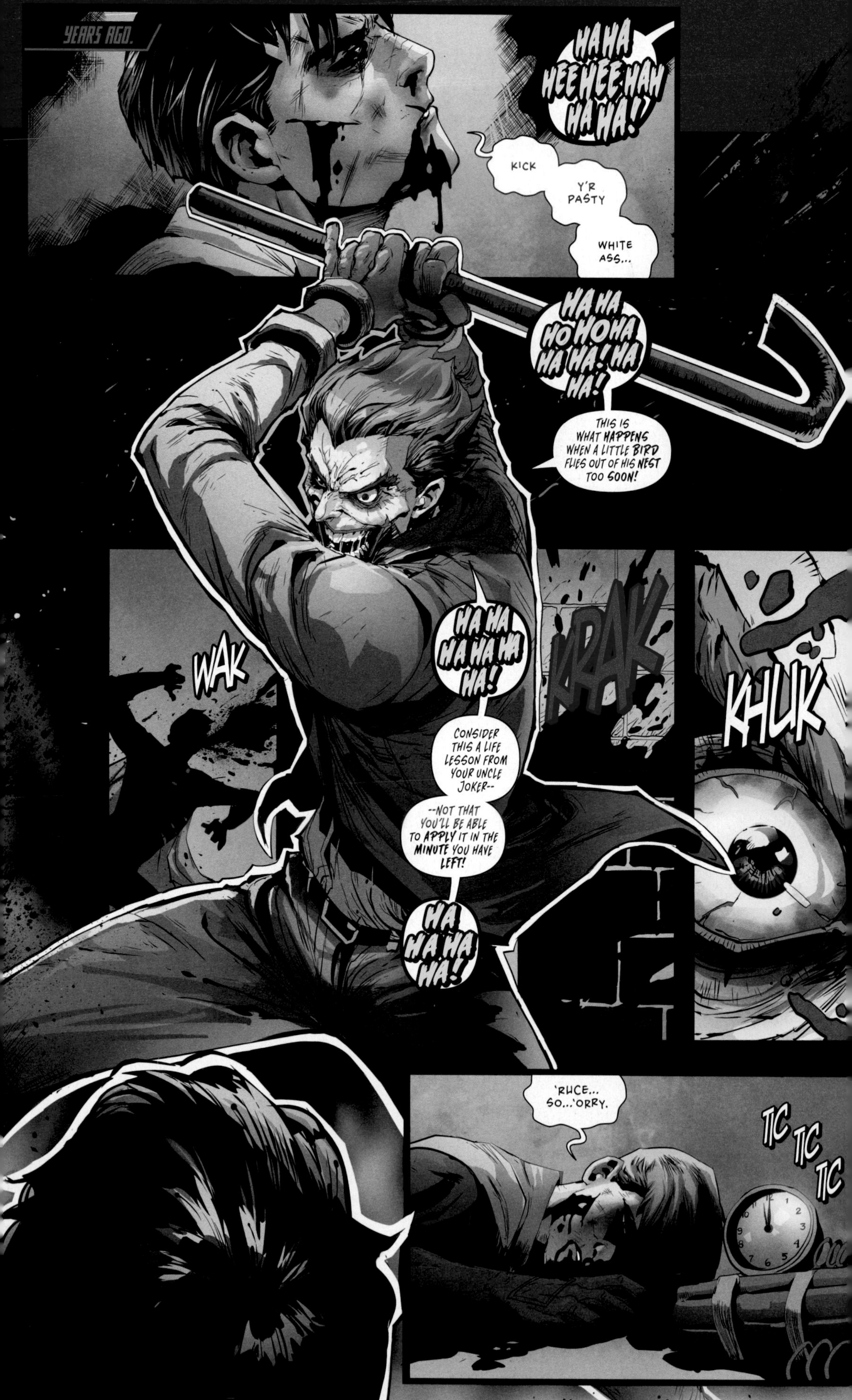
YEARS AGO.
HA HA HEE HEE HAH HA HA!
KICK
Y'R PASTY
WHITE ASS...
HA HA HO HO HA HA HA! HA HA!
THIS IS WHAT HAPPENS WHEN A LITTLE BIRD FLIES OUT OF HIS NEST TOO SOON!
WAK
HA HA HA HA HA HA!
KRAK
KHUK
CONSIDER THIS A LIFE LESSON FROM YOUR UNCLE JOKER--
--NOT THAT YOU'LL BE ABLE TO APPLY IT IN THE MINUTE YOU HAVE LEFT!
HA HA HA HA!
'RUCE... SO...'ORRY.
TIC TIC TIC

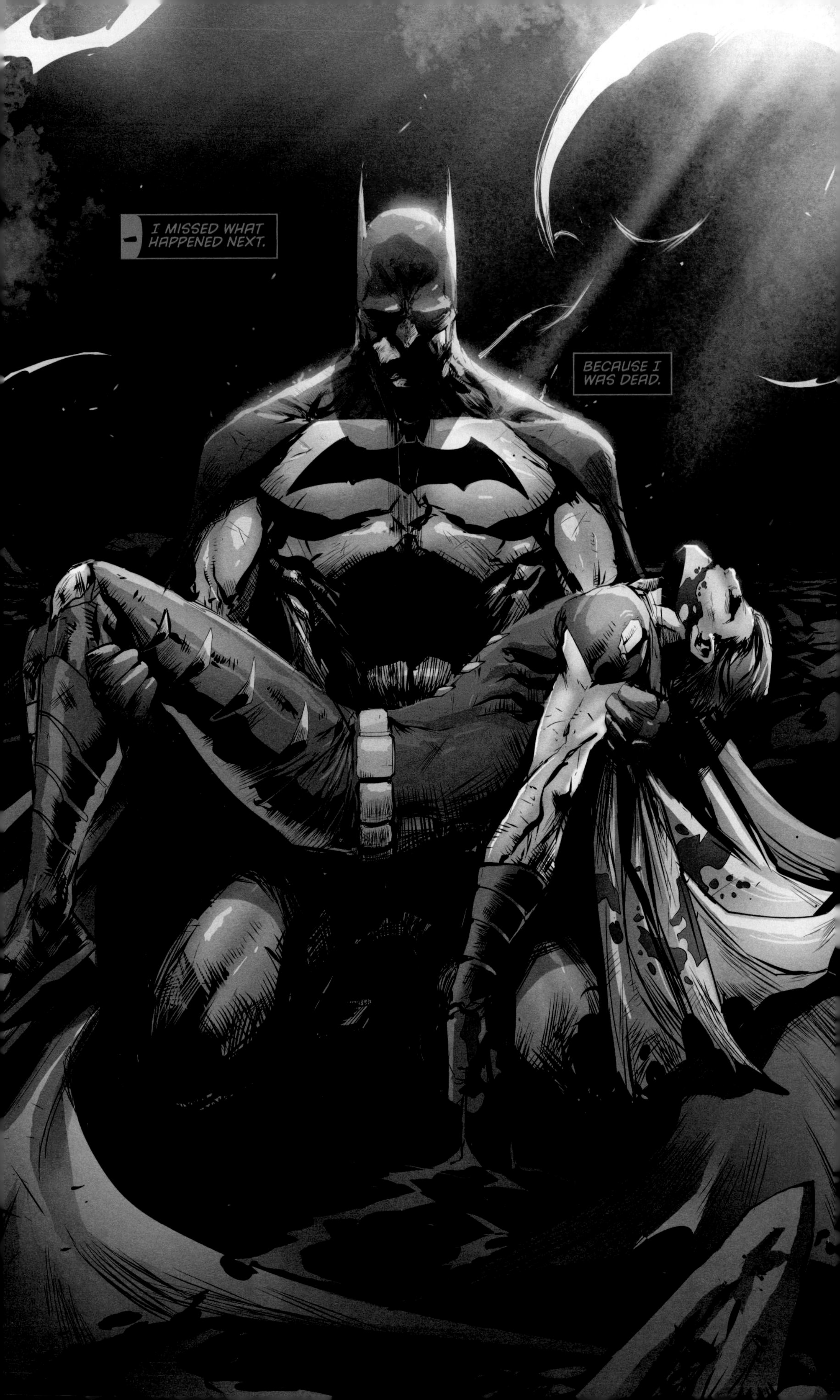
I MISSED WHAT HAPPENED NEXT.
BECAUSE I WAS DEAD.

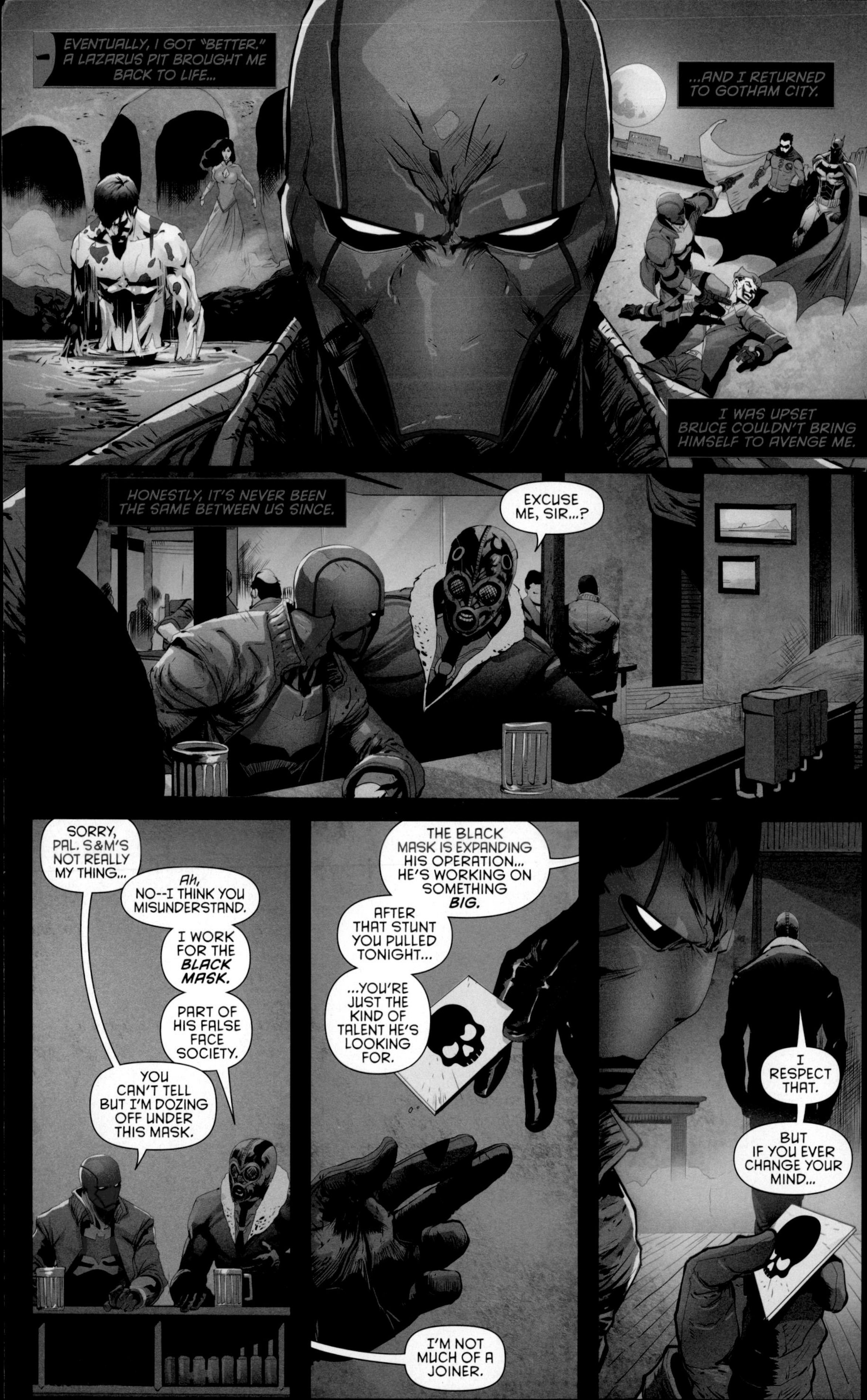
EVENTUALLY, I GOT "BETTER." A LAZARUS PIT BROUGHT ME BACK TO LIFE...
...AND I RETURNED TO GOTHAM CITY.
I WAS UPSET BRUCE COULDN'T BRING HIMSELF TO AVENGE ME.
HONESTLY, IT'S NEVER BEEN THE SAME BETWEEN US SINCE.
EXCUSE ME, SIR...?
SORRY, PAL. S&M'S NOT REALLY MY THING...
Ah, NO--I THINK YOU MISUNDERSTAND.
I WORK FOR THE BLACK MASK.
PART OF HIS FALSE FACE SOCIETY.
YOU CAN'T TELL BUT I'M DOZING OFF UNDER THIS MASK.
THE BLACK MASK IS EXPANDING HIS OPERATION... HE'S WORKING ON SOMETHING BIG.
AFTER THAT STUNT YOU PULLED TONIGHT...
...YOU'RE JUST THE KIND OF TALENT HE'S LOOKING FOR.
I'M NOT MUCH OF A JOINER.
I RESPECT THAT.
BUT IF YOU EVER CHANGE YOUR MIND...

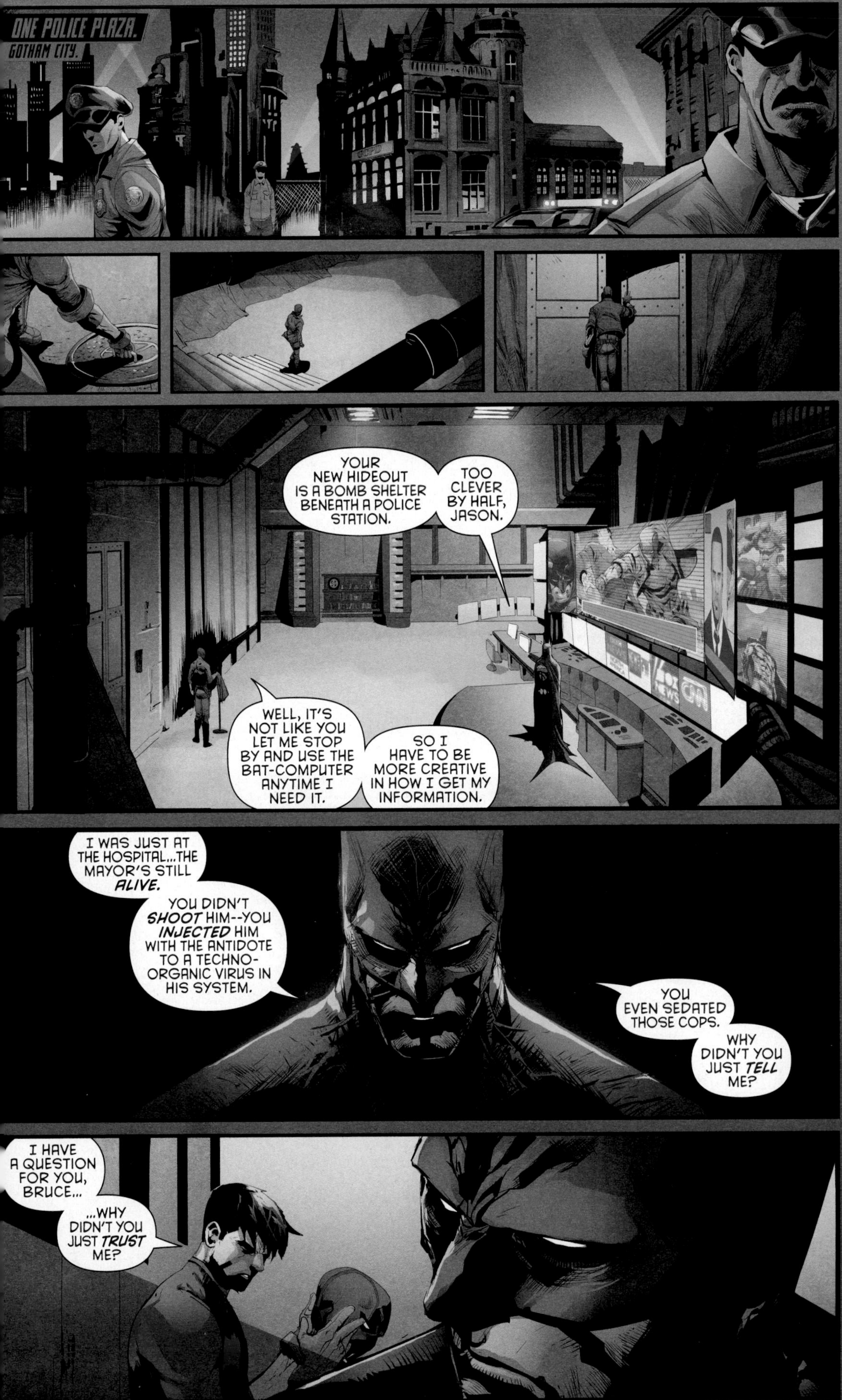
ONE POLICE PLAZA.
GOTHAM CITY.
YOUR NEW HIDEOUT IS A BOMB SHELTER BENEATH A POLICE STATION.
TOO CLEVER BY HALF, JASON.
WELL, IT'S NOT LIKE YOU LET ME STOP BY AND USE THE BAT-COMPUTER ANYTIME I NEED IT.
SO I HAVE TO BE MORE CREATIVE IN HOW I GET MY INFORMATION.
I WAS JUST AT THE HOSPITAL...THE MAYOR'S STILL *ALIVE.*
YOU DIDN'T *SHOOT* HIM--YOU *INJECTED* HIM WITH THE ANTIDOTE TO A TECHNO-ORGANIC VIRUS IN HIS SYSTEM.
YOU EVEN SEDATED THOSE COPS.
WHY DIDN'T YOU JUST *TELL* ME?
I HAVE A QUESTION FOR YOU, BRUCE...
...WHY DIDN'T YOU JUST *TRUST* ME?

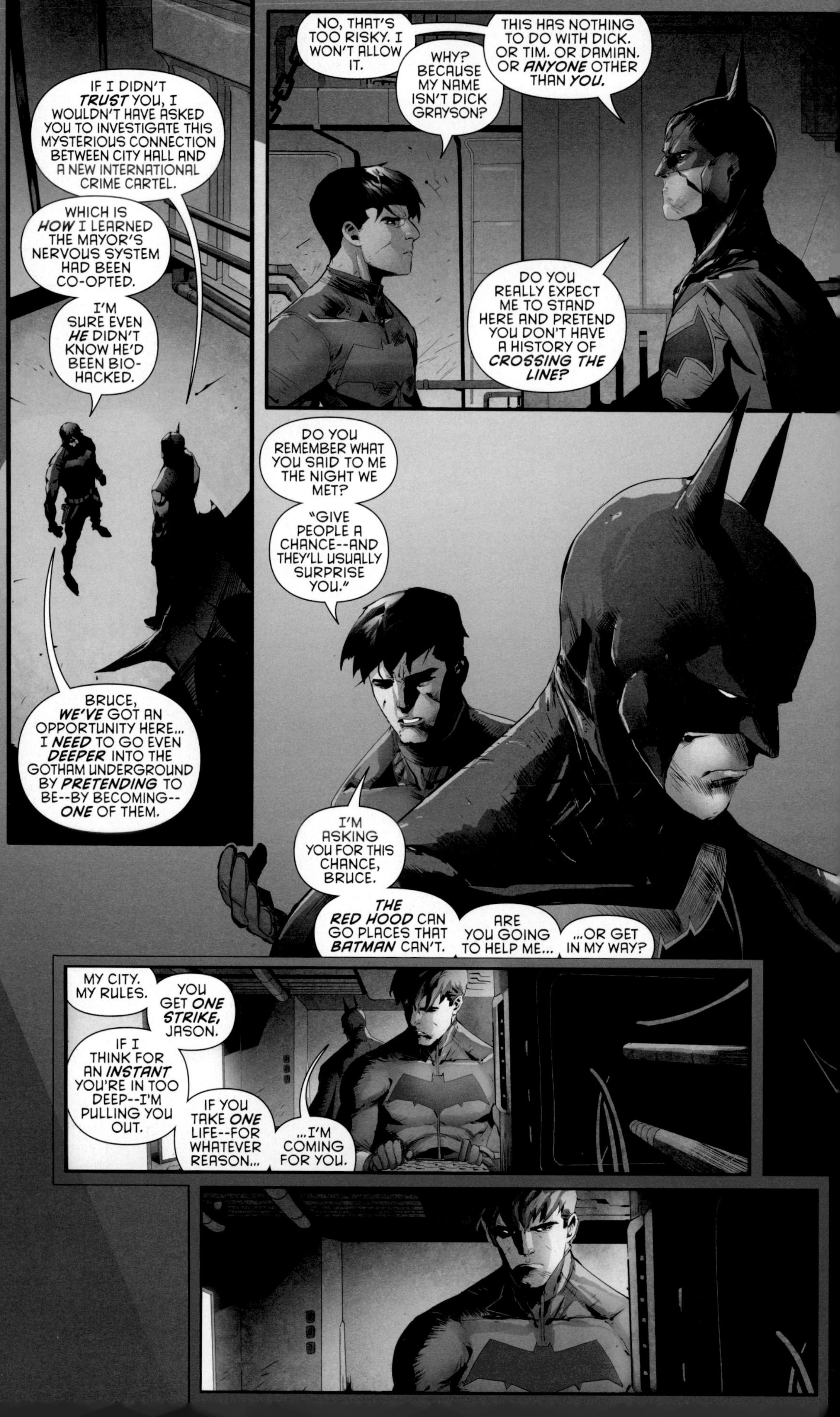
IF I DIDN'T TRUST YOU, I WOULDN'T HAVE ASKED YOU TO INVESTIGATE THIS MYSTERIOUS CONNECTION BETWEEN CITY HALL AND A NEW INTERNATIONAL CRIME CARTEL.
WHICH IS HOW I LEARNED THE MAYOR'S NERVOUS SYSTEM HAD BEEN CO-OPTED.
I'M SURE EVEN HE DIDN'T KNOW HE'D BEEN BIO-HACKED.
BRUCE, WE'VE GOT AN OPPORTUNITY HERE... I NEED TO GO EVEN DEEPER INTO THE GOTHAM UNDERGROUND BY PRETENDING TO BE--BY BECOMING--ONE OF THEM.
NO, THAT'S TOO RISKY. I WON'T ALLOW IT.
WHY? BECAUSE MY NAME ISN'T DICK GRAYSON?
THIS HAS NOTHING TO DO WITH DICK. OR TIM. OR DAMIAN. OR ANYONE OTHER THAN YOU.
DO YOU REALLY EXPECT ME TO STAND HERE AND PRETEND YOU DON'T HAVE A HISTORY OF CROSSING THE LINE?
DO YOU REMEMBER WHAT YOU SAID TO ME THE NIGHT WE MET?
"GIVE PEOPLE A CHANCE--AND THEY'LL USUALLY SURPRISE YOU."
I'M ASKING YOU FOR THIS CHANCE, BRUCE.
THE RED HOOD CAN GO PLACES THAT BATMAN CAN'T.
ARE YOU GOING TO HELP ME...
...OR GET IN MY WAY?
MY CITY. MY RULES.
YOU GET ONE STRIKE, JASON.
IF I THINK FOR AN INSTANT YOU'RE IN TOO DEEP--I'M PULLING YOU OUT.
IF YOU TAKE ONE LIFE--FOR WHATEVER REASON...
...I'M COMING FOR YOU.

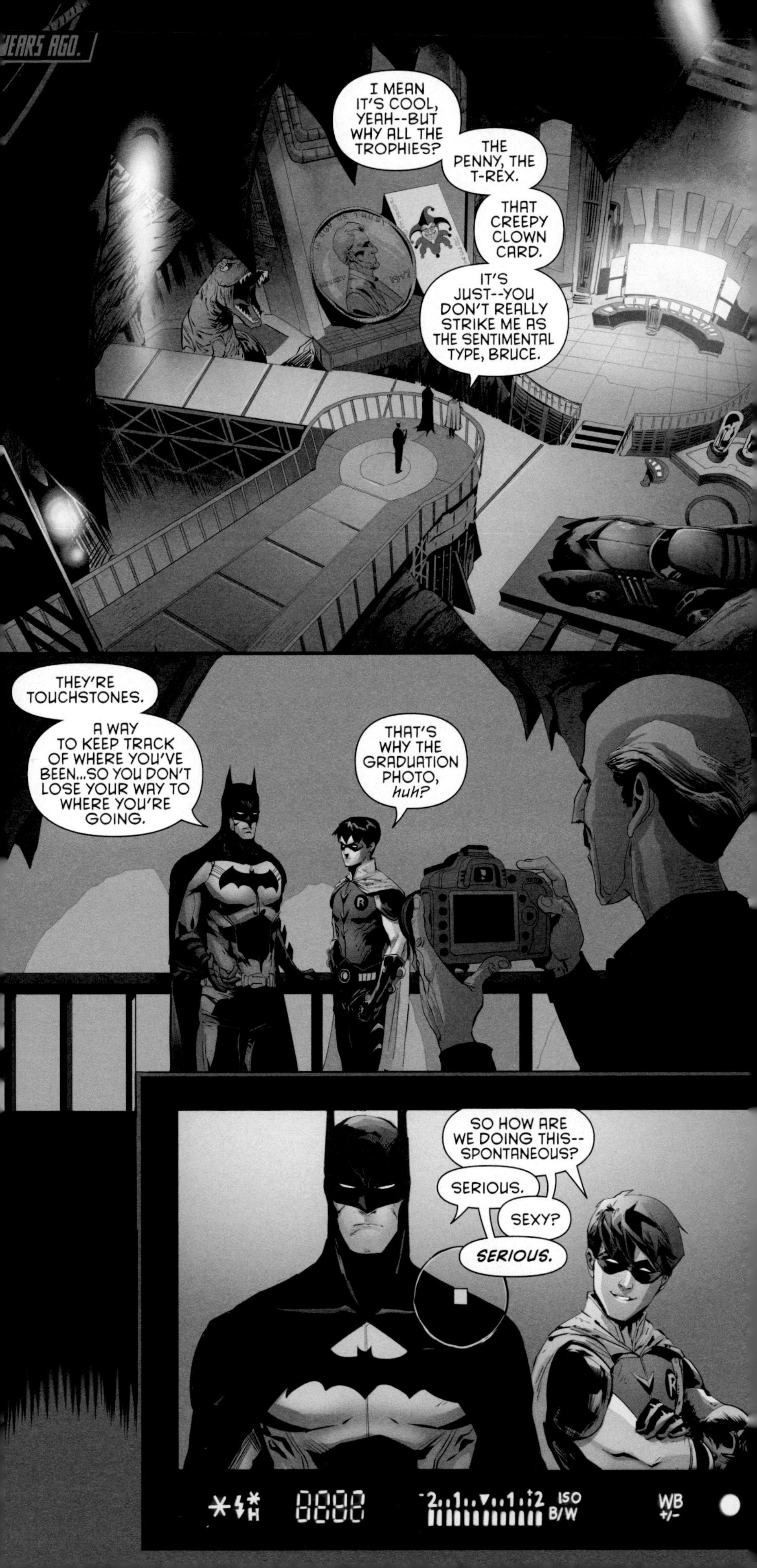
YEARS AGO.
I MEAN IT'S COOL, YEAH--BUT WHY ALL THE TROPHIES?
THE PENNY, THE T-REX.
THAT CREEPY CLOWN CARD.
IT'S JUST--YOU DON'T REALLY STRIKE ME AS THE SENTIMENTAL TYPE, BRUCE.
THEY'RE TOUCHSTONES.
A WAY TO KEEP TRACK OF WHERE YOU'VE BEEN...SO YOU DON'T LOSE YOUR WAY TO WHERE YOU'RE GOING.
THAT'S WHY THE GRADUATION PHOTO, *huh?*
SO HOW ARE WE DOING THIS--SPONTANEOUS?
SERIOUS.
SEXY?
SERIOUS.
ISO B/W
WB +/-

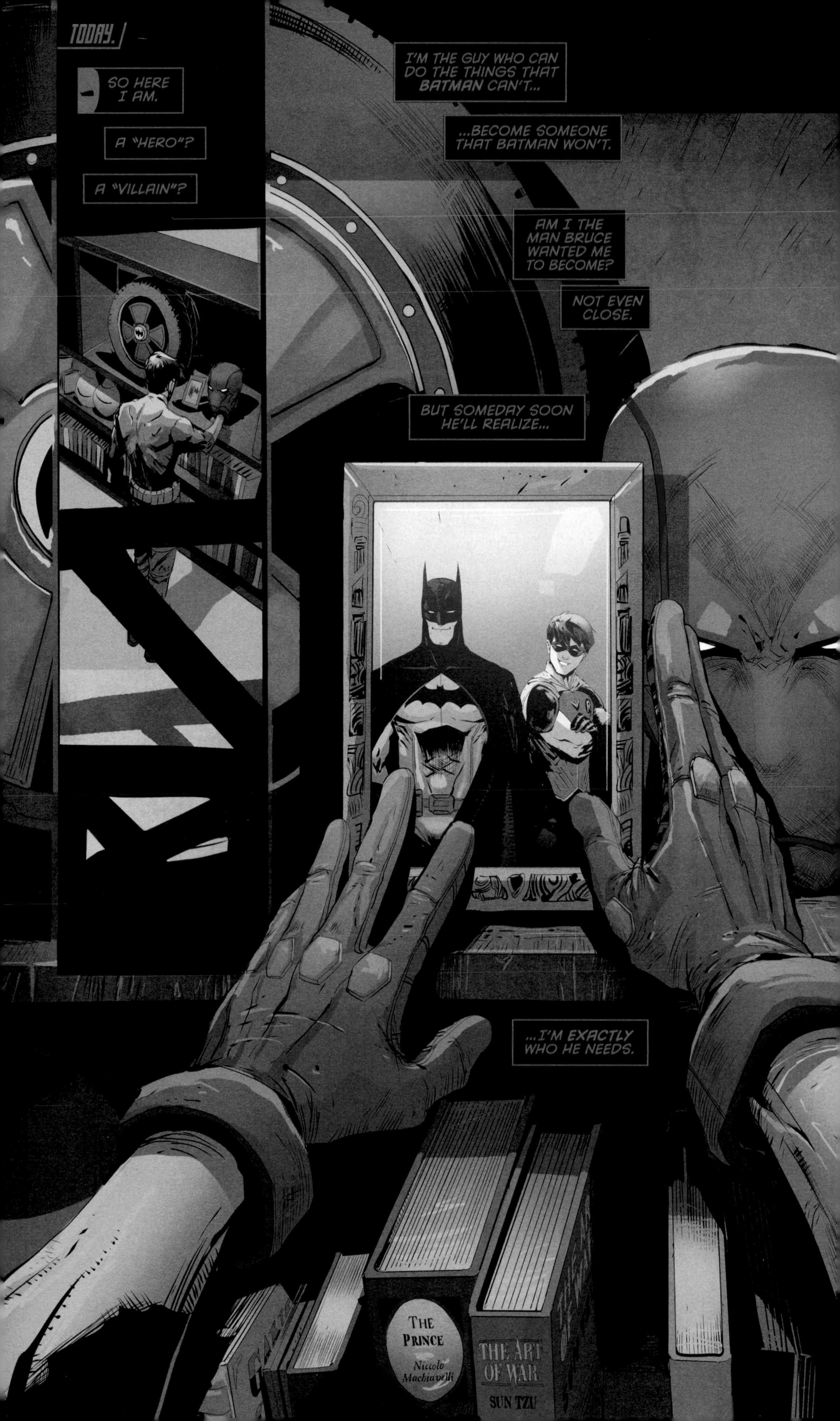
TODAY.
SO HERE I AM.
A "HERO"?
A "VILLAIN"?
I'M THE GUY WHO CAN DO THE THINGS THAT BATMAN CAN'T...
...BECOME SOMEONE THAT BATMAN WON'T.
AM I THE MAN BRUCE WANTED ME TO BECOME?
NOT EVEN CLOSE.
BUT SOMEDAY SOON HE'LL REALIZE...
...I'M EXACTLY WHO HE NEEDS.
THE PRINCE
Niccolo Machiavelli
THE ART OF WAR
SUN TZU

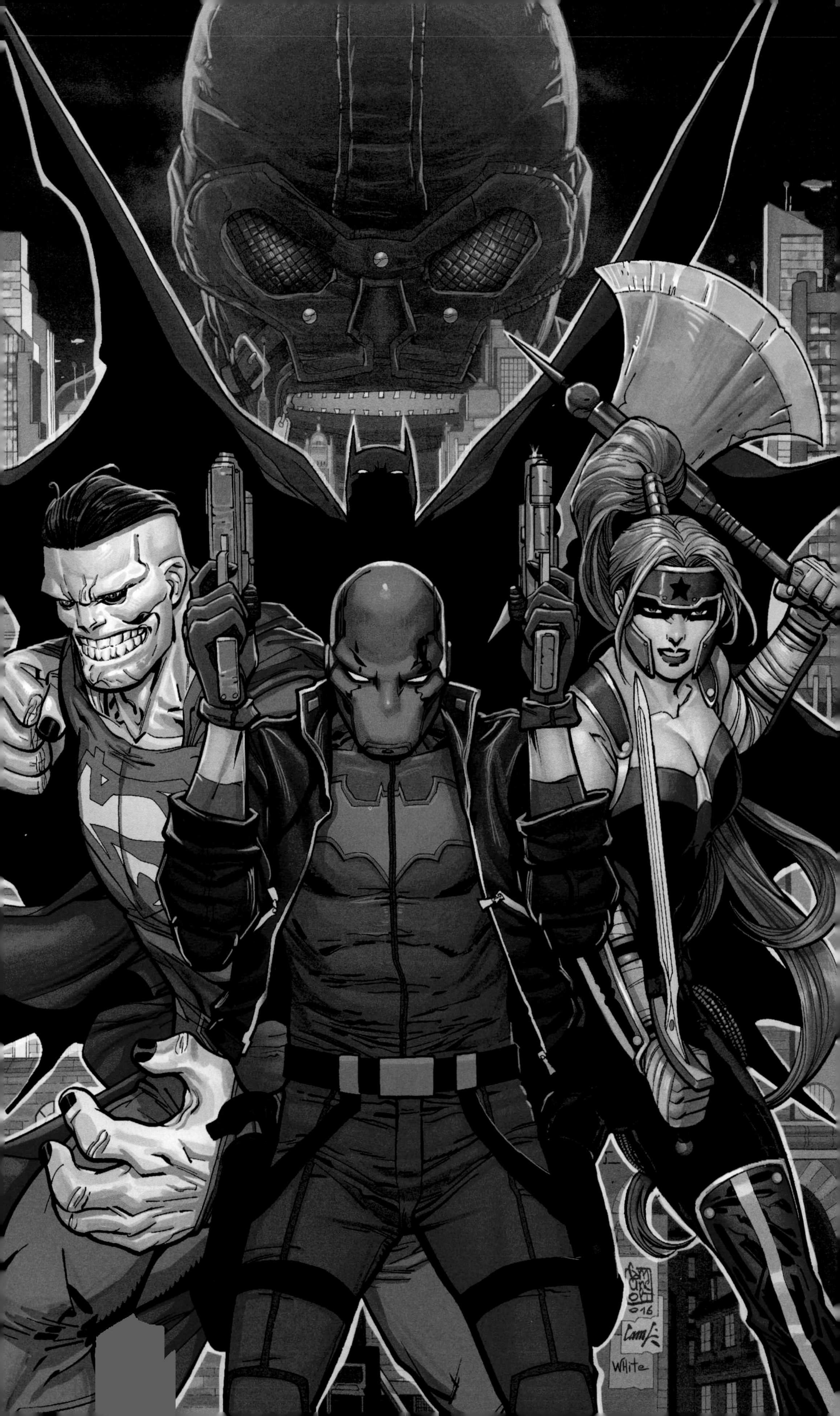
WHITE

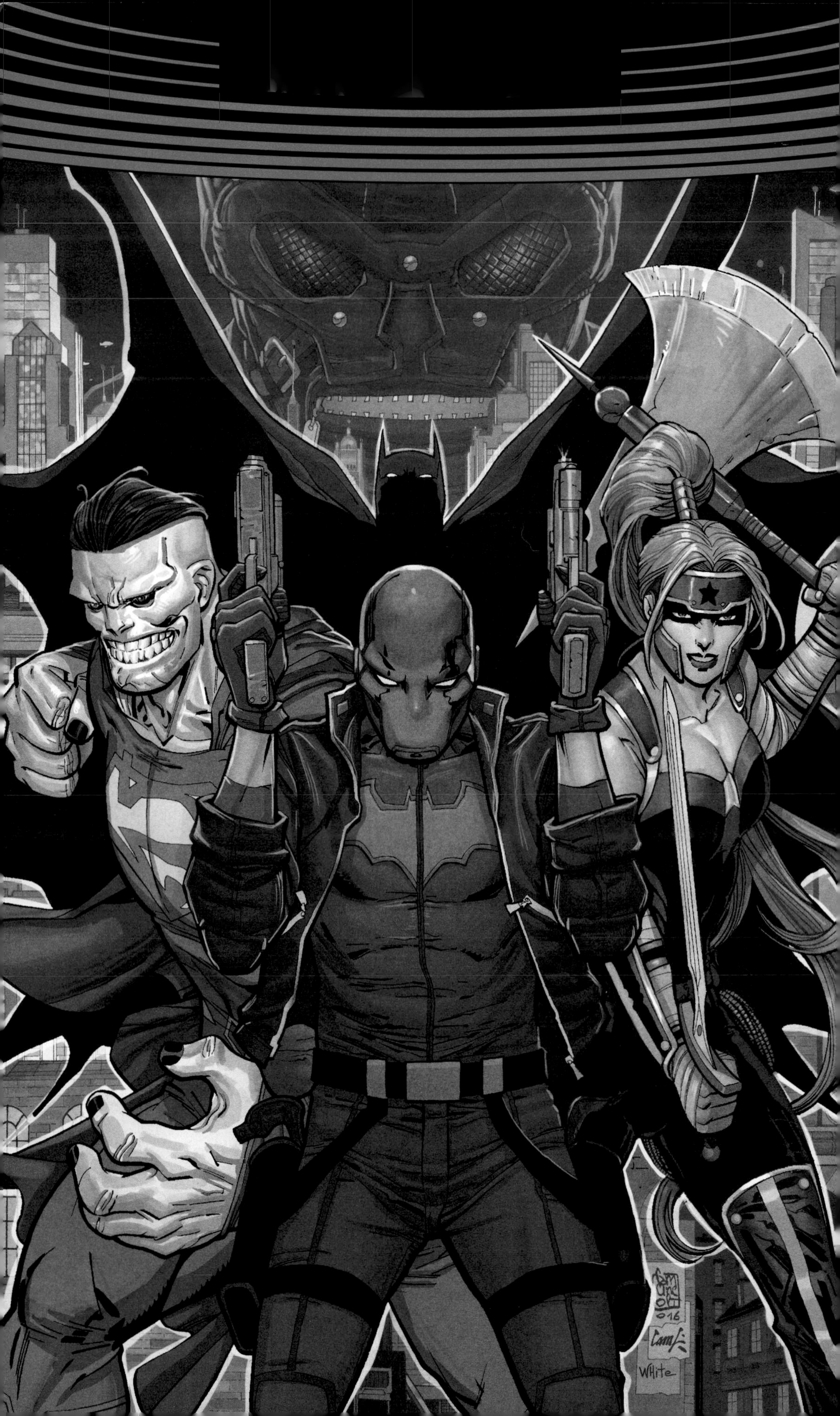

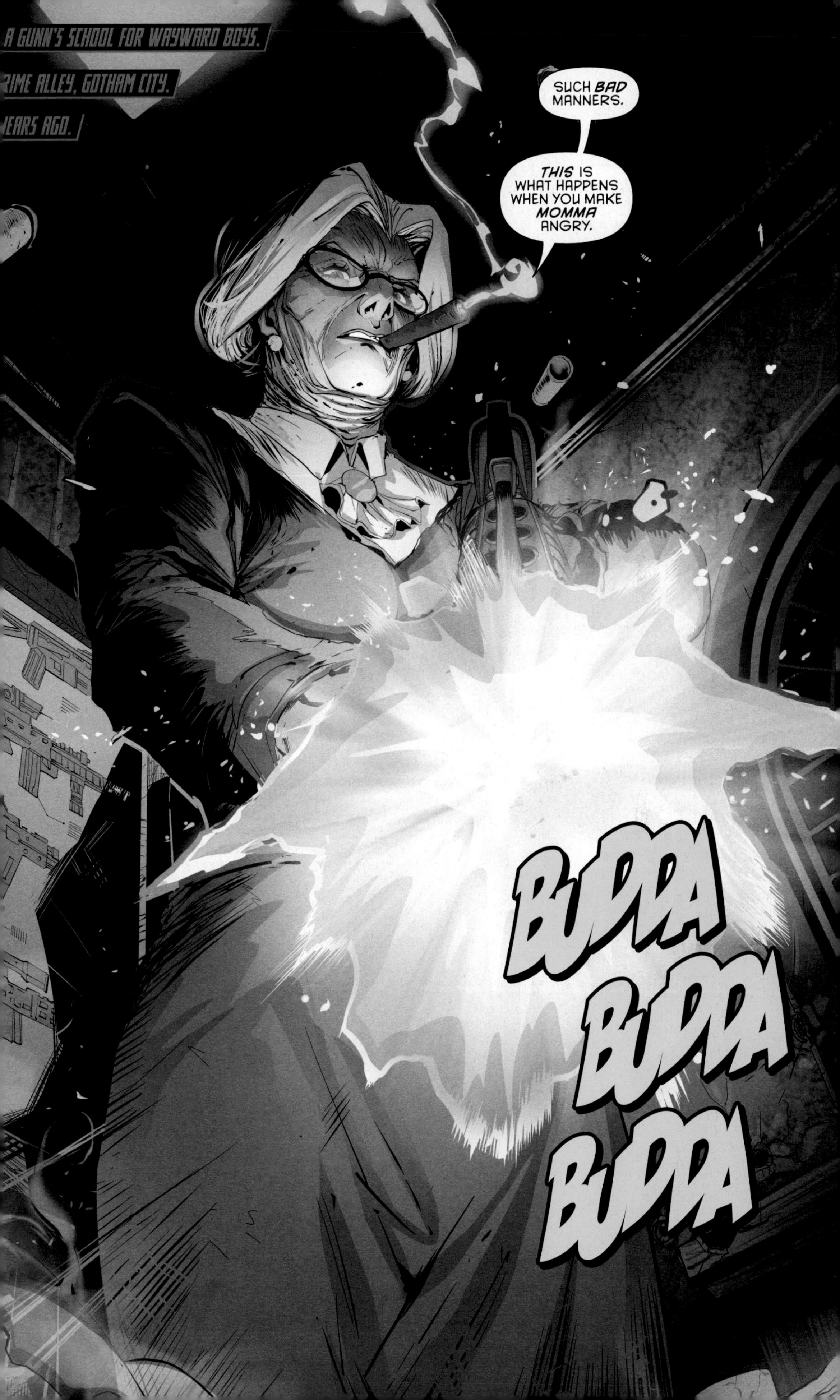

A GUNN'S SCHOOL FOR WAYWARD BOYS.
RIME ALLEY, GOTHAM CITY.
EARS AGO.
SUCH BAD MANNERS.
THIS IS WHAT HAPPENS WHEN YOU MAKE MOMMA ANGRY.
BUDDA BUDDA BUDDA

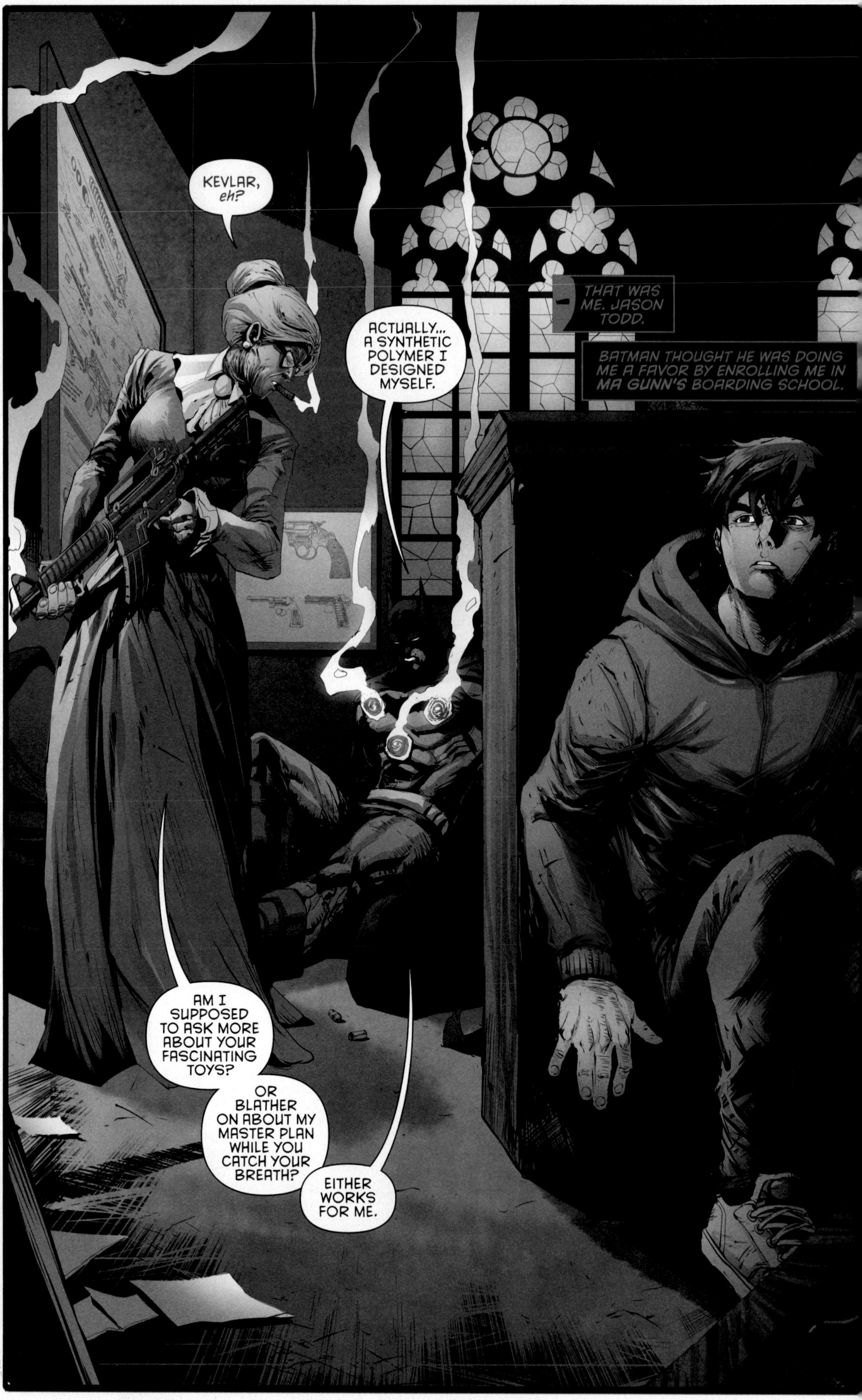
KEVLAR, eh?
THAT WAS ME. JASON TODD.
BATMAN THOUGHT HE WAS DOING ME A FAVOR BY ENROLLING ME IN MA GUNN'S BOARDING SCHOOL.
ACTUALLY... A SYNTHETIC POLYMER I DESIGNED MYSELF.
AM I SUPPOSED TO ASK MORE ABOUT YOUR FASCINATING TOYS?
OR BLATHER ON ABOUT MY MASTER PLAN WHILE YOU CATCH YOUR BREATH?
EITHER WORKS FOR ME.

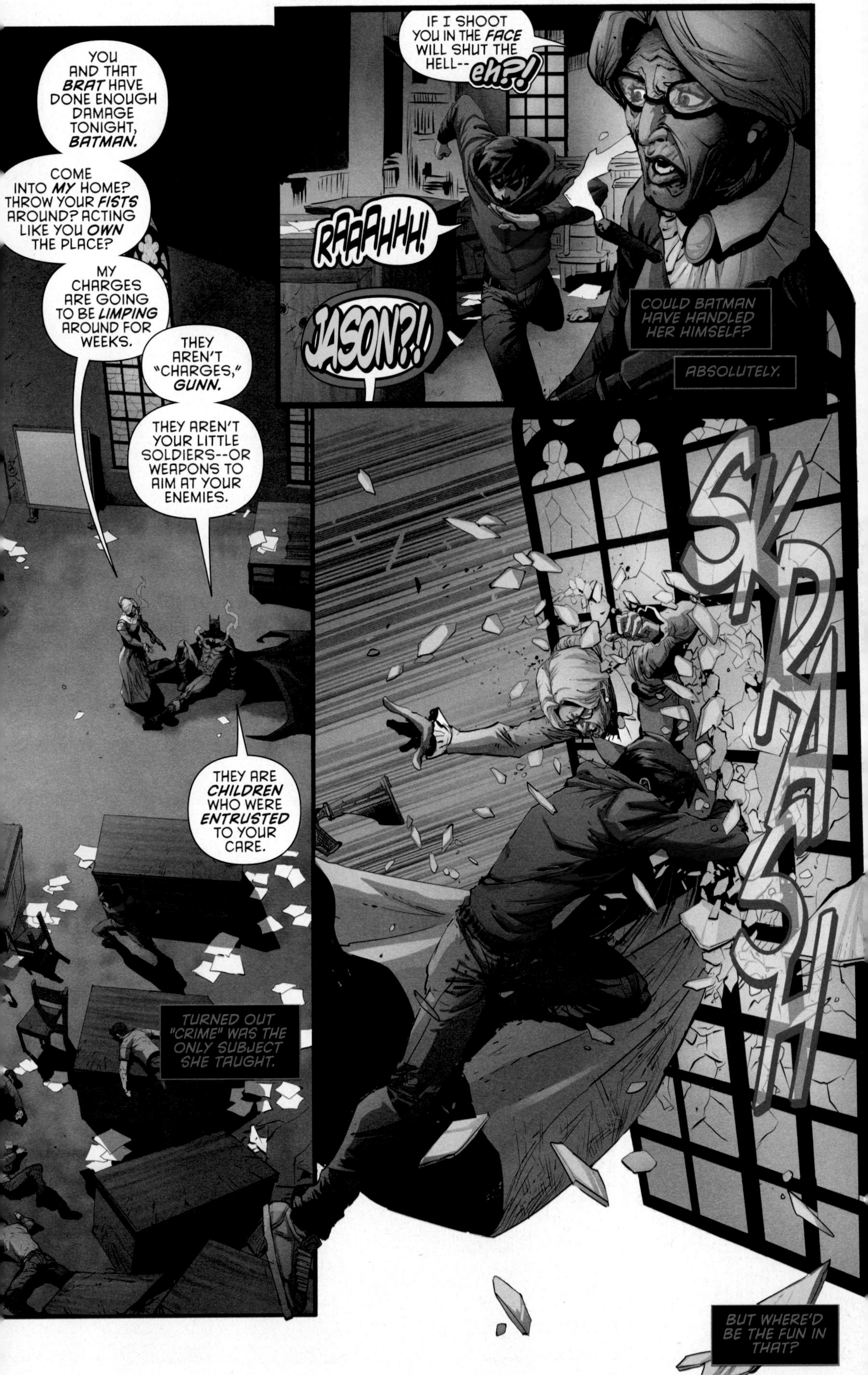
YOU AND THAT *BRAT* HAVE DONE ENOUGH DAMAGE TONIGHT, *BATMAN.*
COME INTO *MY* HOME? THROW YOUR *FISTS* AROUND? ACTING LIKE YOU *OWN* THE PLACE?
MY CHARGES ARE GOING TO BE *LIMPING* AROUND FOR WEEKS.
THEY AREN'T "CHARGES," *GUNN.*
THEY AREN'T YOUR LITTLE SOLDIERS--OR WEAPONS TO AIM AT YOUR ENEMIES.
THEY ARE *CHILDREN* WHO WERE *ENTRUSTED* TO YOUR CARE.
TURNED OUT "CRIME" WAS THE ONLY SUBJECT SHE TAUGHT.
IF I SHOOT YOU IN THE *FACE* WILL SHUT THE HELL-- *eh?!*
RAAAHHH!
JASON?!
COULD BATMAN HAVE HANDLED HER HIMSELF?
ABSOLUTELY.
SKRAASH
BUT WHERE'D BE THE FUN IN THAT?

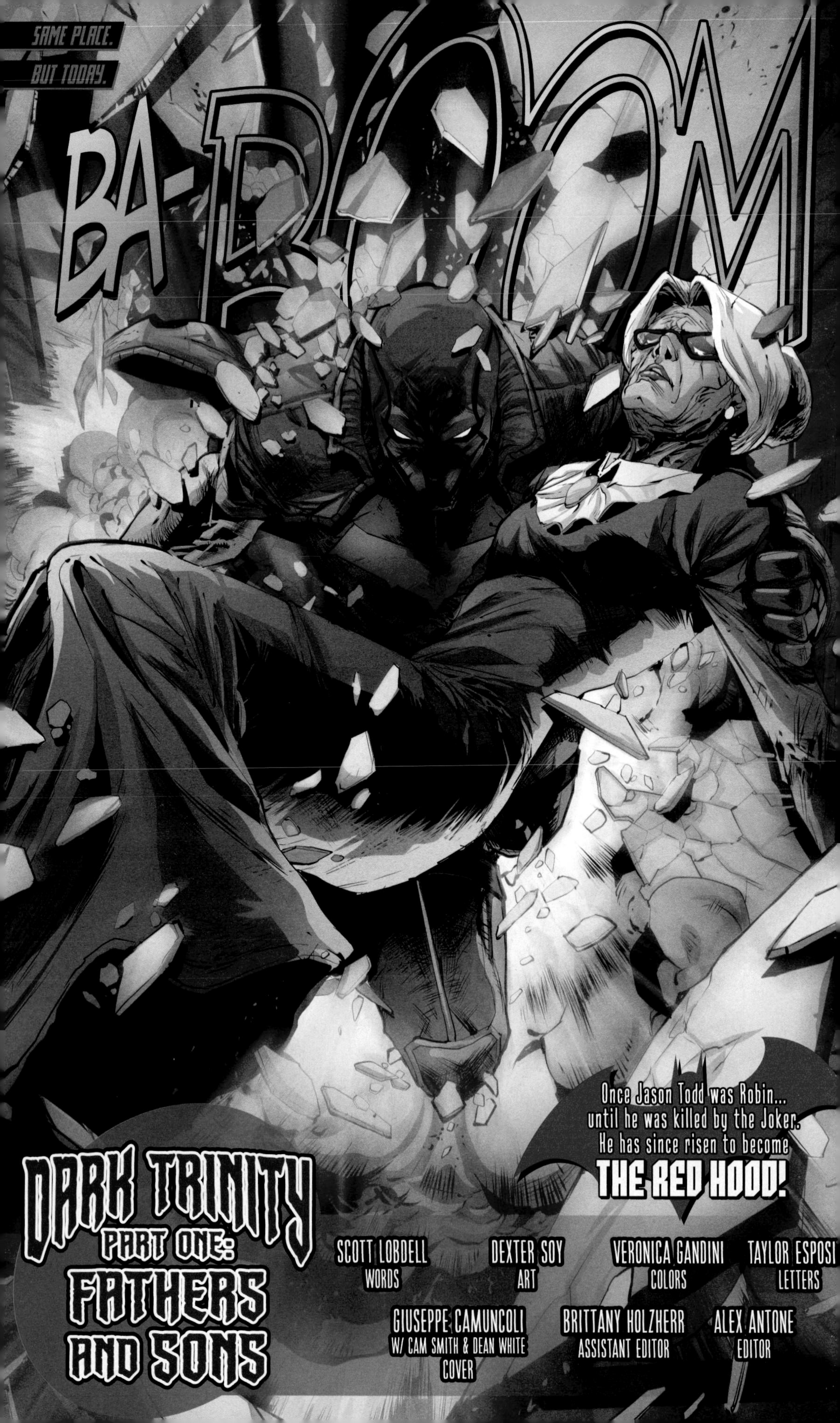
SAME PLACE.
BUT TODAY.
BA-BOOM
Once Jason Todd was Robin... until he was killed by the Joker. He has since risen to become THE RED HOOD!
DARK TRINITY PART ONE: FATHERS AND SONS
SCOTT LOBDELL WORDS
DEXTER SOY ART
VERONICA GANDINI COLORS
TAYLOR ESPOSI LETTERS
GIUSEPPE CAMUNCOLI W/ CAM SMITH & DEAN WHITE COVER
BRITTANY HOLZHERR ASSISTANT EDITOR
ALEX ANTONE EDITOR

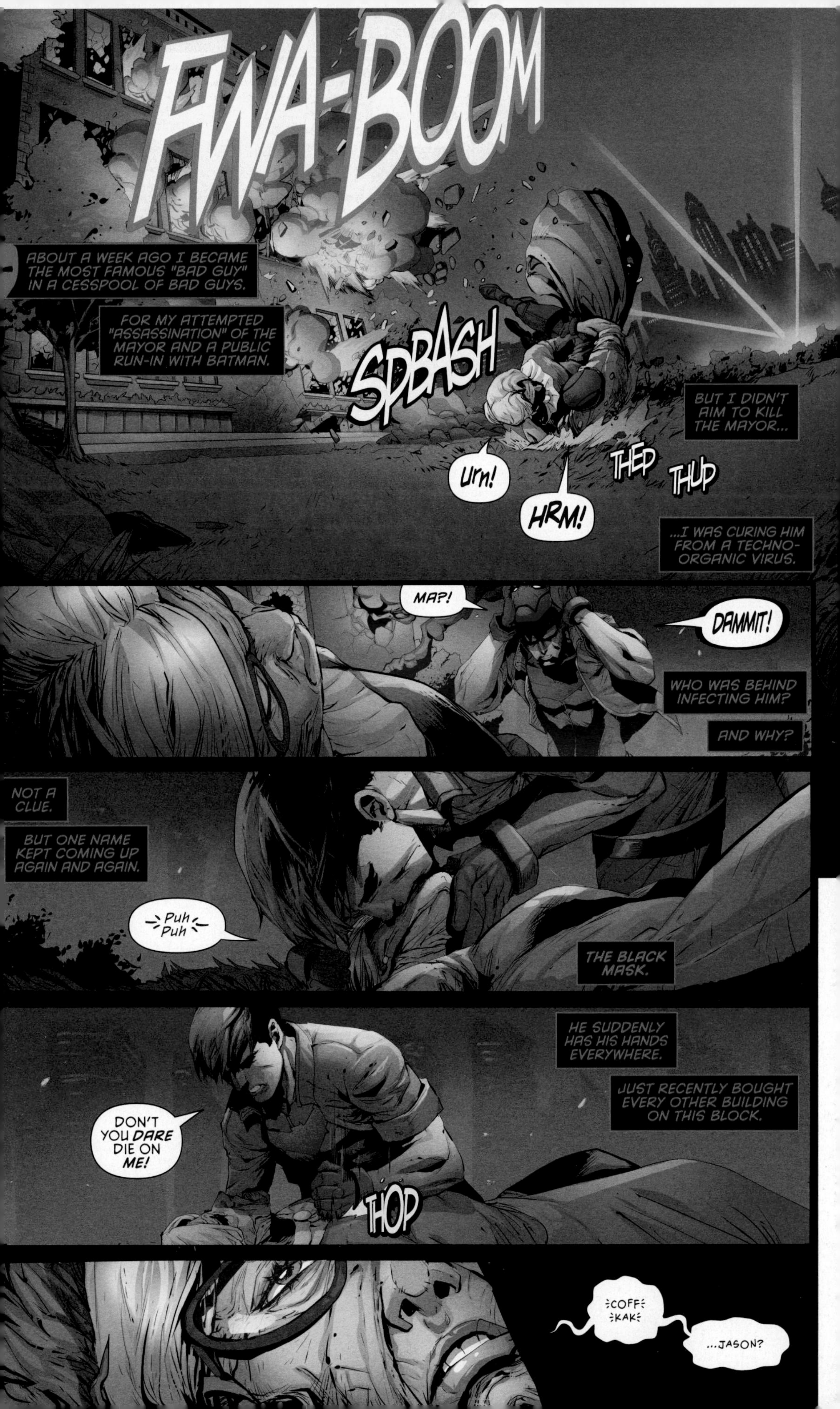
FWA-BOOM
ABOUT A WEEK AGO I BECAME THE MOST FAMOUS "BAD GUY" IN A CESSPOOL OF BAD GUYS.
FOR MY ATTEMPTED "ASSASSINATION" OF THE MAYOR AND A PUBLIC RUN-IN WITH BATMAN.
SPBASH
BUT I DIDN'T AIM TO KILL THE MAYOR...
Urn!
HRM!
THEP
THUP
...I WAS CURING HIM FROM A TECHNO-ORGANIC VIRUS.
MA?!
DAMMIT!
WHO WAS BEHIND INFECTING HIM?
AND WHY?
NOT A CLUE.
BUT ONE NAME KEPT COMING UP AGAIN AND AGAIN.
Puh Puh
THE BLACK MASK.
HE SUDDENLY HAS HIS HANDS EVERYWHERE.
JUST RECENTLY BOUGHT EVERY OTHER BUILDING ON THIS BLOCK.
DON'T YOU DARE DIE ON ME!
THOP
COFF KAK
...JASON?

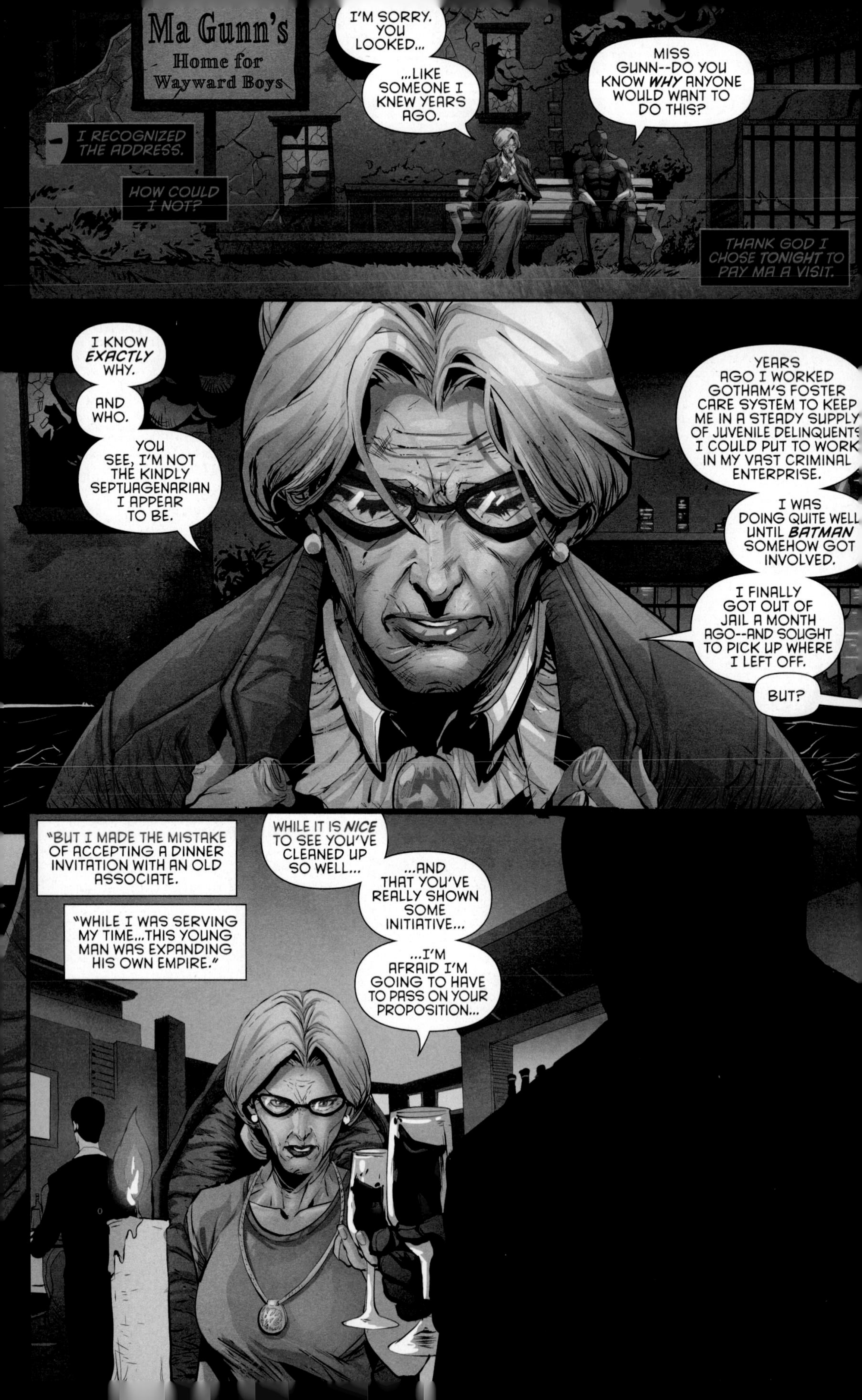

Ma Gunn's
Home for Wayward Boys
I RECOGNIZED THE ADDRESS.
HOW COULD I NOT?
I'M SORRY. YOU LOOKED...
...LIKE SOMEONE I KNEW YEARS AGO.
MISS GUNN--DO YOU KNOW WHY ANYONE WOULD WANT TO DO THIS?
THANK GOD I CHOSE TONIGHT TO PAY MA A VISIT.
I KNOW EXACTLY WHY.
AND WHO.
YOU SEE, I'M NOT THE KINDLY SEPTUAGENARIAN I APPEAR TO BE.
YEARS AGO I WORKED GOTHAM'S FOSTER CARE SYSTEM TO KEEP ME IN A STEADY SUPPLY OF JUVENILE DELINQUENTS I COULD PUT TO WORK IN MY VAST CRIMINAL ENTERPRISE.
I WAS DOING QUITE WELL UNTIL BATMAN SOMEHOW GOT INVOLVED.
I FINALLY GOT OUT OF JAIL A MONTH AGO--AND SOUGHT TO PICK UP WHERE I LEFT OFF.
BUT?
"BUT I MADE THE MISTAKE OF ACCEPTING A DINNER INVITATION WITH AN OLD ASSOCIATE.
"WHILE I WAS SERVING MY TIME...THIS YOUNG MAN WAS EXPANDING HIS OWN EMPIRE."
WHILE IT IS NICE TO SEE YOU'VE CLEANED UP SO WELL...
...AND THAT YOU'VE REALLY SHOWN SOME INITIATIVE...
...I'M AFRAID I'M GOING TO HAVE TO PASS ON YOUR PROPOSITION...

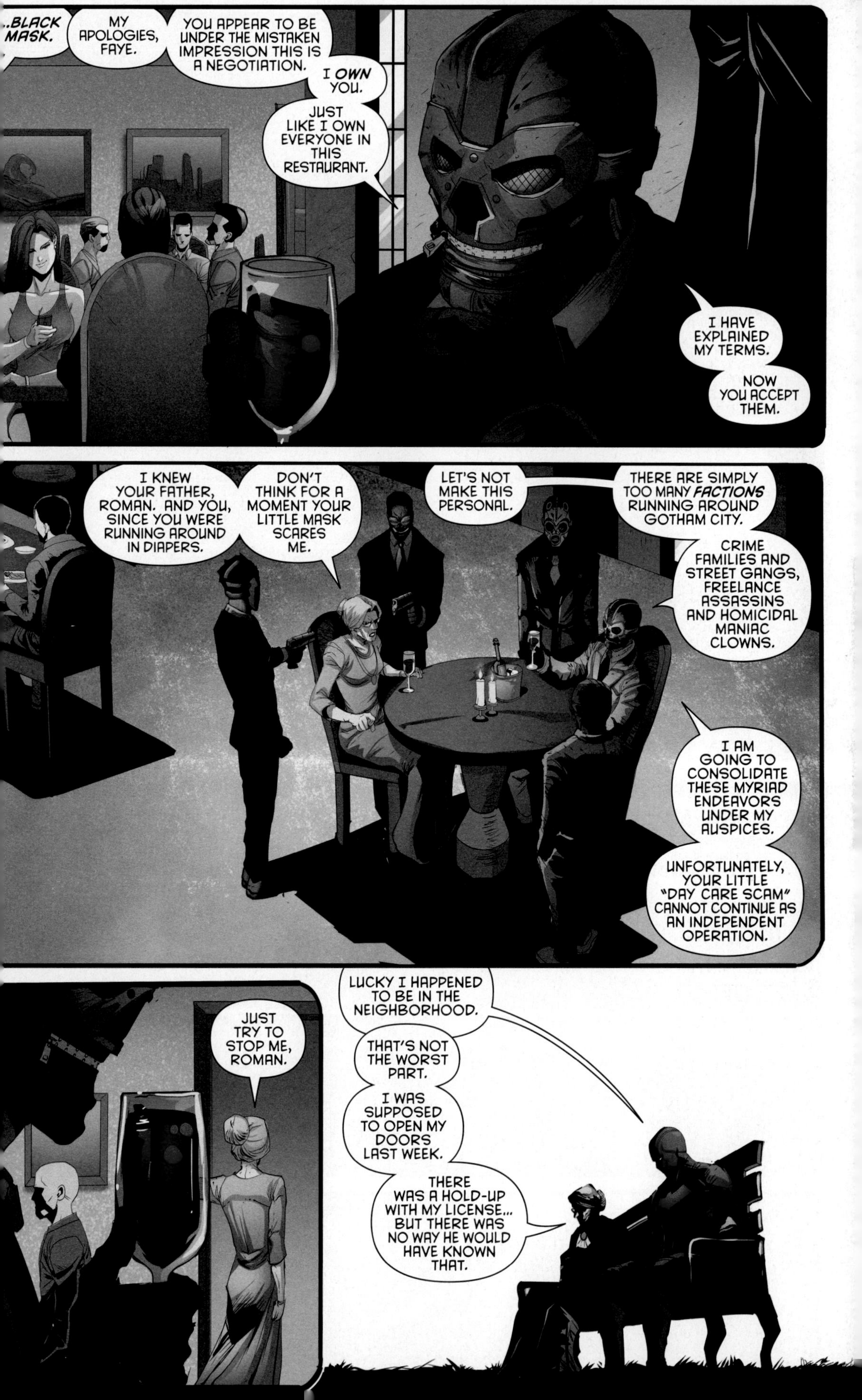

...BLACK MASK.
MY APOLOGIES, FAYE.
YOU APPEAR TO BE UNDER THE MISTAKEN IMPRESSION THIS IS A NEGOTIATION.
I OWN YOU.
JUST LIKE I OWN EVERYONE IN THIS RESTAURANT.
I HAVE EXPLAINED MY TERMS.
NOW YOU ACCEPT THEM.
I KNEW YOUR FATHER, ROMAN. AND YOU, SINCE YOU WERE RUNNING AROUND IN DIAPERS.
DON'T THINK FOR A MOMENT YOUR LITTLE MASK SCARES ME.
LET'S NOT MAKE THIS PERSONAL.
THERE ARE SIMPLY TOO MANY FACTIONS RUNNING AROUND GOTHAM CITY.
CRIME FAMILIES AND STREET GANGS, FREELANCE ASSASSINS AND HOMICIDAL MANIAC CLOWNS.
I AM GOING TO CONSOLIDATE THESE MYRIAD ENDEAVORS UNDER MY AUSPICES.
UNFORTUNATELY, YOUR LITTLE "DAY CARE SCAM" CANNOT CONTINUE AS AN INDEPENDENT OPERATION.
JUST TRY TO STOP ME, ROMAN.
LUCKY I HAPPENED TO BE IN THE NEIGHBORHOOD.
THAT'S NOT THE WORST PART.
I WAS SUPPOSED TO OPEN MY DOORS LAST WEEK.
THERE WAS A HOLD-UP WITH MY LICENSE... BUT THERE WAS NO WAY HE WOULD HAVE KNOWN THAT.

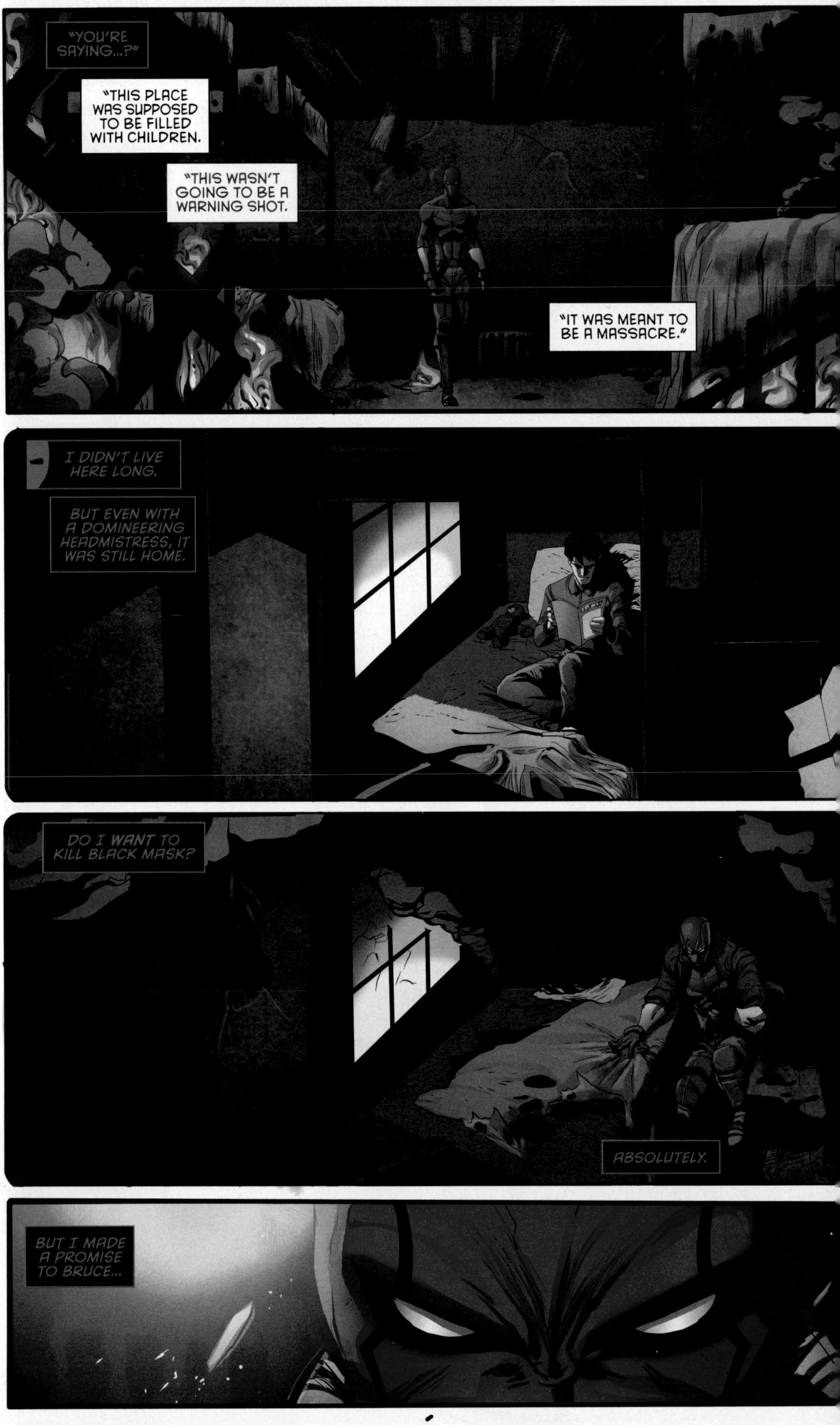
"YOU'RE SAYING...?"
"THIS PLACE WAS SUPPOSED TO BE FILLED WITH CHILDREN.
"THIS WASN'T GOING TO BE A WARNING SHOT.
"IT WAS MEANT TO BE A MASSACRE."
I DIDN'T LIVE HERE LONG.
BUT EVEN WITH A DOMINEERING HEADMISTRESS, IT WAS STILL HOME.
DO I WANT TO KILL BLACK MASK?
ABSOLUTELY.
BUT I MADE A PROMISE TO BRUCE...

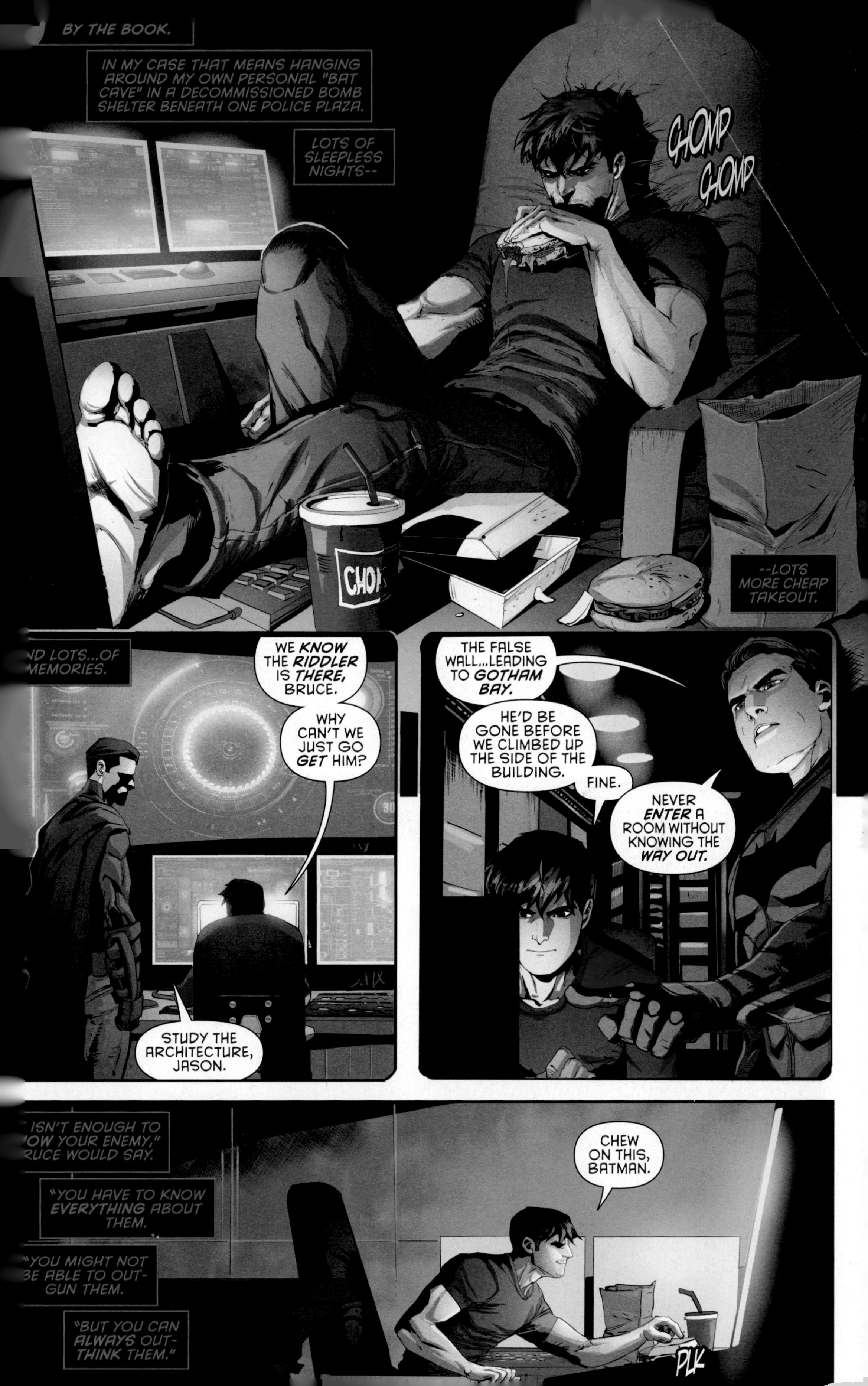
BY THE BOOK.
IN MY CASE THAT MEANS HANGING AROUND MY OWN PERSONAL "BAT CAVE" IN A DECOMMISSIONED BOMB SHELTER BENEATH ONE POLICE PLAZA.
LOTS OF SLEEPLESS NIGHTS--
CHOMP CHOMP
--LOTS MORE CHEAP TAKEOUT.
ND LOTS...OF MEMORIES.
WE KNOW THE RIDDLER IS THERE, BRUCE.
WHY CAN'T WE JUST GO GET HIM?
STUDY THE ARCHITECTURE, JASON.
THE FALSE WALL...LEADING TO GOTHAM BAY.
HE'D BE GONE BEFORE WE CLIMBED UP THE SIDE OF THE BUILDING.
FINE.
NEVER ENTER A ROOM WITHOUT KNOWING THE WAY OUT.
ISN'T ENOUGH TO OW YOUR ENEMY," RUCE WOULD SAY.
"YOU HAVE TO KNOW EVERYTHING ABOUT THEM.
"YOU MIGHT NOT BE ABLE TO OUT-GUN THEM.
"BUT YOU CAN ALWAYS OUT-THINK THEM."
CHEW ON THIS, BATMAN.
PLIK

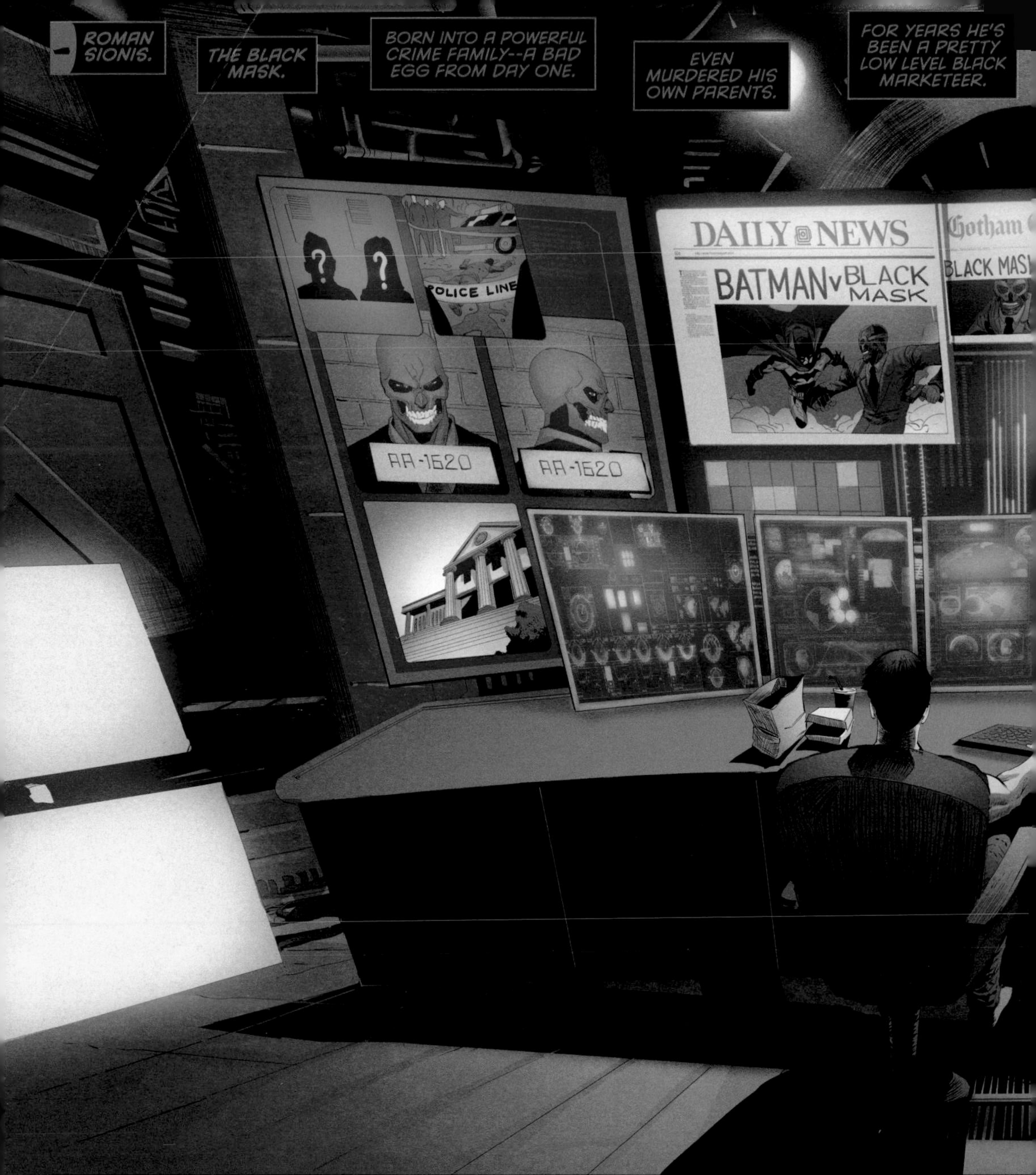
ROMAN SIONIS.
THE BLACK MASK.
BORN INTO A POWERFUL CRIME FAMILY--A BAD EGG FROM DAY ONE.
EVEN MURDERED HIS OWN PARENTS.
FOR YEARS HE'S BEEN A PRETTY LOW LEVEL BLACK MARKETEER.
POLICE LINE
AA-1620
AA-1620
DAILY NEWS
BATMAN v BLACK MASK
Gotham
BLACK MAS

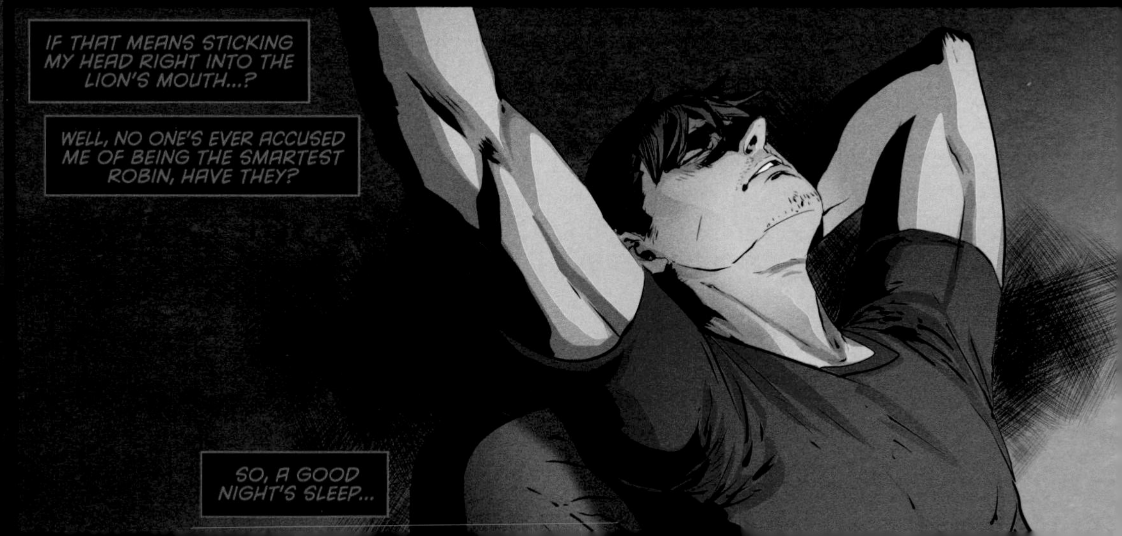
IF THAT MEANS STICKING MY HEAD RIGHT INTO THE LION'S MOUTH...?
WELL, NO ONE'S EVER ACCUSED ME OF BEING THE SMARTEST ROBIN, HAVE THEY?
SO, A GOOD NIGHT'S SLEEP...

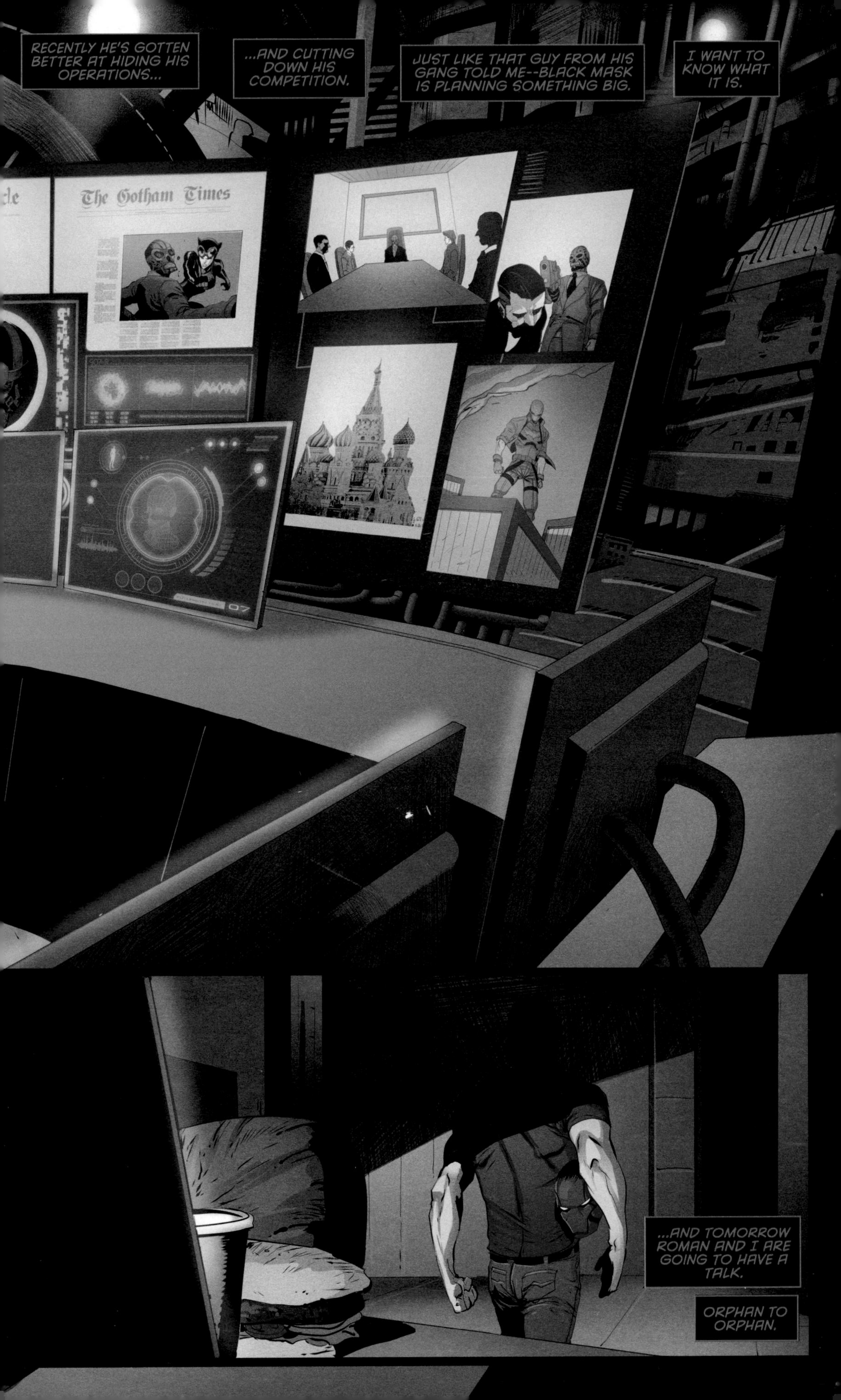

RECENTLY HE'S GOTTEN BETTER AT HIDING HIS OPERATIONS...
...AND CUTTING DOWN HIS COMPETITION.
JUST LIKE THAT GUY FROM HIS GANG TOLD ME--BLACK MASK IS PLANNING SOMETHING BIG.
I WANT TO KNOW WHAT IT IS.
The Gotham Times
...AND TOMORROW ROMAN AND I ARE GOING TO HAVE A TALK.
ORPHAN TO ORPHAN.

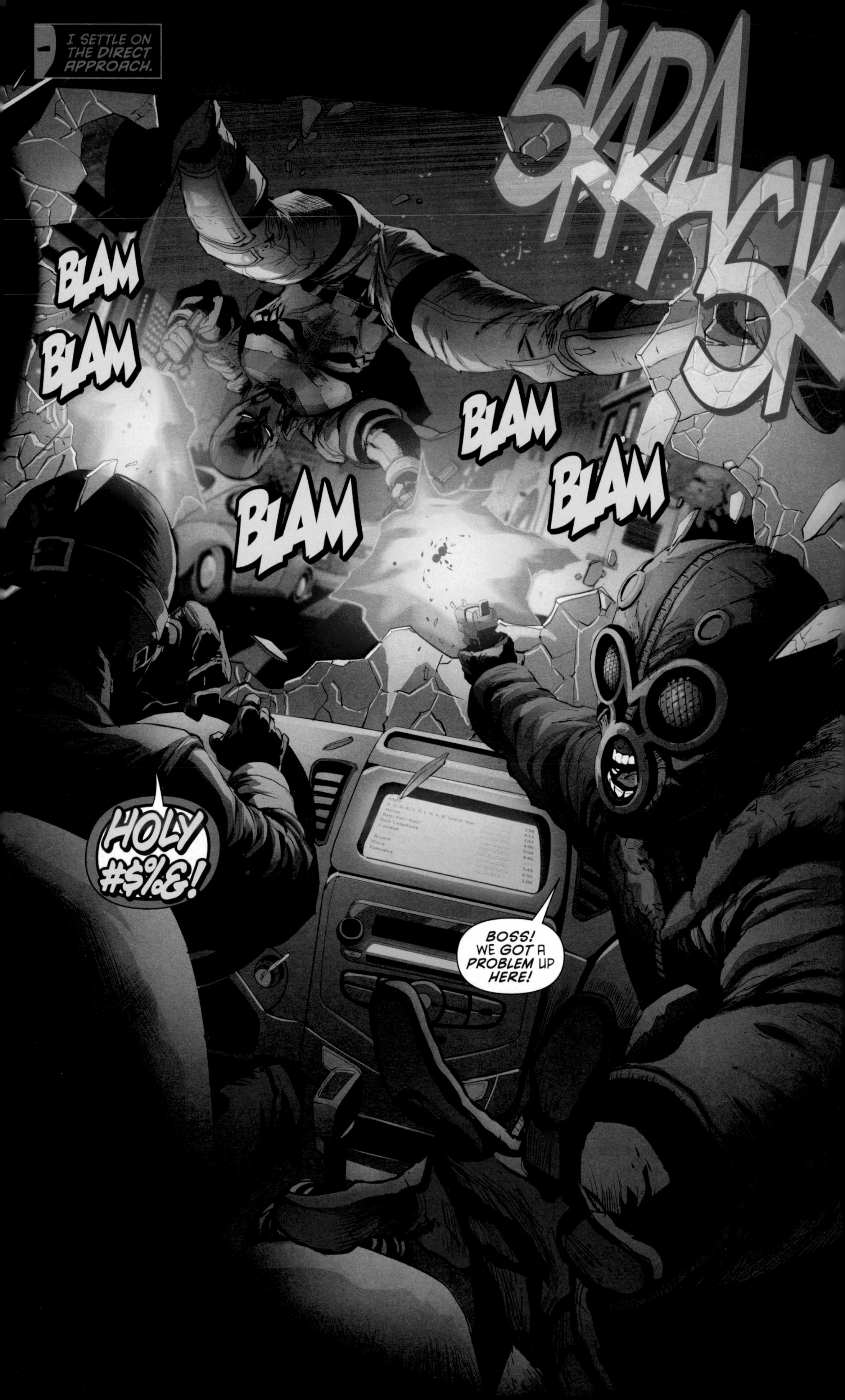
I SETTLE ON THE DIRECT APPROACH.
BLAM
BLAM
BLAM
BLAM
BLAM
HOLY #$%&!
BOSS! WE GOT A PROBLEM UP HERE!

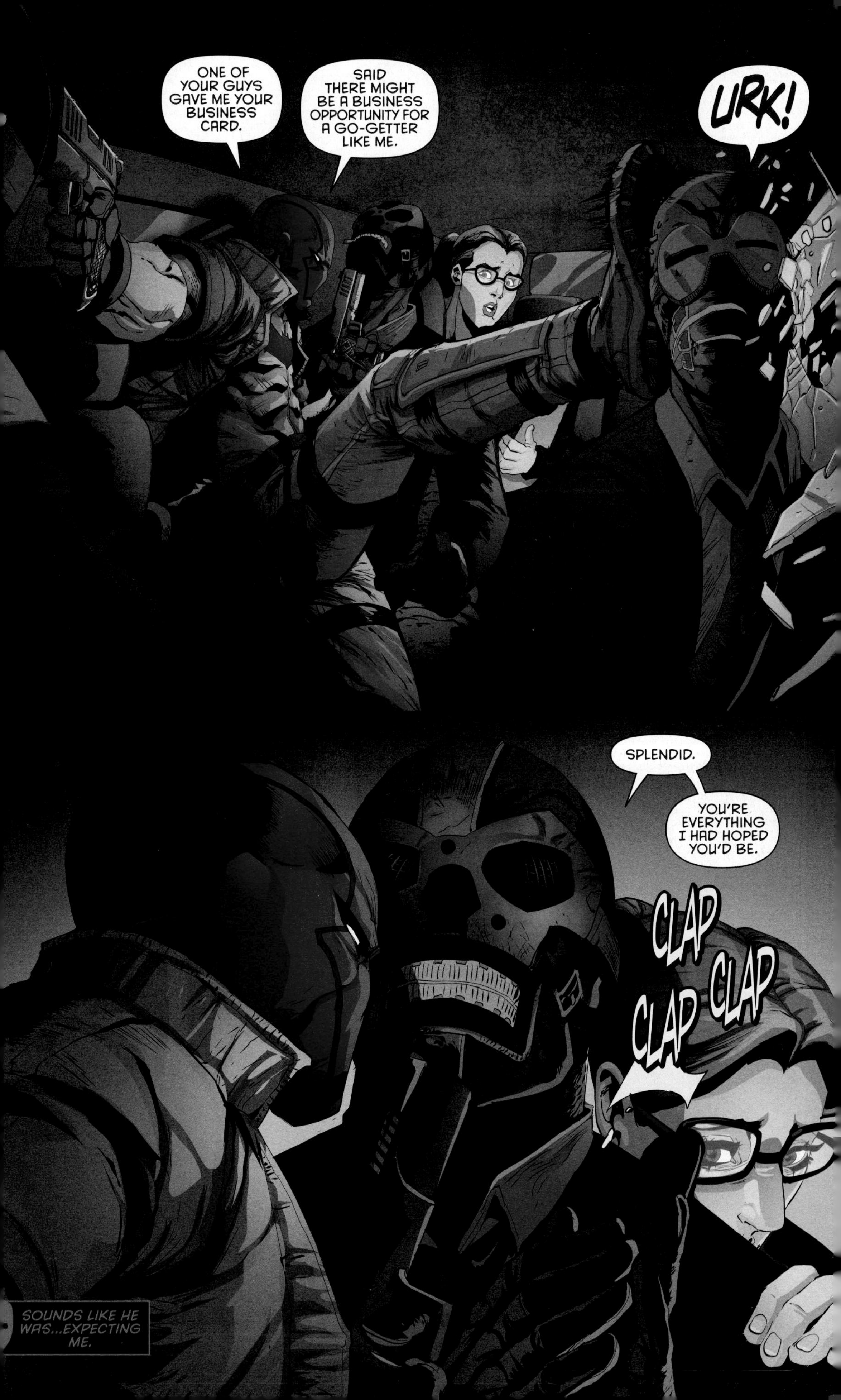
ONE OF YOUR GUYS GAVE ME YOUR BUSINESS CARD.
SAID THERE MIGHT BE A BUSINESS OPPORTUNITY FOR A GO-GETTER LIKE ME.
URK!
SPLENDID.
YOU'RE EVERYTHING I HAD HOPED YOU'D BE.
CLAP
CLAP CLAP
CLAP
SOUNDS LIKE HE WAS...EXPECTING ME.

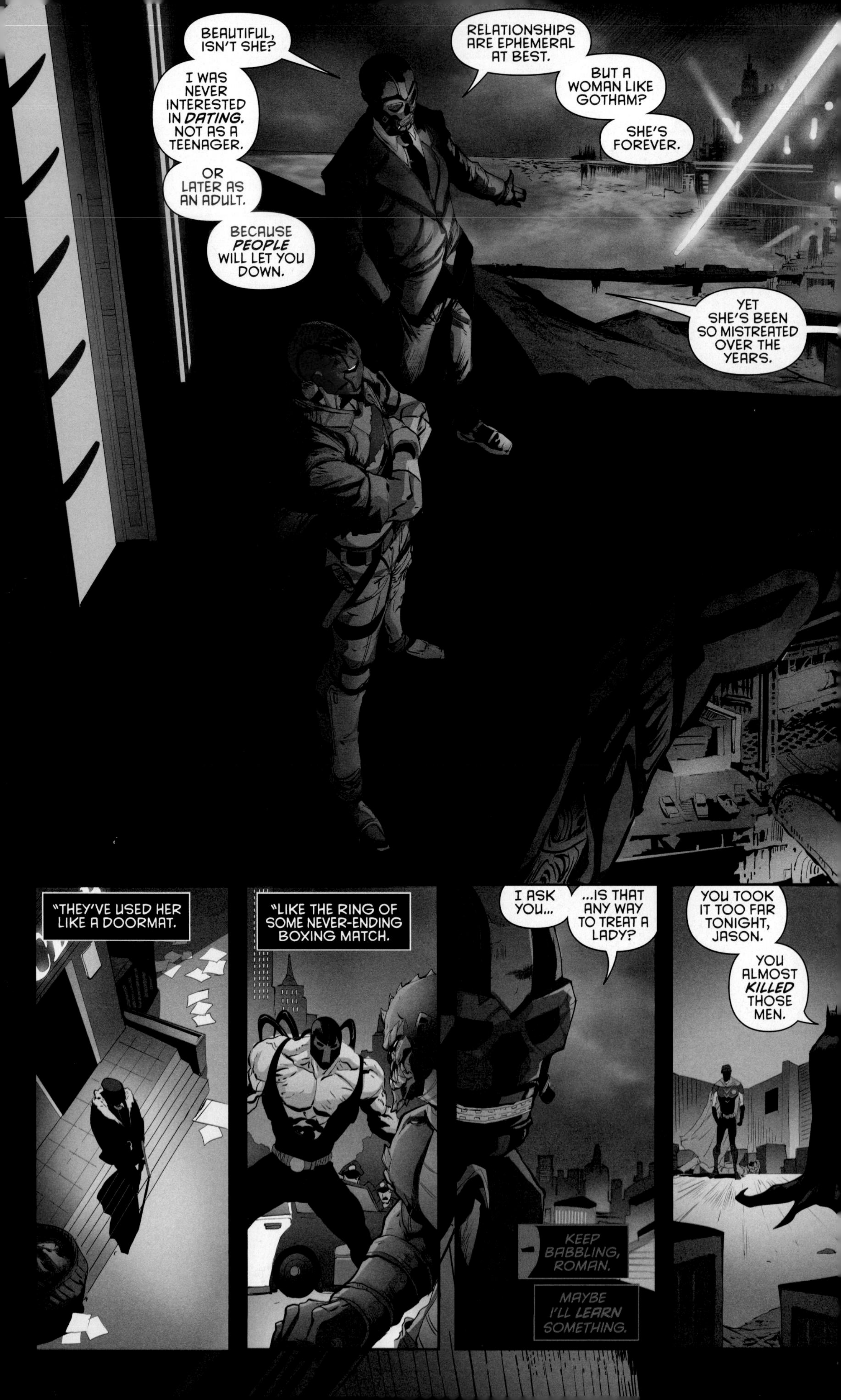

BEAUTIFUL, ISN'T SHE?
I WAS NEVER INTERESTED IN *DATING.* NOT AS A TEENAGER.
OR LATER AS AN ADULT.
BECAUSE *PEOPLE* WILL LET YOU DOWN.
RELATIONSHIPS ARE EPHEMERAL AT BEST.
BUT A WOMAN LIKE GOTHAM?
SHE'S FOREVER.
YET SHE'S BEEN SO MISTREATED OVER THE YEARS.
"THEY'VE USED HER LIKE A DOORMAT.
"LIKE THE RING OF SOME NEVER-ENDING BOXING MATCH.
I ASK YOU...
...IS THAT ANY WAY TO TREAT A LADY?
KEEP BABBLING, ROMAN.
MAYBE I'LL LEARN SOMETHING.
YOU TOOK IT TOO FAR TONIGHT, JASON.
YOU ALMOST *KILLED* THOSE MEN.

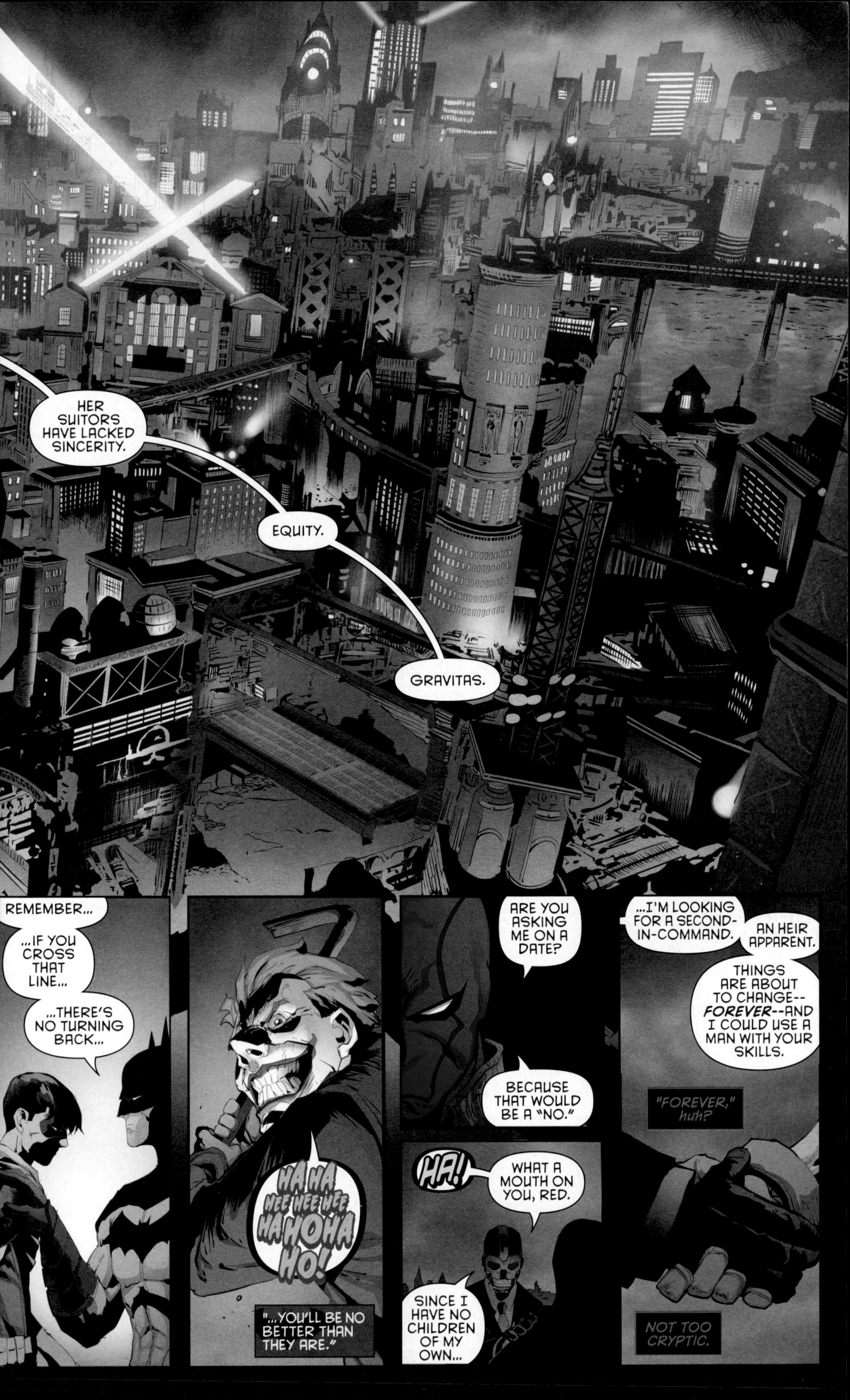

HER SUITORS HAVE LACKED SINCERITY.
EQUITY.
GRAVITAS.
REMEMBER...
...IF YOU CROSS THAT LINE...
...THERE'S NO TURNING BACK...
HA HA HEE HEE HEE HA HOHA HO!
"...YOU'LL BE NO BETTER THAN THEY ARE."
ARE YOU ASKING ME ON A DATE?
BECAUSE THAT WOULD BE A "NO."
HA!
WHAT A MOUTH ON YOU, RED.
SINCE I HAVE NO CHILDREN OF MY OWN...
...I'M LOOKING FOR A SECOND-IN-COMMAND.
AN HEIR APPARENT.
THINGS ARE ABOUT TO CHANGE--FOREVER--AND I COULD USE A MAN WITH YOUR SKILLS.
"FOREVER," huh?
NOT TOO CRYPTIC.

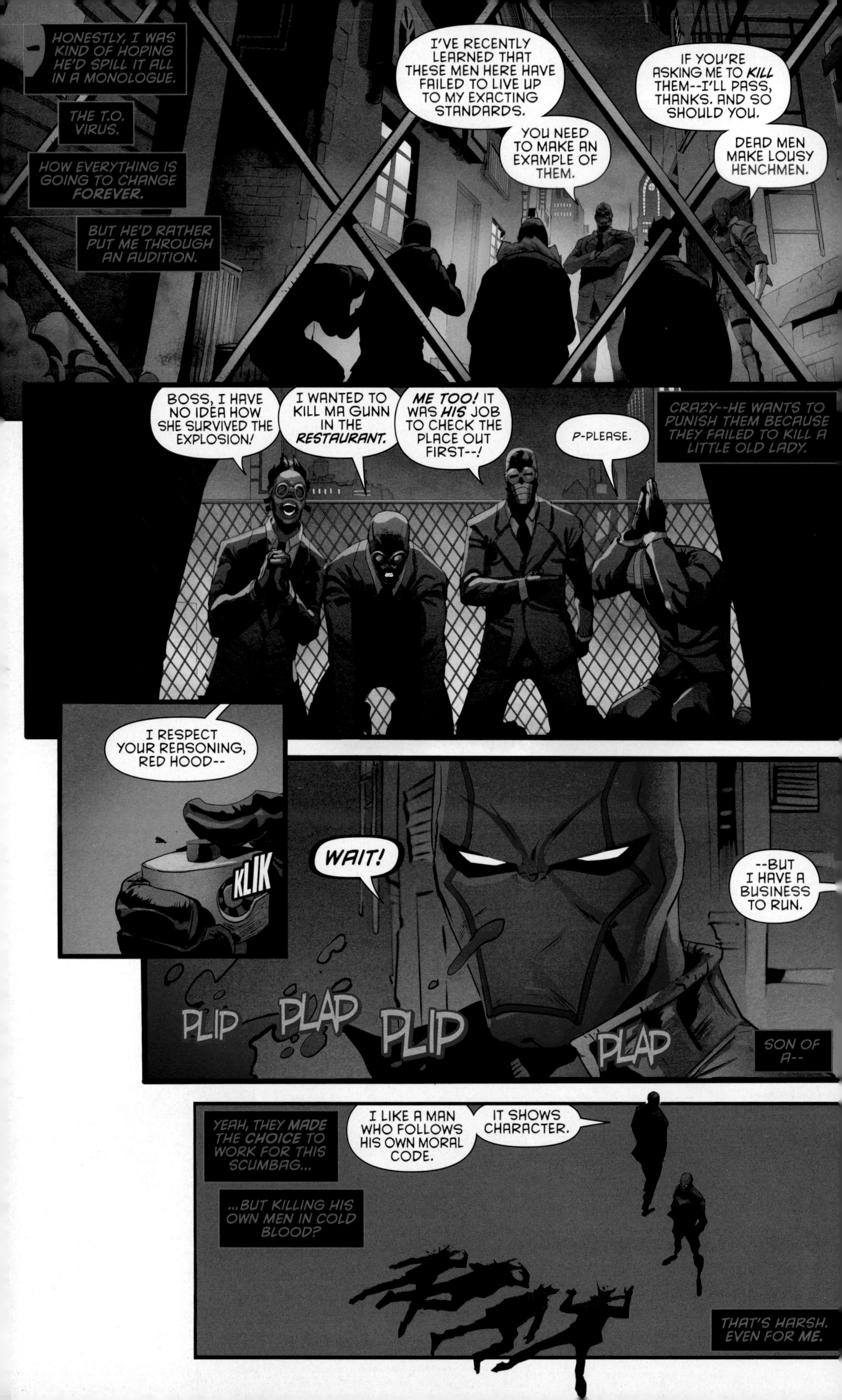
HONESTLY, I WAS KIND OF HOPING HE'D SPILL IT ALL IN A MONOLOGUE.
THE T.O. VIRUS.
HOW EVERYTHING IS GOING TO CHANGE FOREVER.
BUT HE'D RATHER PUT ME THROUGH AN AUDITION.
I'VE RECENTLY LEARNED THAT THESE MEN HERE HAVE FAILED TO LIVE UP TO MY EXACTING STANDARDS.
YOU NEED TO MAKE AN EXAMPLE OF THEM.
IF YOU'RE ASKING ME TO KILL THEM--I'LL PASS, THANKS. AND SO SHOULD YOU.
DEAD MEN MAKE LOUSY HENCHMEN.
BOSS, I HAVE NO IDEA HOW SHE SURVIVED THE EXPLOSION!
I WANTED TO KILL MA GUNN IN THE RESTAURANT.
ME TOO! IT WAS HIS JOB TO CHECK THE PLACE OUT FIRST--!
P-PLEASE.
CRAZY--HE WANTS TO PUNISH THEM BECAUSE THEY FAILED TO KILL A LITTLE OLD LADY.
I RESPECT YOUR REASONING, RED HOOD--
KLIK
WAIT!
--BUT I HAVE A BUSINESS TO RUN.
PLIP PLAP PLIP PLAP
SON OF A--
YEAH, THEY MADE THE CHOICE TO WORK FOR THIS SCUMBAG...
...BUT KILLING HIS OWN MEN IN COLD BLOOD?
I LIKE A MAN WHO FOLLOWS HIS OWN MORAL CODE.
IT SHOWS CHARACTER.
THAT'S HARSH. EVEN FOR ME.

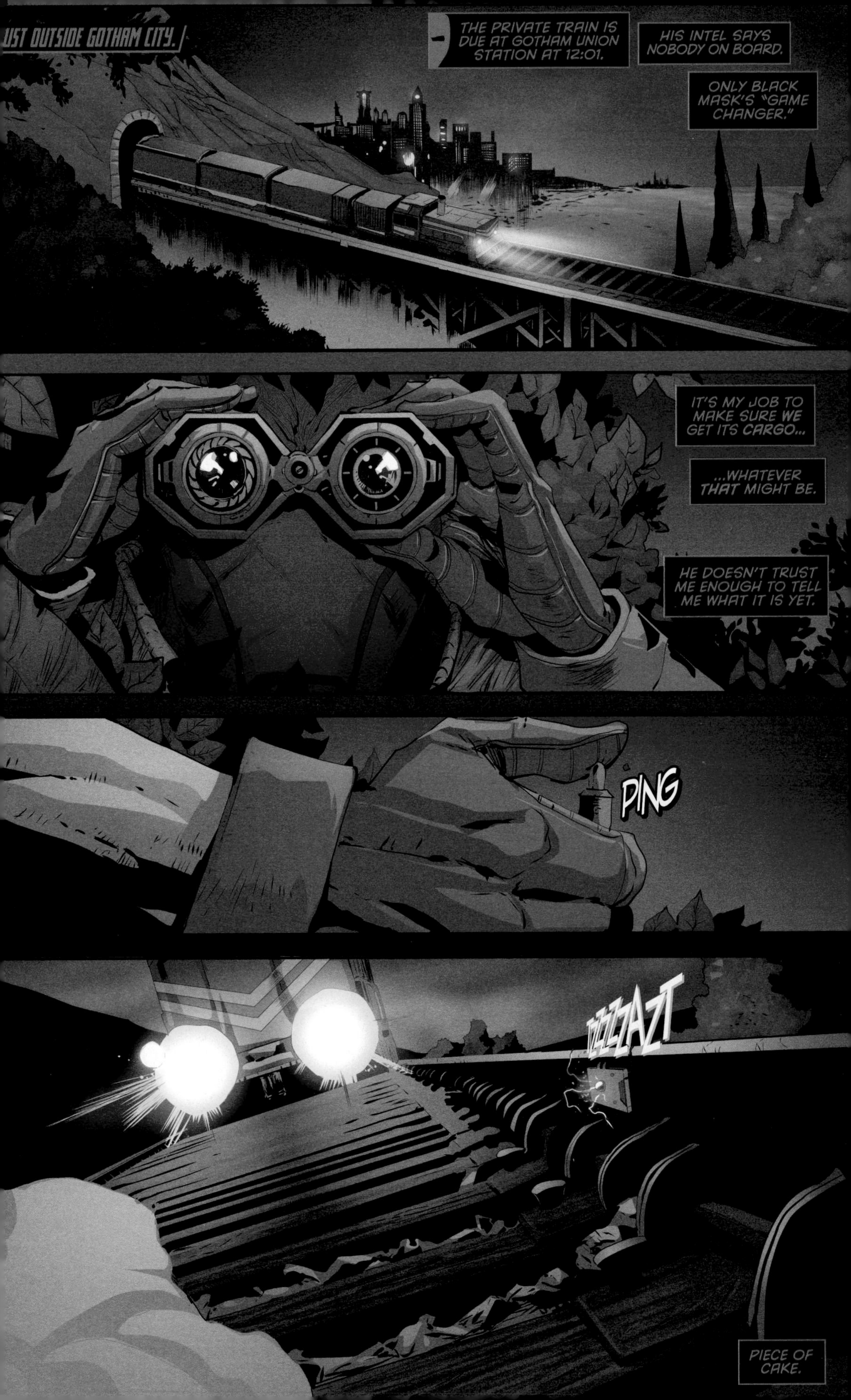
UST OUTSIDE GOTHAM CITY.
THE PRIVATE TRAIN IS DUE AT GOTHAM UNION STATION AT 12:01.
HIS INTEL SAYS NOBODY ON BOARD.
ONLY BLACK MASK'S "GAME CHANGER."
IT'S MY JOB TO MAKE SURE WE GET ITS CARGO...
...WHATEVER THAT MIGHT BE.
HE DOESN'T TRUST ME ENOUGH TO TELL ME WHAT IT IS YET.
PING
TZZZZAZT
PIECE OF CAKE.

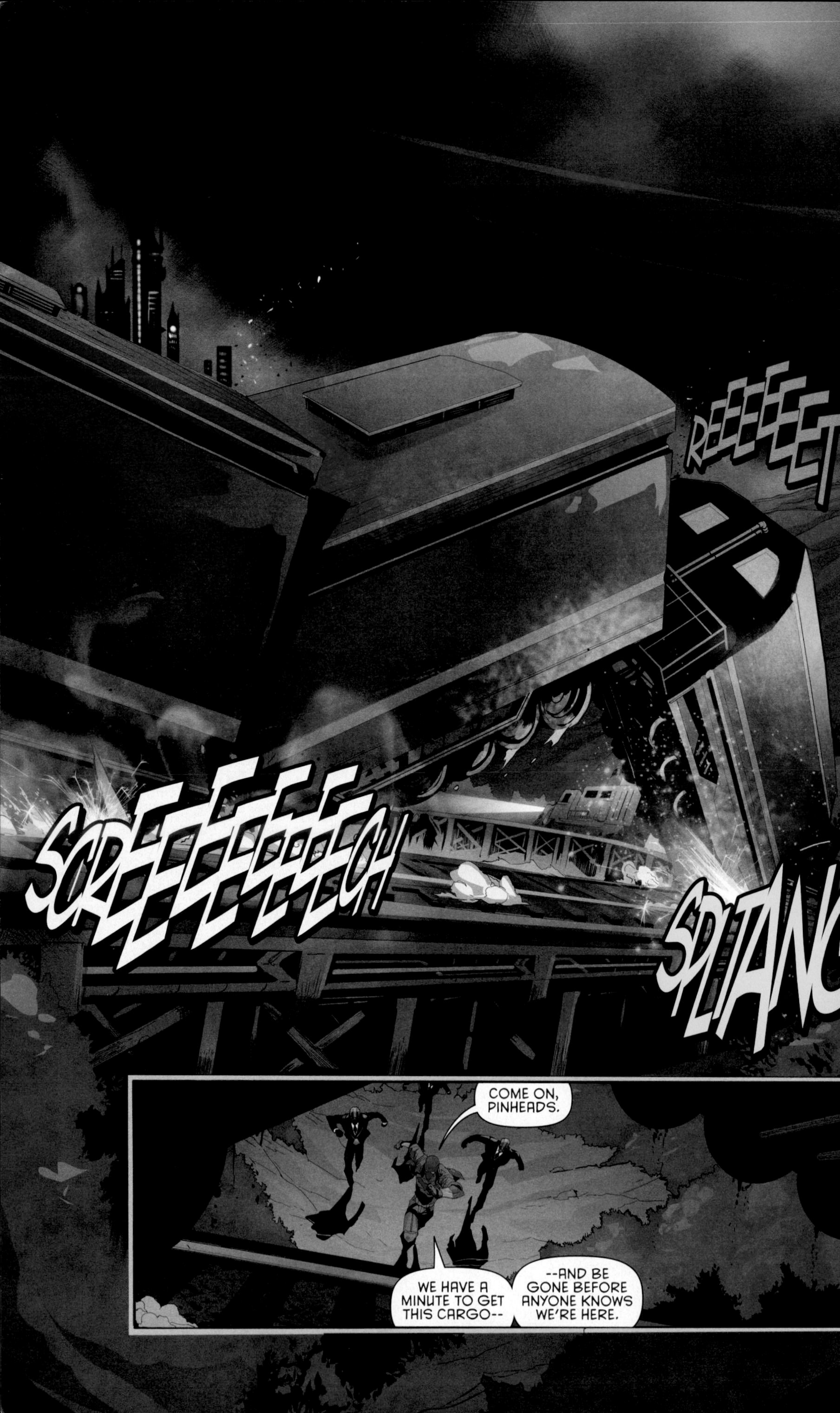
REEEEEET
SCREEEEEEEECH
SPLTANG
COME ON, PINHEADS.
WE HAVE A MINUTE TO GET THIS CARGO--
--AND BE GONE BEFORE ANYONE KNOWS WE'RE HERE.

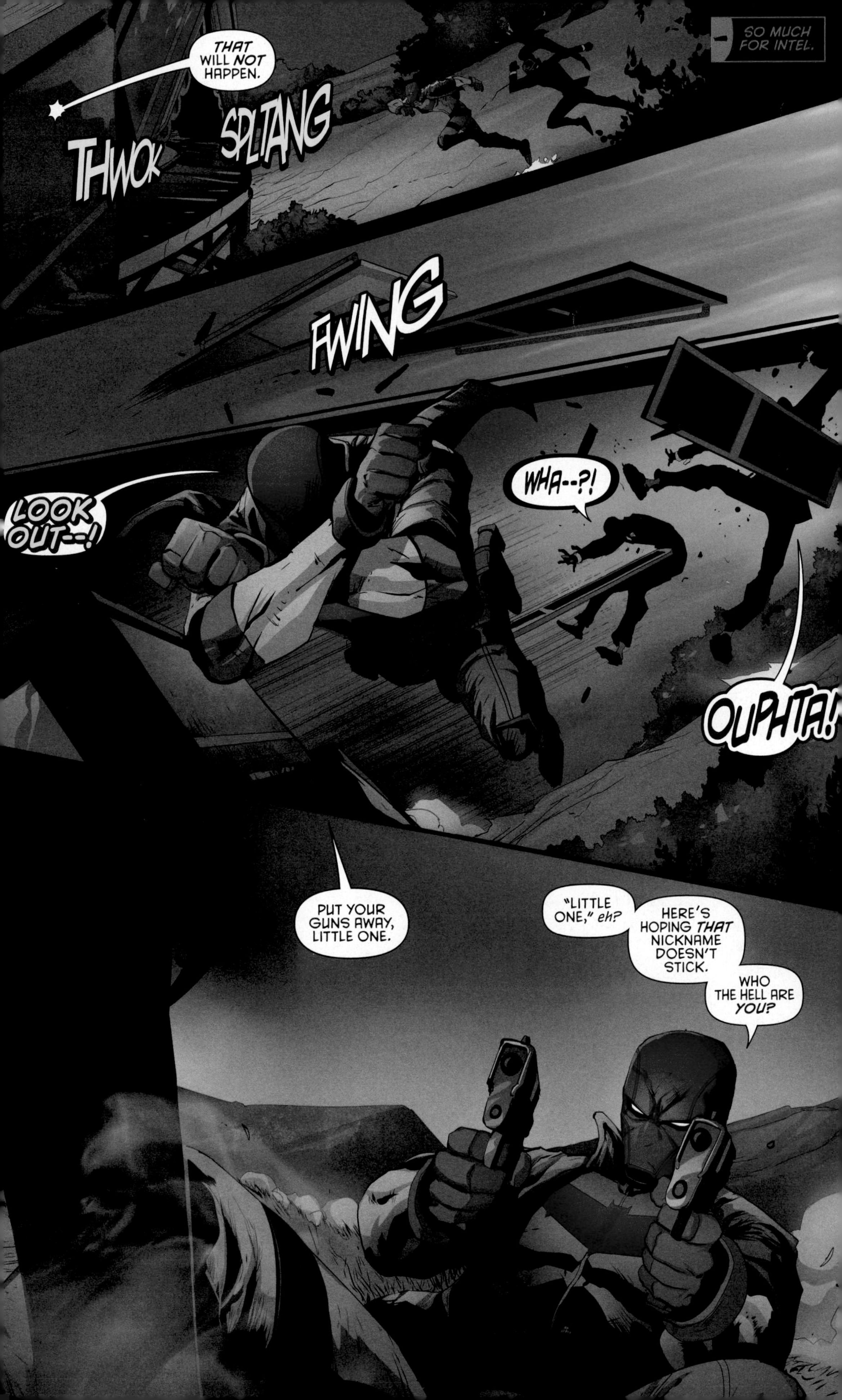
SO MUCH FOR INTEL.
THAT WILL NOT HAPPEN.
THWOK
SPLTANG
FWING
LOOK OUT--!
WHA--?!
OUPHTA!
PUT YOUR GUNS AWAY, LITTLE ONE.
"LITTLE ONE," eh?
HERE'S HOPING THAT NICKNAME DOESN'T STICK.
WHO THE HELL ARE YOU?

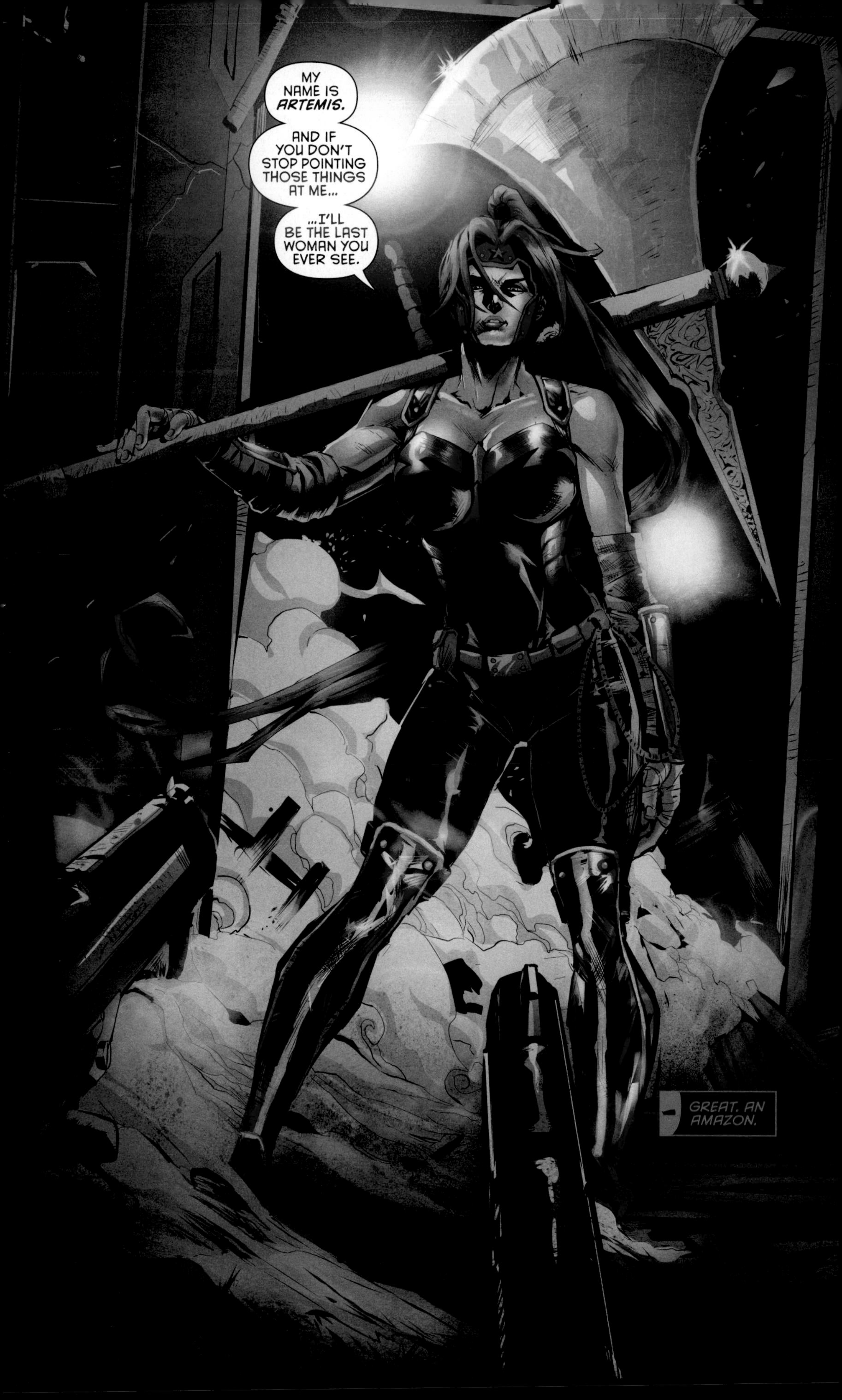
MY NAME IS ARTEMIS.
AND IF YOU DON'T STOP POINTING THOSE THINGS AT ME...
...I'LL BE THE LAST WOMAN YOU EVER SEE.
GREAT. AN AMAZON.

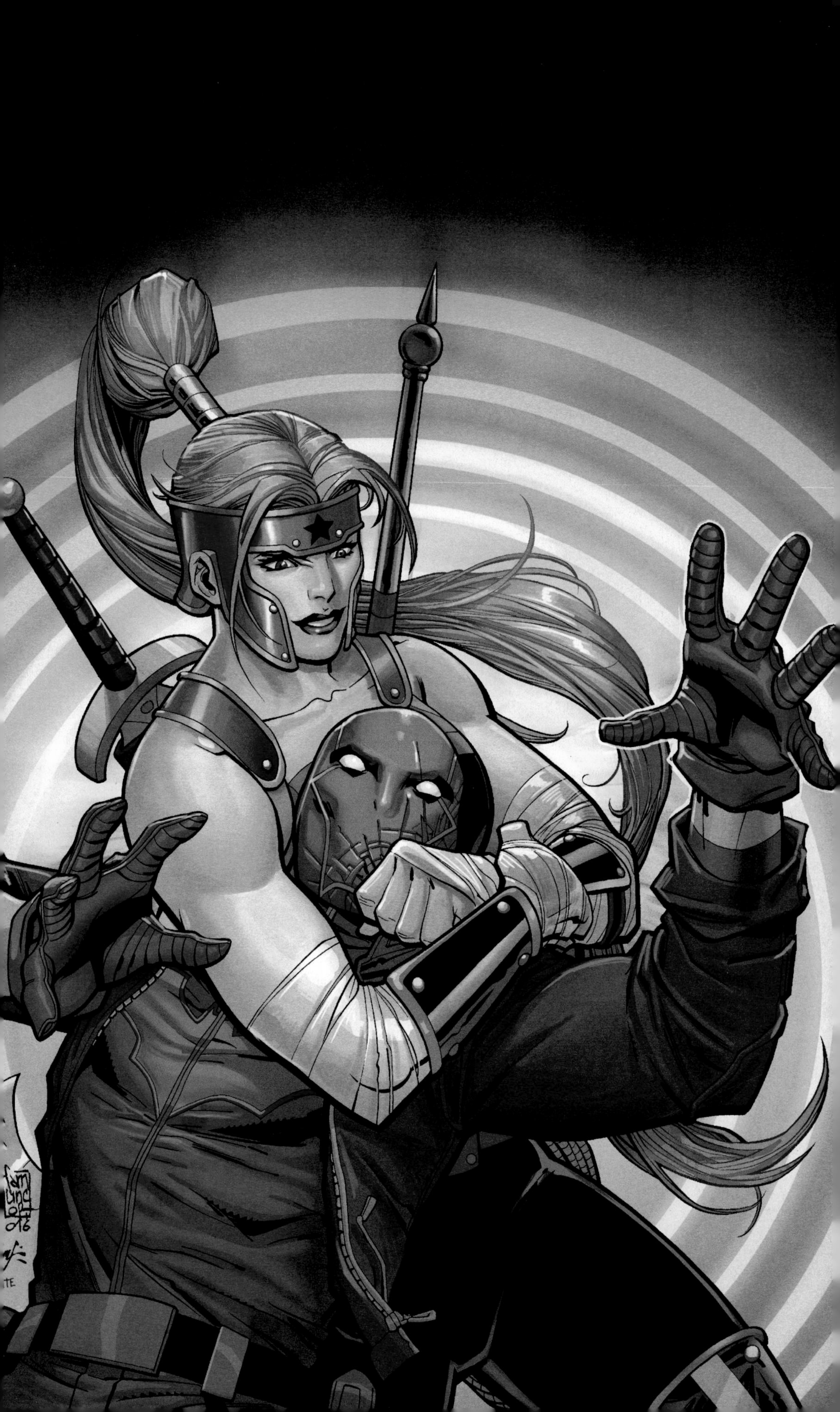

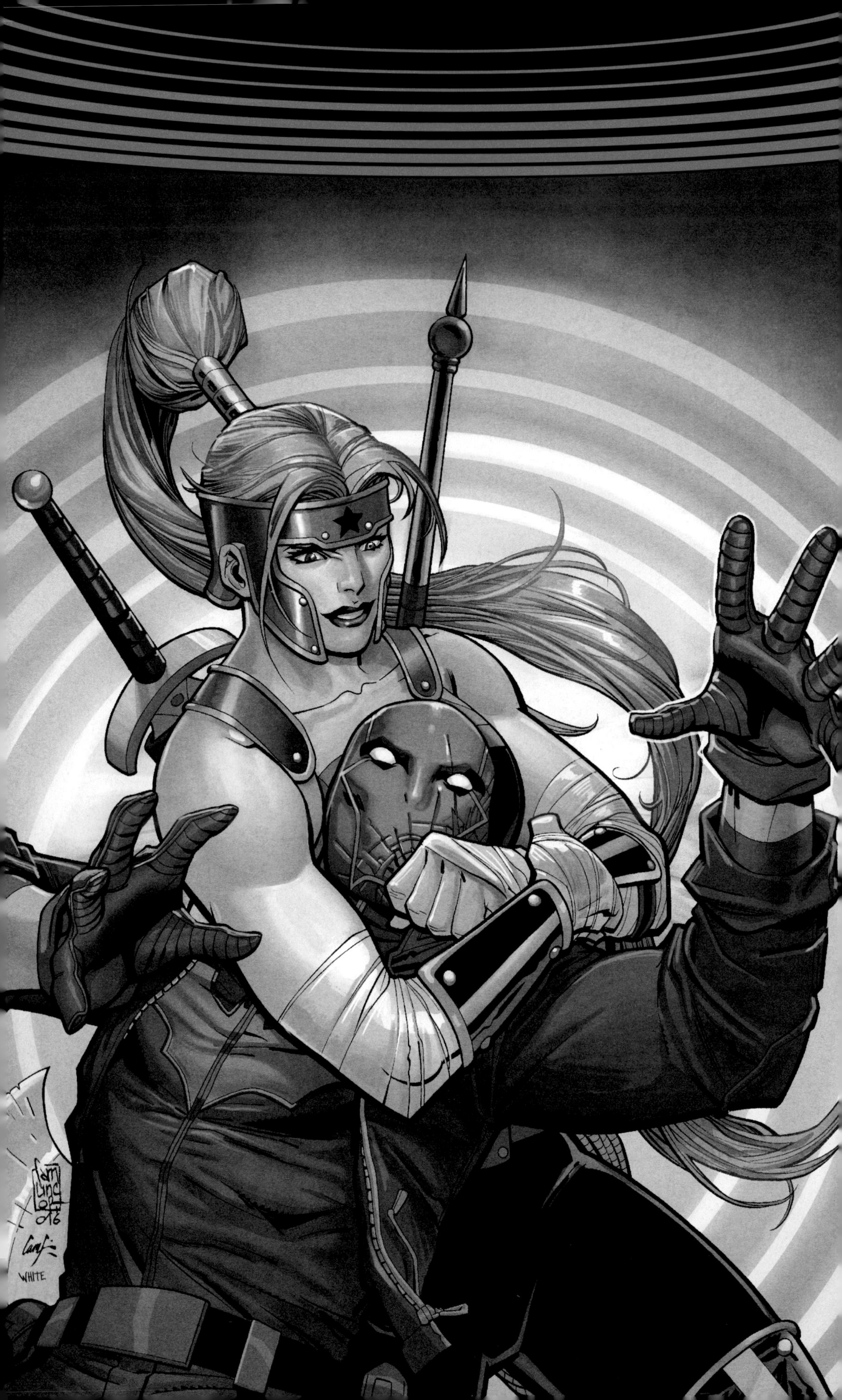
WHITE

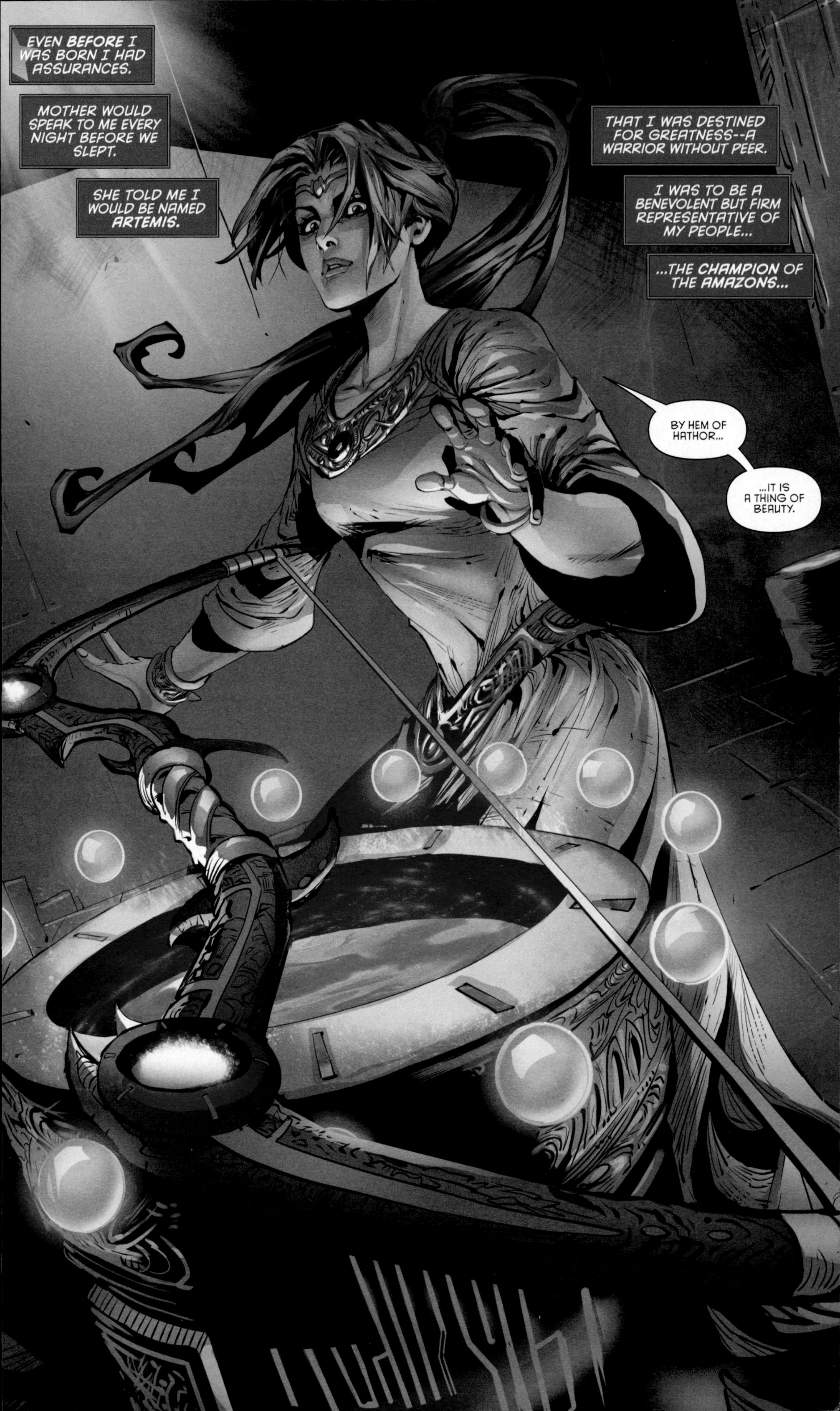

EVEN BEFORE I WAS BORN I HAD ASSURANCES.
MOTHER WOULD SPEAK TO ME EVERY NIGHT BEFORE WE SLEPT.
SHE TOLD ME I WOULD BE NAMED ARTEMIS.
THAT I WAS DESTINED FOR GREATNESS--A WARRIOR WITHOUT PEER.
I WAS TO BE A BENEVOLENT BUT FIRM REPRESENTATIVE OF MY PEOPLE...
...THE CHAMPION OF THE AMAZONS...
BY HEM OF HATHOR...
...IT IS A THING OF BEAUTY.

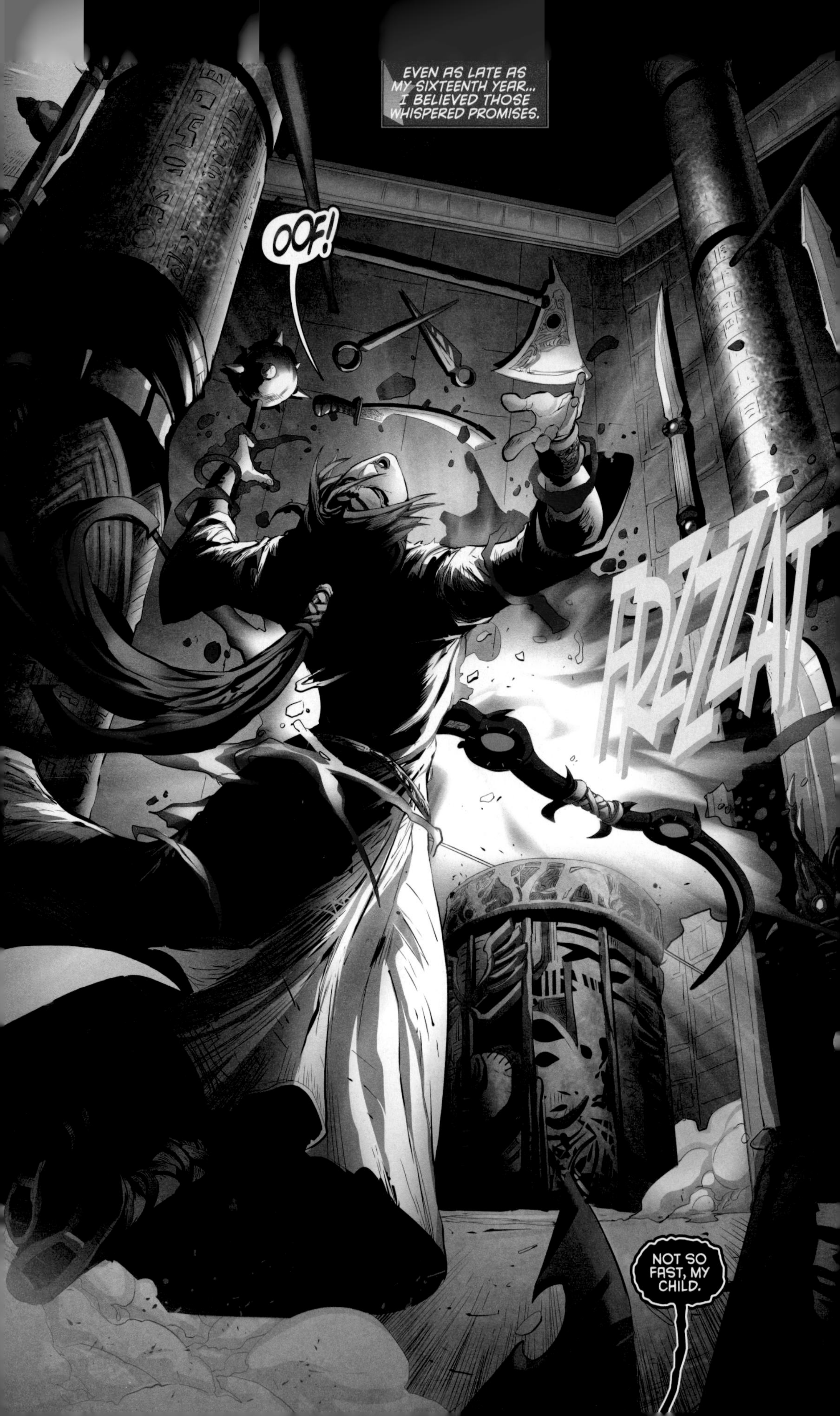
EVEN AS LATE AS MY SIXTEENTH YEAR... I BELIEVED THOSE WHISPERED PROMISES.
OOF!
FRZZAT
NOT SO FAST, MY CHILD.

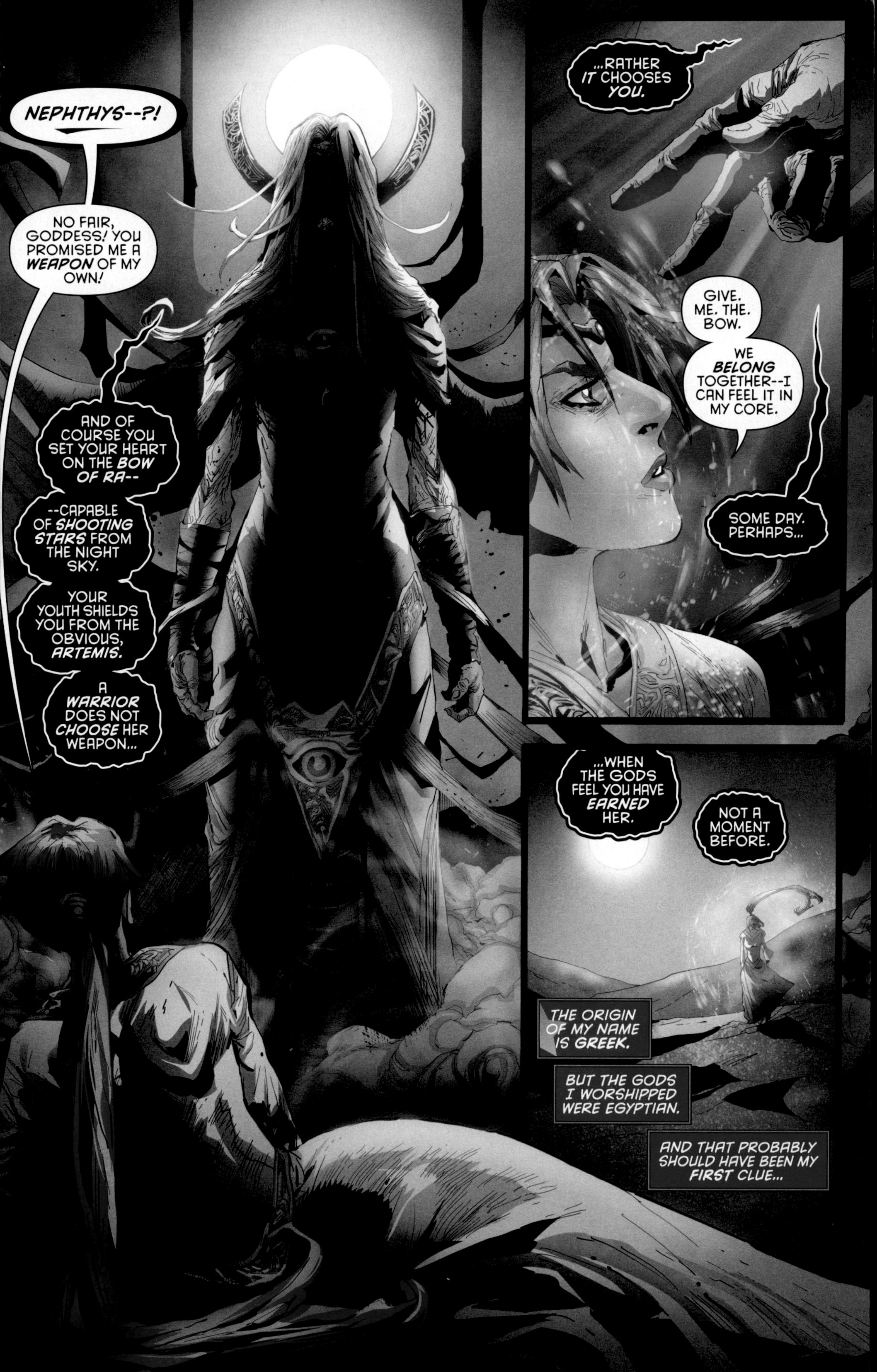
NEPHTHYS--?!
NO FAIR, GODDESS! YOU PROMISED ME A WEAPON OF MY OWN!
AND OF COURSE YOU SET YOUR HEART ON THE BOW OF RA--
--CAPABLE OF SHOOTING STARS FROM THE NIGHT SKY.
YOUR YOUTH SHIELDS YOU FROM THE OBVIOUS, ARTEMIS.
A WARRIOR DOES NOT CHOOSE HER WEAPON...
...RATHER IT CHOOSES YOU.
GIVE. ME. THE. BOW.
WE BELONG TOGETHER--I CAN FEEL IT IN MY CORE.
SOME DAY. PERHAPS...
...WHEN THE GODS FEEL YOU HAVE EARNED HER.
NOT A MOMENT BEFORE.
THE ORIGIN OF MY NAME IS GREEK.
BUT THE GODS I WORSHIPPED WERE EGYPTIAN.
AND THAT PROBABLY SHOULD HAVE BEEN MY FIRST CLUE...

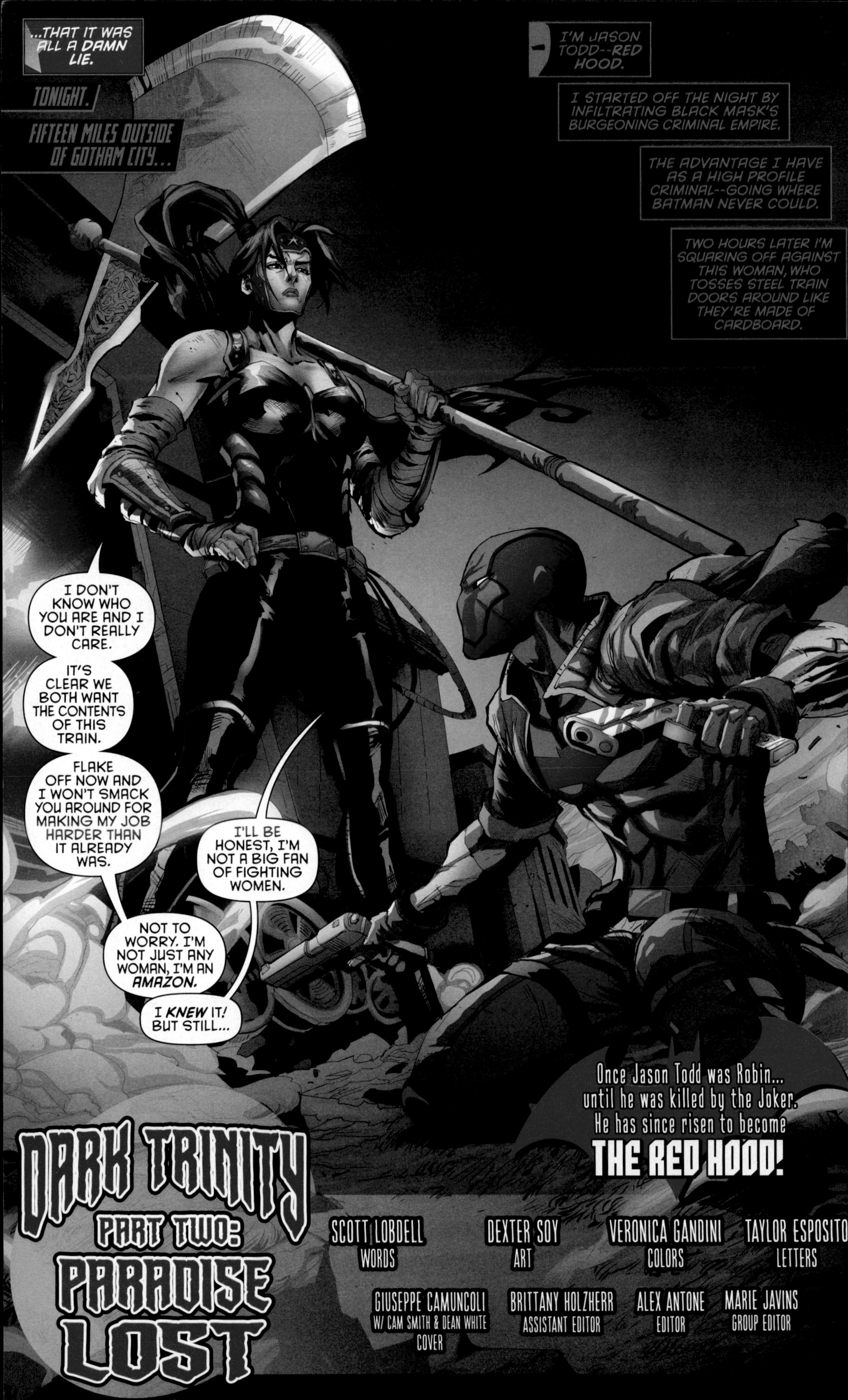
...THAT IT WAS ALL A DAMN LIE.
TONIGHT.
FIFTEEN MILES OUTSIDE OF GOTHAM CITY...
I'M JASON TODD--RED HOOD.
I STARTED OFF THE NIGHT BY INFILTRATING BLACK MASK'S BURGEONING CRIMINAL EMPIRE.
THE ADVANTAGE I HAVE AS A HIGH PROFILE CRIMINAL--GOING WHERE BATMAN NEVER COULD.
TWO HOURS LATER I'M SQUARING OFF AGAINST THIS WOMAN, WHO TOSSES STEEL TRAIN DOORS AROUND LIKE THEY'RE MADE OF CARDBOARD.
I DON'T KNOW WHO YOU ARE AND I DON'T REALLY CARE.
IT'S CLEAR WE BOTH WANT THE CONTENTS OF THIS TRAIN.
FLAKE OFF NOW AND I WON'T SMACK YOU AROUND FOR MAKING MY JOB HARDER THAN IT ALREADY WAS.
I'LL BE HONEST, I'M NOT A BIG FAN OF FIGHTING WOMEN.
NOT TO WORRY. I'M NOT JUST ANY WOMAN, I'M AN AMAZON.
I KNEW IT! BUT STILL...
Once Jason Todd was Robin... until he was killed by the Joker. He has since risen to become
THE RED HOOD!
DARK TRINITY
PART TWO: PARADISE LOST
SCOTT LOBDELL WORDS
DEXTER SOY ART
VERONICA GANDINI COLORS
TAYLOR ESPOSITO LETTERS
GIUSEPPE CAMUNCOLI W/ CAM SMITH & DEAN WHITE COVER
BRITTANY HOLZHERR ASSISTANT EDITOR
ALEX ANTONE EDITOR
MARIE JAVINS GROUP EDITOR

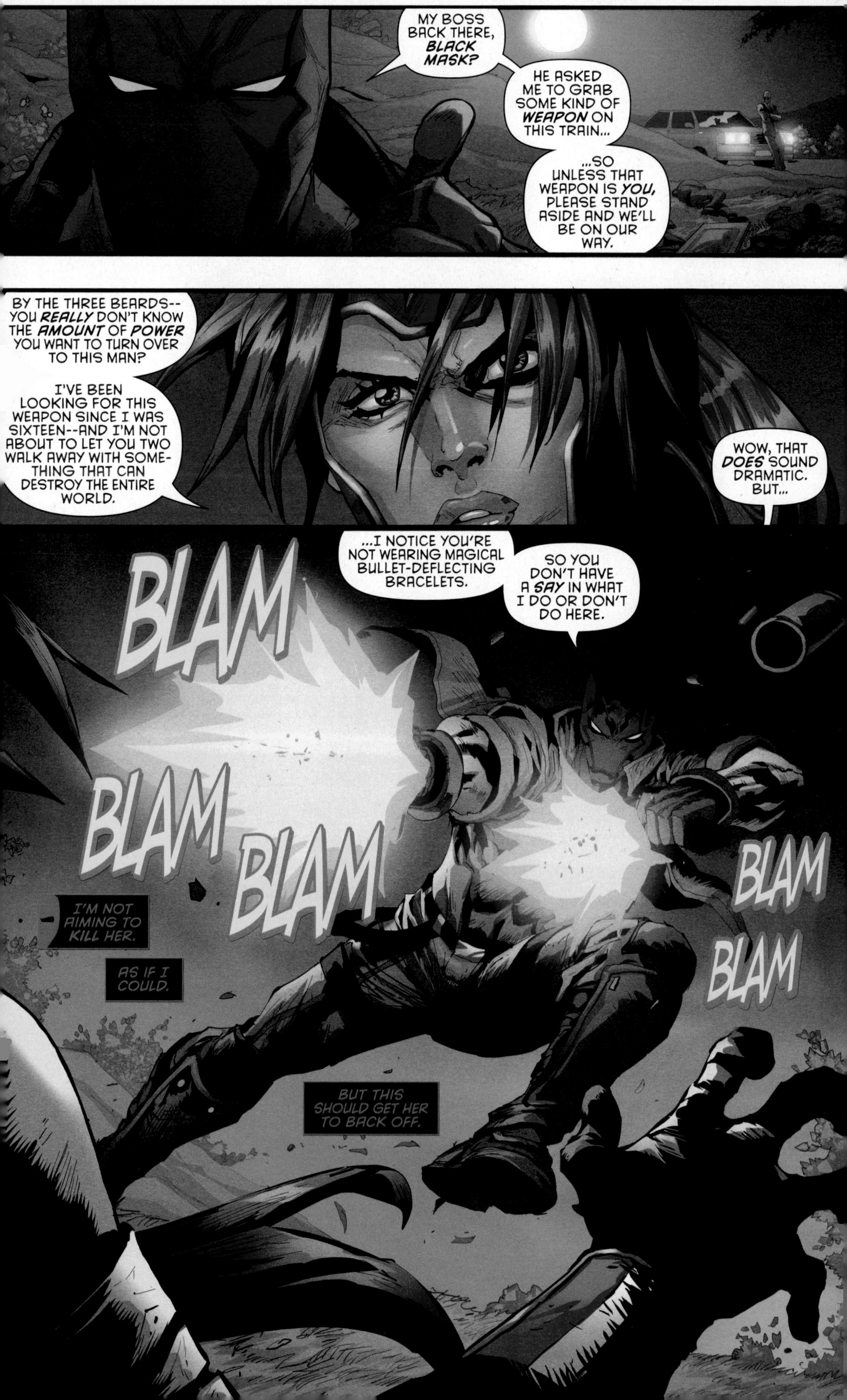
MY BOSS BACK THERE, BLACK MASK?
HE ASKED ME TO GRAB SOME KIND OF WEAPON ON THIS TRAIN...
...SO UNLESS THAT WEAPON IS YOU, PLEASE STAND ASIDE AND WE'LL BE ON OUR WAY.
BY THE THREE BEARDS--YOU REALLY DON'T KNOW THE AMOUNT OF POWER YOU WANT TO TURN OVER TO THIS MAN?
I'VE BEEN LOOKING FOR THIS WEAPON SINCE I WAS SIXTEEN--AND I'M NOT ABOUT TO LET YOU TWO WALK AWAY WITH SOMETHING THAT CAN DESTROY THE ENTIRE WORLD.
WOW, THAT DOES SOUND DRAMATIC. BUT...
...I NOTICE YOU'RE NOT WEARING MAGICAL BULLET-DEFLECTING BRACELETS.
SO YOU DON'T HAVE A SAY IN WHAT I DO OR DON'T DO HERE.
BLAM
BLAM
BLAM
BLAM
BLAM
I'M NOT AIMING TO KILL HER.
AS IF I COULD.
BUT THIS SHOULD GET HER TO BACK OFF.

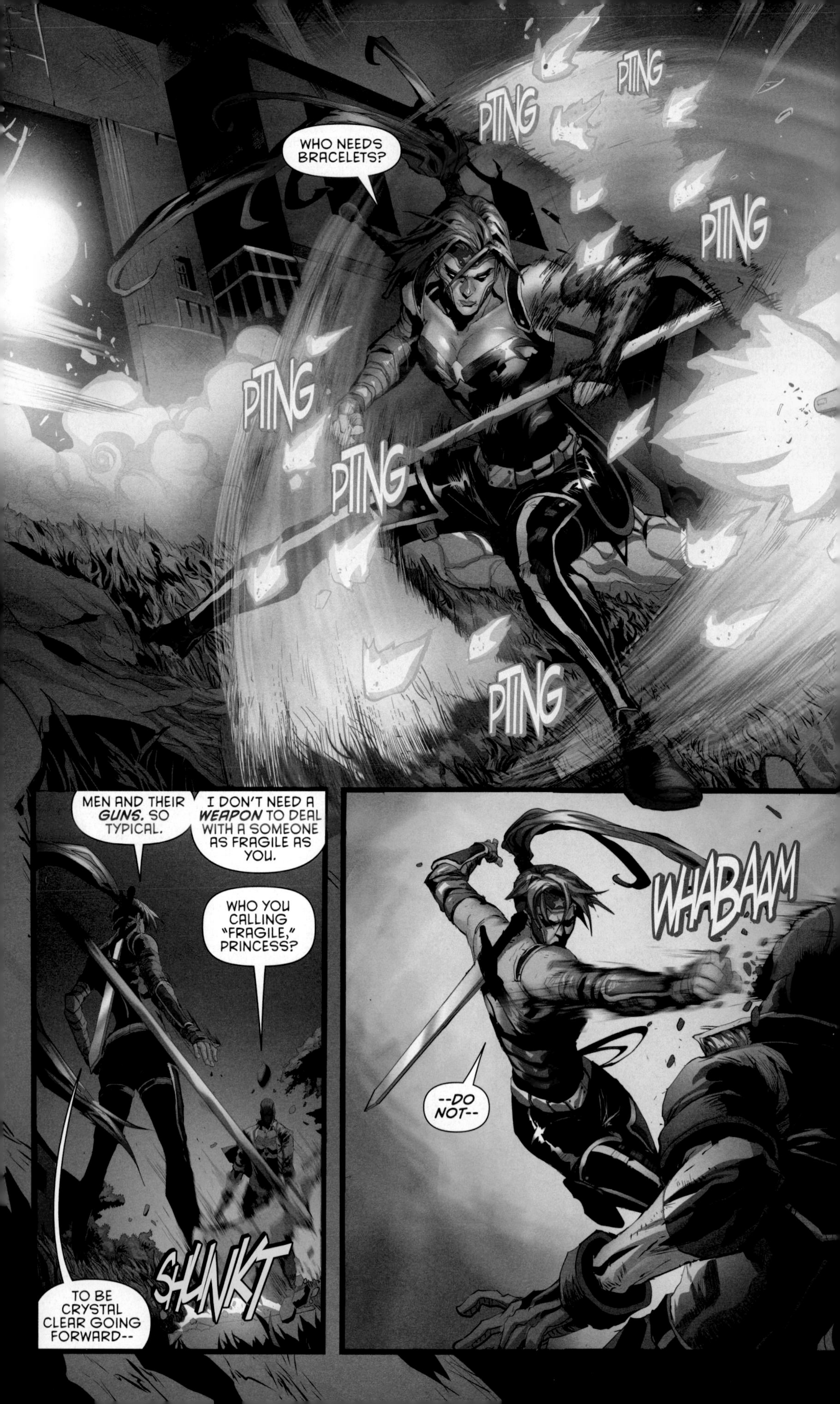
WHO NEEDS BRACELETS?
PTING
PTING
PTING
PTING
PTING
PTING
MEN AND THEIR GUNS. SO TYPICAL.
I DON'T NEED A WEAPON TO DEAL WITH A SOMEONE AS FRAGILE AS YOU.
WHO YOU CALLING "FRAGILE," PRINCESS?
SHUNKT
TO BE CRYSTAL CLEAR GOING FORWARD--
WHABAAM
--DO NOT--

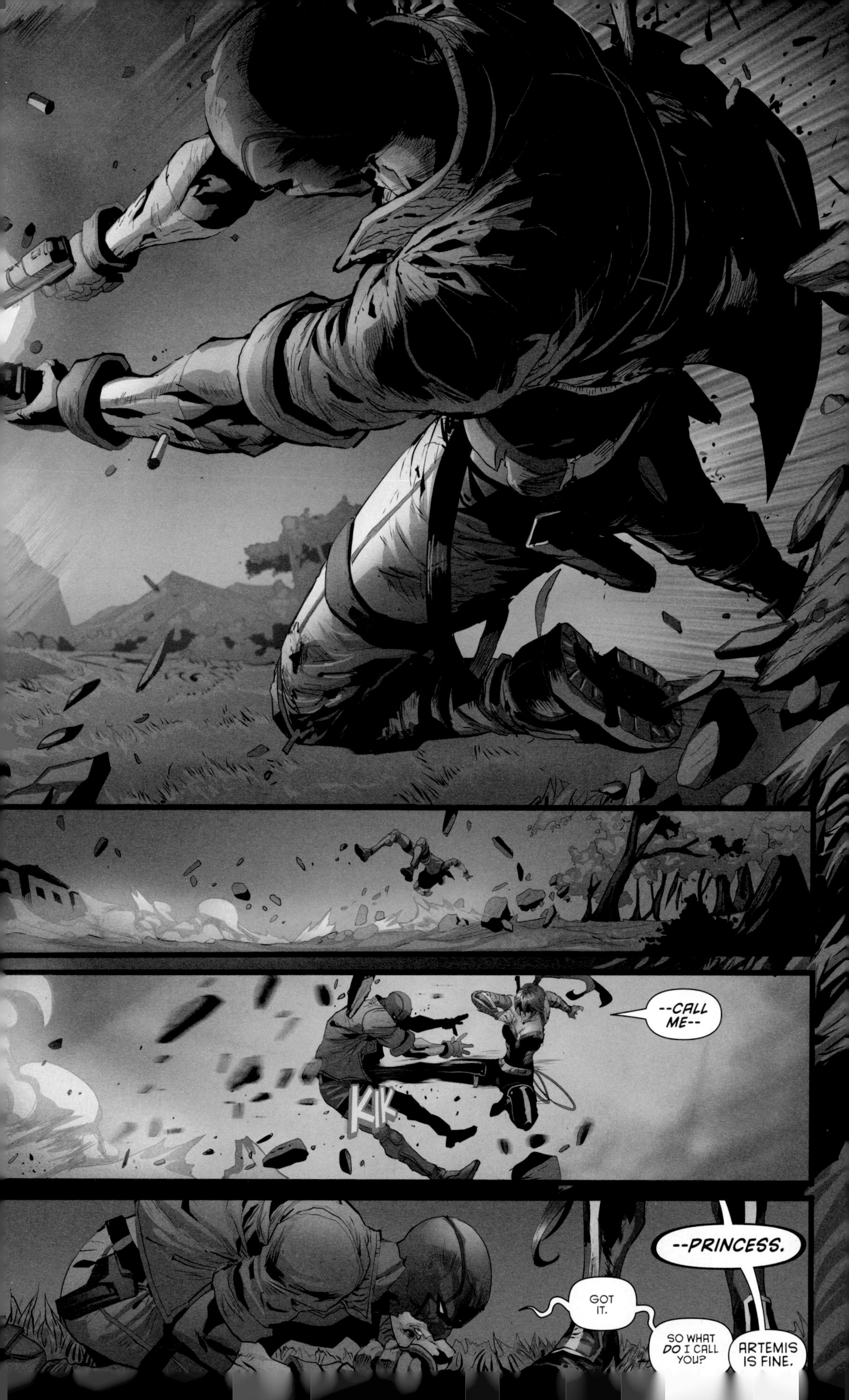
--CALL ME--
KIK
--PRINCESS.
GOT IT.
SO WHAT DO I CALL YOU?
ARTEMIS IS FINE.

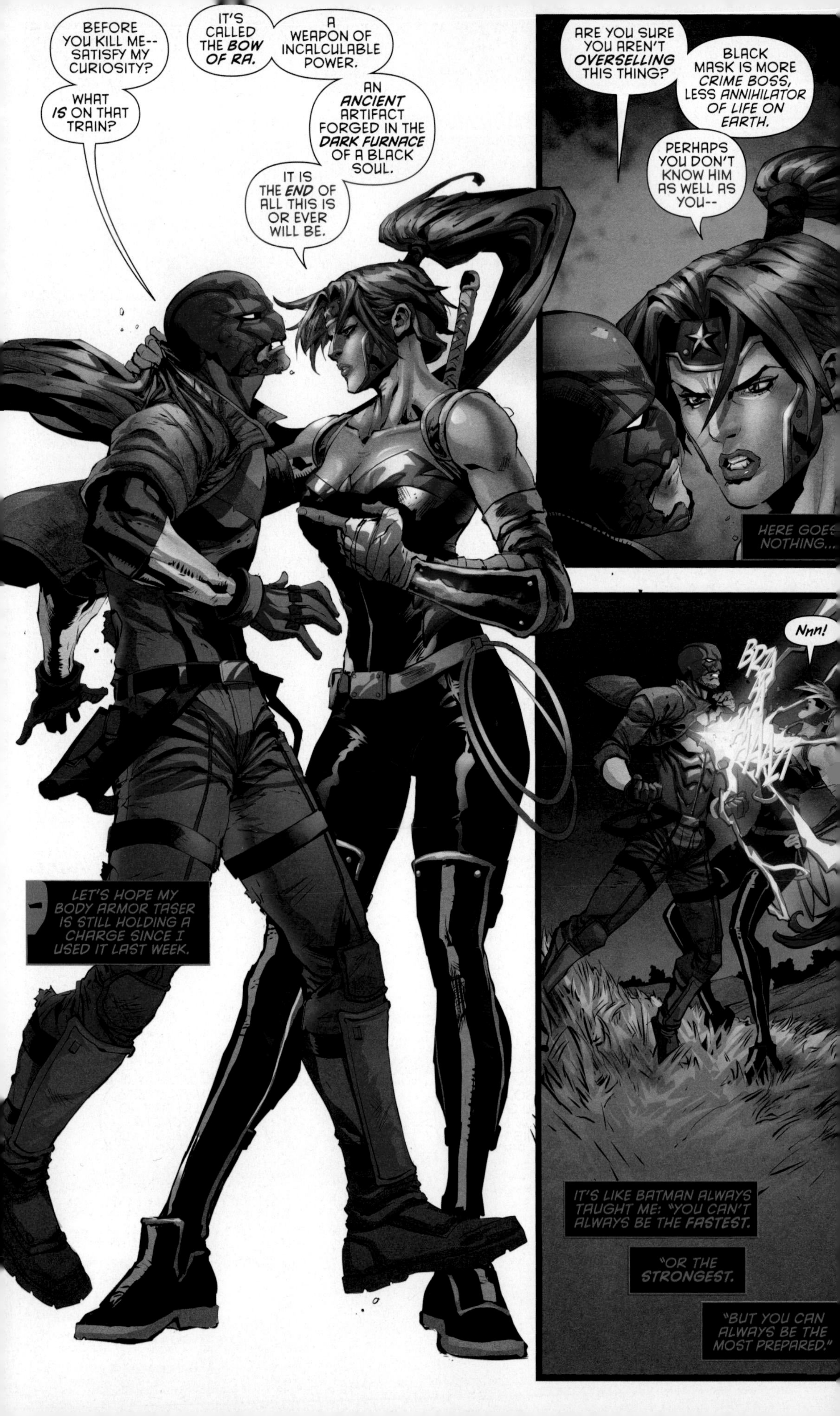
BEFORE YOU KILL ME-- SATISFY MY CURIOSITY?
WHAT *IS* ON THAT TRAIN?
IT'S CALLED THE ***BOW OF RA.***
A WEAPON OF INCALCULABLE POWER.
AN ***ANCIENT*** ARTIFACT FORGED IN THE ***DARK FURNACE*** OF A BLACK SOUL.
IT IS THE ***END*** OF ALL THIS IS OR EVER WILL BE.
LET'S HOPE MY BODY ARMOR TASER IS STILL HOLDING A CHARGE SINCE I USED IT LAST WEEK.
ARE YOU SURE YOU AREN'T ***OVERSELLING*** THIS THING?
BLACK MASK IS MORE *CRIME BOSS,* LESS *ANNIHILATOR OF LIFE ON EARTH.*
PERHAPS YOU DON'T KNOW HIM AS WELL AS YOU--
HERE GOES NOTHING...
Nnn!
IT'S LIKE BATMAN ALWAYS TAUGHT ME: "YOU CAN'T ALWAYS BE THE ***FASTEST.***
"OR THE ***STRONGEST.***
"BUT YOU CAN ALWAYS BE THE ***MOST PREPARED.***"

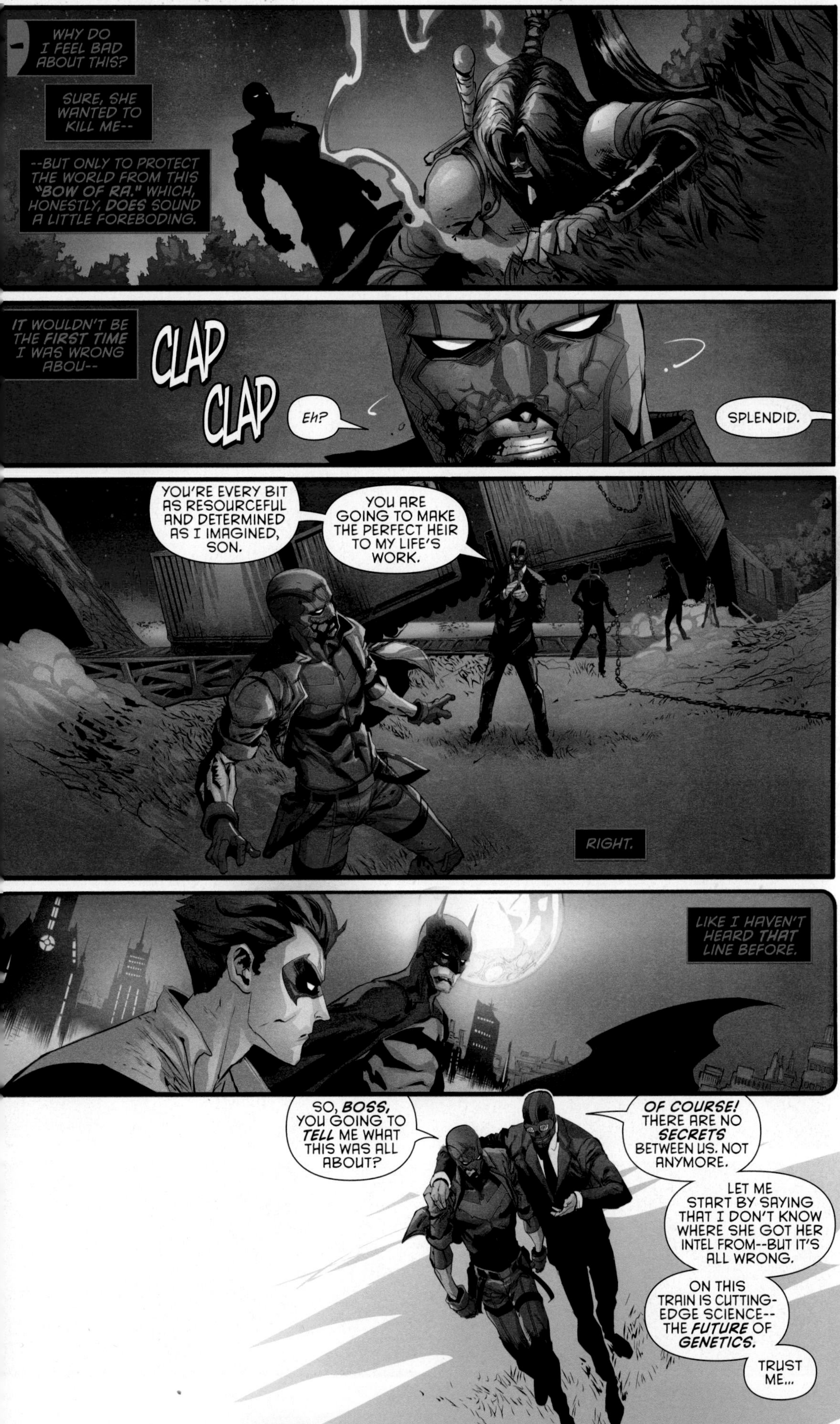

WHY DO I FEEL BAD ABOUT THIS?
SURE, SHE WANTED TO KILL ME--
--BUT ONLY TO PROTECT THE WORLD FROM THIS "BOW OF RA." WHICH, HONESTLY, DOES SOUND A LITTLE FOREBODING.
IT WOULDN'T BE THE FIRST TIME I WAS WRONG ABOU--
CLAP CLAP
Eh?
SPLENDID.
YOU'RE EVERY BIT AS RESOURCEFUL AND DETERMINED AS I IMAGINED, SON.
YOU ARE GOING TO MAKE THE PERFECT HEIR TO MY LIFE'S WORK.
RIGHT.
LIKE I HAVEN'T HEARD THAT LINE BEFORE.
SO, BOSS, YOU GOING TO TELL ME WHAT THIS WAS ALL ABOUT?
OF COURSE! THERE ARE NO SECRETS BETWEEN US. NOT ANYMORE.
LET ME START BY SAYING THAT I DON'T KNOW WHERE SHE GOT HER INTEL FROM--BUT IT'S ALL WRONG.
ON THIS TRAIN IS CUTTING-EDGE SCIENCE--THE FUTURE OF GENETICS.
TRUST ME...

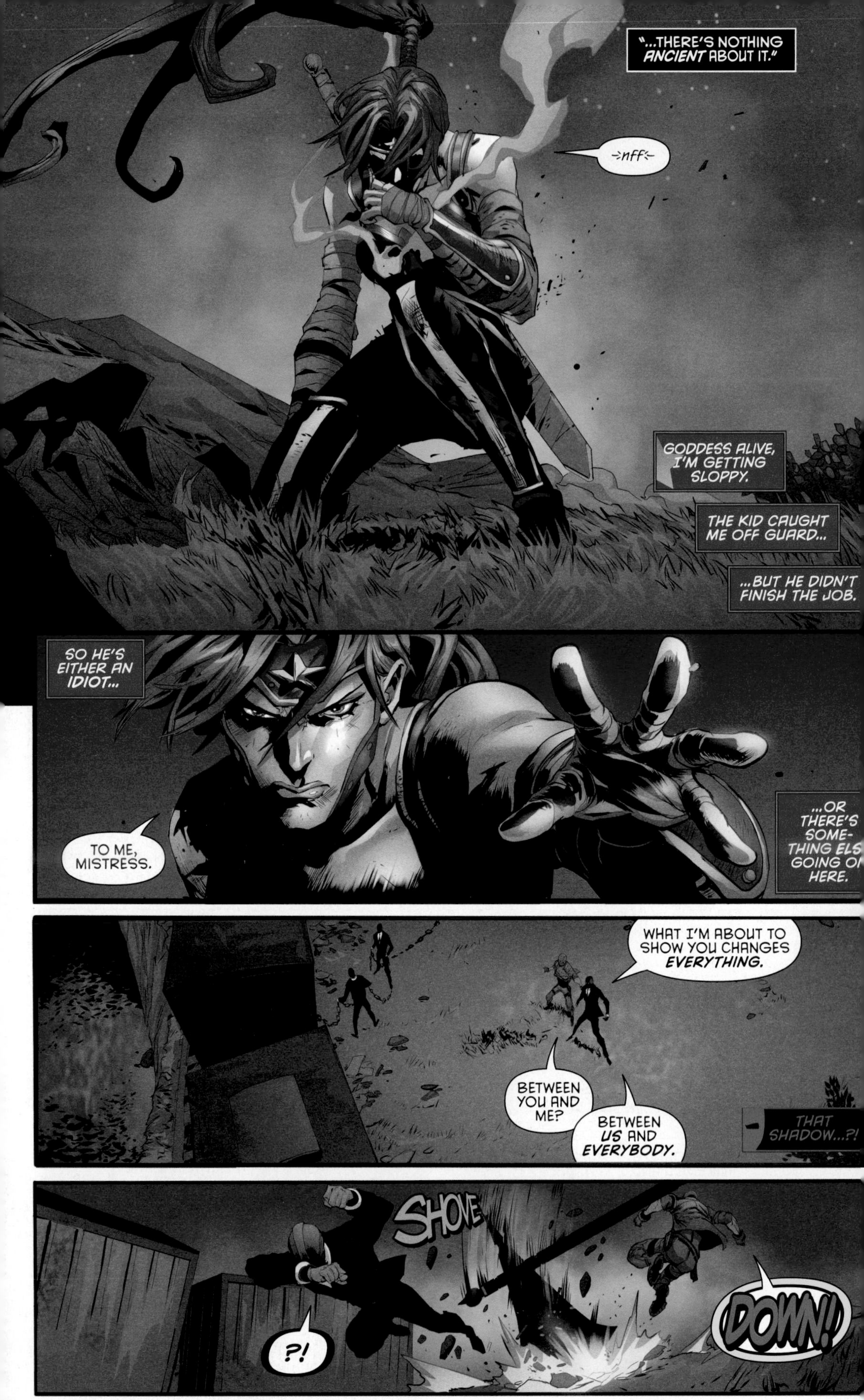
"...THERE'S NOTHING ANCIENT ABOUT IT."
nff
GODDESS ALIVE, I'M GETTING SLOPPY.
THE KID CAUGHT ME OFF GUARD...
...BUT HE DIDN'T FINISH THE JOB.
SO HE'S EITHER AN IDIOT...
TO ME, MISTRESS.
...OR THERE'S SOME-THING ELS GOING ON HERE.
WHAT I'M ABOUT TO SHOW YOU CHANGES EVERYTHING.
BETWEEN YOU AND ME?
BETWEEN US AND EVERYBODY.
THAT SHADOW...?!
SHOVE
?!
DOWN!

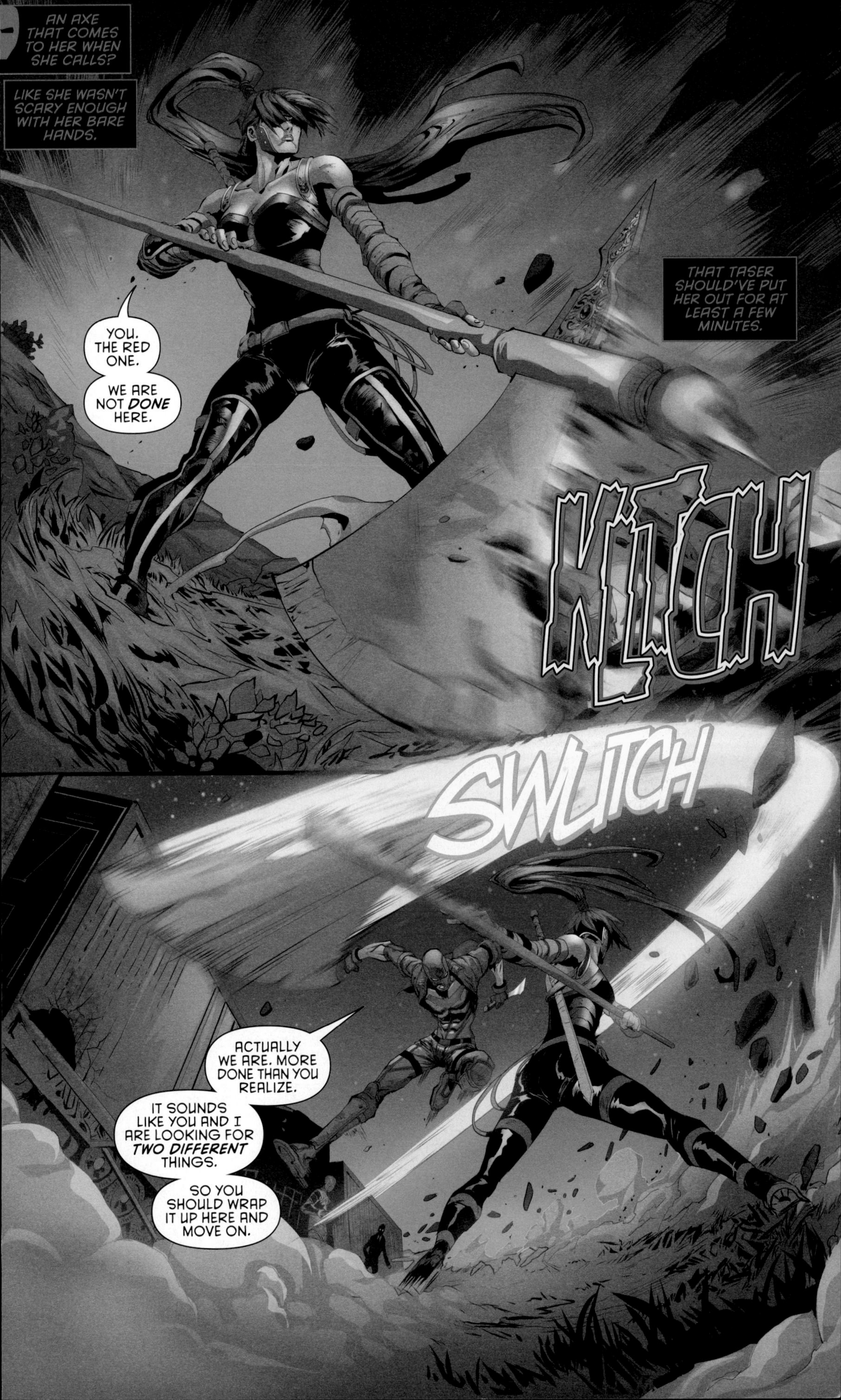
AN AXE THAT COMES TO HER WHEN SHE CALLS?
LIKE SHE WASN'T SCARY ENOUGH WITH HER BARE HANDS.
YOU. THE RED ONE.
WE ARE NOT *DONE* HERE.
THAT TASER SHOULD'VE PUT HER OUT FOR AT LEAST A FEW MINUTES.
KLTCH
SWLTCH
ACTUALLY WE ARE. MORE DONE THAN YOU REALIZE.
IT SOUNDS LIKE YOU AND I ARE LOOKING FOR *TWO DIFFERENT* THINGS.
SO YOU SHOULD WRAP IT UP HERE AND MOVE ON.

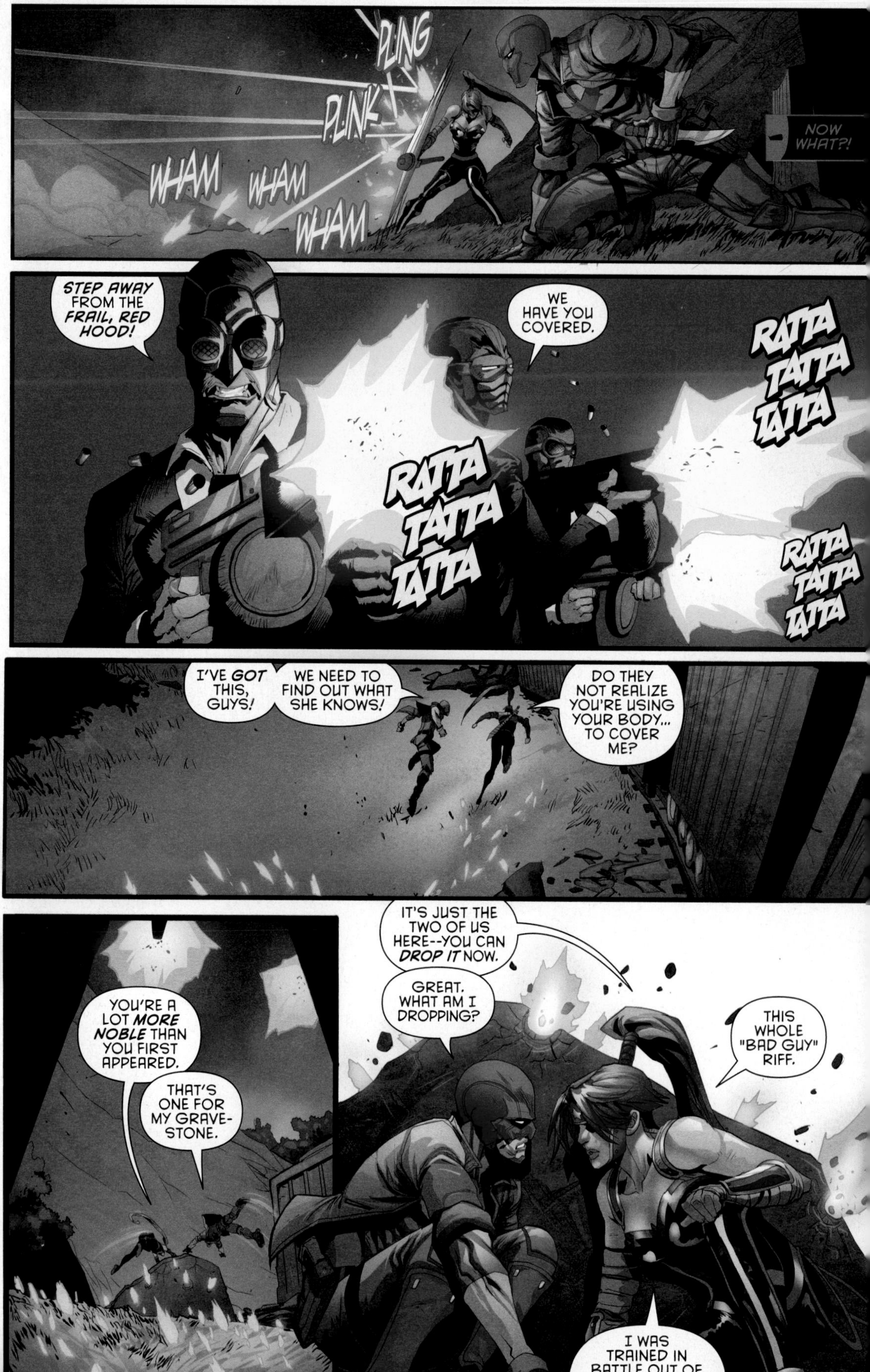
PLING
PLINK
WHAM
WHAM
WHAM
NOW WHAT?!
STEP AWAY FROM THE FRAIL, RED HOOD!
WE HAVE YOU COVERED.
RATTA TATTA TATTA
RATTA TATTA TATTA
RATTA TATTA TATTA
I'VE GOT THIS, GUYS!
WE NEED TO FIND OUT WHAT SHE KNOWS!
DO THEY NOT REALIZE YOU'RE USING YOUR BODY... TO COVER ME?
YOU'RE A LOT MORE NOBLE THAN YOU FIRST APPEARED.
THAT'S ONE FOR MY GRAVE-STONE.
IT'S JUST THE TWO OF US HERE--YOU CAN DROP IT NOW.
GREAT. WHAT AM I DROPPING?
THIS WHOLE "BAD GUY" RIFF.
I WAS TRAINED IN BATTLE OUT OF THE WOMB--I KNOW WHEN SOMEONE IS PULLING THEIR PUNCHES.

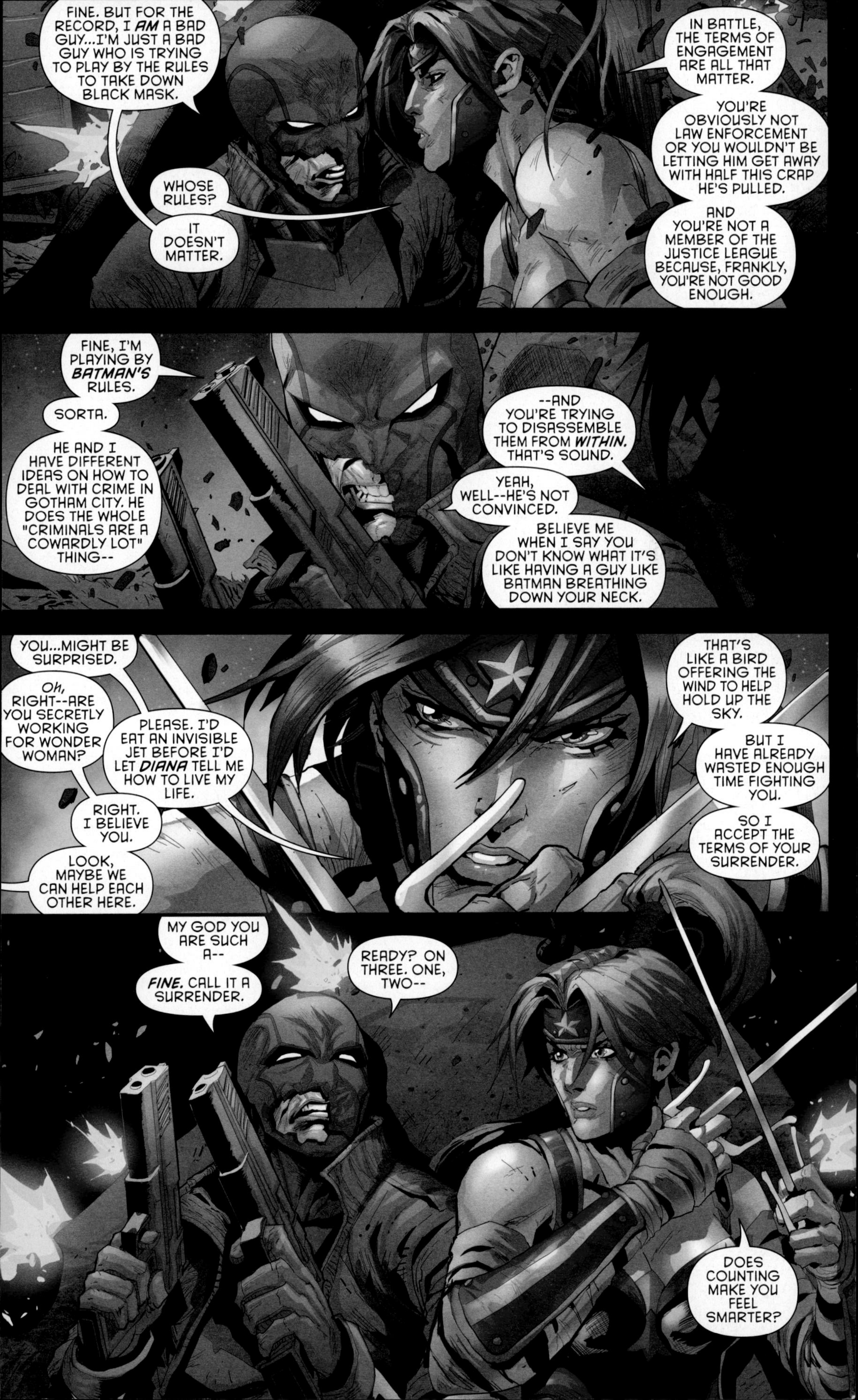
FINE. BUT FOR THE RECORD, I AM A BAD GUY...I'M JUST A BAD GUY WHO IS TRYING TO PLAY BY THE RULES TO TAKE DOWN BLACK MASK.
IN BATTLE, THE TERMS OF ENGAGEMENT ARE ALL THAT MATTER.
YOU'RE OBVIOUSLY NOT LAW ENFORCEMENT OR YOU WOULDN'T BE LETTING HIM GET AWAY WITH HALF THIS CRAP HE'S PULLED.
AND YOU'RE NOT A MEMBER OF THE JUSTICE LEAGUE BECAUSE, FRANKLY, YOU'RE NOT GOOD ENOUGH.
WHOSE RULES?
IT DOESN'T MATTER.
FINE, I'M PLAYING BY BATMAN'S RULES.
SORTA.
HE AND I HAVE DIFFERENT IDEAS ON HOW TO DEAL WITH CRIME IN GOTHAM CITY. HE DOES THE WHOLE "CRIMINALS ARE A COWARDLY LOT" THING--
--AND YOU'RE TRYING TO DISASSEMBLE THEM FROM WITHIN. THAT'S SOUND.
YEAH, WELL--HE'S NOT CONVINCED.
BELIEVE ME WHEN I SAY YOU DON'T KNOW WHAT IT'S LIKE HAVING A GUY LIKE BATMAN BREATHING DOWN YOUR NECK.
YOU...MIGHT BE SURPRISED.
Oh, RIGHT--ARE YOU SECRETLY WORKING FOR WONDER WOMAN?
PLEASE. I'D EAT AN INVISIBLE JET BEFORE I'D LET DIANA TELL ME HOW TO LIVE MY LIFE.
RIGHT. I BELIEVE YOU.
LOOK, MAYBE WE CAN HELP EACH OTHER HERE.
THAT'S LIKE A BIRD OFFERING THE WIND TO HELP HOLD UP THE SKY.
BUT I HAVE ALREADY WASTED ENOUGH TIME FIGHTING YOU.
SO I ACCEPT THE TERMS OF YOUR SURRENDER.
MY GOD YOU ARE SUCH A--
FINE. CALL IT A SURRENDER.
READY? ON THREE. ONE, TWO--
DOES COUNTING MAKE YOU FEEL SMARTER?

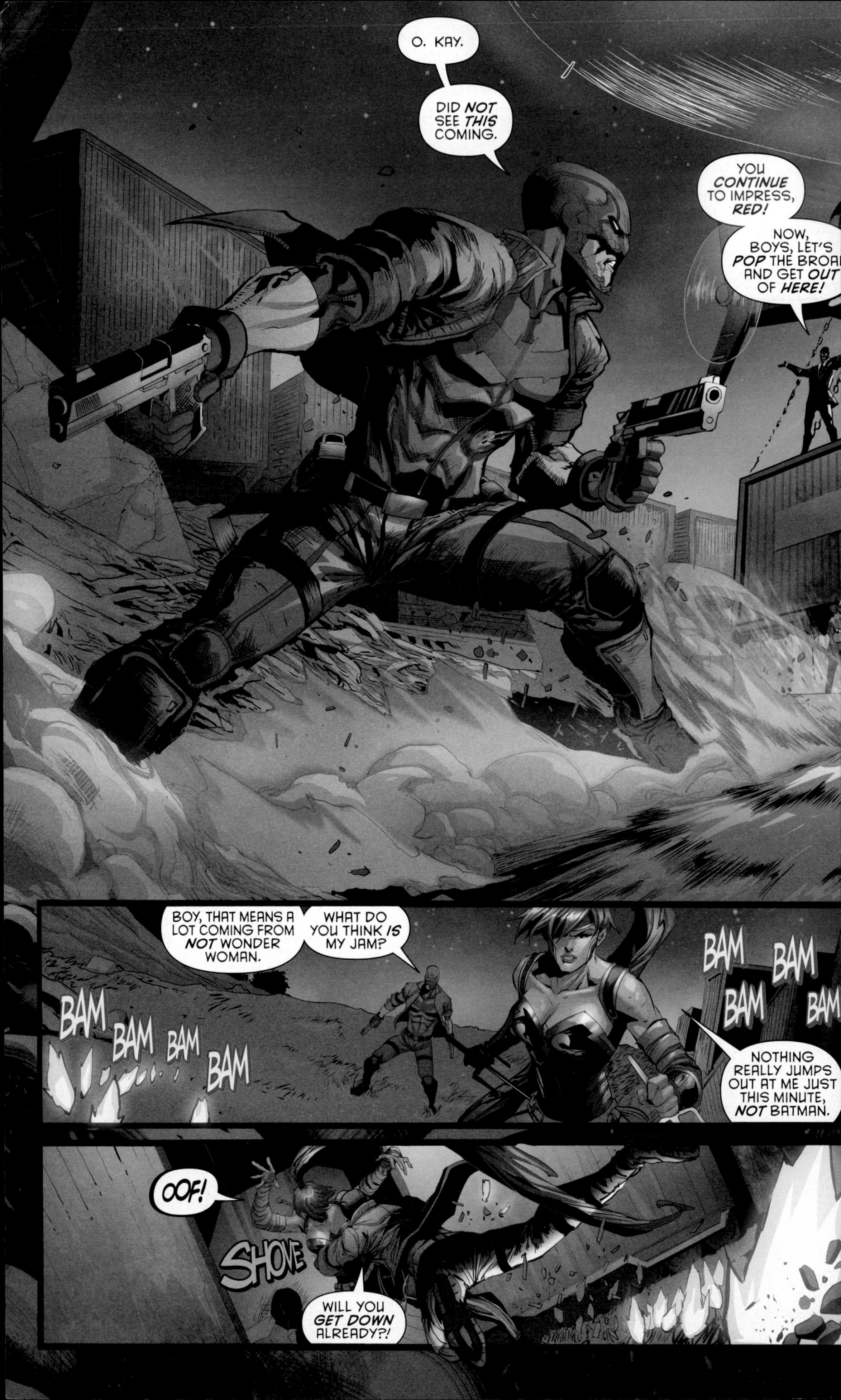
O. KAY.
DID NOT SEE THIS COMING.
YOU CONTINUE TO IMPRESS, RED!
NOW, BOYS, LET'S POP THE BROA
AND GET OUT OF HERE!
BOY, THAT MEANS A LOT COMING FROM NOT WONDER WOMAN.
WHAT DO YOU THINK IS MY JAM?
BAM BAM BAM BAM
BAM BAM BAM BAM
NOTHING REALLY JUMPS OUT AT ME JUST THIS MINUTE, NOT BATMAN.
OOF!
SHOVE
WILL YOU GET DOWN ALREADY?!

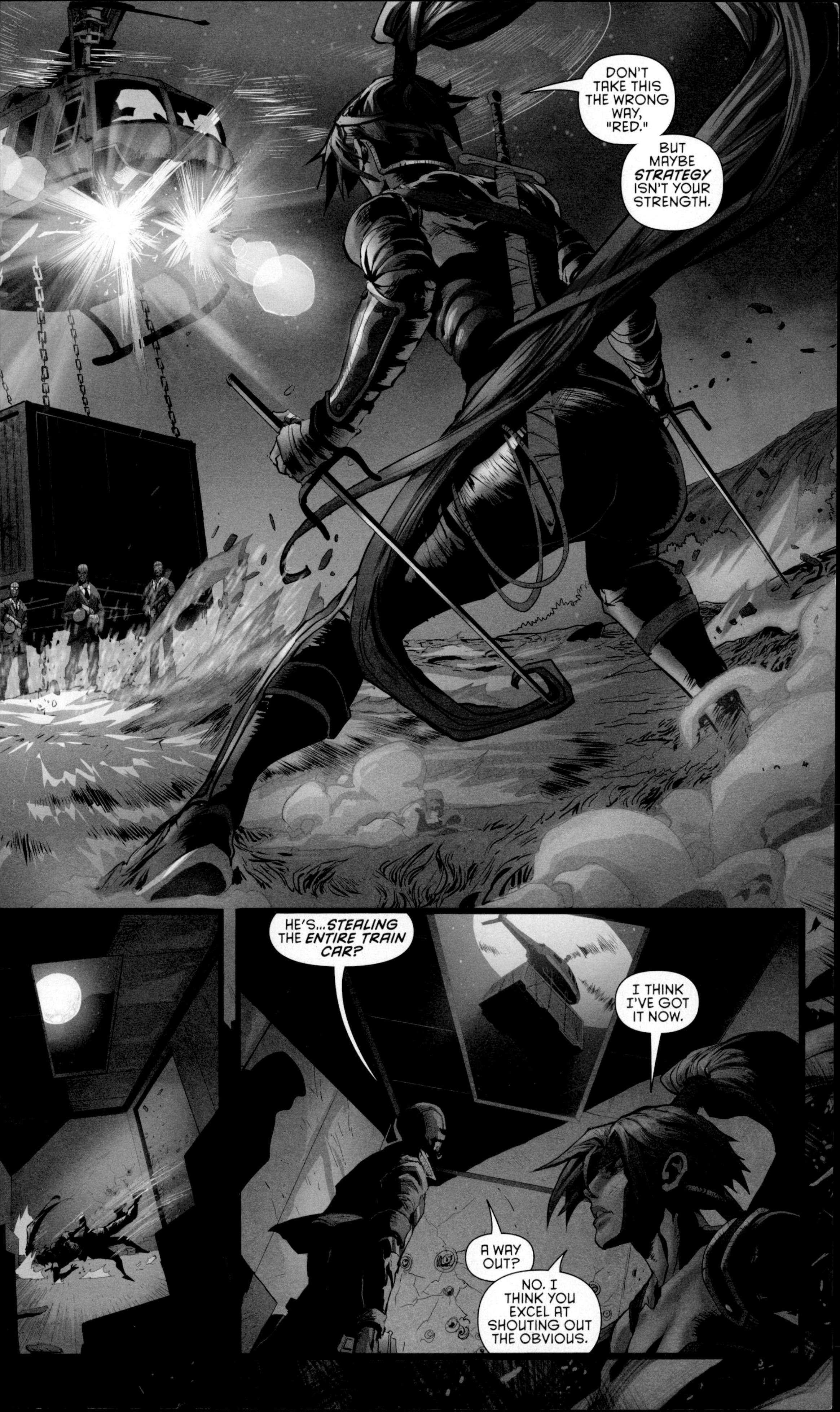

DON'T TAKE THIS THE WRONG WAY, "RED."
BUT MAYBE STRATEGY ISN'T YOUR STRENGTH.
HE'S...STEALING THE ENTIRE TRAIN CAR?
I THINK I'VE GOT IT NOW.
A WAY OUT?
NO. I THINK YOU EXCEL AT SHOUTING OUT THE OBVIOUS.

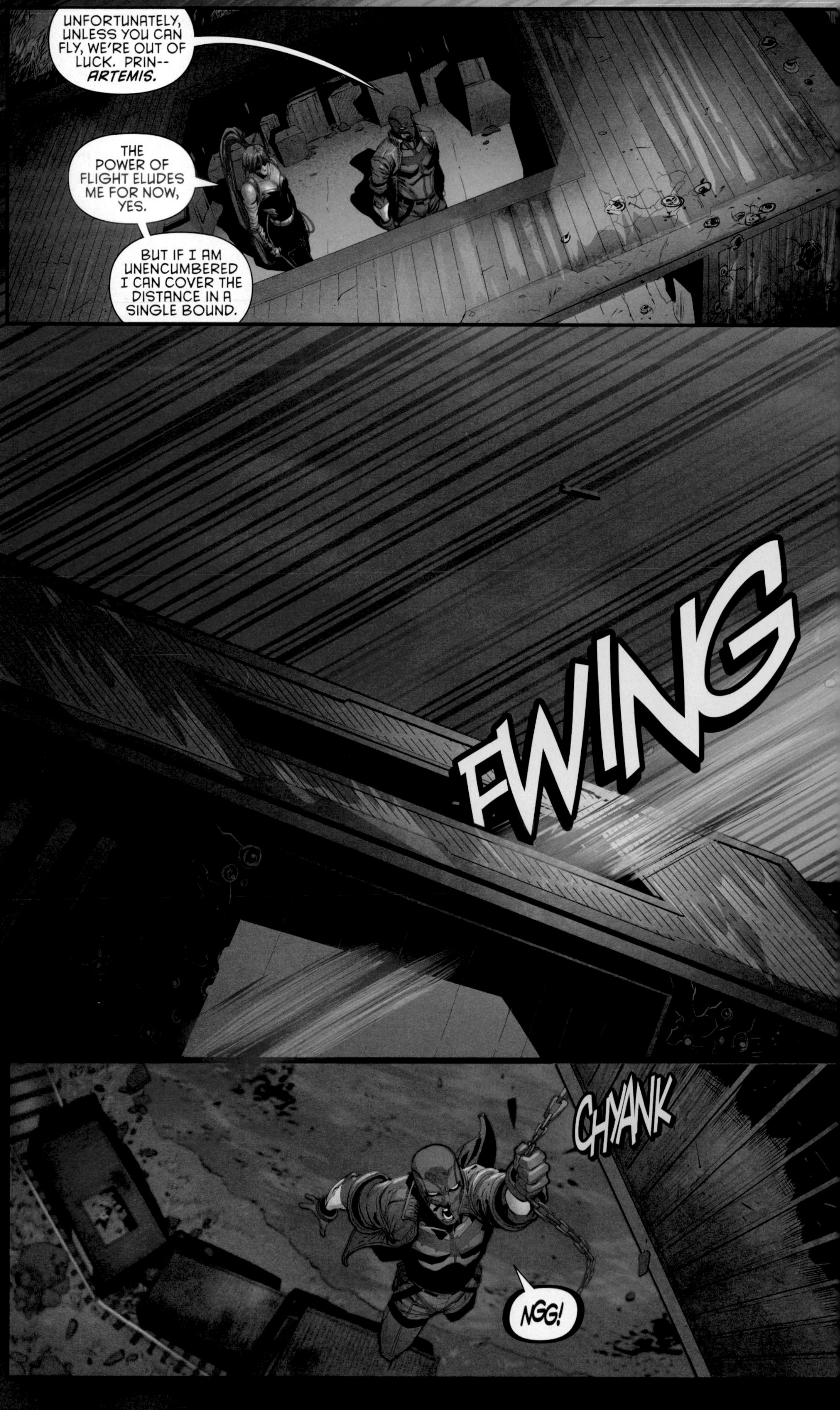

UNFORTUNATELY, UNLESS YOU CAN FLY, WE'RE OUT OF LUCK. PRIN-- ARTEMIS.
THE POWER OF FLIGHT ELUDES ME FOR NOW, YES.
BUT IF I AM UNENCUMBERED I CAN COVER THE DISTANCE IN A SINGLE BOUND.
FWING
CHYANK
NGG!

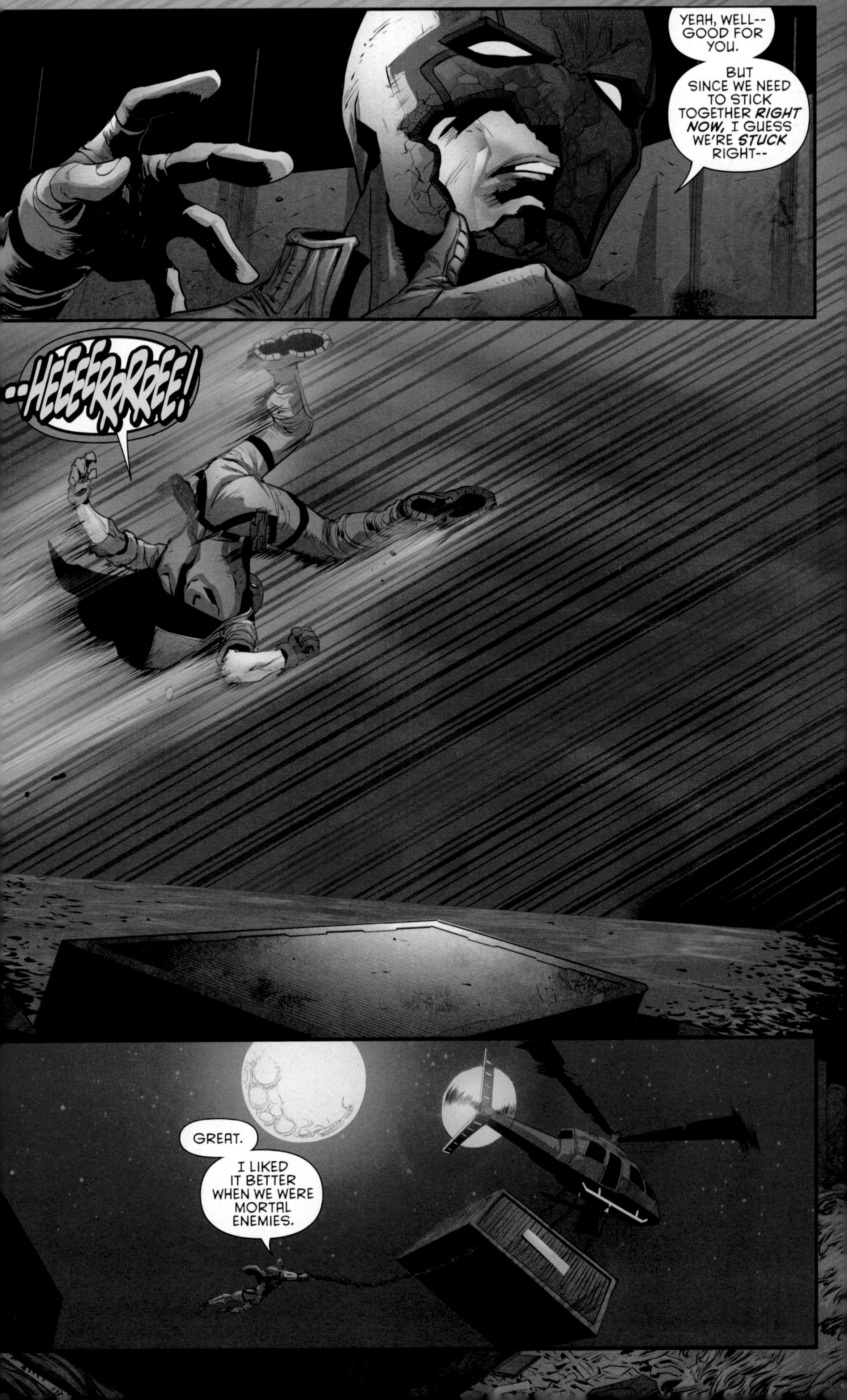
YEAH, WELL-- GOOD FOR YOU.
BUT SINCE WE NEED TO STICK TOGETHER RIGHT NOW, I GUESS WE'RE STUCK RIGHT--
--HEEEERRRREE!
GREAT.
I LIKED IT BETTER WHEN WE WERE MORTAL ENEMIES.

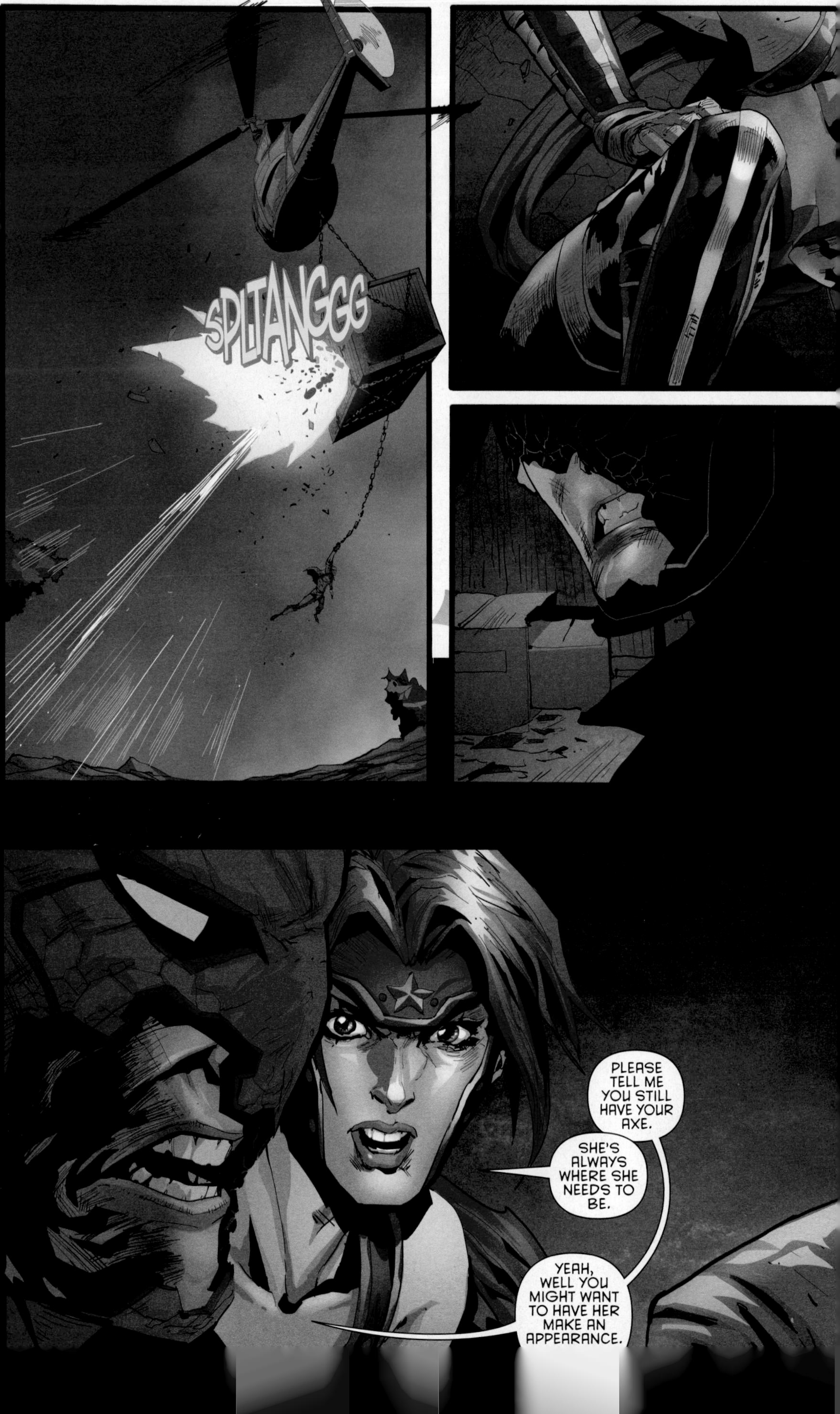
SPLITANGGG
PLEASE TELL ME YOU STILL HAVE YOUR AXE.
SHE'S ALWAYS WHERE SHE NEEDS TO BE.
YEAH, WELL YOU MIGHT WANT TO HAVE HER MAKE AN APPEARANCE.

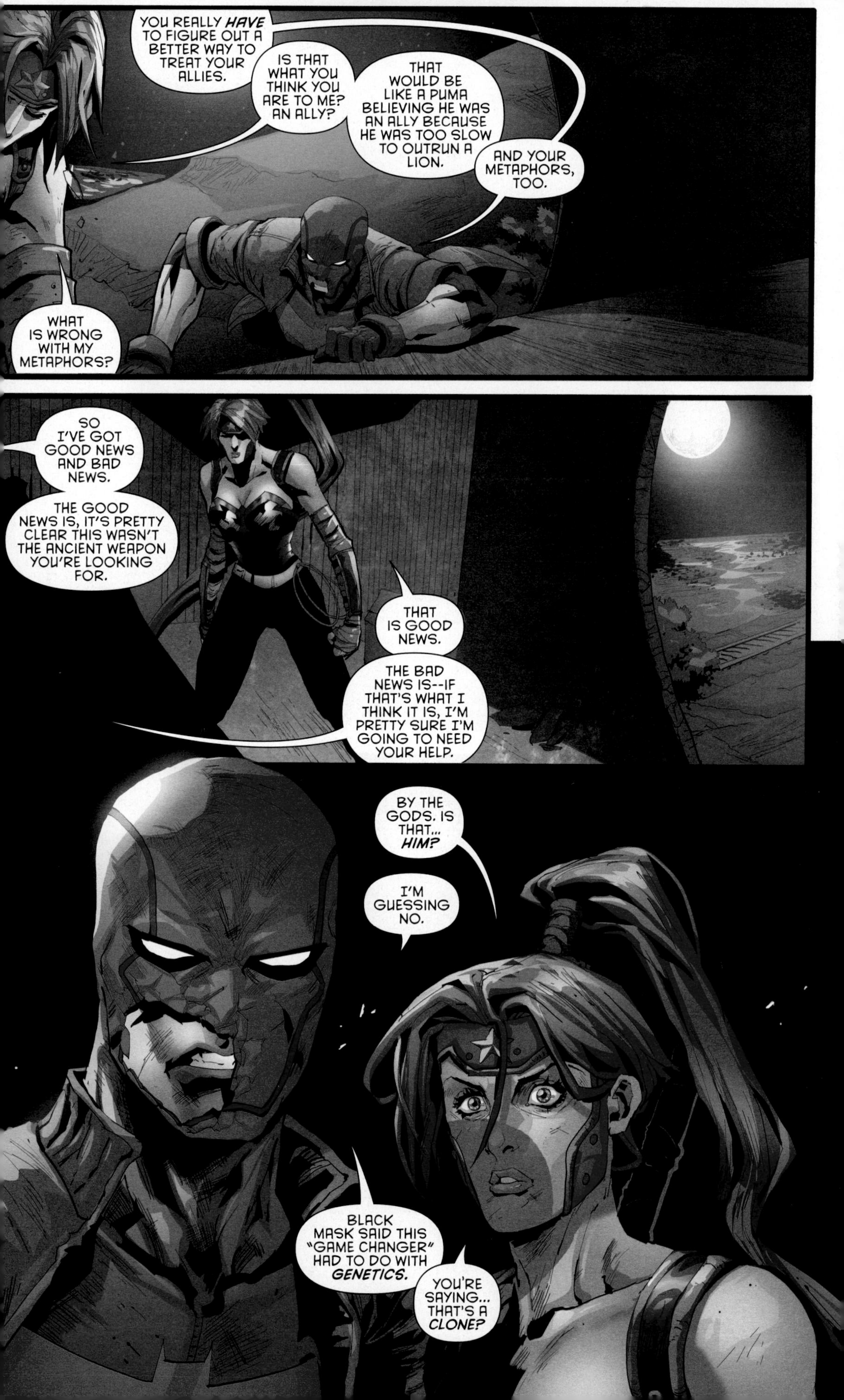
YOU REALLY HAVE TO FIGURE OUT A BETTER WAY TO TREAT YOUR ALLIES.
IS THAT WHAT YOU THINK YOU ARE TO ME? AN ALLY?
THAT WOULD BE LIKE A PUMA BELIEVING HE WAS AN ALLY BECAUSE HE WAS TOO SLOW TO OUTRUN A LION.
AND YOUR METAPHORS, TOO.
WHAT IS WRONG WITH MY METAPHORS?
SO I'VE GOT GOOD NEWS AND BAD NEWS.
THE GOOD NEWS IS, IT'S PRETTY CLEAR THIS WASN'T THE ANCIENT WEAPON YOU'RE LOOKING FOR.
THAT IS GOOD NEWS.
THE BAD NEWS IS--IF THAT'S WHAT I THINK IT IS, I'M PRETTY SURE I'M GOING TO NEED YOUR HELP.
BY THE GODS. IS THAT... HIM?
I'M GUESSING NO.
BLACK MASK SAID THIS "GAME CHANGER" HAD TO DO WITH GENETICS.
YOU'RE SAYING... THAT'S A CLONE?

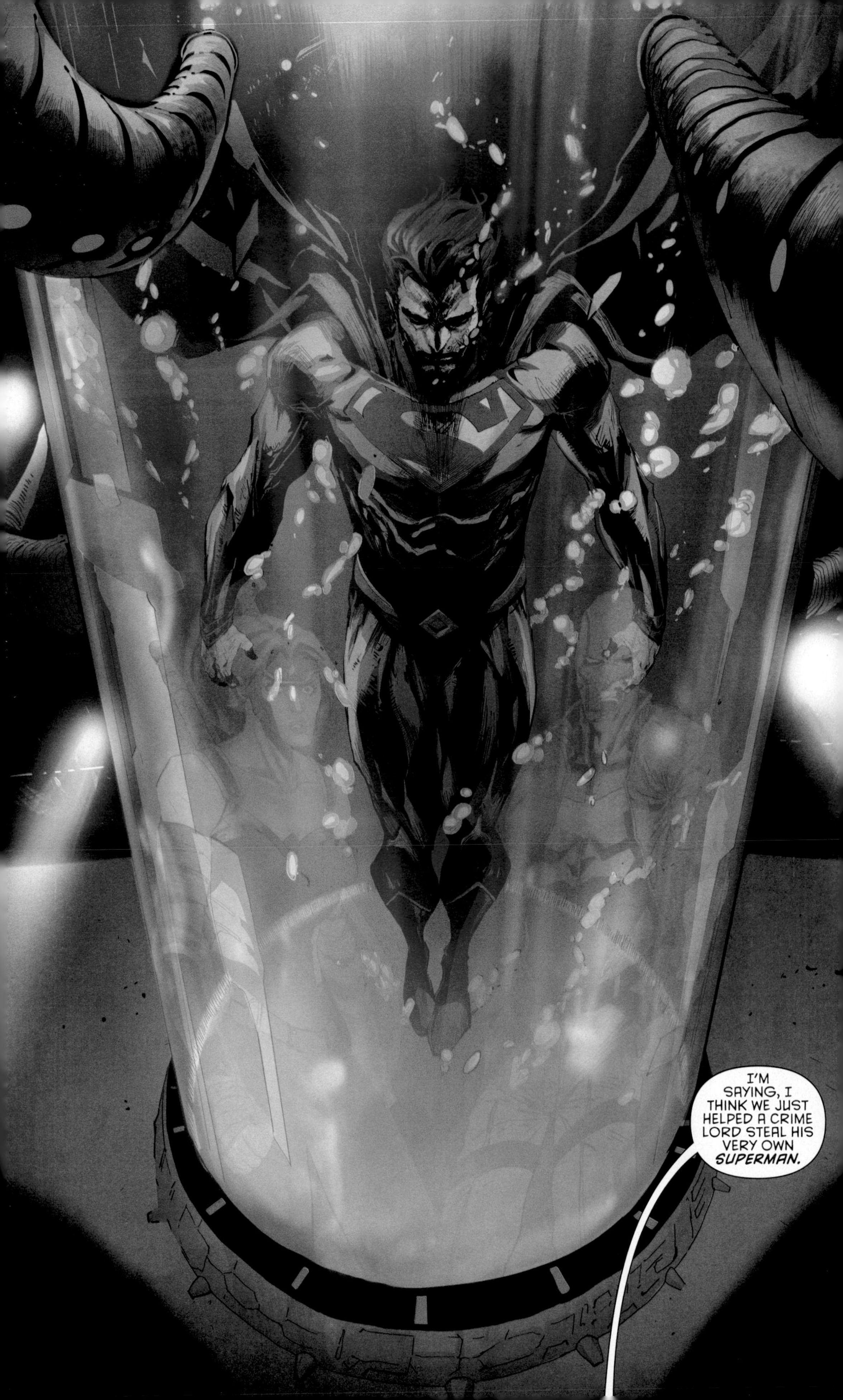
I'M SAYING, I THINK WE JUST HELPED A CRIME LORD STEAL HIS VERY OWN *SUPERMAN.*

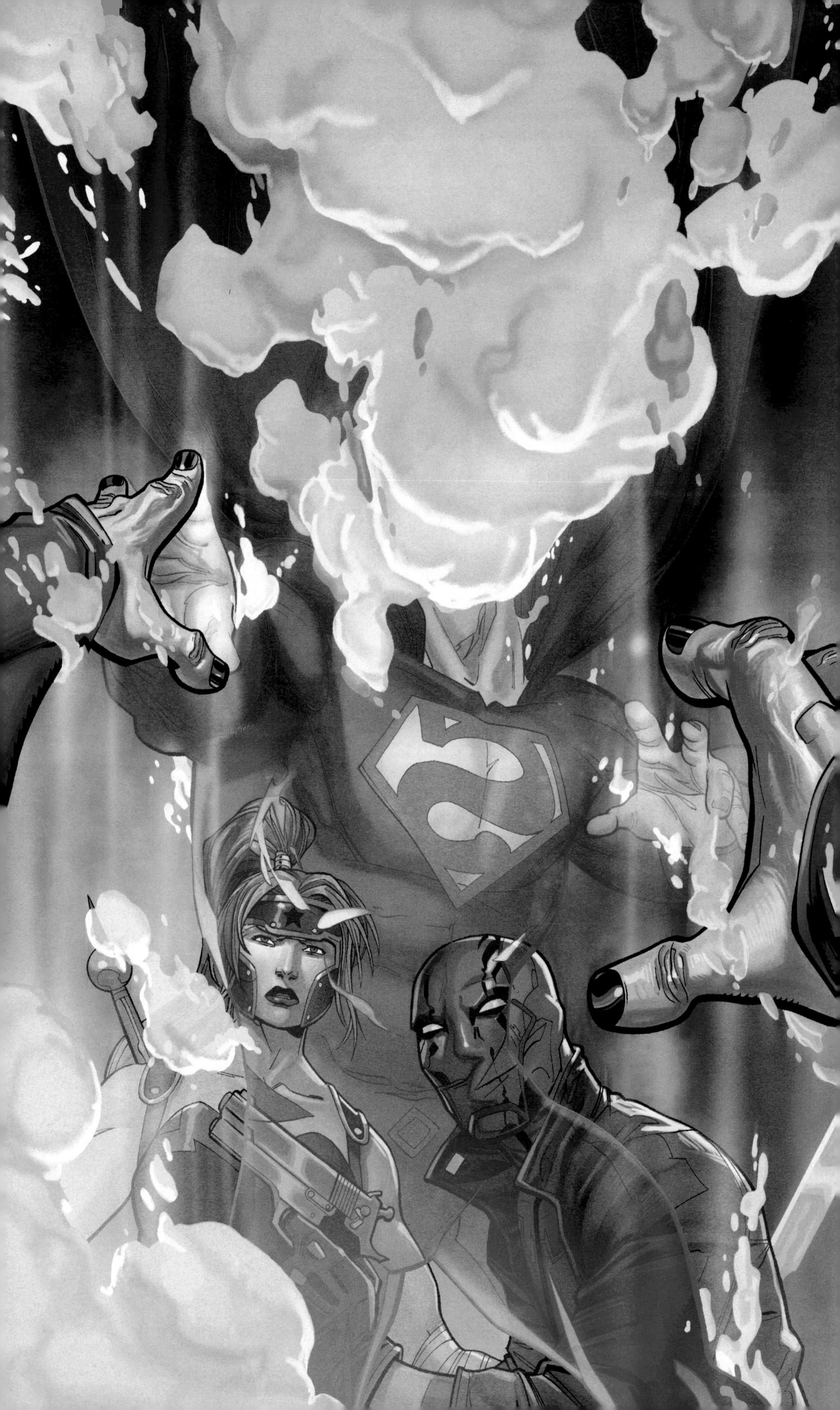

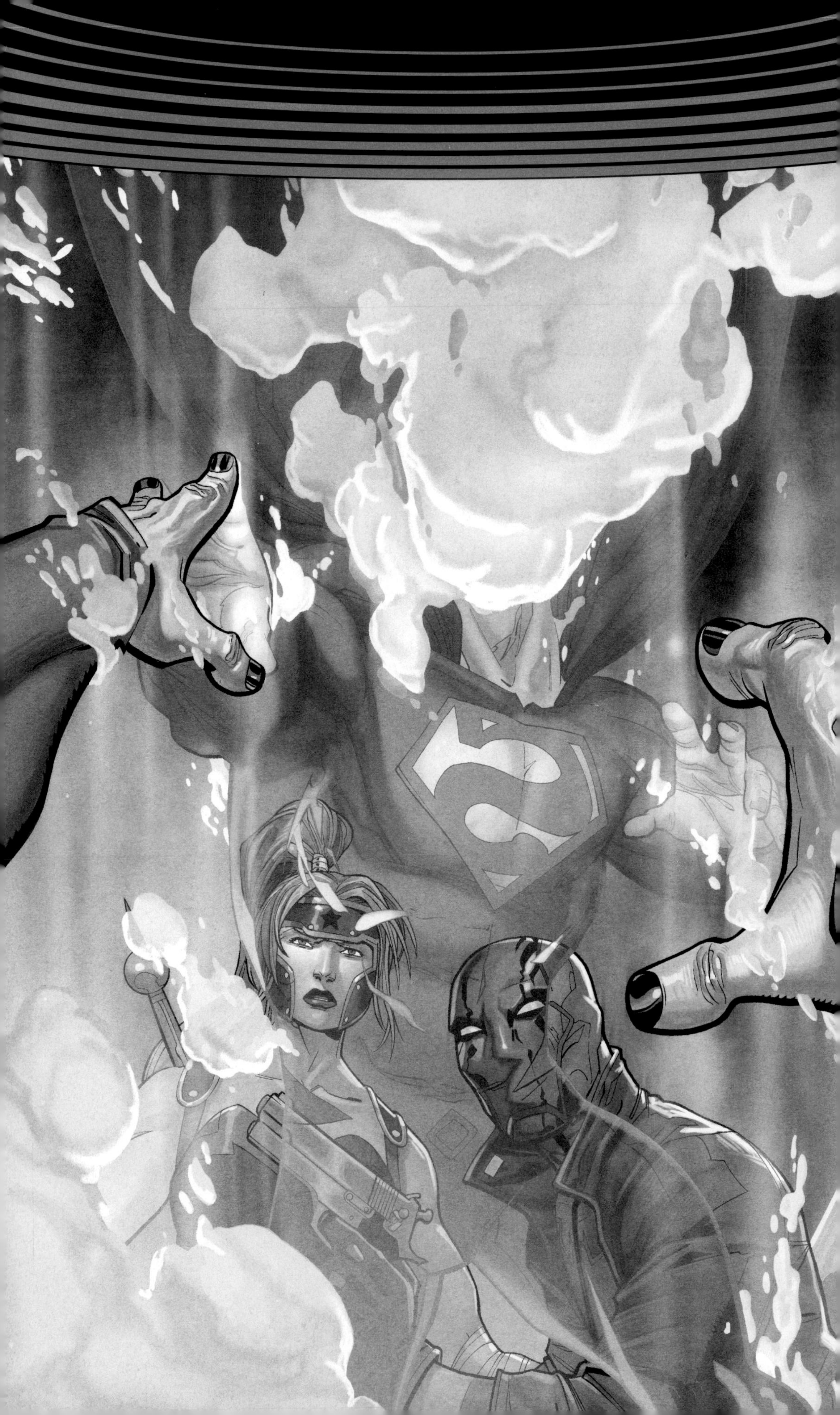

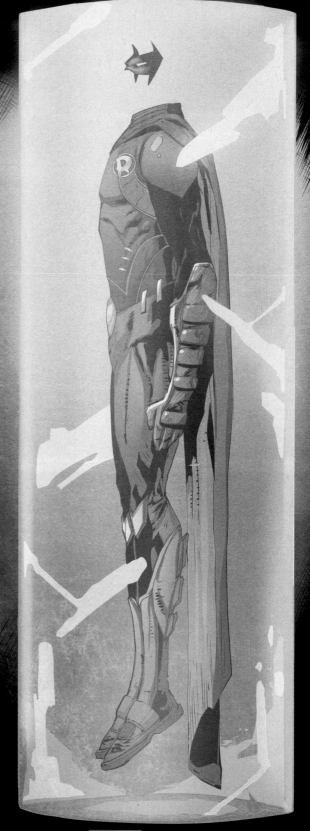

IT WAS MY FIRST NIGHT AS ROBIN ON MY OWN.

TOTALLY UNAUTHORIZED.

TO THE SURPRISE OF NO ONE--IT DID *NOT* GO WELL.

WHAT ARE *YOU* LOOKING AT?

"RED HOOD?

"HELLO?"

Huhn?

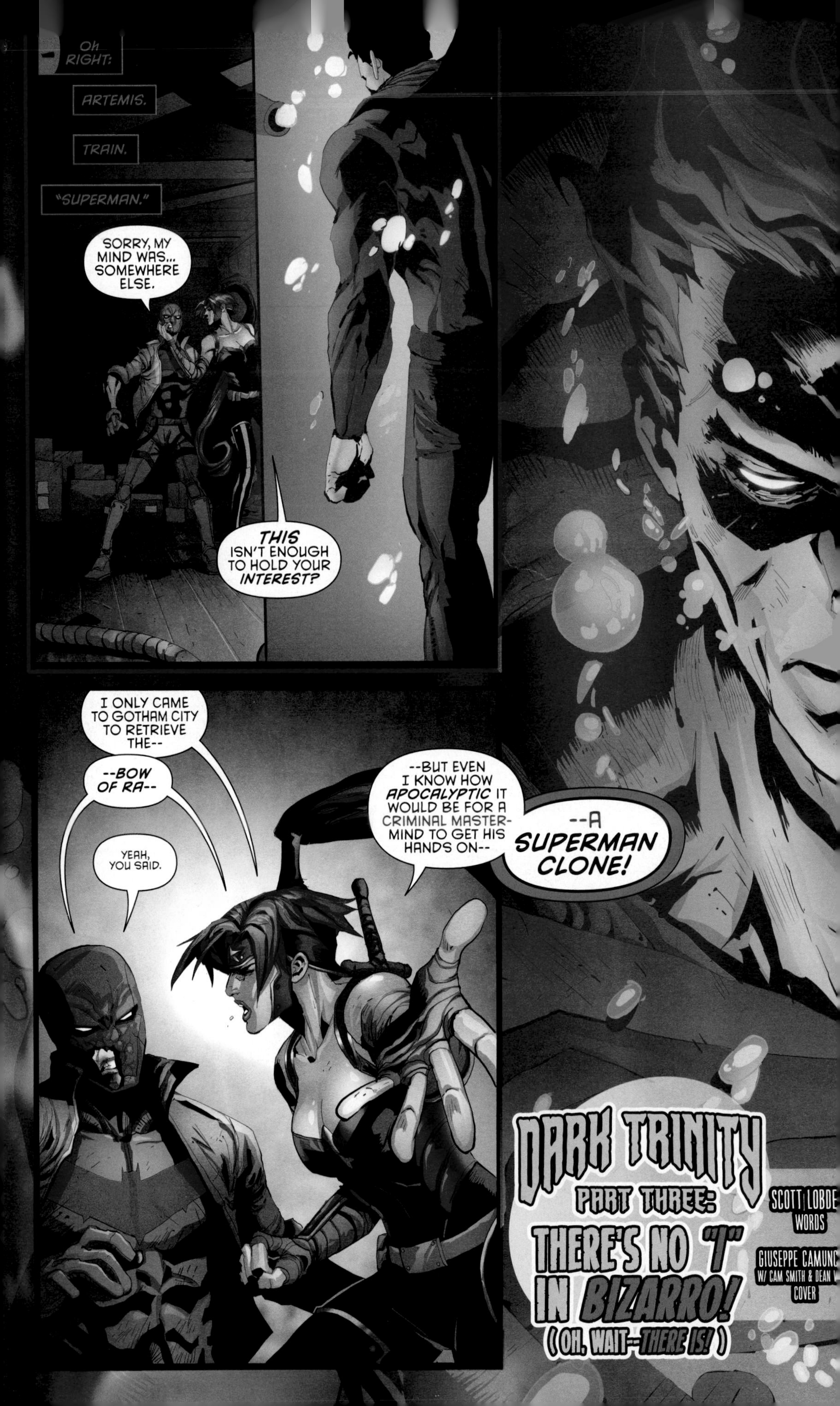

Oh RIGHT:
ARTEMIS.
TRAIN.
"SUPERMAN."
SORRY, MY MIND WAS... SOMEWHERE ELSE.
THIS ISN'T ENOUGH TO HOLD YOUR INTEREST?
I ONLY CAME TO GOTHAM CITY TO RETRIEVE THE--
--BOW OF RA--
YEAH, YOU SAID.
--BUT EVEN I KNOW HOW APOCALYPTIC IT WOULD BE FOR A CRIMINAL MASTER-MIND TO GET HIS HANDS ON--
--A SUPERMAN CLONE!
DARK TRINITY
PART THREE:
THERE'S NO "I" IN BIZARRO!
(OH, WAIT--THERE IS!)
SCOTT LOBDE
WORDS
GIUSEPPE CAMUNC
W/ CAM SMITH & DEAN
COVER

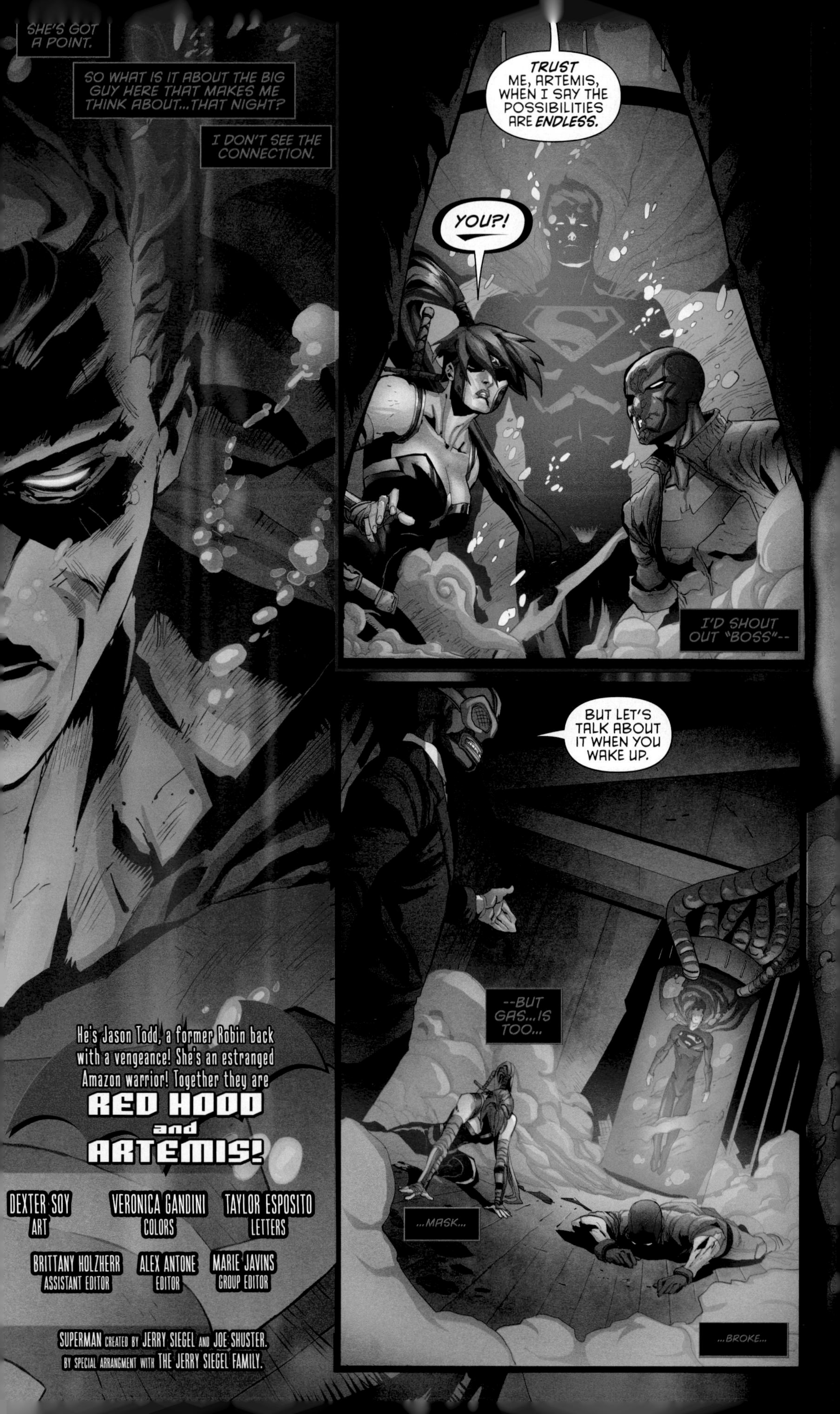

SHE'S GOT A POINT.
SO WHAT IS IT ABOUT THE BIG GUY HERE THAT MAKES ME THINK ABOUT...THAT NIGHT?
I DON'T SEE THE CONNECTION.
TRUST ME, ARTEMIS, WHEN I SAY THE POSSIBILITIES ARE ENDLESS.
YOU?!
I'D SHOUT OUT "BOSS"--
BUT LET'S TALK ABOUT IT WHEN YOU WAKE UP.
--BUT GAS...IS TOO...
...MASK...
...BROKE...
He's Jason Todd, a former Robin back with a vengeance! She's an estranged Amazon warrior! Together they are
RED HOOD and ARTEMIS!
DEXTER SOY ART
VERONICA GANDINI COLORS
TAYLOR ESPOSITO LETTERS
BRITTANY HOLZHERR ASSISTANT EDITOR
ALEX ANTONE EDITOR
MARIE JAVINS GROUP EDITOR
SUPERMAN CREATED BY JERRY SIEGEL AND JOE SHUSTER.
BY SPECIAL ARRANGMENT WITH THE JERRY SIEGEL FAMILY.

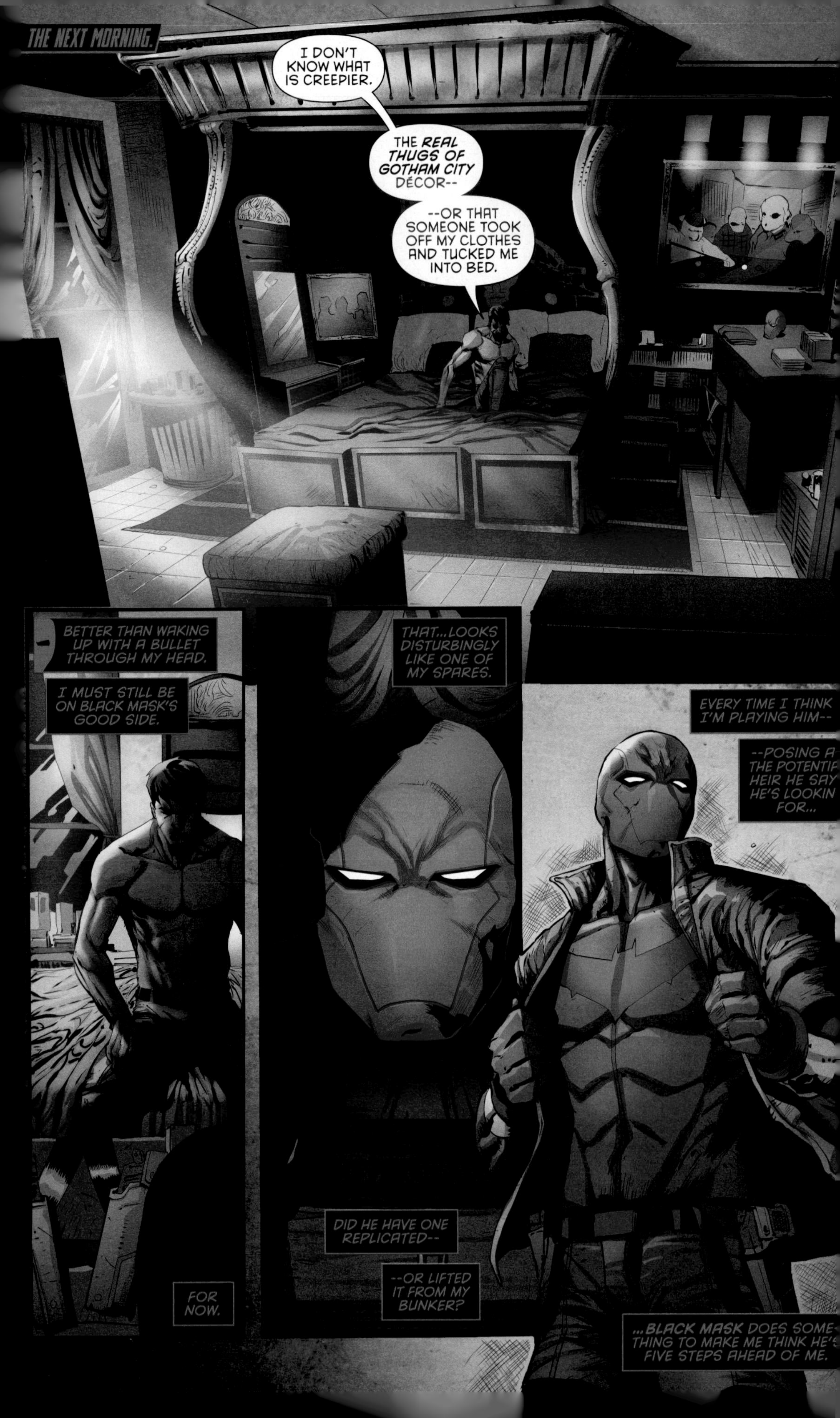

THE NEXT MORNING.
I DON'T KNOW WHAT IS CREEPIER.
THE REAL THUGS OF GOTHAM CITY DÉCOR--
--OR THAT SOMEONE TOOK OFF MY CLOTHES AND TUCKED ME INTO BED.
BETTER THAN WAKING UP WITH A BULLET THROUGH MY HEAD.
I MUST STILL BE ON BLACK MASK'S GOOD SIDE.
FOR NOW.
THAT...LOOKS DISTURBINGLY LIKE ONE OF MY SPARES.
DID HE HAVE ONE REPLICATED--
--OR LIFTED IT FROM MY BUNKER?
EVERY TIME I THINK I'M PLAYING HIM--
--POSING A THE POTENTIA HEIR HE SAY HE'S LOOKIN FOR...
...BLACK MASK DOES SOME-THING TO MAKE ME THINK HE'S FIVE STEPS AHEAD OF ME.

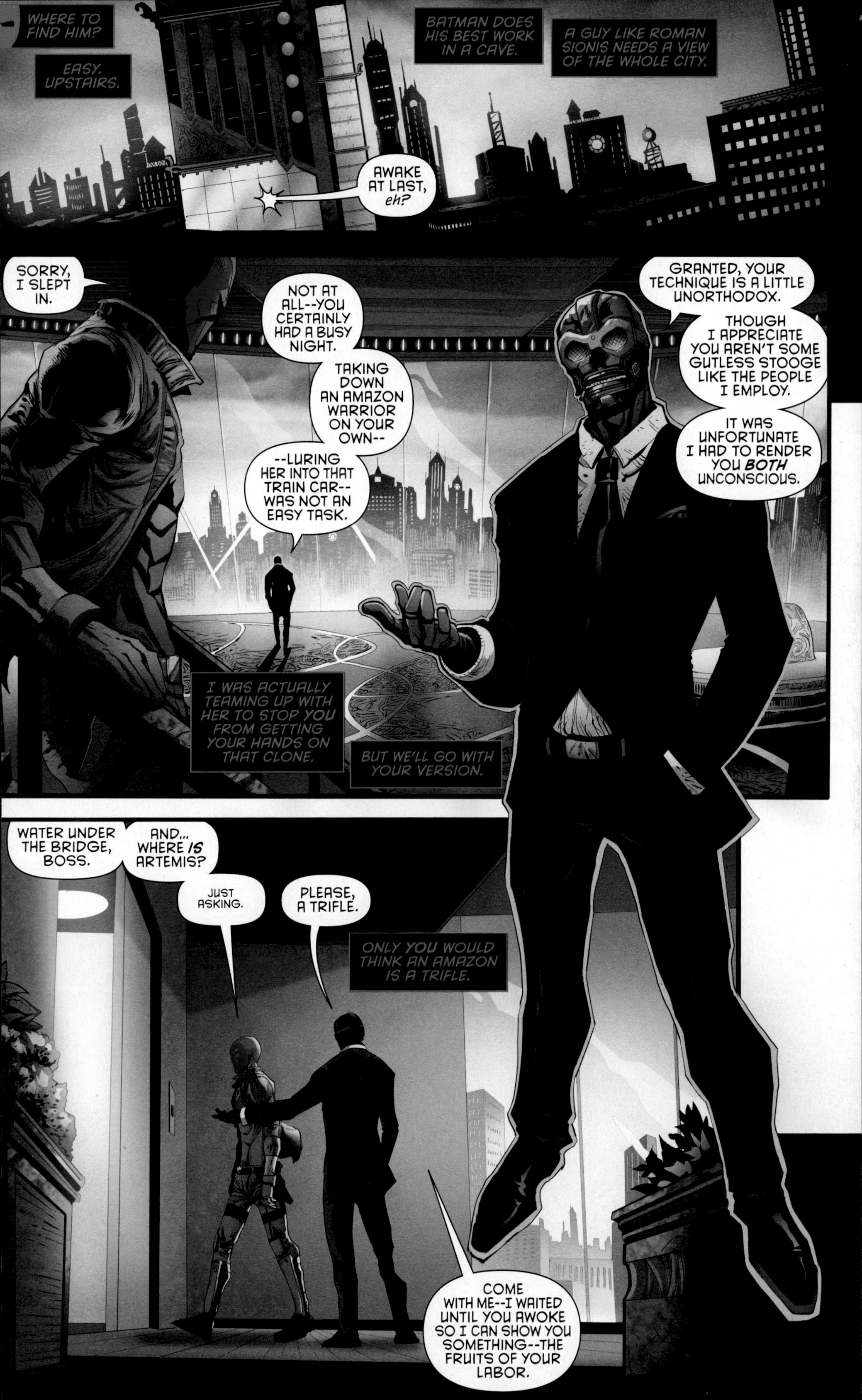

WHERE TO FIND HIM?
EASY. UPSTAIRS.
BATMAN DOES HIS BEST WORK IN A CAVE.
A GUY LIKE ROMAN SIONIS NEEDS A VIEW OF THE WHOLE CITY.
AWAKE AT LAST, eh?
SORRY, I SLEPT IN.
NOT AT ALL--YOU CERTAINLY HAD A BUSY NIGHT.
TAKING DOWN AN AMAZON WARRIOR ON YOUR OWN--
--LURING HER INTO THAT TRAIN CAR--WAS NOT AN EASY TASK.
I WAS ACTUALLY TEAMING UP WITH HER TO STOP YOU FROM GETTING YOUR HANDS ON THAT CLONE.
BUT WE'LL GO WITH YOUR VERSION.
GRANTED, YOUR TECHNIQUE IS A LITTLE UNORTHODOX.
THOUGH I APPRECIATE YOU AREN'T SOME GUTLESS STOOGE LIKE THE PEOPLE I EMPLOY.
IT WAS UNFORTUNATE I HAD TO RENDER YOU BOTH UNCONSCIOUS.
WATER UNDER THE BRIDGE, BOSS.
AND... WHERE IS ARTEMIS?
JUST ASKING.
PLEASE, A TRIFLE.
ONLY YOU WOULD THINK AN AMAZON IS A TRIFLE.
COME WITH ME--I WAITED UNTIL YOU AWOKE SO I CAN SHOW YOU SOMETHING--THE FRUITS OF YOUR LABOR.

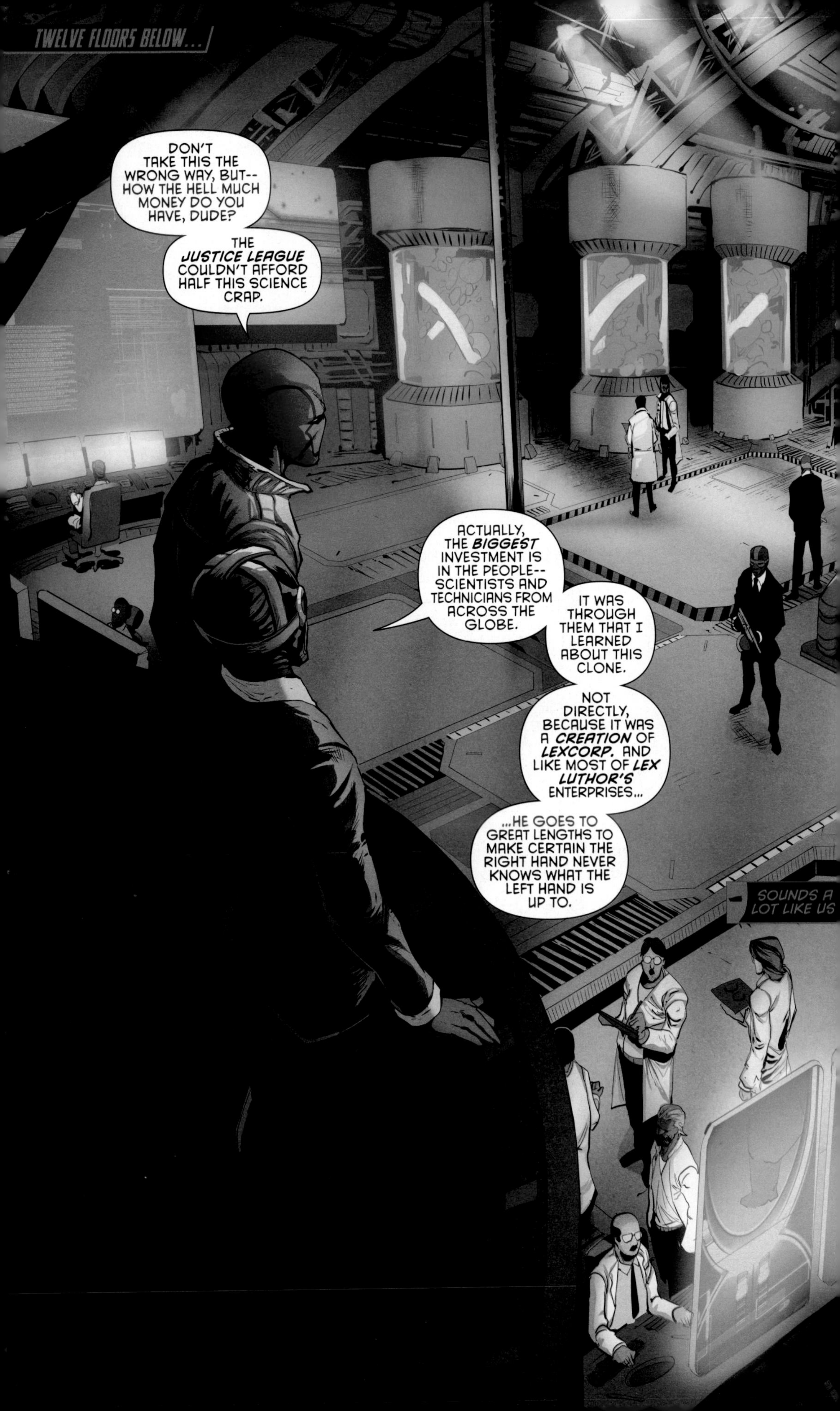
TWELVE FLOORS BELOW...
DON'T TAKE THIS THE WRONG WAY, BUT-- HOW THE HELL MUCH MONEY DO YOU HAVE, DUDE?
THE JUSTICE LEAGUE COULDN'T AFFORD HALF THIS SCIENCE CRAP.
ACTUALLY, THE BIGGEST INVESTMENT IS IN THE PEOPLE-- SCIENTISTS AND TECHNICIANS FROM ACROSS THE GLOBE.
IT WAS THROUGH THEM THAT I LEARNED ABOUT THIS CLONE.
NOT DIRECTLY, BECAUSE IT WAS A CREATION OF LEXCORP. AND LIKE MOST OF LEX LUTHOR'S ENTERPRISES...
...HE GOES TO GREAT LENGTHS TO MAKE CERTAIN THE RIGHT HAND NEVER KNOWS WHAT THE LEFT HAND IS UP TO.
SOUNDS A LOT LIKE US

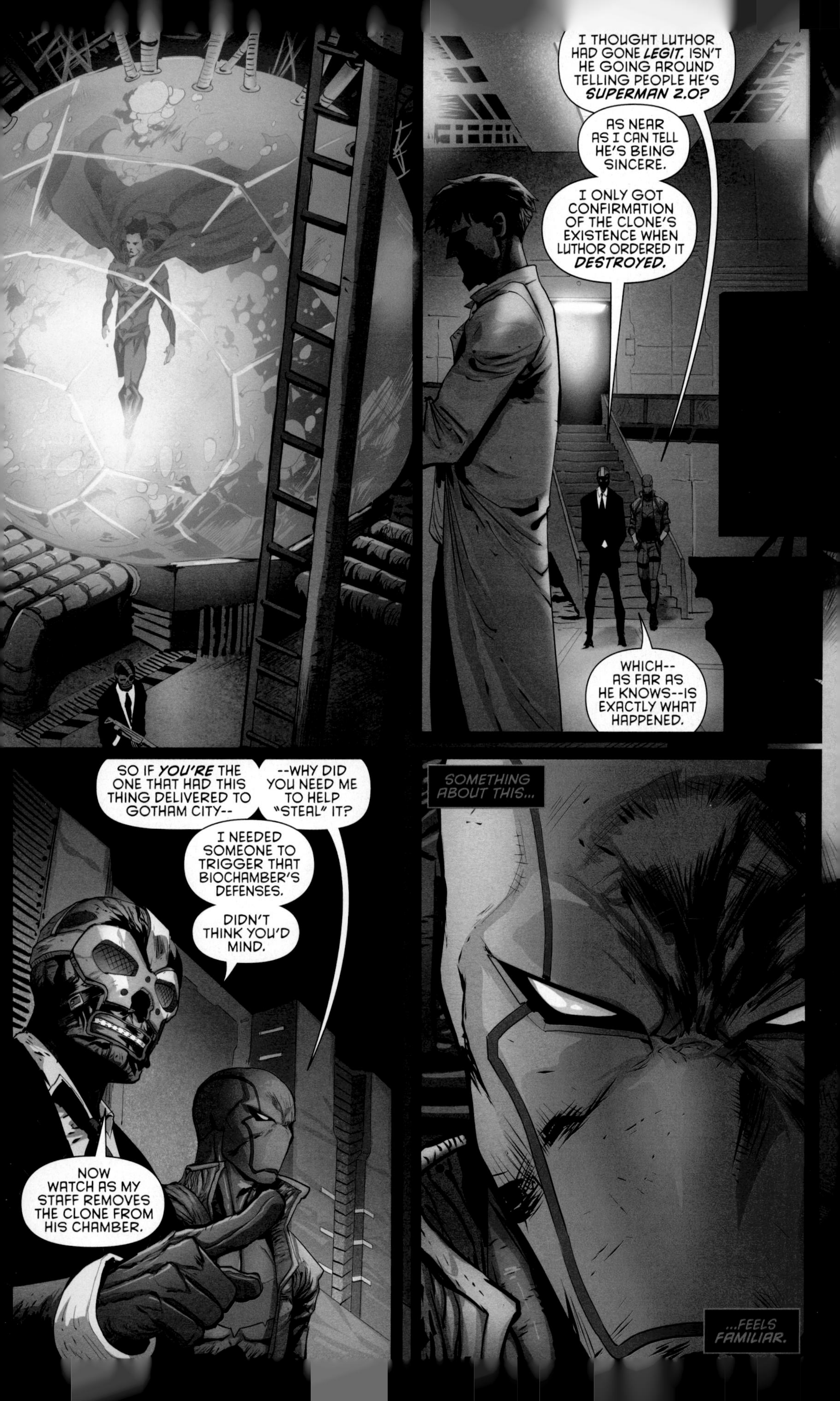
I THOUGHT LUTHOR HAD GONE *LEGIT.* ISN'T HE GOING AROUND TELLING PEOPLE HE'S *SUPERMAN 2.0?*
AS NEAR AS I CAN TELL HE'S BEING SINCERE.
I ONLY GOT CONFIRMATION OF THE CLONE'S EXISTENCE WHEN LUTHOR ORDERED IT *DESTROYED.*
WHICH-- AS FAR AS HE KNOWS--IS EXACTLY WHAT HAPPENED.
SO IF *YOU'RE* THE ONE THAT HAD THIS THING DELIVERED TO GOTHAM CITY--
--WHY DID YOU NEED ME TO HELP "STEAL" IT?
I NEEDED SOMEONE TO TRIGGER THAT BIOCHAMBER'S DEFENSES.
DIDN'T THINK YOU'D MIND.
NOW WATCH AS MY STAFF REMOVES THE CLONE FROM HIS CHAMBER.
SOMETHING ABOUT THIS...
...FEELS FAMILIAR.

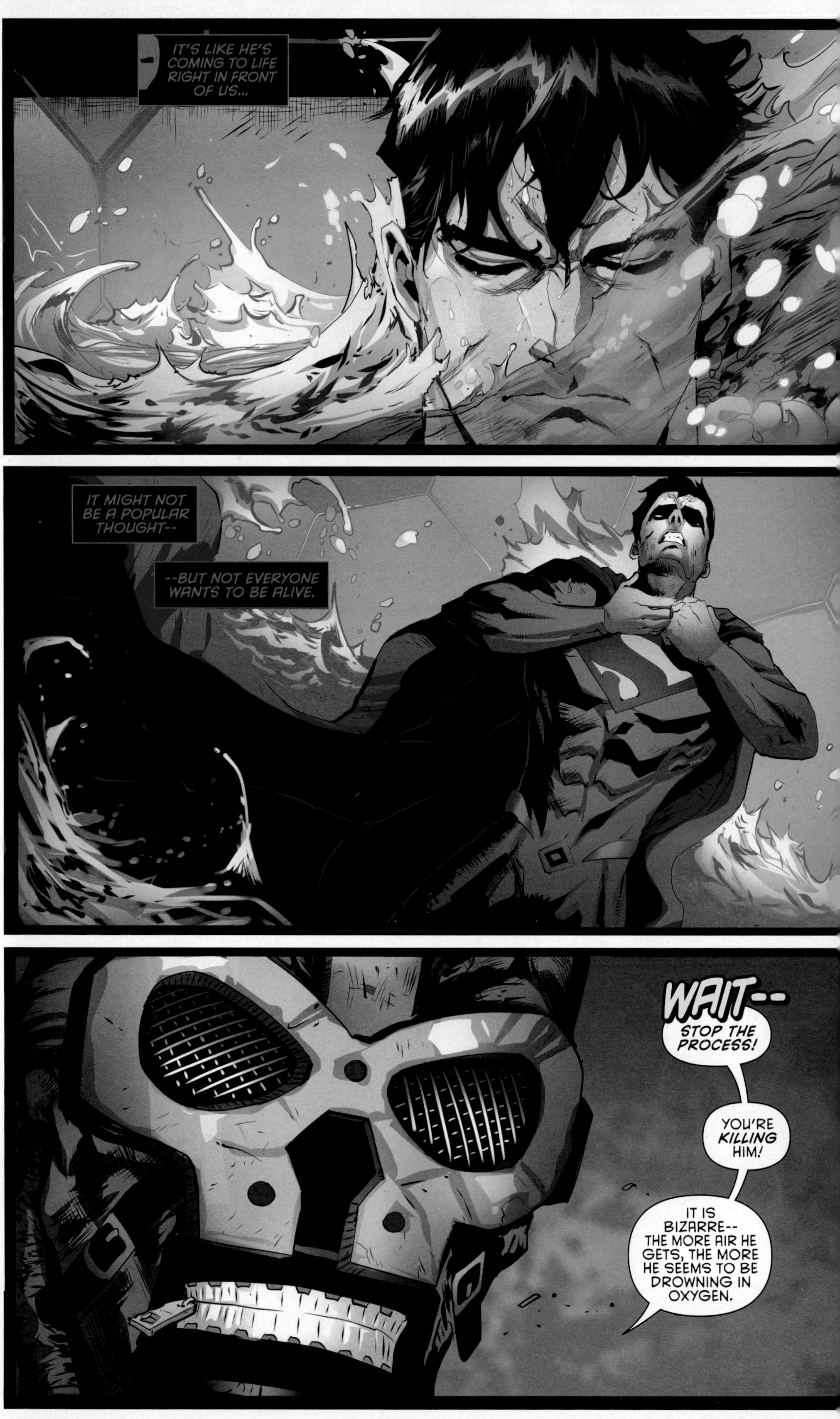

IT'S LIKE HE'S COMING TO LIFE RIGHT IN FRONT OF US...
IT MIGHT NOT BE A POPULAR THOUGHT--
--BUT NOT EVERYONE WANTS TO BE ALIVE.
WAIT--
STOP THE PROCESS!
YOU'RE KILLING HIM!
IT IS BIZARRE-- THE MORE AIR HE GETS, THE MORE HE SEEMS TO BE DROWNING IN OXYGEN.

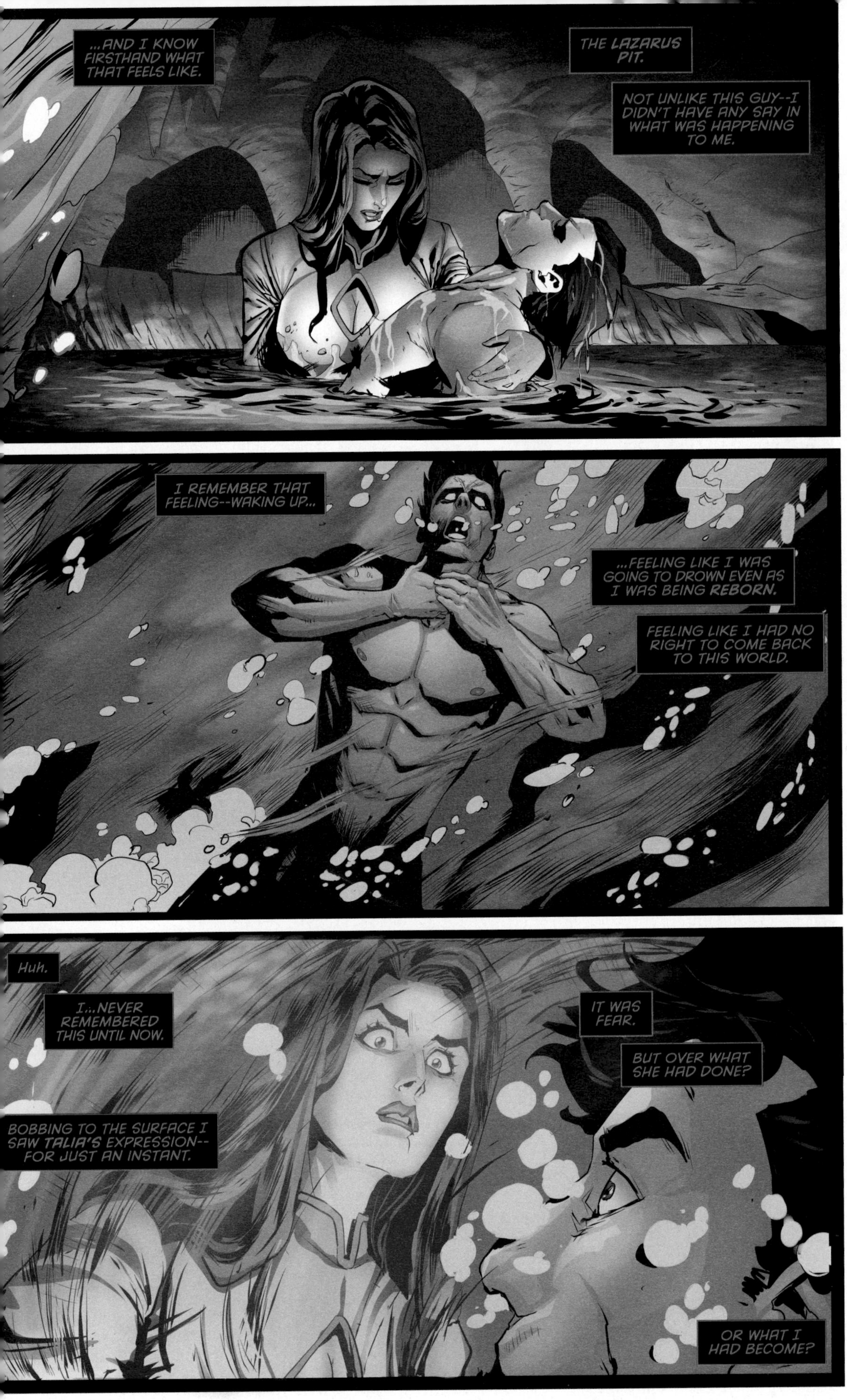
...AND I KNOW FIRSTHAND WHAT THAT FEELS LIKE.
THE LAZARUS PIT.
NOT UNLIKE THIS GUY--I DIDN'T HAVE ANY SAY IN WHAT WAS HAPPENING TO ME.
I REMEMBER THAT FEELING--WAKING UP...
...FEELING LIKE I WAS GOING TO DROWN EVEN AS I WAS BEING REBORN.
FEELING LIKE I HAD NO RIGHT TO COME BACK TO THIS WORLD.
Huh.
I...NEVER REMEMBERED THIS UNTIL NOW.
BOBBING TO THE SURFACE I SAW TALIA'S EXPRESSION--FOR JUST AN INSTANT.
IT WAS FEAR.
BUT OVER WHAT SHE HAD DONE?
OR WHAT I HAD BECOME?

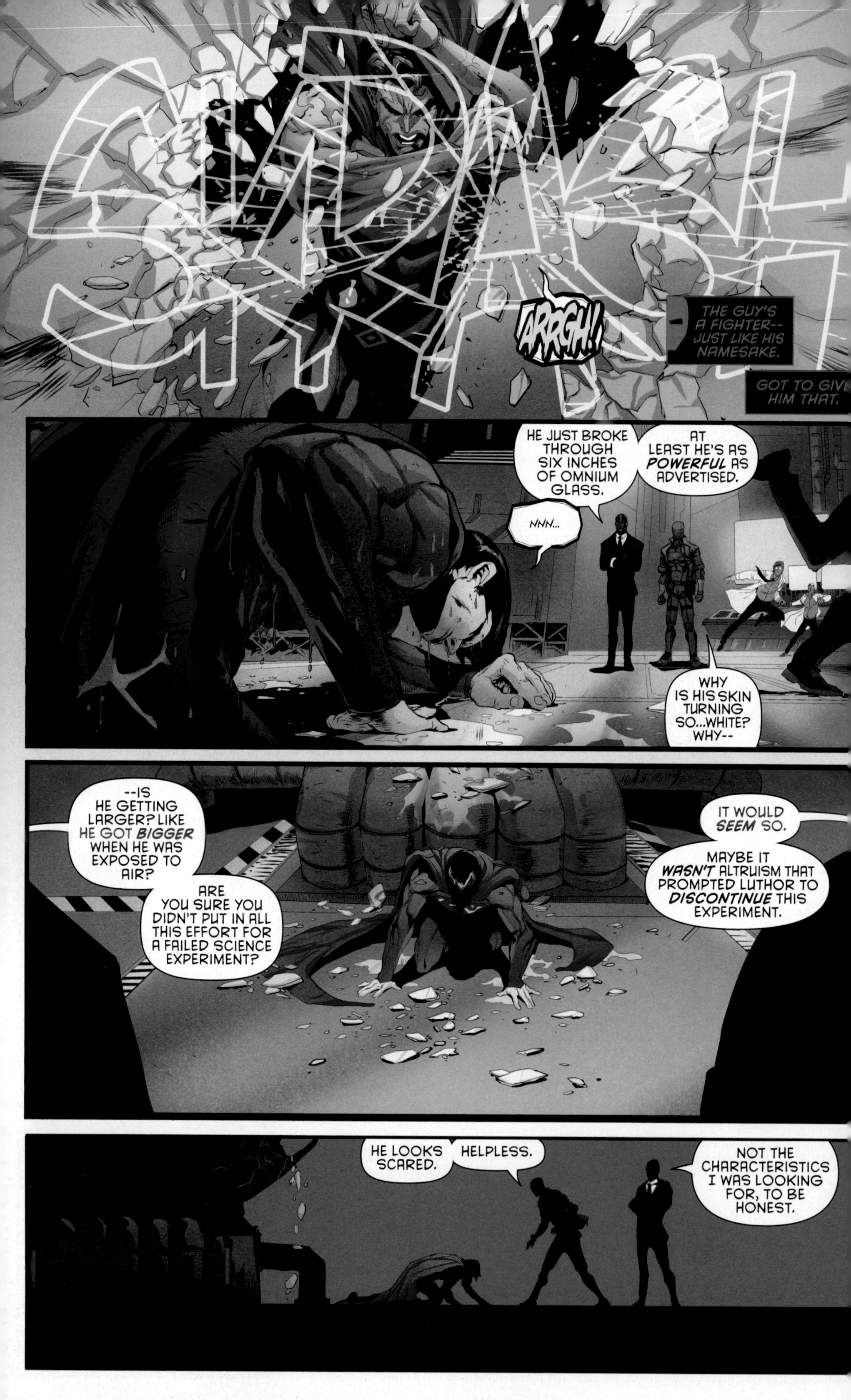
SMASH
ARRGH!
THE GUY'S A FIGHTER-- JUST LIKE HIS NAMESAKE.
GOT TO GIV HIM THAT.
HE JUST BROKE THROUGH SIX INCHES OF OMNIUM GLASS.
AT LEAST HE'S AS POWERFUL AS ADVERTISED.
NNN...
WHY IS HIS SKIN TURNING SO...WHITE? WHY--
--IS HE GETTING LARGER? LIKE HE GOT BIGGER WHEN HE WAS EXPOSED TO AIR?
ARE YOU SURE YOU DIDN'T PUT IN ALL THIS EFFORT FOR A FAILED SCIENCE EXPERIMENT?
IT WOULD SEEM SO.
MAYBE IT WASN'T ALTRUISM THAT PROMPTED LUTHOR TO DISCONTINUE THIS EXPERIMENT.
HE LOOKS SCARED.
HELPLESS.
NOT THE CHARACTERISTICS I WAS LOOKING FOR, TO BE HONEST.

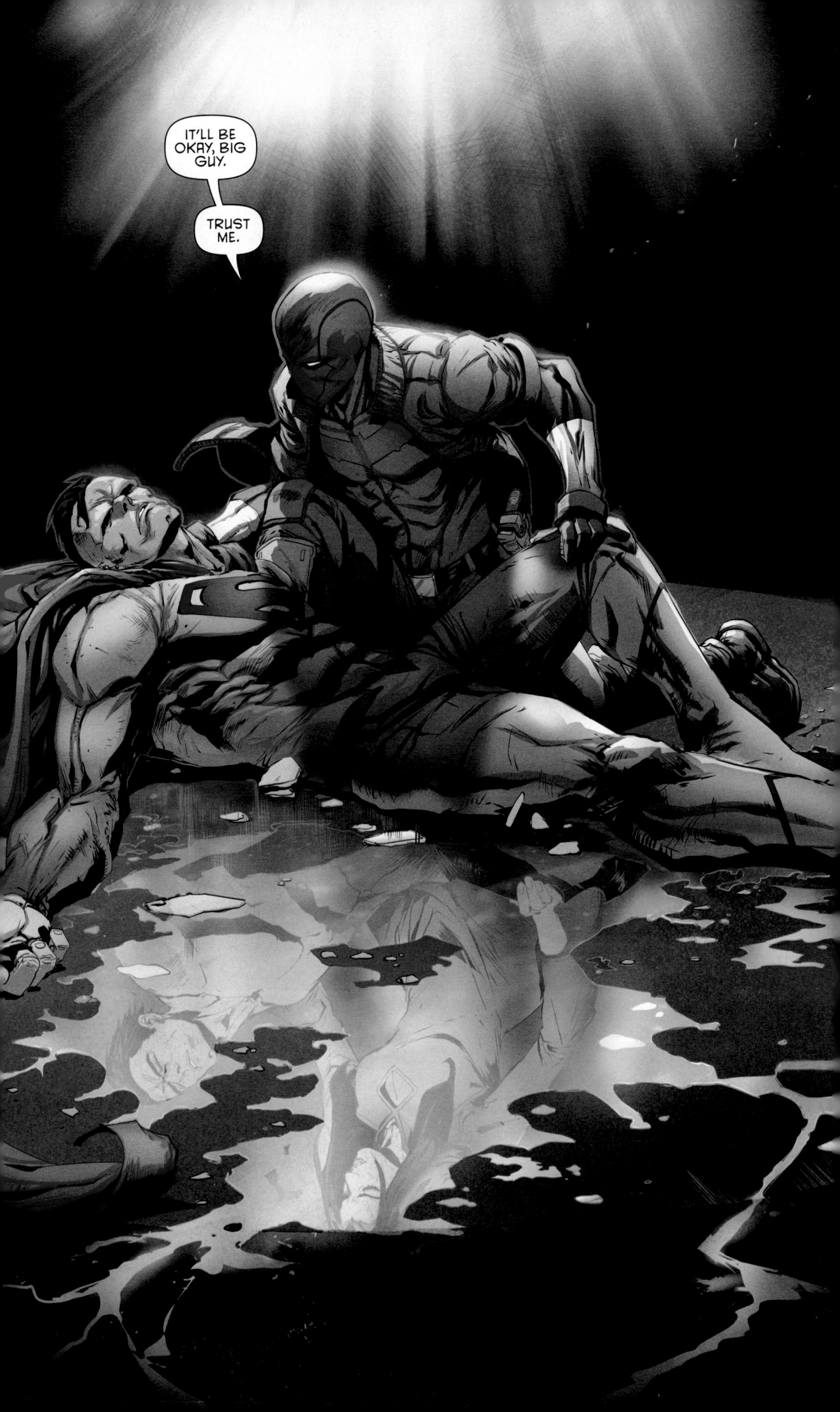
IT'LL BE OKAY, BIG GUY.
TRUST ME.

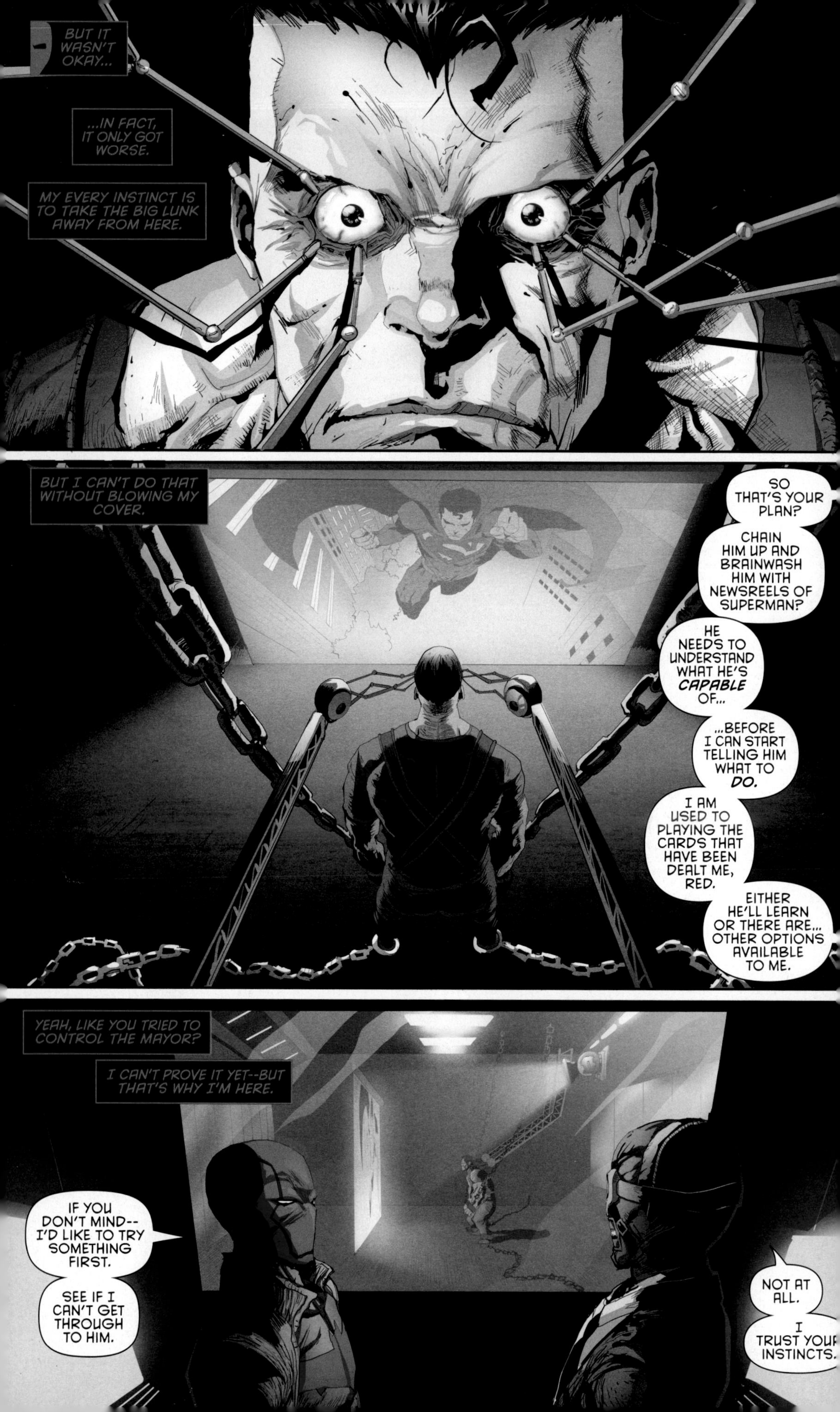

BUT IT WASN'T OKAY...
...IN FACT, IT ONLY GOT WORSE.
MY EVERY INSTINCT IS TO TAKE THE BIG LUNK AWAY FROM HERE.
BUT I CAN'T DO THAT WITHOUT BLOWING MY COVER.
SO THAT'S YOUR PLAN?
CHAIN HIM UP AND BRAINWASH HIM WITH NEWSREELS OF SUPERMAN?
HE NEEDS TO UNDERSTAND WHAT HE'S CAPABLE OF...
...BEFORE I CAN START TELLING HIM WHAT TO DO.
I AM USED TO PLAYING THE CARDS THAT HAVE BEEN DEALT ME, RED.
EITHER HE'LL LEARN OR THERE ARE... OTHER OPTIONS AVAILABLE TO ME.
YEAH, LIKE YOU TRIED TO CONTROL THE MAYOR?
I CAN'T PROVE IT YET--BUT THAT'S WHY I'M HERE.
IF YOU DON'T MIND--I'D LIKE TO TRY SOMETHING FIRST.
SEE IF I CAN'T GET THROUGH TO HIM.
NOT AT ALL.
I TRUST YOUR INSTINCTS.

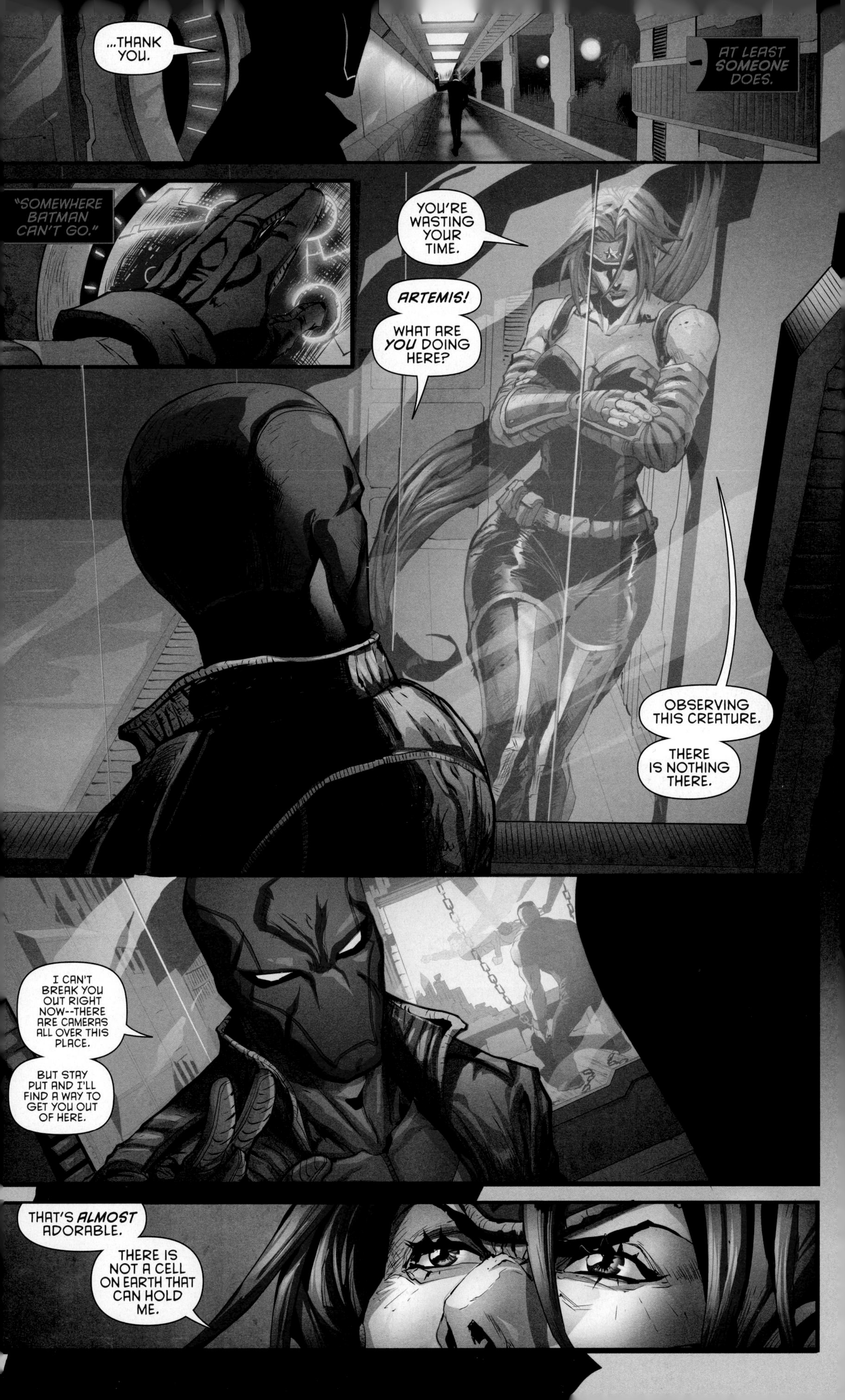
...THANK YOU.
AT LEAST SOMEONE DOES.
"SOMEWHERE BATMAN CAN'T GO."
YOU'RE WASTING YOUR TIME.
ARTEMIS!
WHAT ARE YOU DOING HERE?
OBSERVING THIS CREATURE.
THERE IS NOTHING THERE.
I CAN'T BREAK YOU OUT RIGHT NOW--THERE ARE CAMERAS ALL OVER THIS PLACE.
BUT STAY PUT AND I'LL FIND A WAY TO GET YOU OUT OF HERE.
THAT'S ALMOST ADORABLE.
THERE IS NOT A CELL ON EARTH THAT CAN HOLD ME.

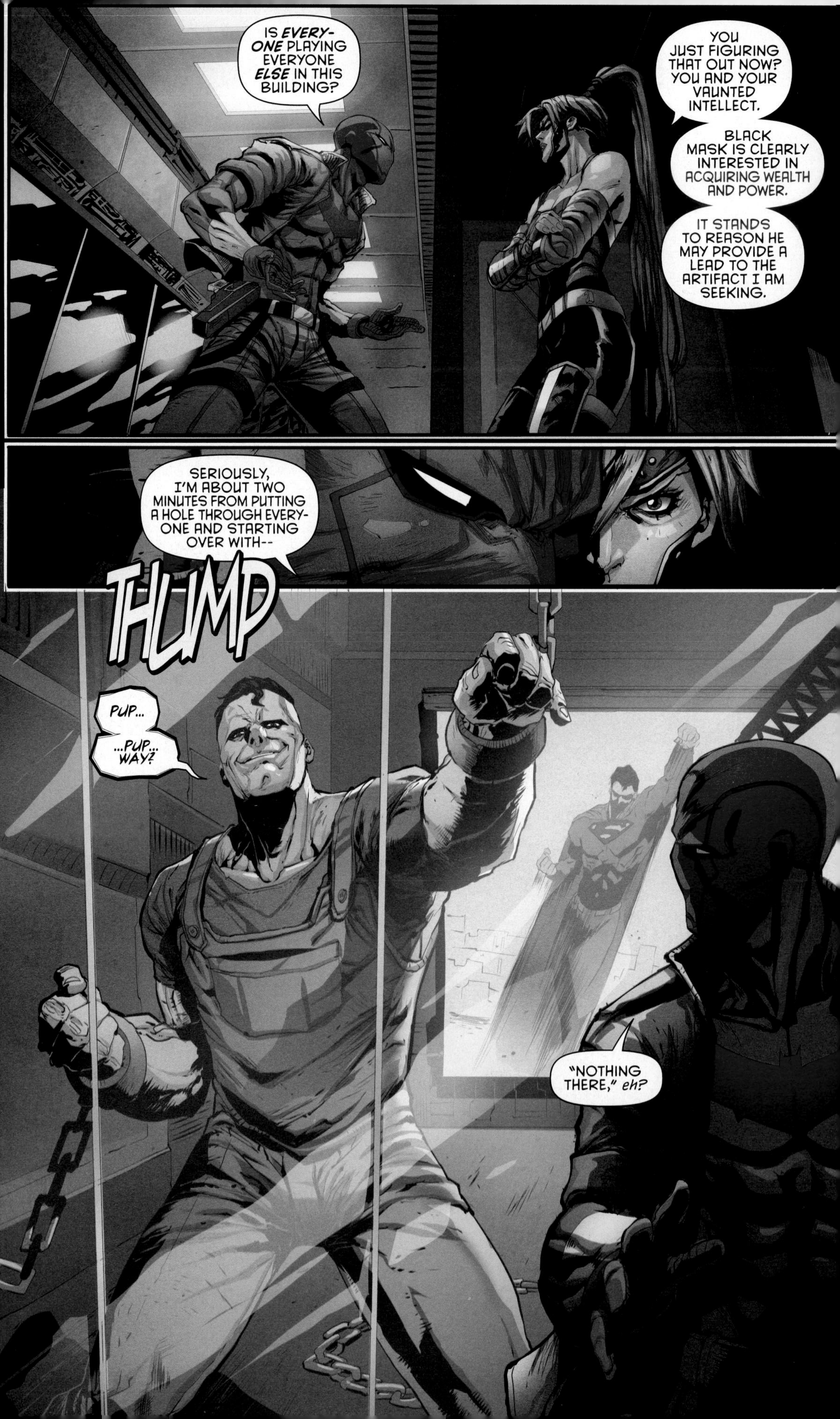
IS *EVERY-ONE* PLAYING EVERYONE *ELSE* IN THIS BUILDING?
YOU JUST FIGURING THAT OUT NOW? YOU AND YOUR VAUNTED INTELLECT.
BLACK MASK IS CLEARLY INTERESTED IN ACQUIRING WEALTH AND POWER.
IT STANDS TO REASON HE MAY PROVIDE A LEAD TO THE ARTIFACT I AM SEEKING.
SERIOUSLY, I'M ABOUT TWO MINUTES FROM PUTTING A HOLE THROUGH EVERY-ONE AND STARTING OVER WITH--
THUMP
PUP...
...PUP... WAY?
"NOTHING THERE," *eh?*

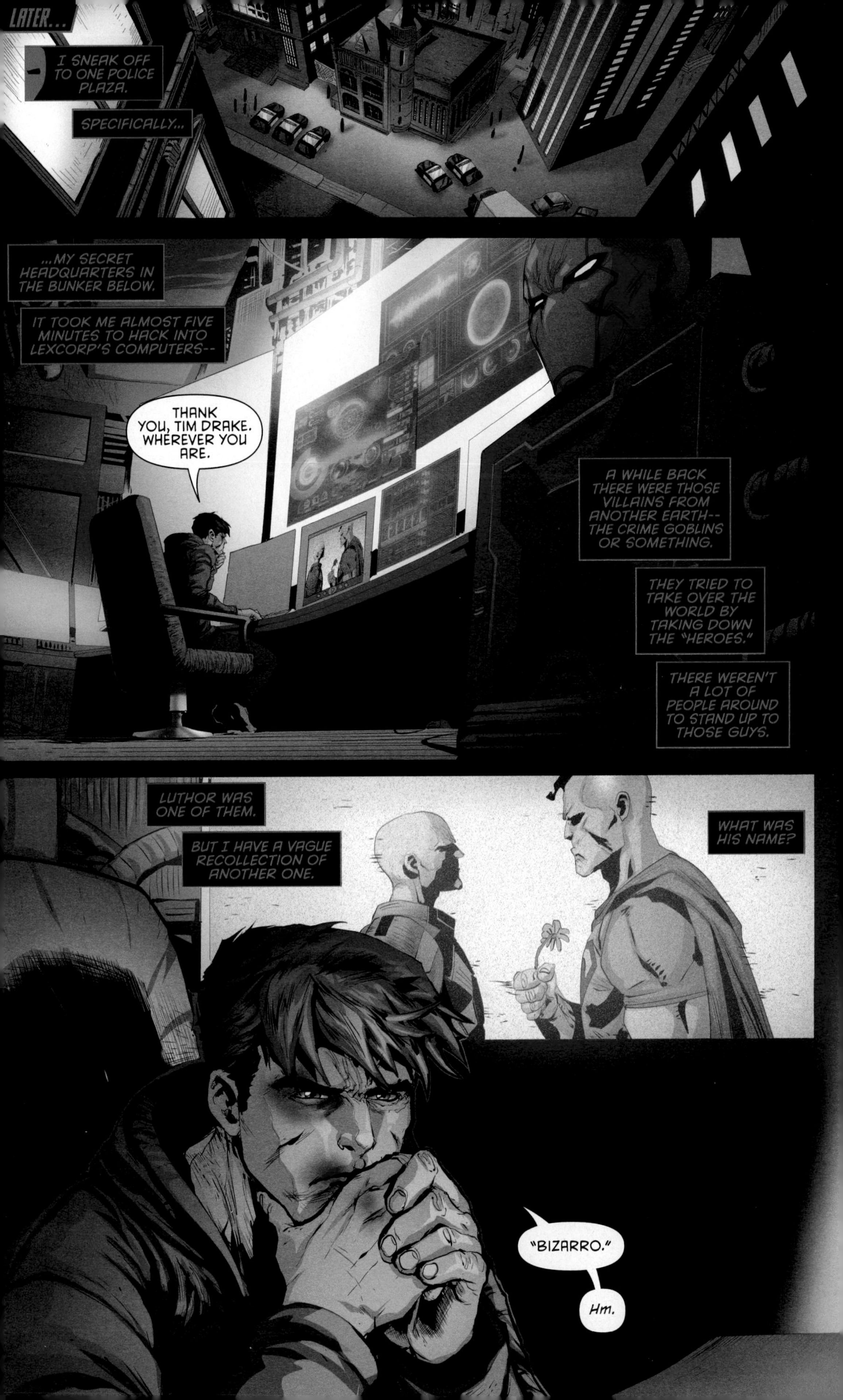
LATER...
I SNEAK OFF TO ONE POLICE PLAZA.
SPECIFICALLY...
...MY SECRET HEADQUARTERS IN THE BUNKER BELOW.
IT TOOK ME ALMOST FIVE MINUTES TO HACK INTO LEXCORP'S COMPUTERS--
THANK YOU, TIM DRAKE. WHEREVER YOU ARE.
A WHILE BACK THERE WERE THOSE VILLAINS FROM ANOTHER EARTH-- THE CRIME GOBLINS OR SOMETHING.
THEY TRIED TO TAKE OVER THE WORLD BY TAKING DOWN THE "HEROES."
THERE WEREN'T A LOT OF PEOPLE AROUND TO STAND UP TO THOSE GUYS.
LUTHOR WAS ONE OF THEM.
BUT I HAVE A VAGUE RECOLLECTION OF ANOTHER ONE.
WHAT WAS HIS NAME?
"BIZARRO."
Hm.

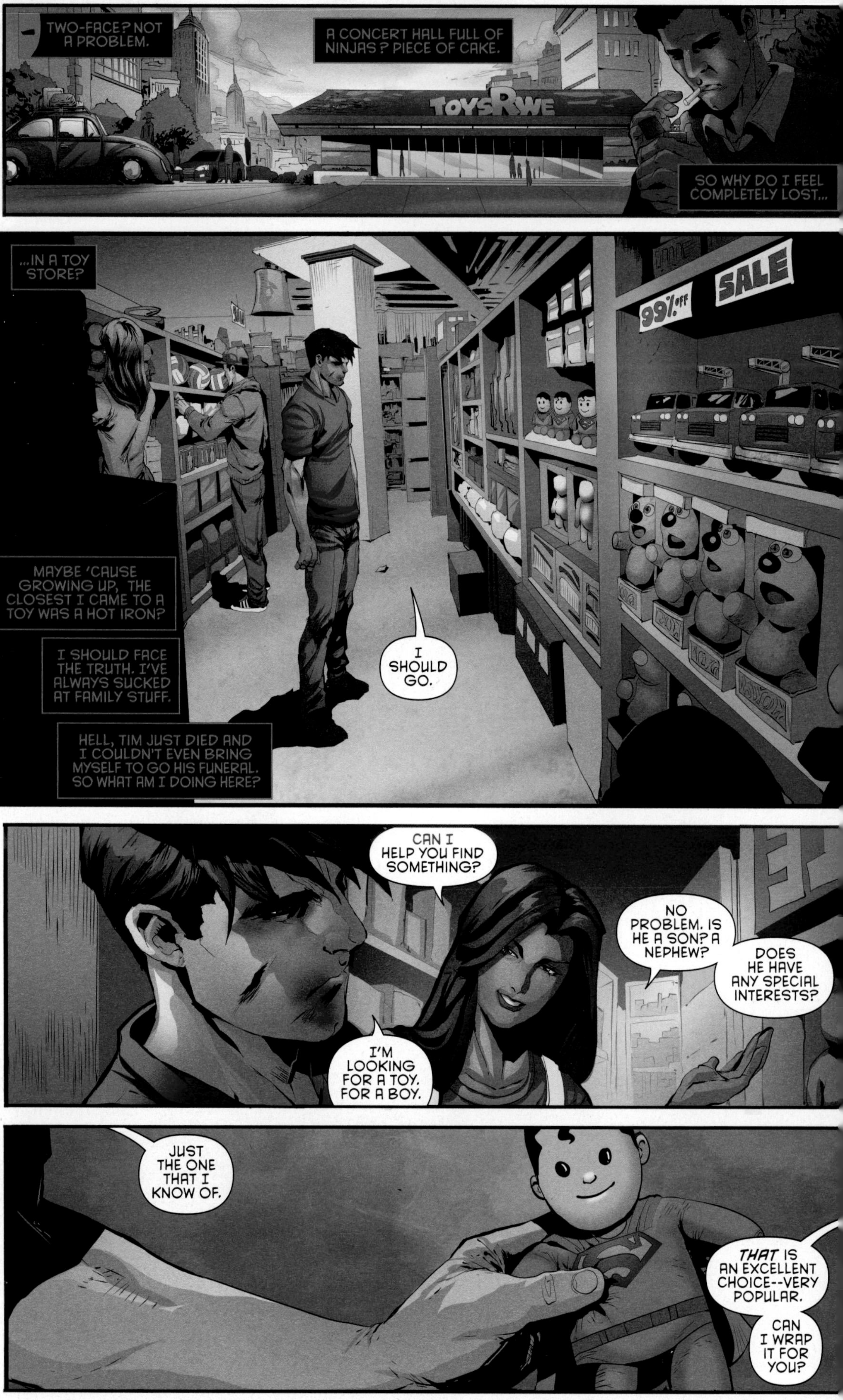
TWO-FACE? NOT A PROBLEM.
A CONCERT HALL FULL OF NINJAS? PIECE OF CAKE.
TOYSRWE
SO WHY DO I FEEL COMPLETELY LOST...
...IN A TOY STORE?
SALE
99% OFF
MAYBE 'CAUSE GROWING UP, THE CLOSEST I CAME TO A TOY WAS A HOT IRON?
I SHOULD FACE THE TRUTH. I'VE ALWAYS SUCKED AT FAMILY STUFF.
HELL, TIM JUST DIED AND I COULDN'T EVEN BRING MYSELF TO GO HIS FUNERAL. SO WHAT AM I DOING HERE?
I SHOULD GO.
CAN I HELP YOU FIND SOMETHING?
I'M LOOKING FOR A TOY. FOR A BOY.
NO PROBLEM. IS HE A SON? A NEPHEW?
DOES HE HAVE ANY SPECIAL INTERESTS?
JUST THE ONE THAT I KNOW OF.
THAT IS AN EXCELLENT CHOICE--VERY POPULAR.
CAN I WRAP IT FOR YOU?

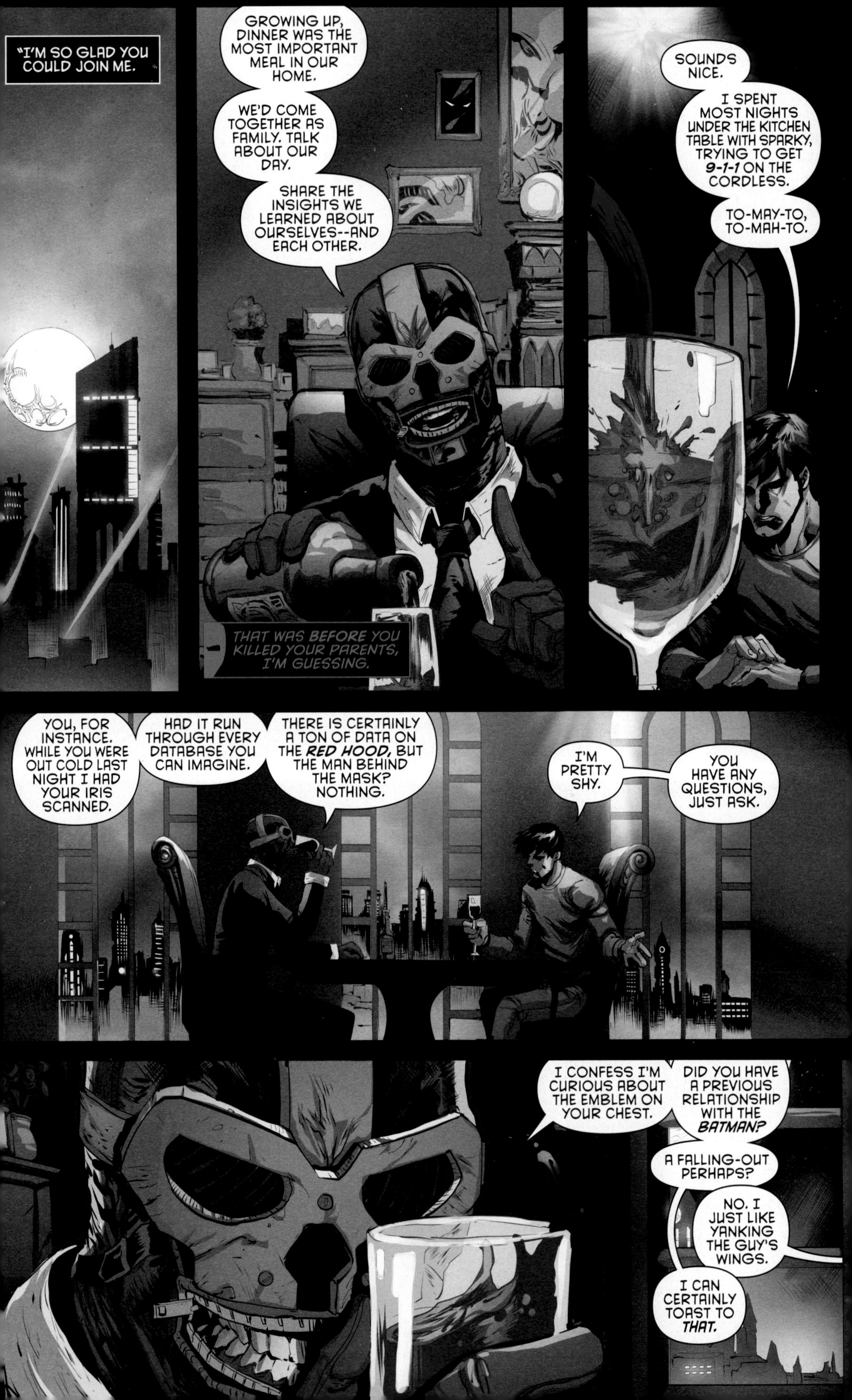
"I'M SO GLAD YOU COULD JOIN ME.
GROWING UP, DINNER WAS THE MOST IMPORTANT MEAL IN OUR HOME.
WE'D COME TOGETHER AS FAMILY. TALK ABOUT OUR DAY.
SHARE THE INSIGHTS WE LEARNED ABOUT OURSELVES--AND EACH OTHER.
THAT WAS BEFORE YOU KILLED YOUR PARENTS, I'M GUESSING.
SOUNDS NICE.
I SPENT MOST NIGHTS UNDER THE KITCHEN TABLE WITH SPARKY, TRYING TO GET 9-1-1 ON THE CORDLESS.
TO-MAY-TO, TO-MAH-TO.
YOU, FOR INSTANCE. WHILE YOU WERE OUT COLD LAST NIGHT I HAD YOUR IRIS SCANNED.
HAD IT RUN THROUGH EVERY DATABASE YOU CAN IMAGINE.
THERE IS CERTAINLY A TON OF DATA ON THE RED HOOD, BUT THE MAN BEHIND THE MASK? NOTHING.
I'M PRETTY SHY.
YOU HAVE ANY QUESTIONS, JUST ASK.
I CONFESS I'M CURIOUS ABOUT THE EMBLEM ON YOUR CHEST.
DID YOU HAVE A PREVIOUS RELATIONSHIP WITH THE BATMAN?
A FALLING-OUT PERHAPS?
NO. I JUST LIKE YANKING THE GUY'S WINGS.
I CAN CERTAINLY TOAST TO THAT.

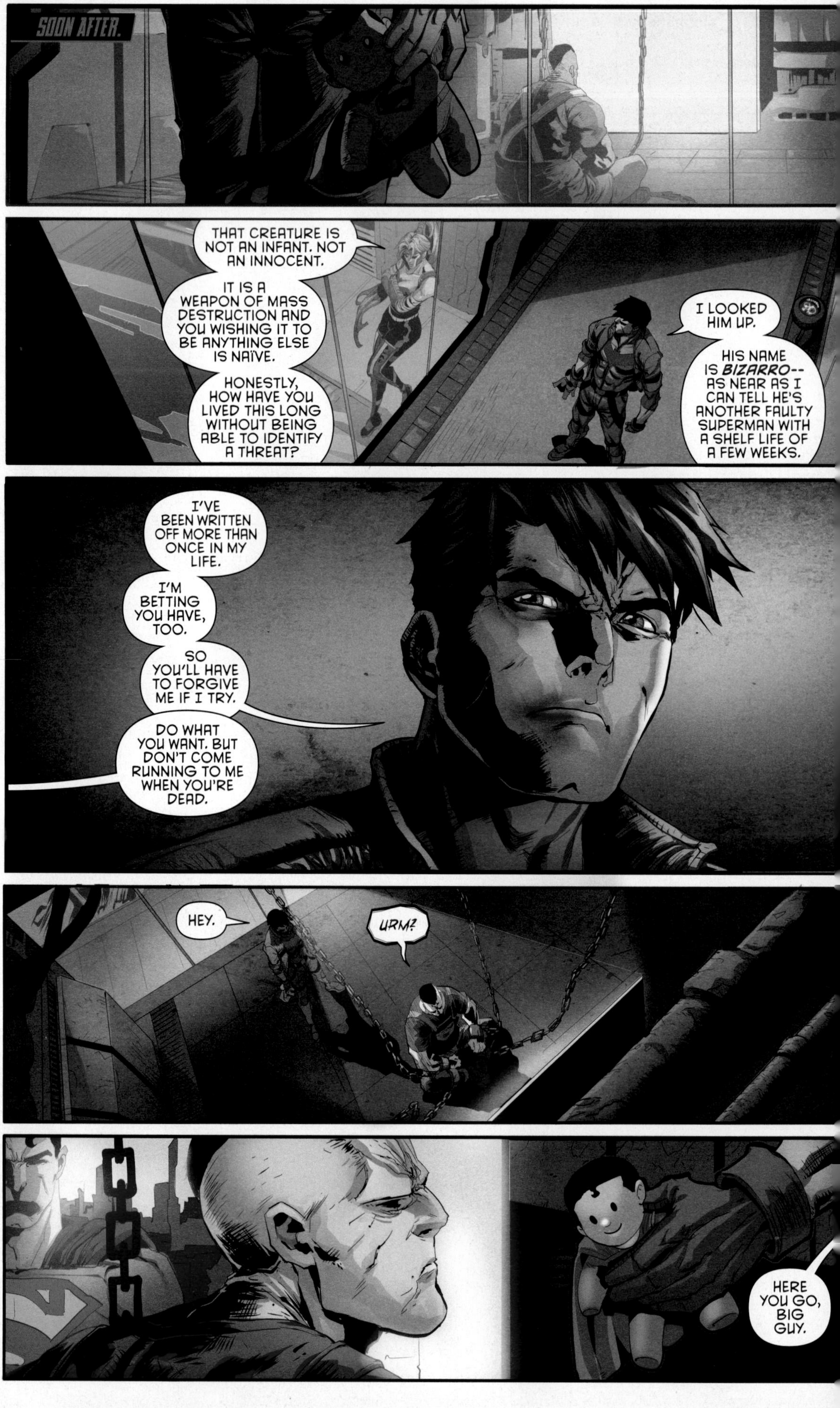
SOON AFTER.
THAT CREATURE IS NOT AN INFANT. NOT AN INNOCENT.
IT IS A WEAPON OF MASS DESTRUCTION AND YOU WISHING IT TO BE ANYTHING ELSE IS NAÏVE.
HONESTLY, HOW HAVE YOU LIVED THIS LONG WITHOUT BEING ABLE TO IDENTIFY A THREAT?
I LOOKED HIM UP.
HIS NAME IS *BIZARRO*-- AS NEAR AS I CAN TELL HE'S ANOTHER FAULTY SUPERMAN WITH A SHELF LIFE OF A FEW WEEKS.
I'VE BEEN WRITTEN OFF MORE THAN ONCE IN MY LIFE.
I'M BETTING YOU HAVE, TOO.
SO YOU'LL HAVE TO FORGIVE ME IF I TRY.
DO WHAT YOU WANT. BUT DON'T COME RUNNING TO ME WHEN YOU'RE DEAD.
HEY.
URM?
HERE YOU GO, BIG GUY.

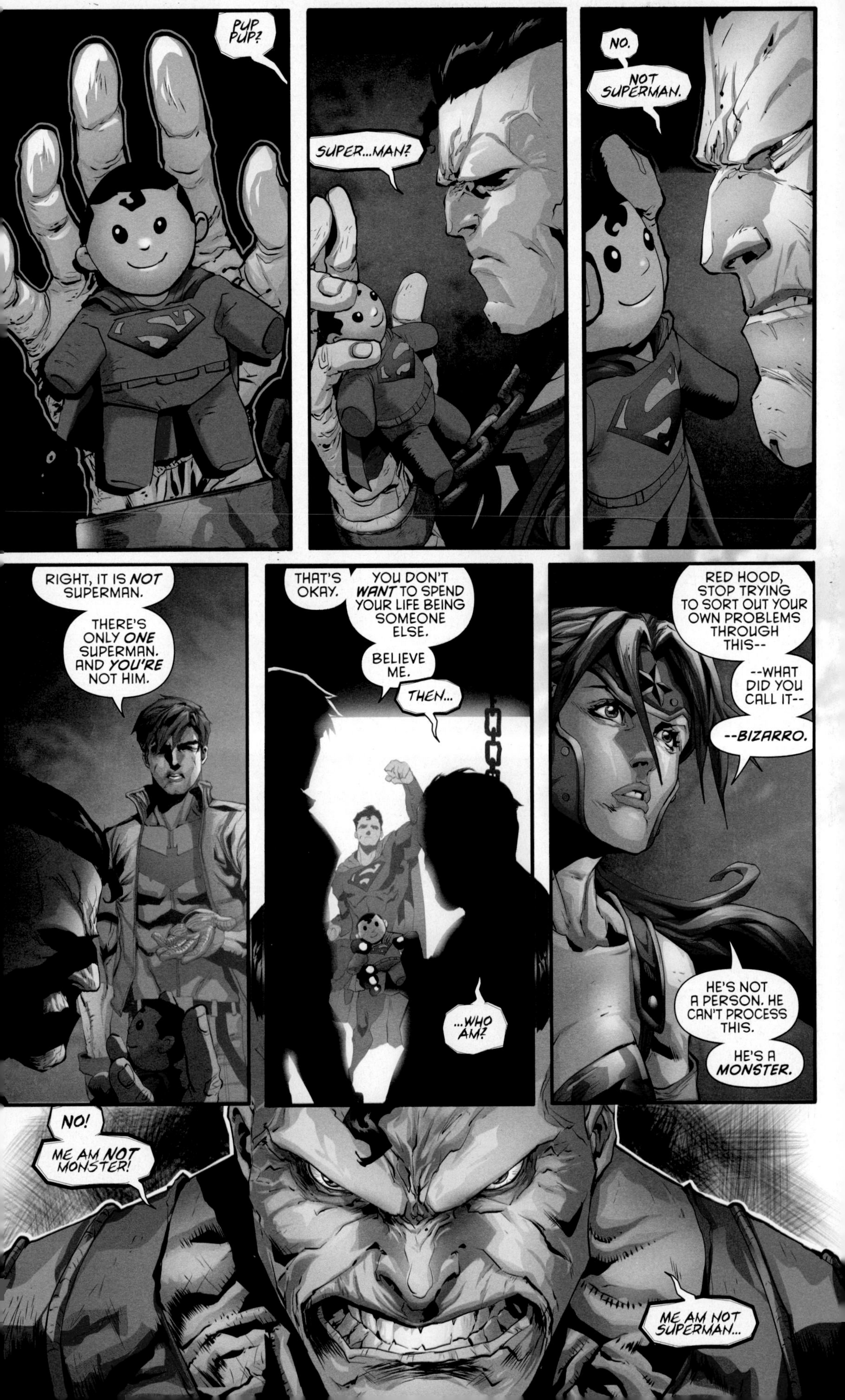
PUP PUP?
SUPER...MAN?
NO.
NOT SUPERMAN.
RIGHT, IT IS NOT SUPERMAN.
THERE'S ONLY ONE SUPERMAN. AND YOU'RE NOT HIM.
THAT'S OKAY.
YOU DON'T WANT TO SPEND YOUR LIFE BEING SOMEONE ELSE.
BELIEVE ME.
THEN...
...WHO AM?
RED HOOD, STOP TRYING TO SORT OUT YOUR OWN PROBLEMS THROUGH THIS--
--WHAT DID YOU CALL IT--
--BIZARRO.
HE'S NOT A PERSON. HE CAN'T PROCESS THIS.
HE'S A MONSTER.
NO!
ME AM NOT MONSTER!
ME AM NOT SUPERMAN...

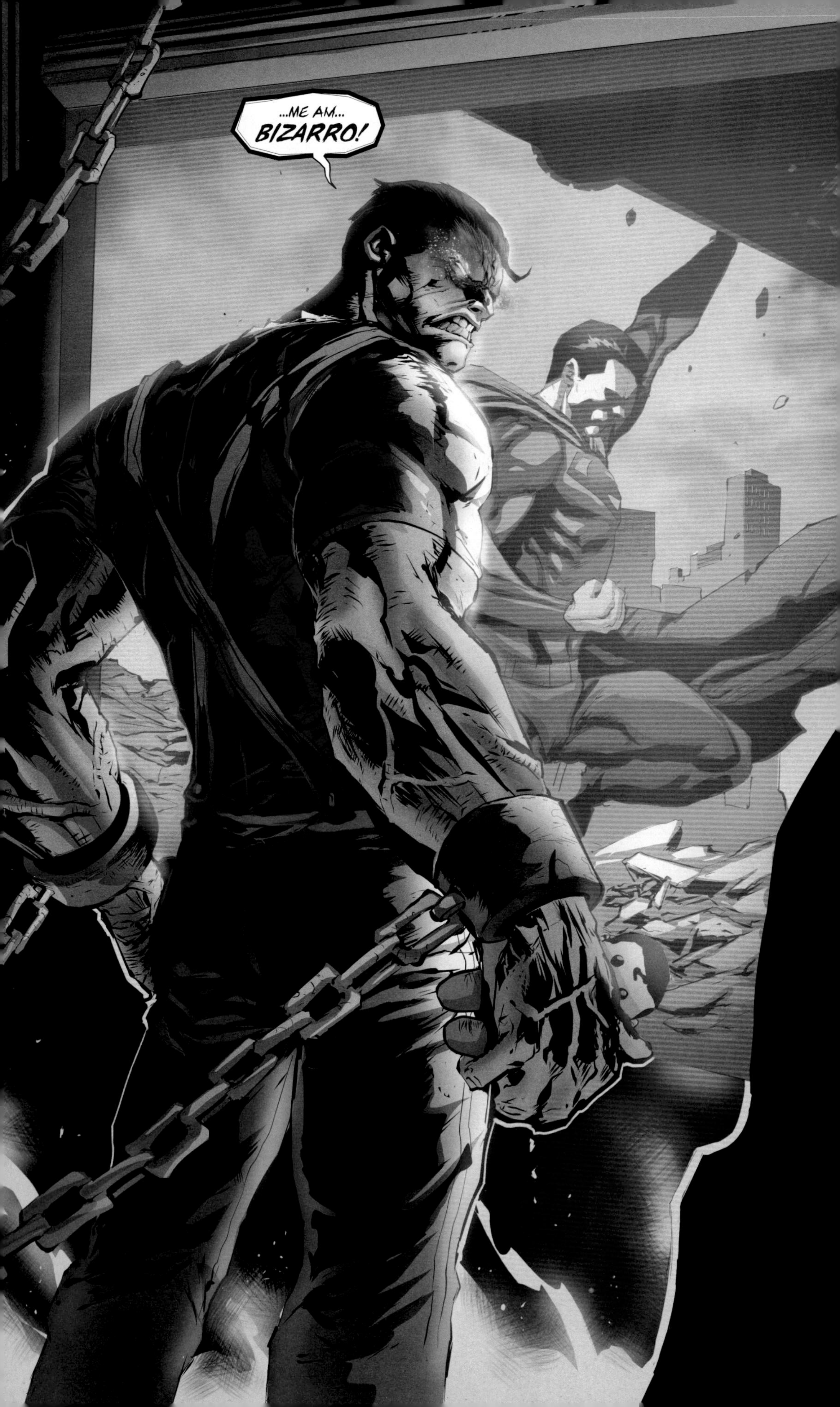
...ME AM... BIZARRO!

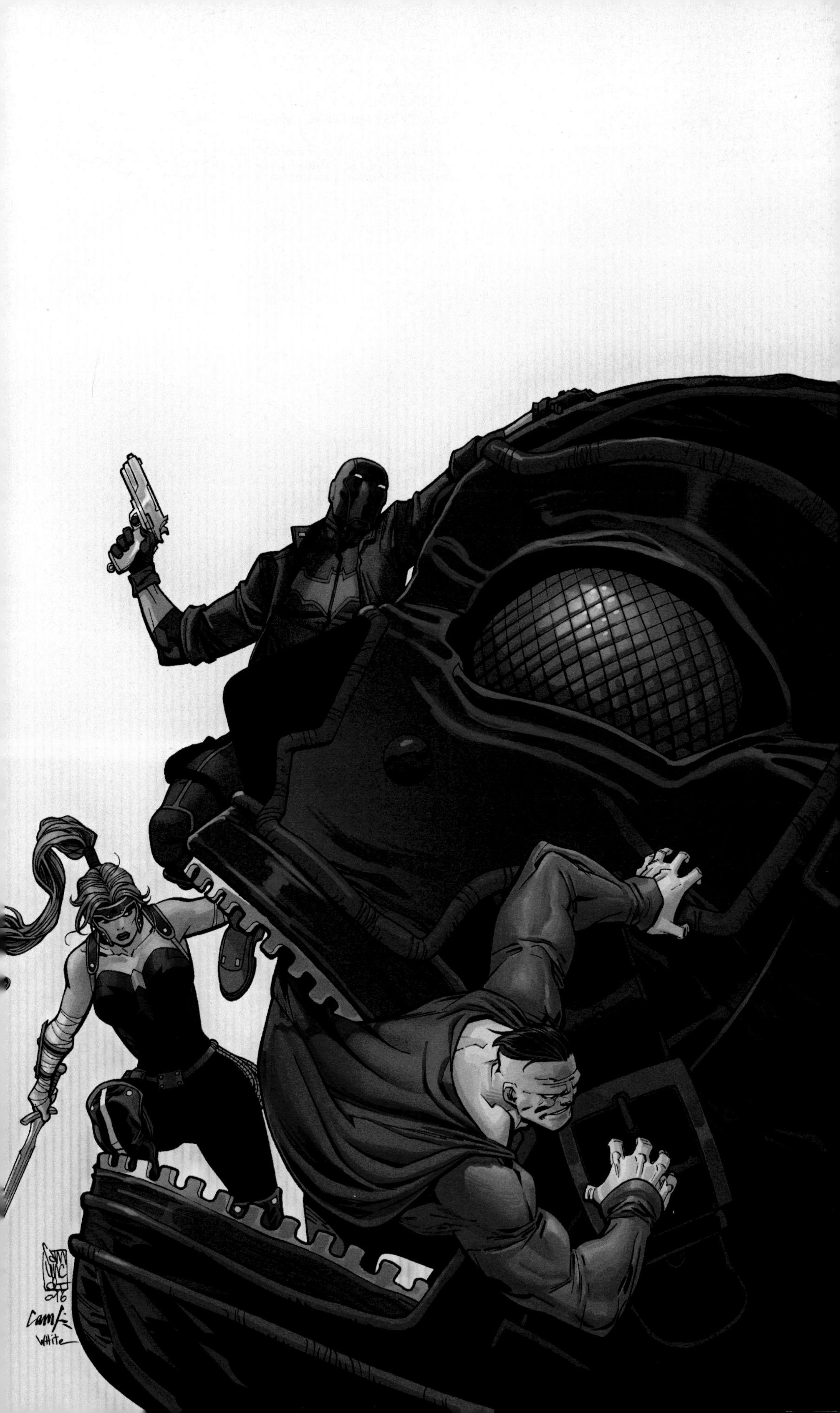

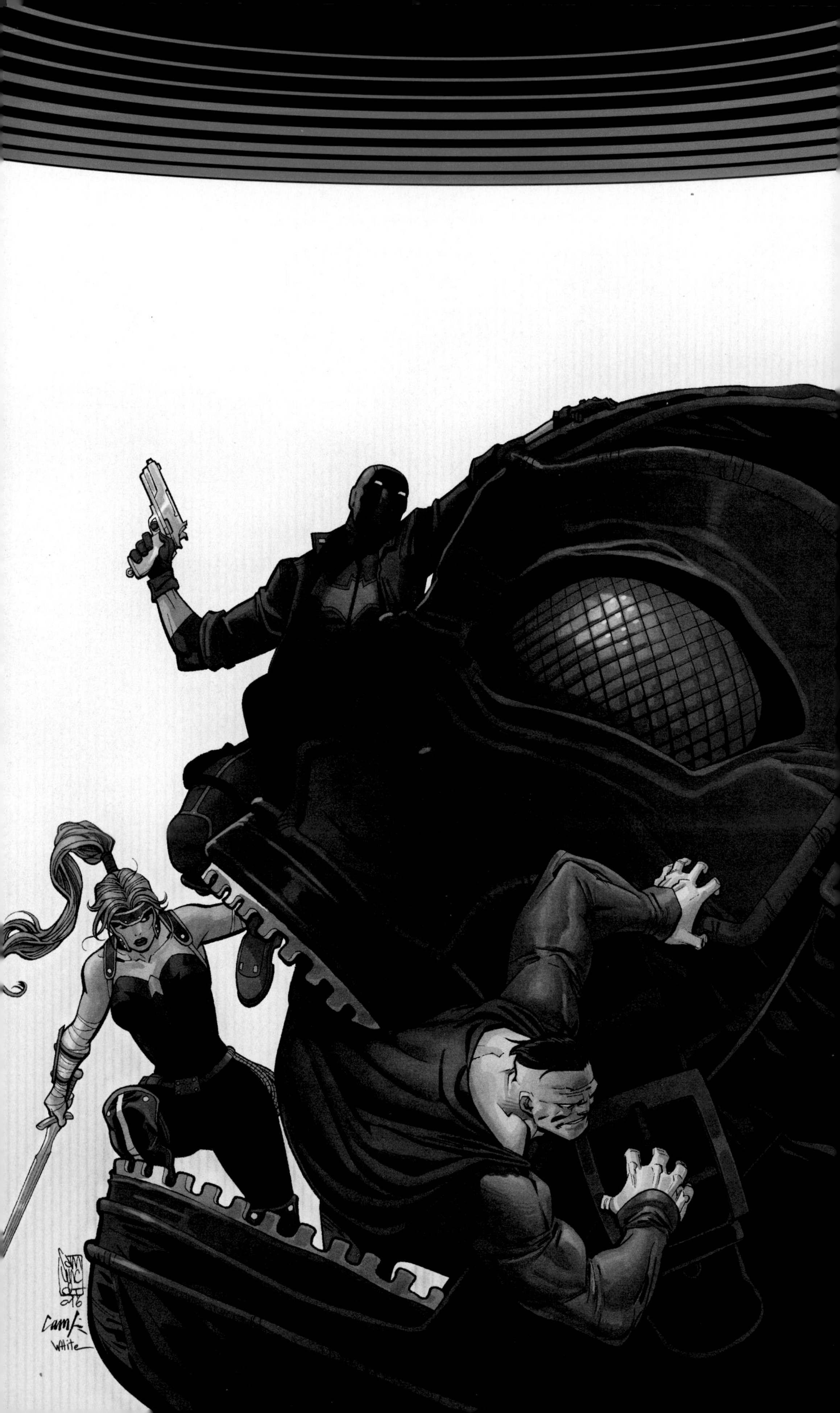

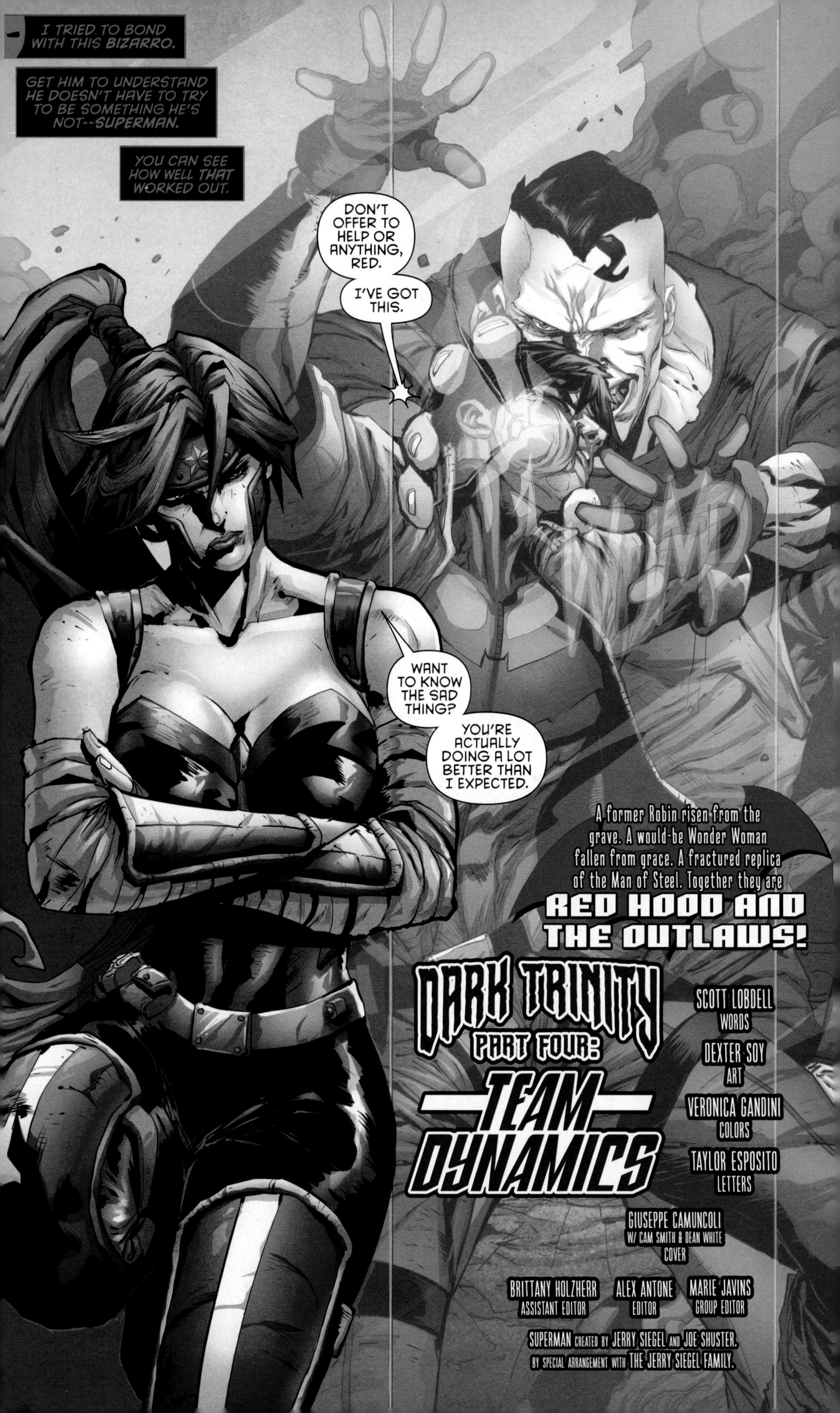
I TRIED TO BOND WITH THIS BIZARRO.
GET HIM TO UNDERSTAND HE DOESN'T HAVE TO TRY TO BE SOMETHING HE'S NOT--SUPERMAN.
YOU CAN SEE HOW WELL THAT WORKED OUT.
DON'T OFFER TO HELP OR ANYTHING, RED.
I'VE GOT THIS.
WANT TO KNOW THE SAD THING?
YOU'RE ACTUALLY DOING A LOT BETTER THAN I EXPECTED.
A former Robin risen from the grave. A would-be Wonder Woman fallen from grace. A fractured replica of the Man of Steel. Together they are
RED HOOD AND THE OUTLAWS!
DARK TRINITY
PART FOUR:
TEAM DYNAMICS
SCOTT LOBDELL WORDS
DEXTER SOY ART
VERONICA GANDINI COLORS
TAYLOR ESPOSITO LETTERS
GIUSEPPE CAMUNCOLI W/ CAM SMITH & DEAN WHITE COVER
BRITTANY HOLZHERR ASSISTANT EDITOR
ALEX ANTONE EDITOR
MARIE JAVINS GROUP EDITOR
SUPERMAN CREATED BY JERRY SIEGEL AND JOE SHUSTER.
BY SPECIAL ARRANGEMENT WITH THE JERRY SIEGEL FAMILY.

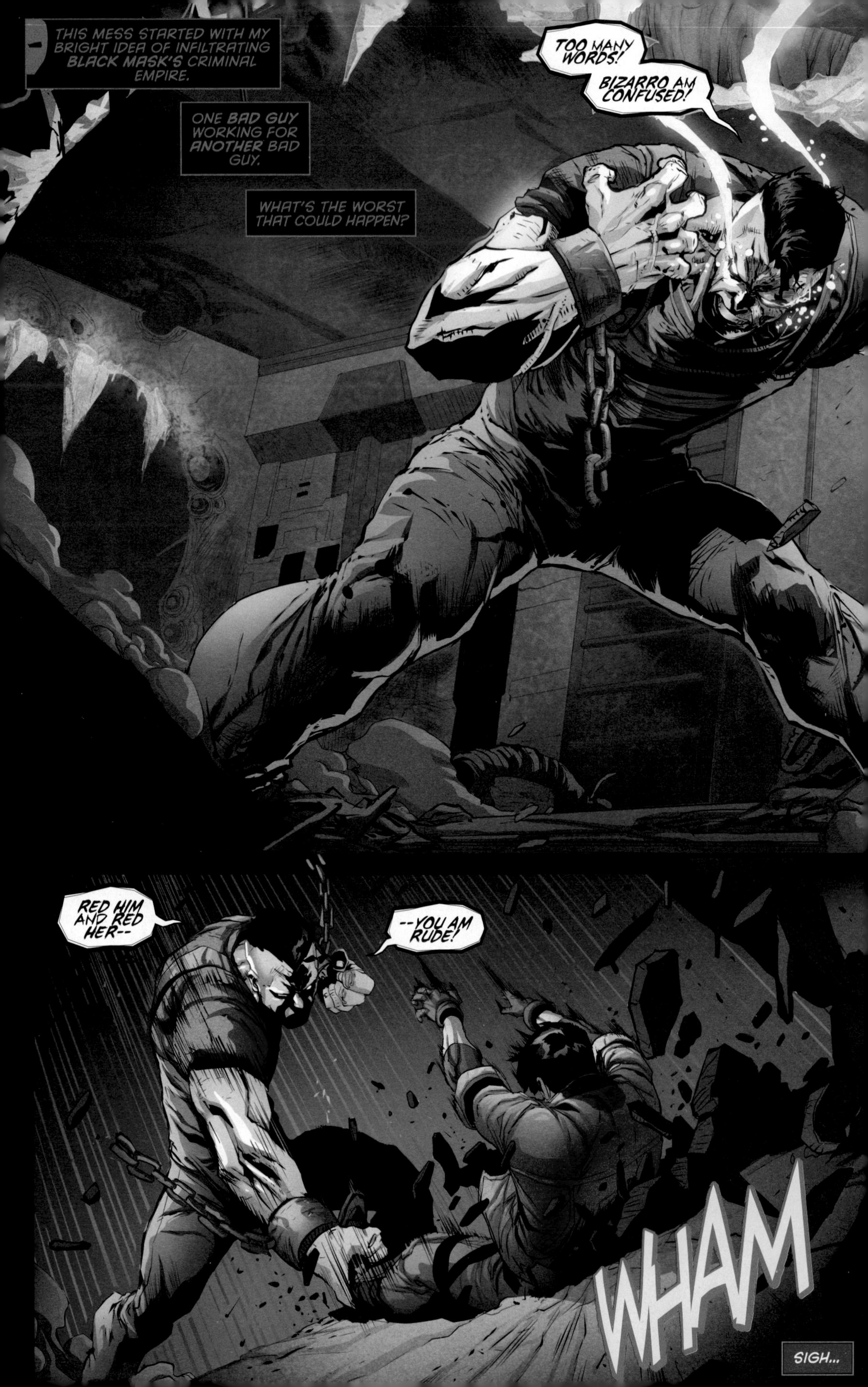
THIS MESS STARTED WITH MY BRIGHT IDEA OF INFILTRATING BLACK MASK'S CRIMINAL EMPIRE.
ONE BAD GUY WORKING FOR ANOTHER BAD GUY.
WHAT'S THE WORST THAT COULD HAPPEN?
TOO MANY WORDS!
BIZARRO AM CONFUSED!
RED HIM AND RED HER--
--YOU AM RUDE!
WHAM
SIGH...

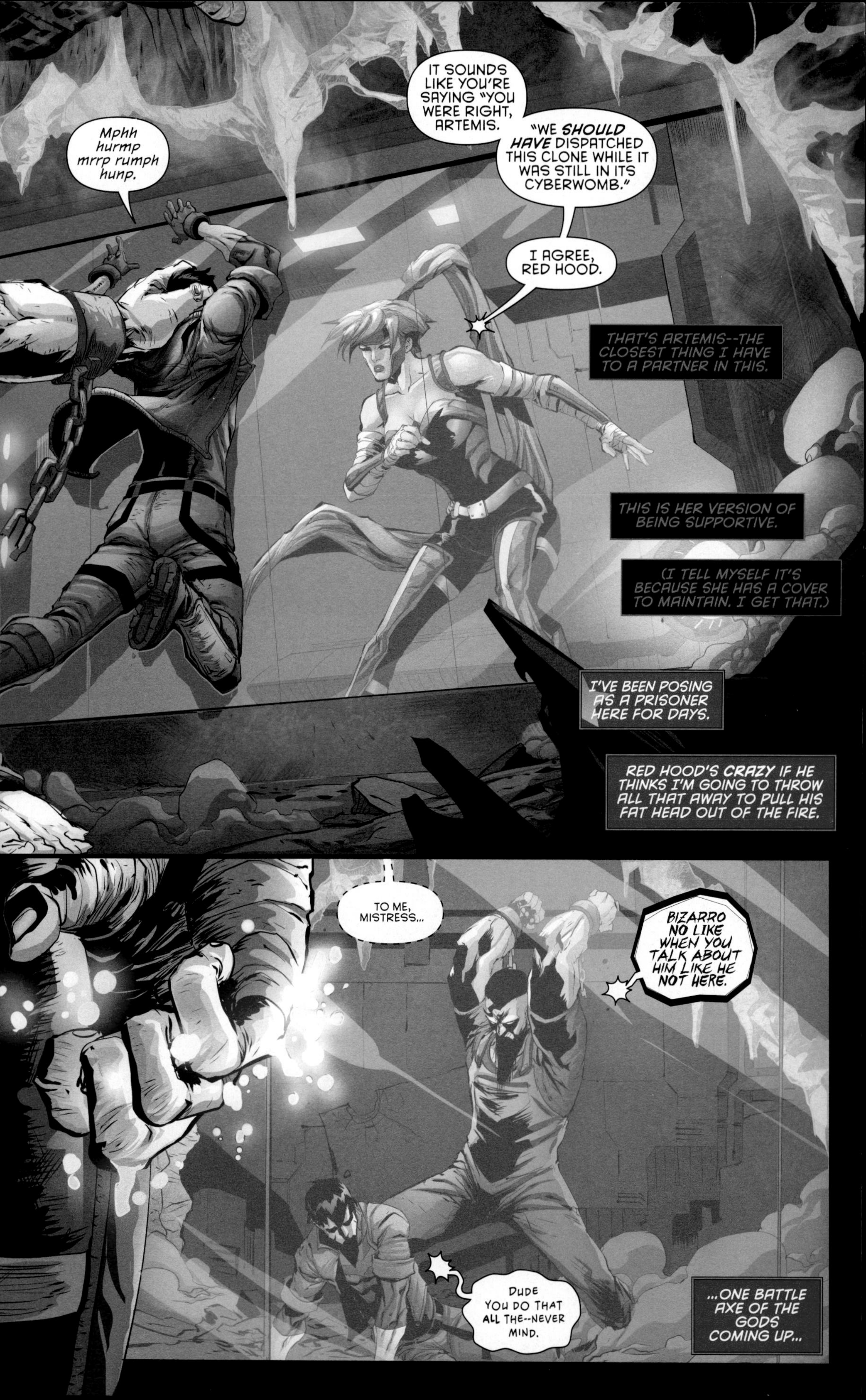

Mphh hurmp mrrp rumph hunp.
IT SOUNDS LIKE YOU'RE SAYING "YOU WERE RIGHT, ARTEMIS.
"WE SHOULD HAVE DISPATCHED THIS CLONE WHILE IT WAS STILL IN ITS CYBERWOMB."
I AGREE, RED HOOD.
THAT'S ARTEMIS--THE CLOSEST THING I HAVE TO A PARTNER IN THIS.
THIS IS HER VERSION OF BEING SUPPORTIVE.
(I TELL MYSELF IT'S BECAUSE SHE HAS A COVER TO MAINTAIN. I GET THAT.)
I'VE BEEN POSING AS A PRISONER HERE FOR DAYS.
RED HOOD'S CRAZY IF HE THINKS I'M GOING TO THROW ALL THAT AWAY TO PULL HIS FAT HEAD OUT OF THE FIRE.
TO ME, MISTRESS...
BIZARRO NO LIKE WHEN YOU TALK ABOUT HIM LIKE HE NOT HERE.
DUDE YOU DO THAT ALL THE--NEVER MIND.
...ONE BATTLE AXE OF THE GODS COMING UP...

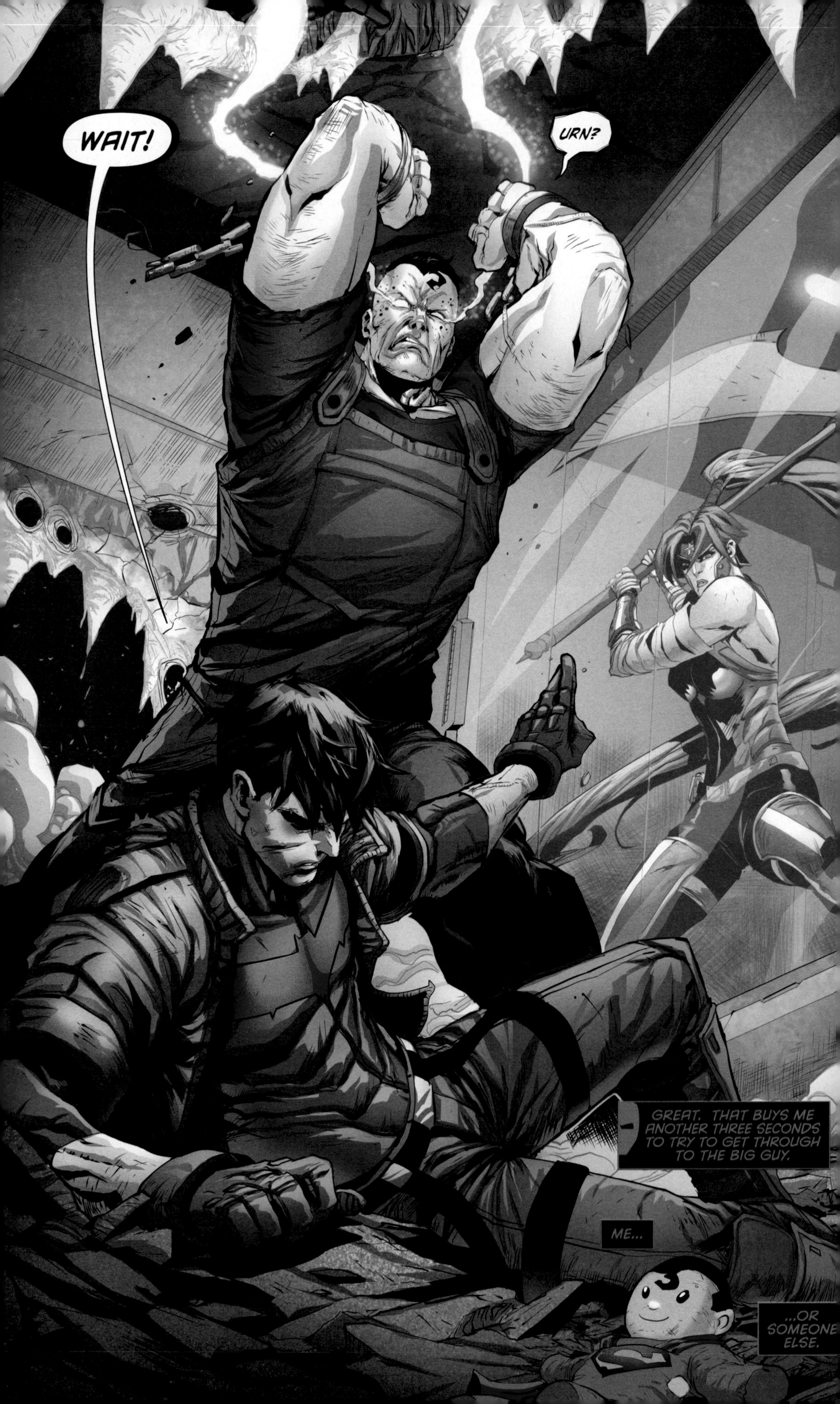
WAIT!
URN?
GREAT. THAT BUYS ME ANOTHER THREE SECONDS TO TRY TO GET THROUGH TO THE BIG GUY.
ME...
...OR SOMEONE ELSE.

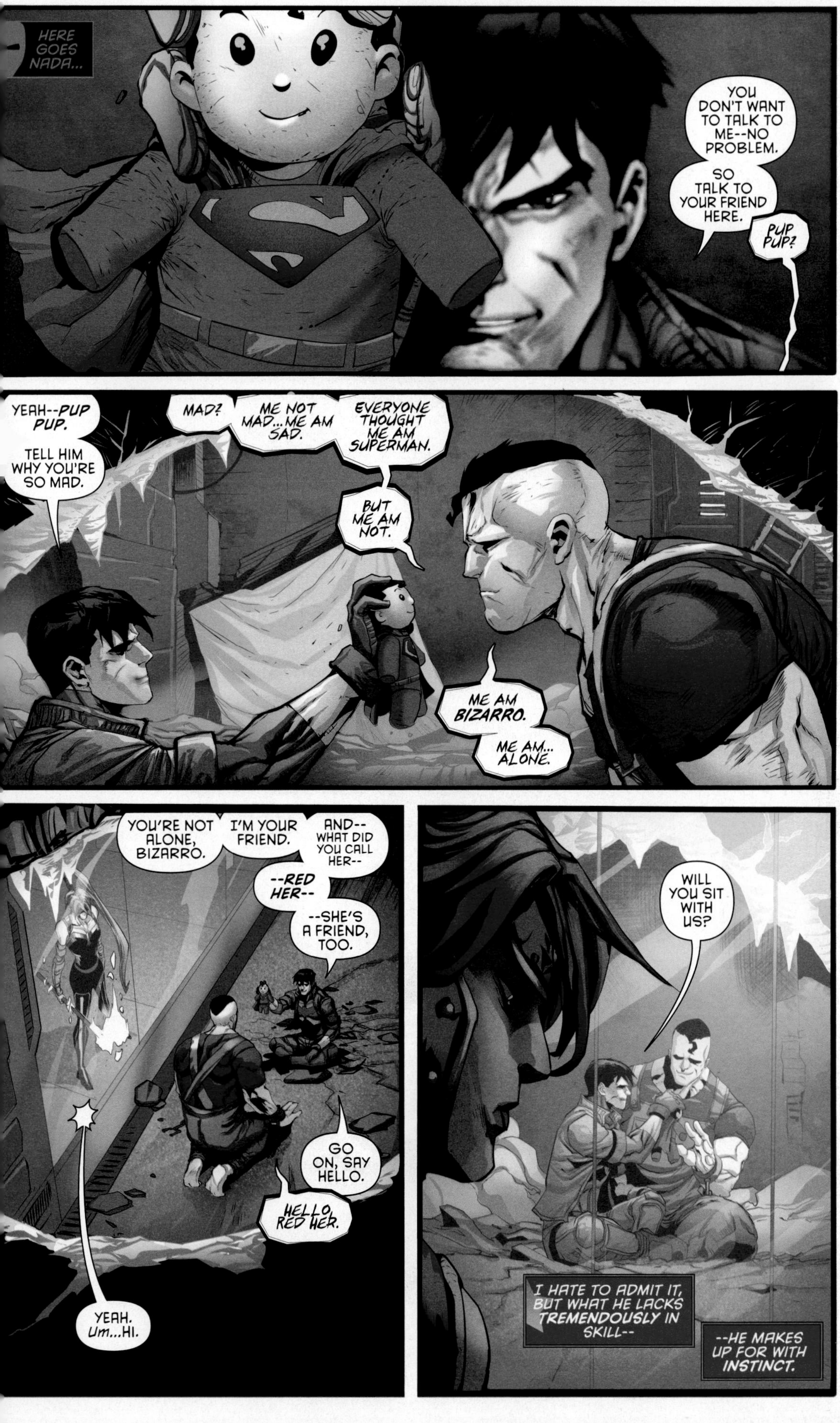
HERE GOES NADA...
YOU DON'T WANT TO TALK TO ME--NO PROBLEM.
SO TALK TO YOUR FRIEND HERE.
PUP PUP?
YEAH--PUP PUP.
TELL HIM WHY YOU'RE SO MAD.
MAD?
ME NOT MAD... ME AM SAD.
EVERYONE THOUGHT ME AM SUPERMAN.
BUT ME AM NOT.
ME AM BIZARRO.
ME AM... ALONE.
YOU'RE NOT ALONE, BIZARRO.
I'M YOUR FRIEND.
AND--WHAT DID YOU CALL HER--
--RED HER--
--SHE'S A FRIEND, TOO.
GO ON, SAY HELLO.
HELLO RED HER.
YEAH. Um...HI.
WILL YOU SIT WITH US?
I HATE TO ADMIT IT, BUT WHAT HE LACKS TREMENDOUSLY IN SKILL--
--HE MAKES UP FOR WITH INSTINCT.

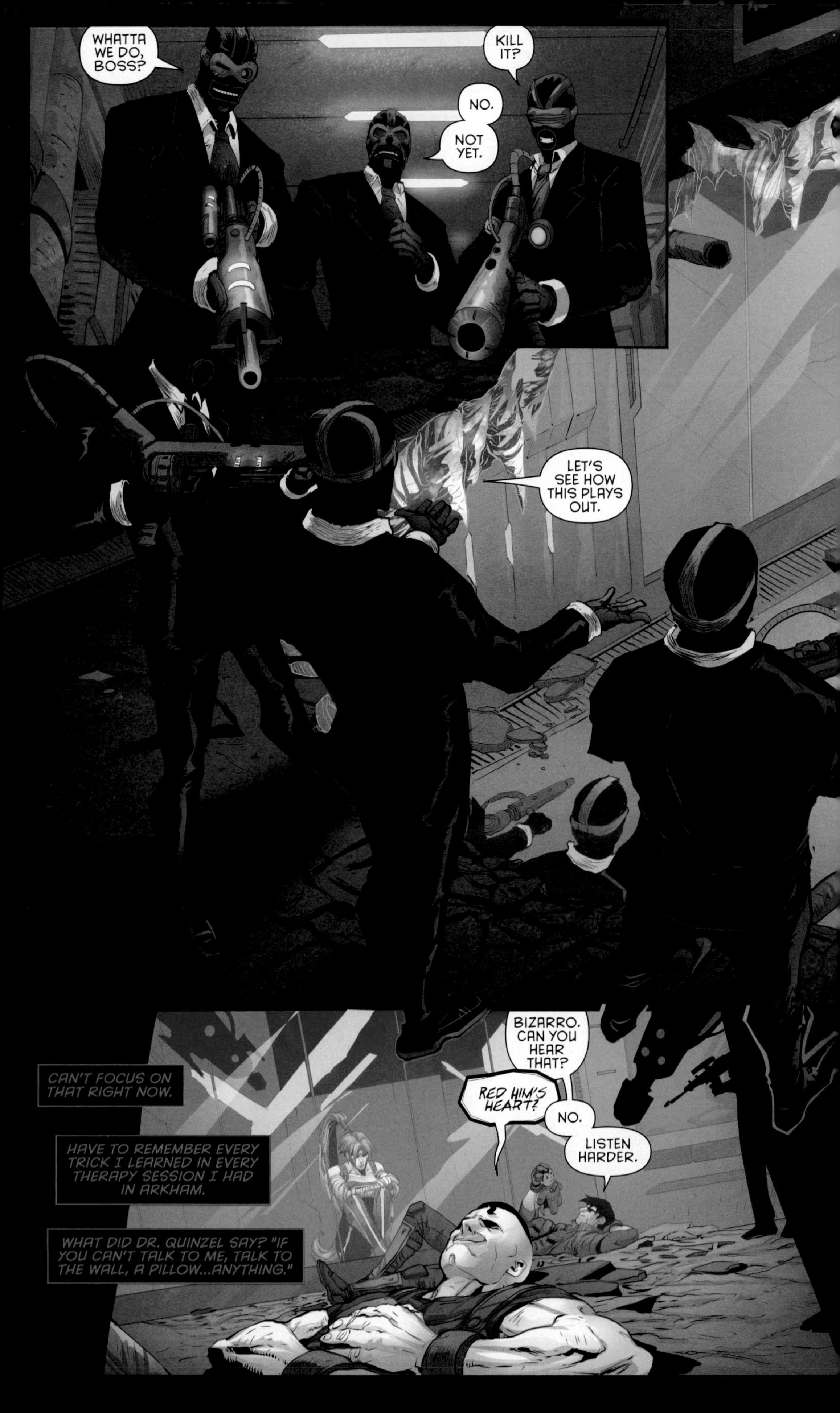
WHATTA WE DO, BOSS?
KILL IT?
NO.
NOT YET.
LET'S SEE HOW THIS PLAYS OUT.
CAN'T FOCUS ON THAT RIGHT NOW.
HAVE TO REMEMBER EVERY TRICK I LEARNED IN EVERY THERAPY SESSION I HAD IN ARKHAM.
WHAT DID DR. QUINZEL SAY? "IF YOU CAN'T TALK TO ME, TALK TO THE WALL, A PILLOW...ANYTHING."
BIZARRO. CAN YOU HEAR THAT?
RED HIM'S HEART?
NO.
LISTEN HARDER.

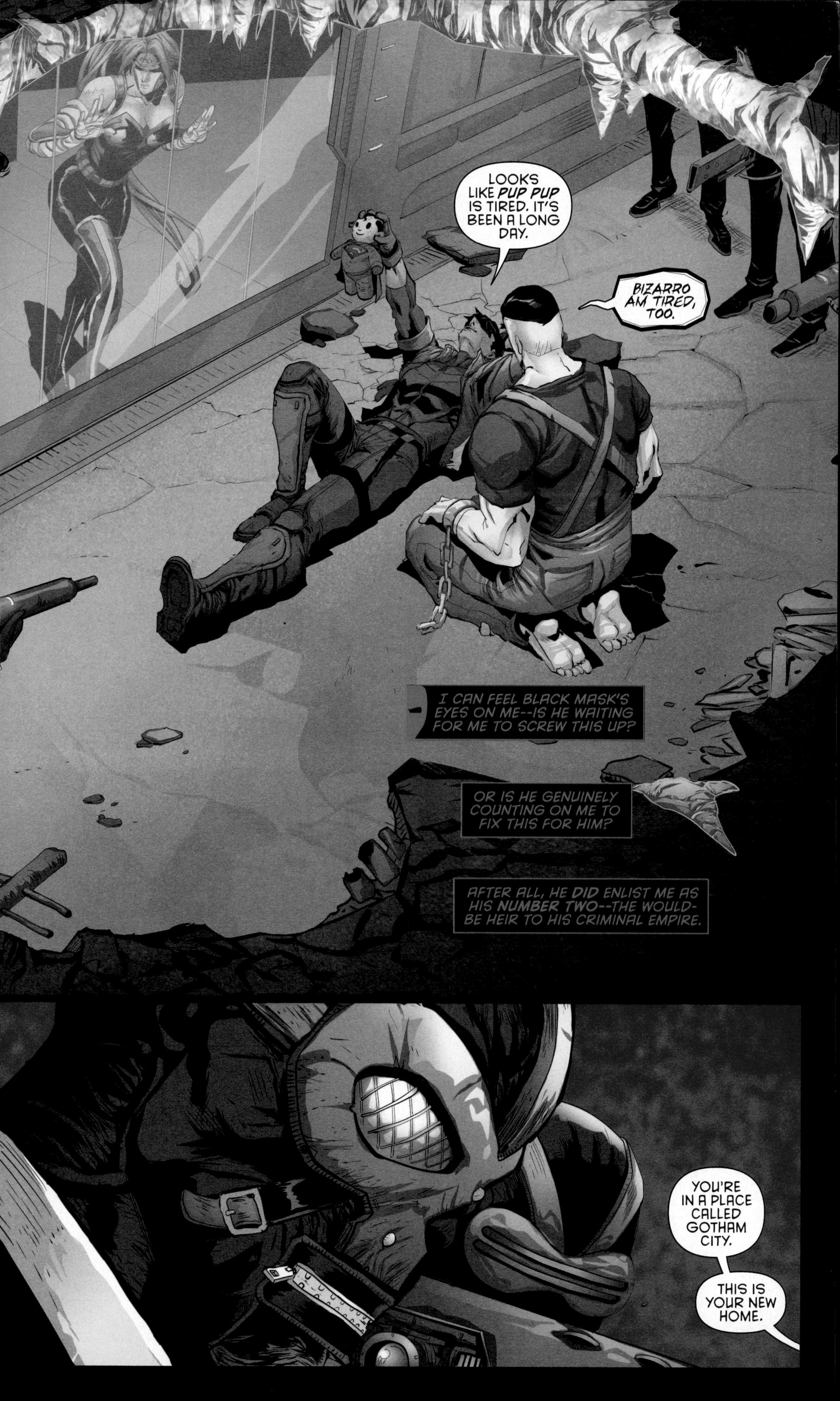

LOOKS LIKE PUP PUP IS TIRED. IT'S BEEN A LONG DAY.
BIZARRO AM TIRED, TOO.
I CAN FEEL BLACK MASK'S EYES ON ME--IS HE WAITING FOR ME TO SCREW THIS UP?
OR IS HE GENUINELY COUNTING ON ME TO FIX THIS FOR HIM?
AFTER ALL, HE DID ENLIST ME AS HIS NUMBER TWO--THE WOULD-BE HEIR TO HIS CRIMINAL EMPIRE.
YOU'RE IN A PLACE CALLED GOTHAM CITY.
THIS IS YOUR NEW HOME.

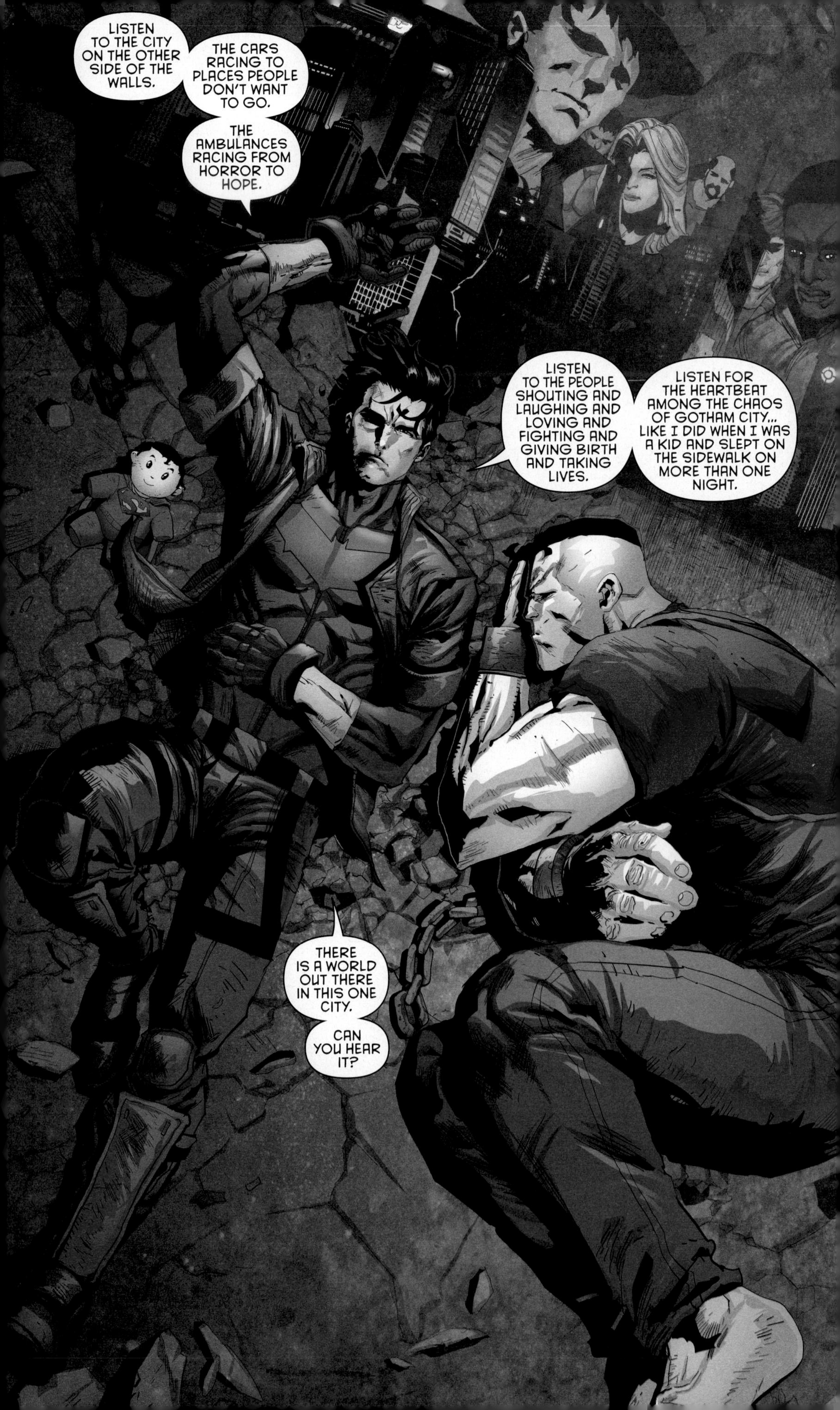

LISTEN TO THE CITY ON THE OTHER SIDE OF THE WALLS.
THE CARS RACING TO PLACES PEOPLE DON'T WANT TO GO.
THE AMBULANCES RACING FROM HORROR TO HOPE.
LISTEN TO THE PEOPLE SHOUTING AND LAUGHING AND LOVING AND FIGHTING AND GIVING BIRTH AND TAKING LIVES.
LISTEN FOR THE HEARTBEAT AMONG THE CHAOS OF GOTHAM CITY... LIKE I DID WHEN I WAS A KID AND SLEPT ON THE SIDEWALK ON MORE THAN ONE NIGHT.
THERE IS A WORLD OUT THERE IN THIS ONE CITY.
CAN YOU HEAR IT?

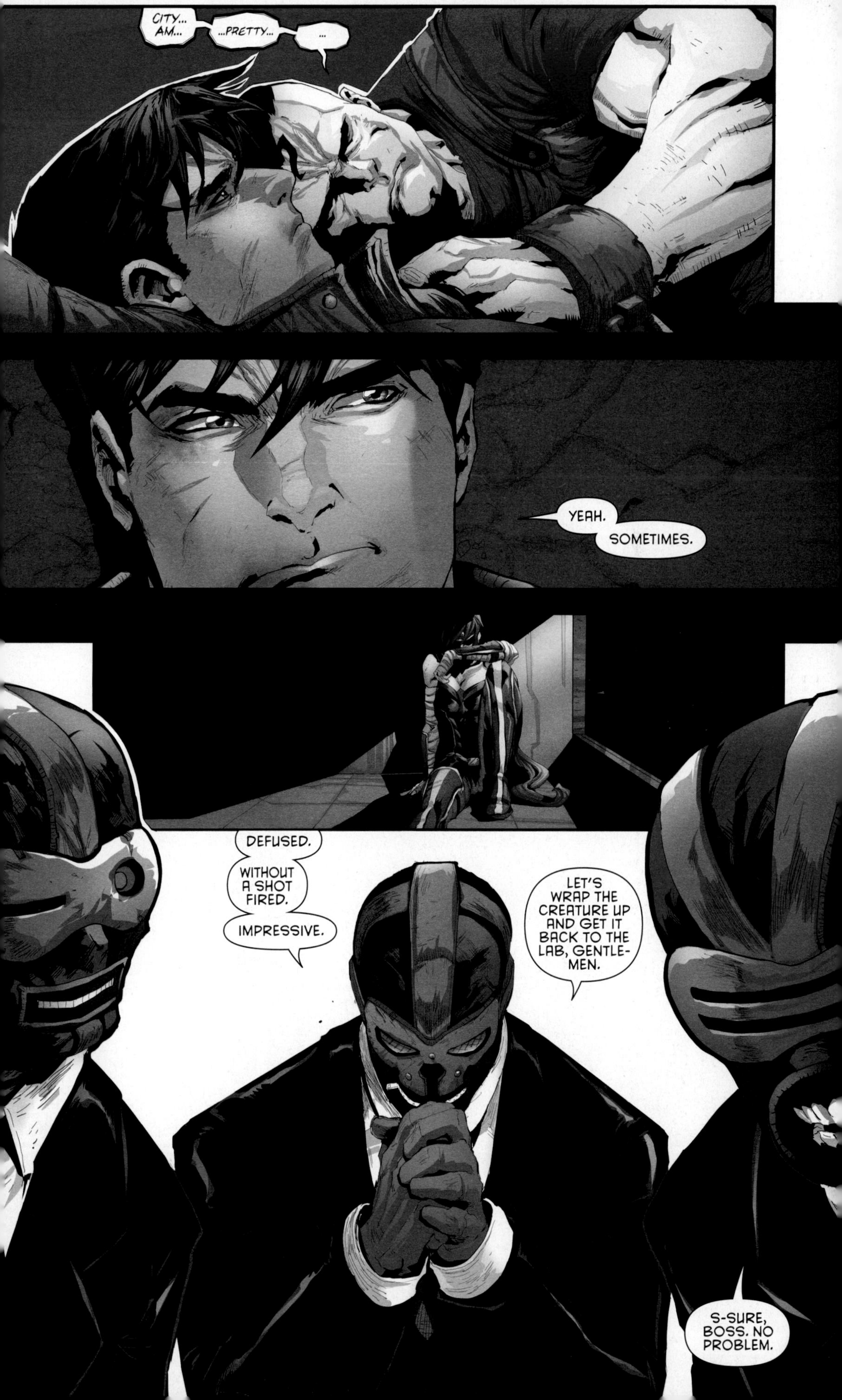
CITY... AM...
...PRETTY...
...
YEAH.
SOMETIMES.
DEFUSED.
WITHOUT A SHOT FIRED.
IMPRESSIVE.
LET'S WRAP THE CREATURE UP AND GET IT BACK TO THE LAB, GENTLE-MEN.
S-SURE, BOSS. NO PROBLEM.

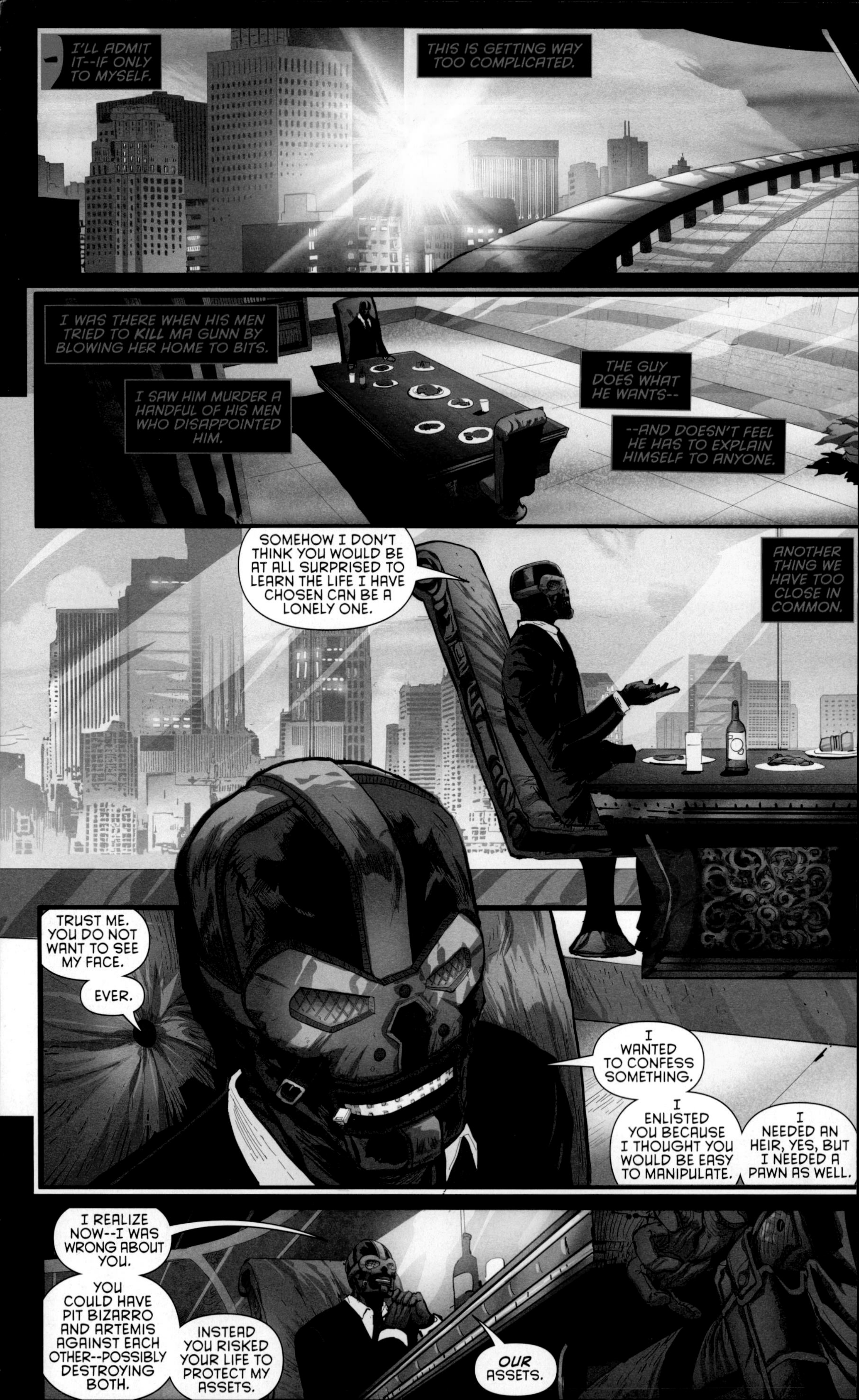
I'LL ADMIT IT--IF ONLY TO MYSELF.
THIS IS GETTING WAY TOO COMPLICATED.
I WAS THERE WHEN HIS MEN TRIED TO KILL MA GUNN BY BLOWING HER HOME TO BITS.
I SAW HIM MURDER A HANDFUL OF HIS MEN WHO DISAPPOINTED HIM.
THE GUY DOES WHAT HE WANTS--
--AND DOESN'T FEEL HE HAS TO EXPLAIN HIMSELF TO ANYONE.
SOMEHOW I DON'T THINK YOU WOULD BE AT ALL SURPRISED TO LEARN THE LIFE I HAVE CHOSEN CAN BE A LONELY ONE.
ANOTHER THING WE HAVE TOO CLOSE IN COMMON.
TRUST ME. YOU DO NOT WANT TO SEE MY FACE.
EVER.
I WANTED TO CONFESS SOMETHING.
I ENLISTED YOU BECAUSE I THOUGHT YOU WOULD BE EASY TO MANIPULATE.
I NEEDED AN HEIR, YES, BUT I NEEDED A PAWN AS WELL.
I REALIZE NOW--I WAS WRONG ABOUT YOU.
YOU COULD HAVE PIT BIZARRO AND ARTEMIS AGAINST EACH OTHER--POSSIBLY DESTROYING BOTH.
INSTEAD YOU RISKED YOUR LIFE TO PROTECT MY ASSETS.
OUR ASSETS.

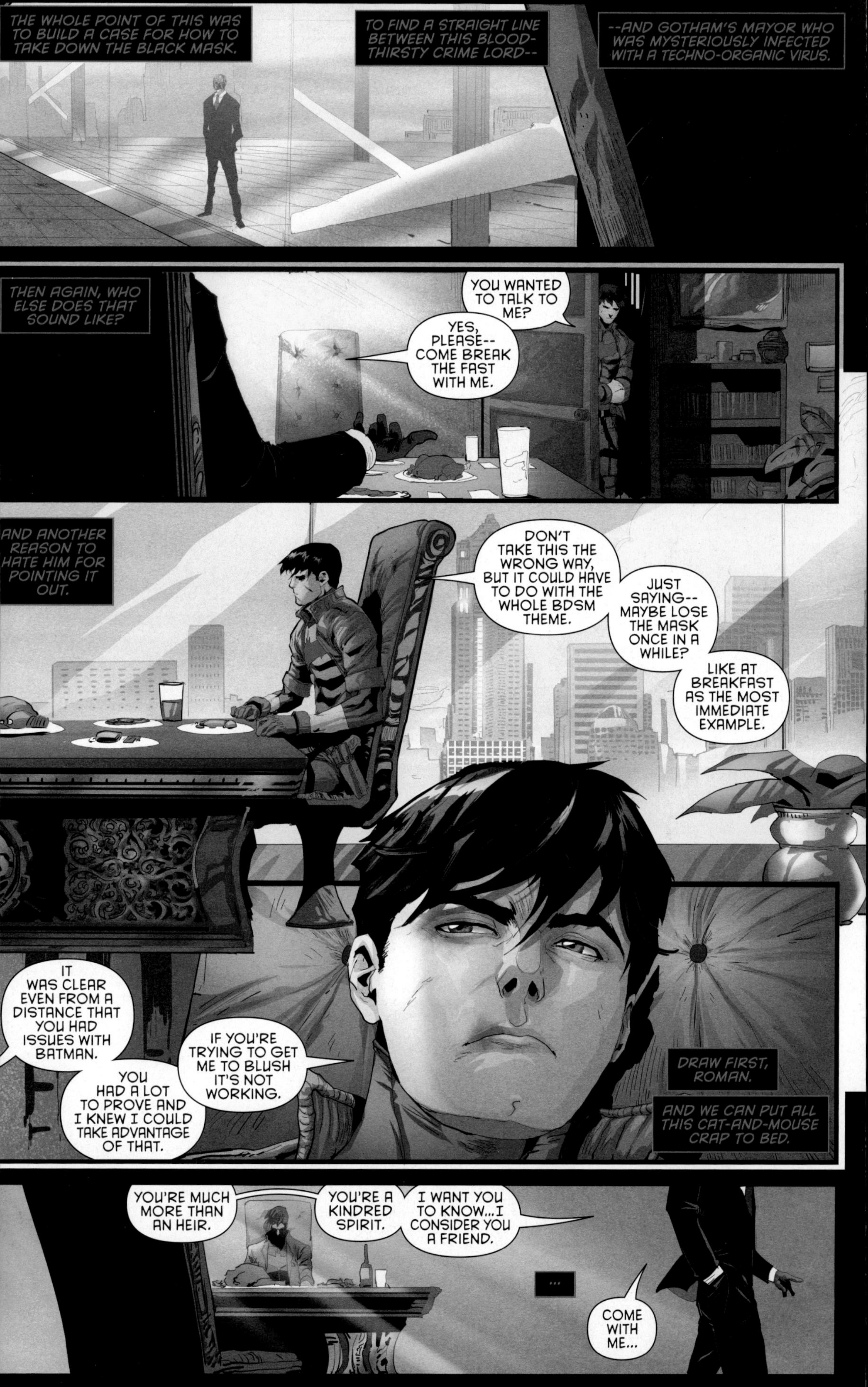
THE WHOLE POINT OF THIS WAS TO BUILD A CASE FOR HOW TO TAKE DOWN THE BLACK MASK.
TO FIND A STRAIGHT LINE BETWEEN THIS BLOOD-THIRSTY CRIME LORD--
--AND GOTHAM'S MAYOR WHO WAS MYSTERIOUSLY INFECTED WITH A TECHNO-ORGANIC VIRUS.
THEN AGAIN, WHO ELSE DOES THAT SOUND LIKE?
YOU WANTED TO TALK TO ME?
YES, PLEASE-- COME BREAK THE FAST WITH ME.
AND ANOTHER REASON TO HATE HIM FOR POINTING IT OUT.
DON'T TAKE THIS THE WRONG WAY, BUT IT COULD HAVE TO DO WITH THE WHOLE BDSM THEME.
JUST SAYING-- MAYBE LOSE THE MASK ONCE IN A WHILE?
LIKE AT BREAKFAST AS THE MOST IMMEDIATE EXAMPLE.
IT WAS CLEAR EVEN FROM A DISTANCE THAT YOU HAD ISSUES WITH BATMAN.
YOU HAD A LOT TO PROVE AND I KNEW I COULD TAKE ADVANTAGE OF THAT.
IF YOU'RE TRYING TO GET ME TO BLUSH IT'S NOT WORKING.
DRAW FIRST, ROMAN.
AND WE CAN PUT ALL THIS CAT-AND-MOUSE CRAP TO BED.
YOU'RE MUCH MORE THAN AN HEIR.
YOU'RE A KINDRED SPIRIT.
I WANT YOU TO KNOW...I CONSIDER YOU A FRIEND.
...
COME WITH ME...

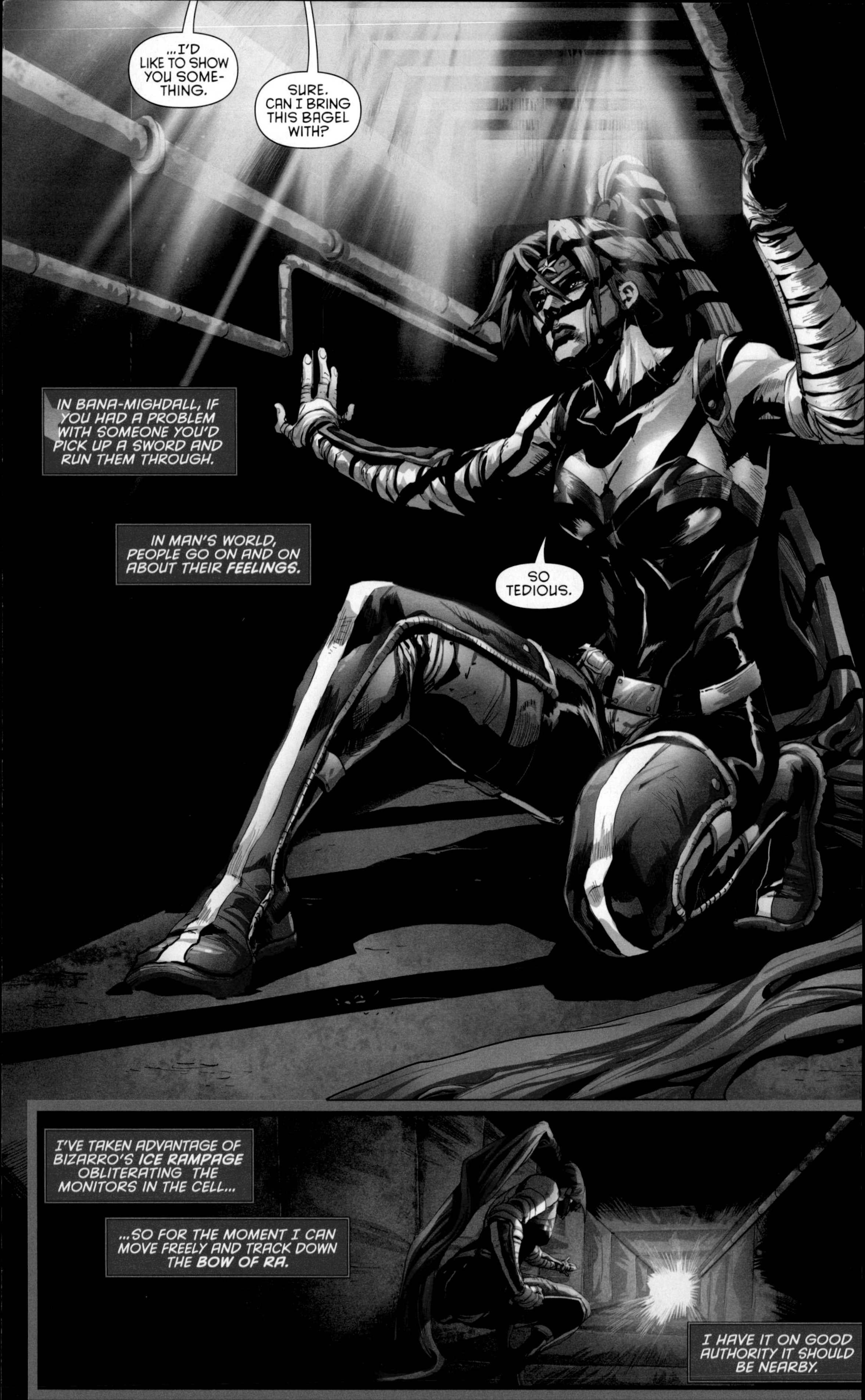
...I'D LIKE TO SHOW YOU SOMETHING.
SURE. CAN I BRING THIS BAGEL WITH?
IN BANA-MIGHDALL, IF YOU HAD A PROBLEM WITH SOMEONE YOU'D PICK UP A SWORD AND RUN THEM THROUGH.
IN MAN'S WORLD, PEOPLE GO ON AND ON ABOUT THEIR FEELINGS.
SO TEDIOUS.
I'VE TAKEN ADVANTAGE OF BIZARRO'S ICE RAMPAGE OBLITERATING THE MONITORS IN THE CELL...
...SO FOR THE MOMENT I CAN MOVE FREELY AND TRACK DOWN THE BOW OF RA.
I HAVE IT ON GOOD AUTHORITY IT SHOULD BE NEARBY.

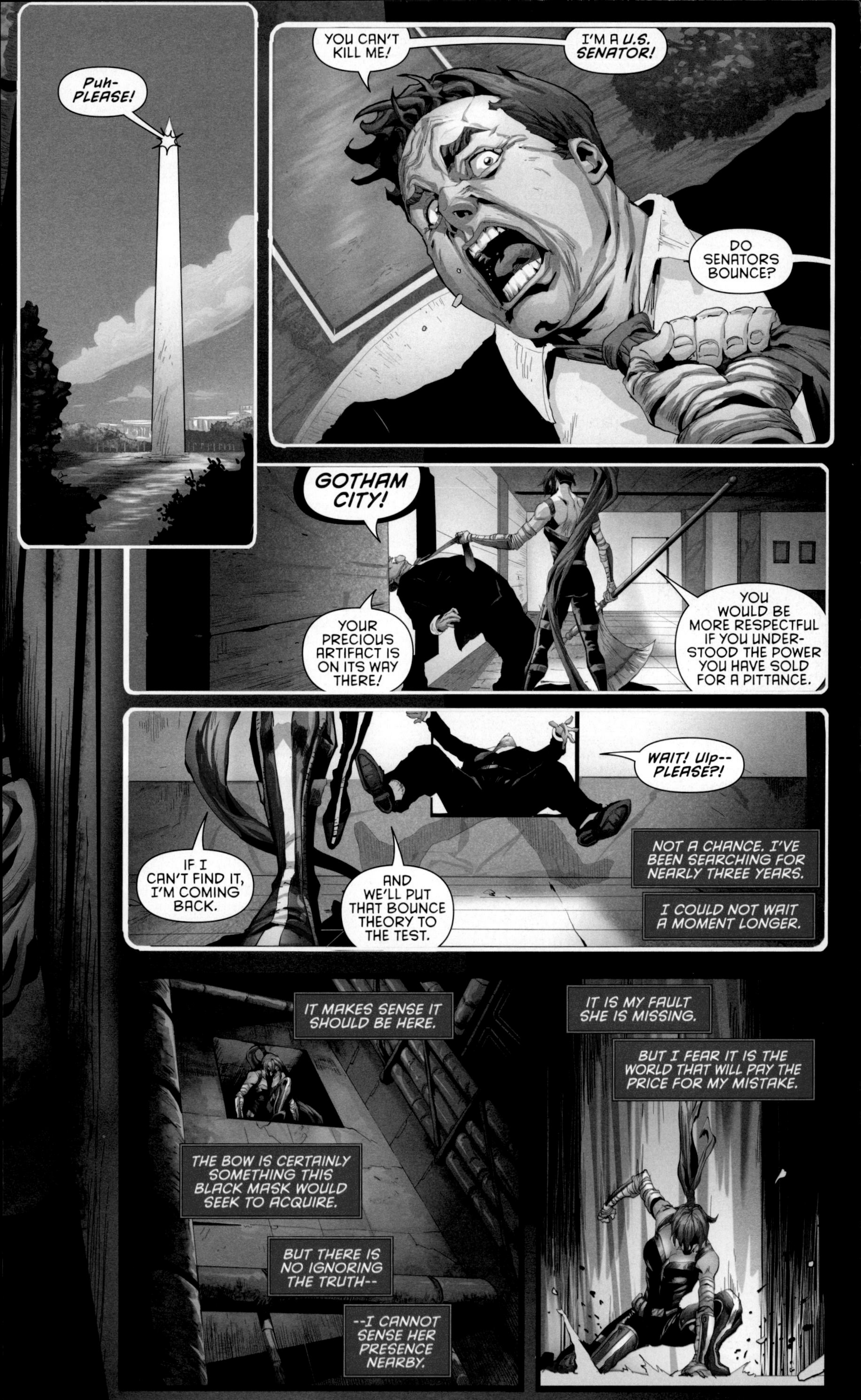
Puh-PLEASE!
YOU CAN'T KILL ME!
I'M A U.S. SENATOR!
DO SENATORS BOUNCE?
GOTHAM CITY!
YOUR PRECIOUS ARTIFACT IS ON ITS WAY THERE!
YOU WOULD BE MORE RESPECTFUL IF YOU UNDER-STOOD THE POWER YOU HAVE SOLD FOR A PITTANCE.
WAIT! Ulp--PLEASE?!
NOT A CHANCE. I'VE BEEN SEARCHING FOR NEARLY THREE YEARS.
I COULD NOT WAIT A MOMENT LONGER.
IF I CAN'T FIND IT, I'M COMING BACK.
AND WE'LL PUT THAT BOUNCE THEORY TO THE TEST.
IT MAKES SENSE IT SHOULD BE HERE.
THE BOW IS CERTAINLY SOMETHING THIS BLACK MASK WOULD SEEK TO ACQUIRE.
BUT THERE IS NO IGNORING THE TRUTH--
--I CANNOT SENSE HER PRESENCE NEARBY.
IT IS MY FAULT SHE IS MISSING.
BUT I FEAR IT IS THE WORLD THAT WILL PAY THE PRICE FOR MY MISTAKE.

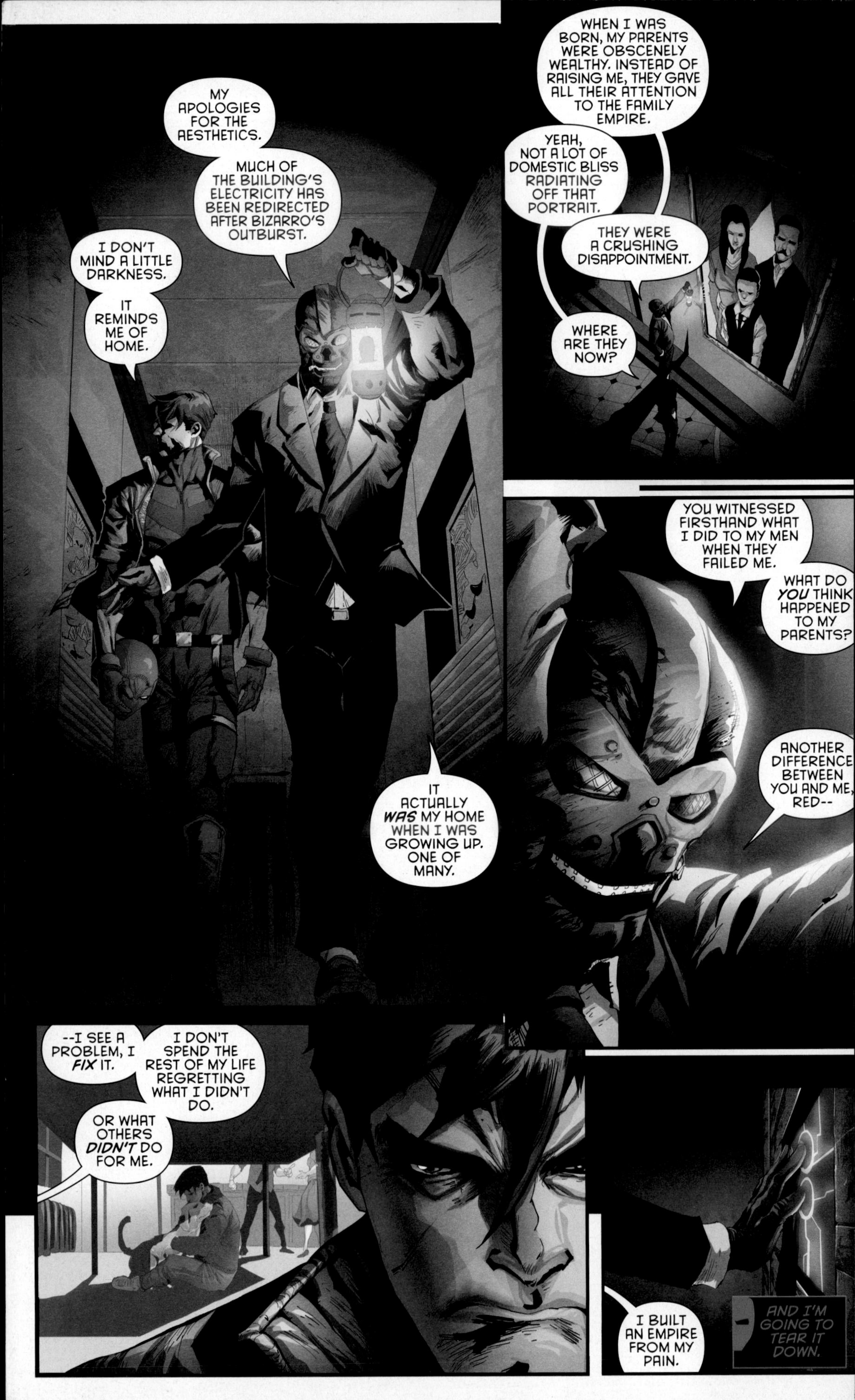
MY APOLOGIES FOR THE AESTHETICS.
MUCH OF THE BUILDING'S ELECTRICITY HAS BEEN REDIRECTED AFTER BIZARRO'S OUTBURST.
I DON'T MIND A LITTLE DARKNESS.
IT REMINDS ME OF HOME.
IT ACTUALLY *WAS* MY HOME WHEN I WAS GROWING UP. ONE OF MANY.
WHEN I WAS BORN, MY PARENTS WERE OBSCENELY WEALTHY. INSTEAD OF RAISING ME, THEY GAVE ALL THEIR ATTENTION TO THE FAMILY EMPIRE.
YEAH, NOT A LOT OF DOMESTIC BLISS RADIATING OFF THAT PORTRAIT.
THEY WERE A CRUSHING DISAPPOINTMENT.
WHERE ARE THEY NOW?
YOU WITNESSED FIRSTHAND WHAT I DID TO MY MEN WHEN THEY FAILED ME.
WHAT DO *YOU* THINK HAPPENED TO MY PARENTS?
ANOTHER DIFFERENCE BETWEEN YOU AND ME, RED--
--I SEE A PROBLEM, I *FIX* IT.
I DON'T SPEND THE REST OF MY LIFE REGRETTING WHAT I DIDN'T DO.
OR WHAT OTHERS *DIDN'T* DO FOR ME.
I BUILT AN EMPIRE FROM MY PAIN.
AND I'M GOING TO TEAR IT DOWN.

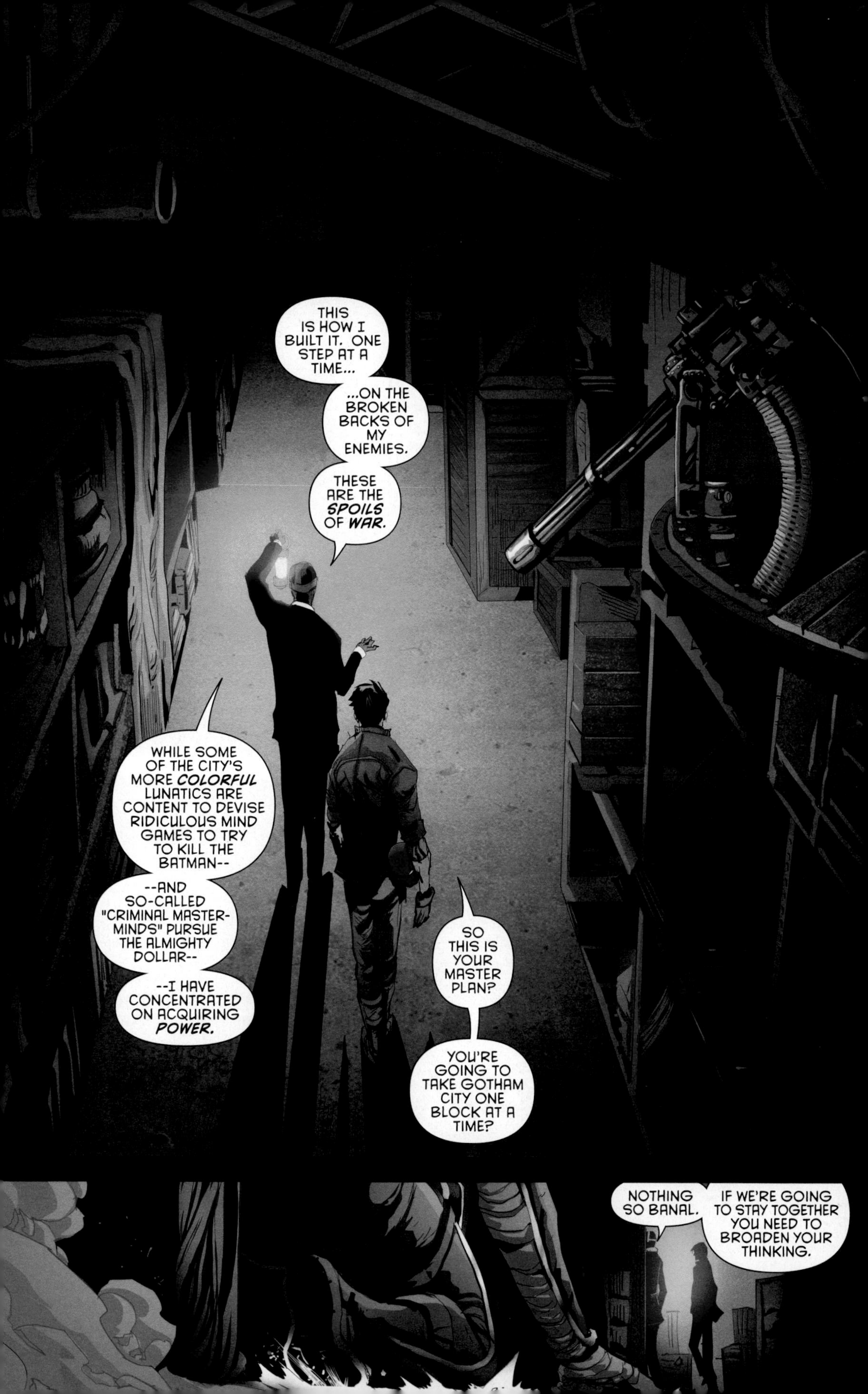
THIS IS HOW I BUILT IT. ONE STEP AT A TIME...
...ON THE BROKEN BACKS OF MY ENEMIES.
THESE ARE THE SPOILS OF WAR.
WHILE SOME OF THE CITY'S MORE COLORFUL LUNATICS ARE CONTENT TO DEVISE RIDICULOUS MIND GAMES TO TRY TO KILL THE BATMAN--
--AND SO-CALLED "CRIMINAL MASTER-MINDS" PURSUE THE ALMIGHTY DOLLAR--
--I HAVE CONCENTRATED ON ACQUIRING POWER.
SO THIS IS YOUR MASTER PLAN?
YOU'RE GOING TO TAKE GOTHAM CITY ONE BLOCK AT A TIME?
NOTHING SO BANAL.
IF WE'RE GOING TO STAY TOGETHER YOU NEED TO BROADEN YOUR THINKING.

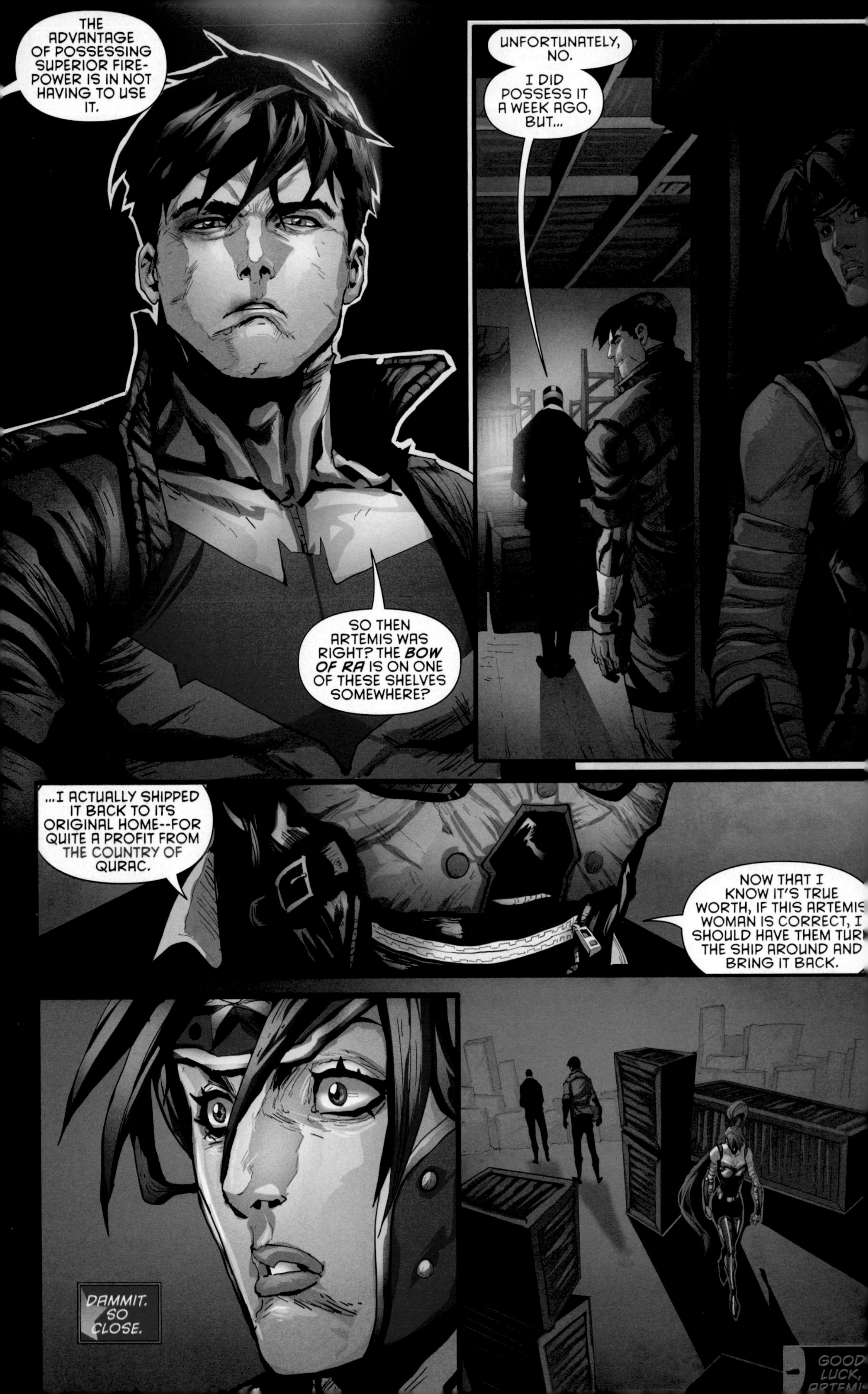
THE ADVANTAGE OF POSSESSING SUPERIOR FIRE-POWER IS IN NOT HAVING TO USE IT.
UNFORTUNATELY, NO.
I DID POSSESS IT A WEEK AGO, BUT...
SO THEN ARTEMIS WAS RIGHT? THE BOW OF RA IS ON ONE OF THESE SHELVES SOMEWHERE?
...I ACTUALLY SHIPPED IT BACK TO ITS ORIGINAL HOME--FOR QUITE A PROFIT FROM THE COUNTRY OF QURAC.
NOW THAT I KNOW IT'S TRUE WORTH, IF THIS ARTEMIS WOMAN IS CORRECT, I SHOULD HAVE THEM TUR THE SHIP AROUND AND BRING IT BACK.
DAMMIT. SO CLOSE.
GOOD LUCK,

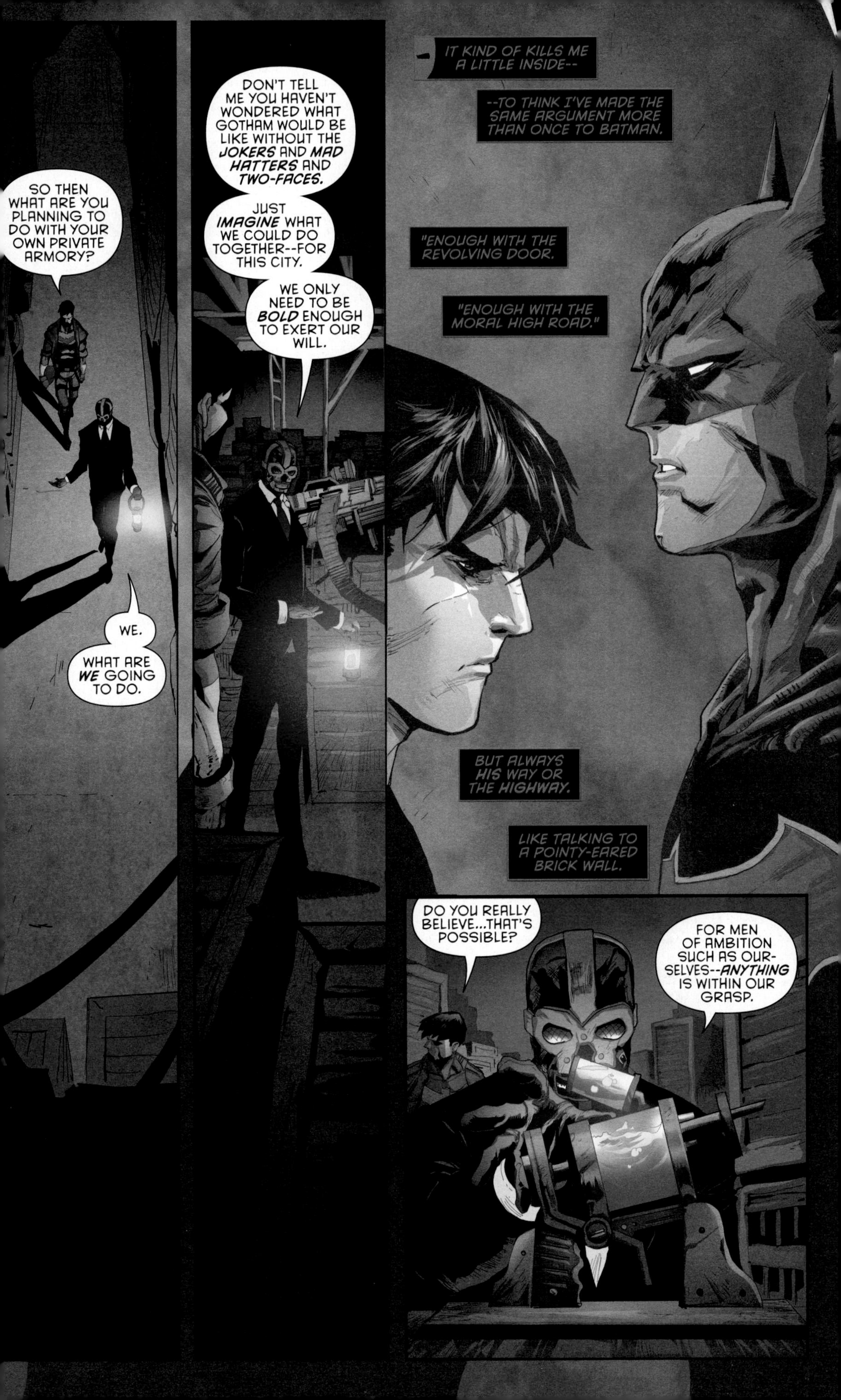
SO THEN WHAT ARE YOU PLANNING TO DO WITH YOUR OWN PRIVATE ARMORY?
WE.
WHAT ARE WE GOING TO DO.
DON'T TELL ME YOU HAVEN'T WONDERED WHAT GOTHAM WOULD BE LIKE WITHOUT THE JOKERS AND MAD HATTERS AND TWO-FACES.
JUST IMAGINE WHAT WE COULD DO TOGETHER--FOR THIS CITY.
WE ONLY NEED TO BE BOLD ENOUGH TO EXERT OUR WILL.
IT KIND OF KILLS ME A LITTLE INSIDE--
--TO THINK I'VE MADE THE SAME ARGUMENT MORE THAN ONCE TO BATMAN.
"ENOUGH WITH THE REVOLVING DOOR.
"ENOUGH WITH THE MORAL HIGH ROAD."
BUT ALWAYS HIS WAY OR THE HIGHWAY.
LIKE TALKING TO A POINTY-EARED BRICK WALL.
DO YOU REALLY BELIEVE...THAT'S POSSIBLE?
FOR MEN OF AMBITION SUCH AS OUR-SELVES--ANYTHING IS WITHIN OUR GRASP.

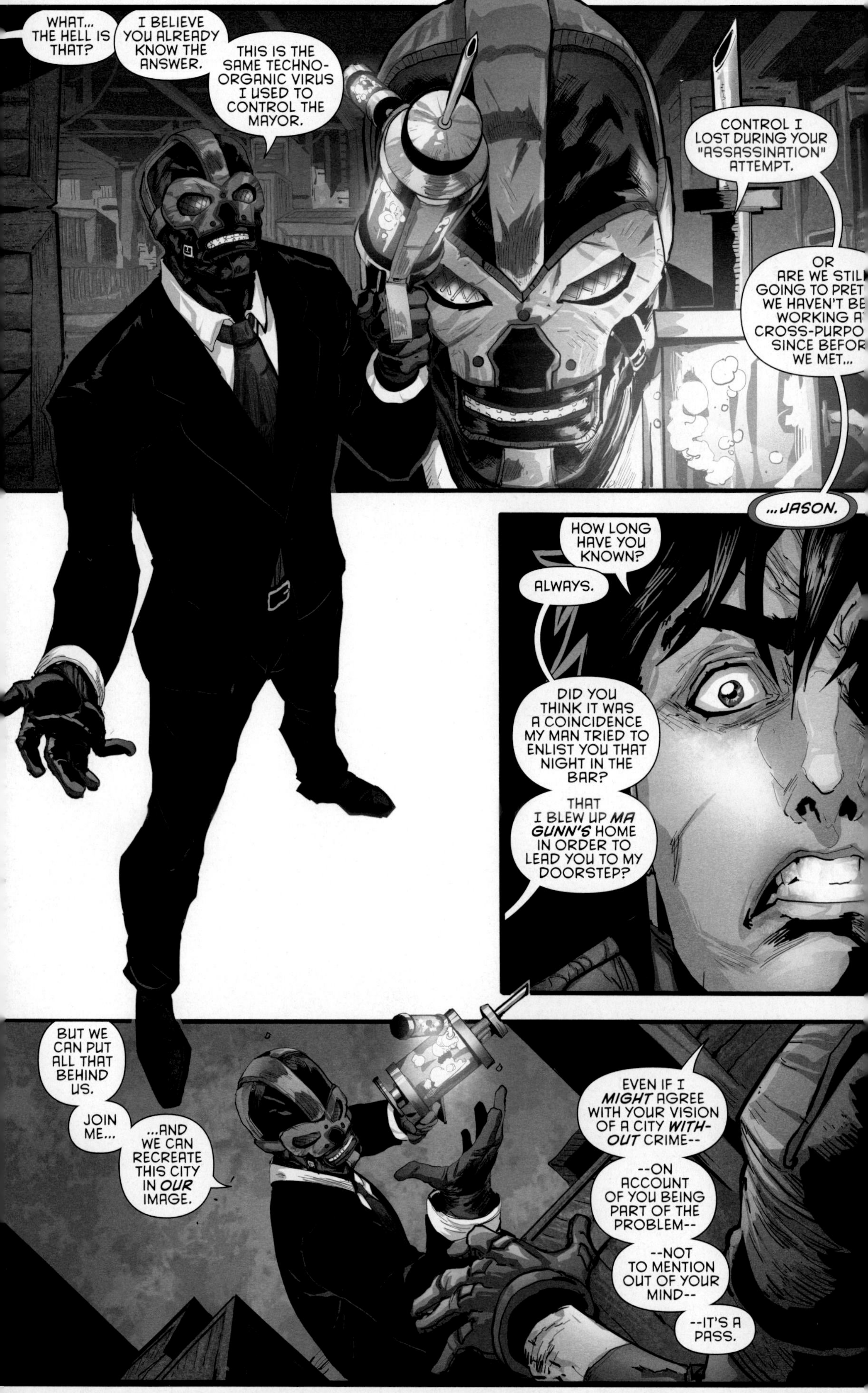

WHAT... THE HELL IS THAT?
I BELIEVE YOU ALREADY KNOW THE ANSWER.
THIS IS THE SAME TECHNO-ORGANIC VIRUS I USED TO CONTROL THE MAYOR.
CONTROL I LOST DURING YOUR "ASSASSINATION" ATTEMPT.
OR ARE WE STIL GOING TO PRET WE HAVEN'T BE WORKING A CROSS-PURPO SINCE BEFOR WE MET...
...JASON.
HOW LONG HAVE YOU KNOWN?
ALWAYS.
DID YOU THINK IT WAS A COINCIDENCE MY MAN TRIED TO ENLIST YOU THAT NIGHT IN THE BAR?
THAT I BLEW UP MA GUNN'S HOME IN ORDER TO LEAD YOU TO MY DOORSTEP?
BUT WE CAN PUT ALL THAT BEHIND US.
JOIN ME...
...AND WE CAN RECREATE THIS CITY IN OUR IMAGE.
EVEN IF I MIGHT AGREE WITH YOUR VISION OF A CITY WITH-OUT CRIME--
--ON ACCOUNT OF YOU BEING PART OF THE PROBLEM--
--NOT TO MENTION OUT OF YOUR MIND--
--IT'S A PASS.

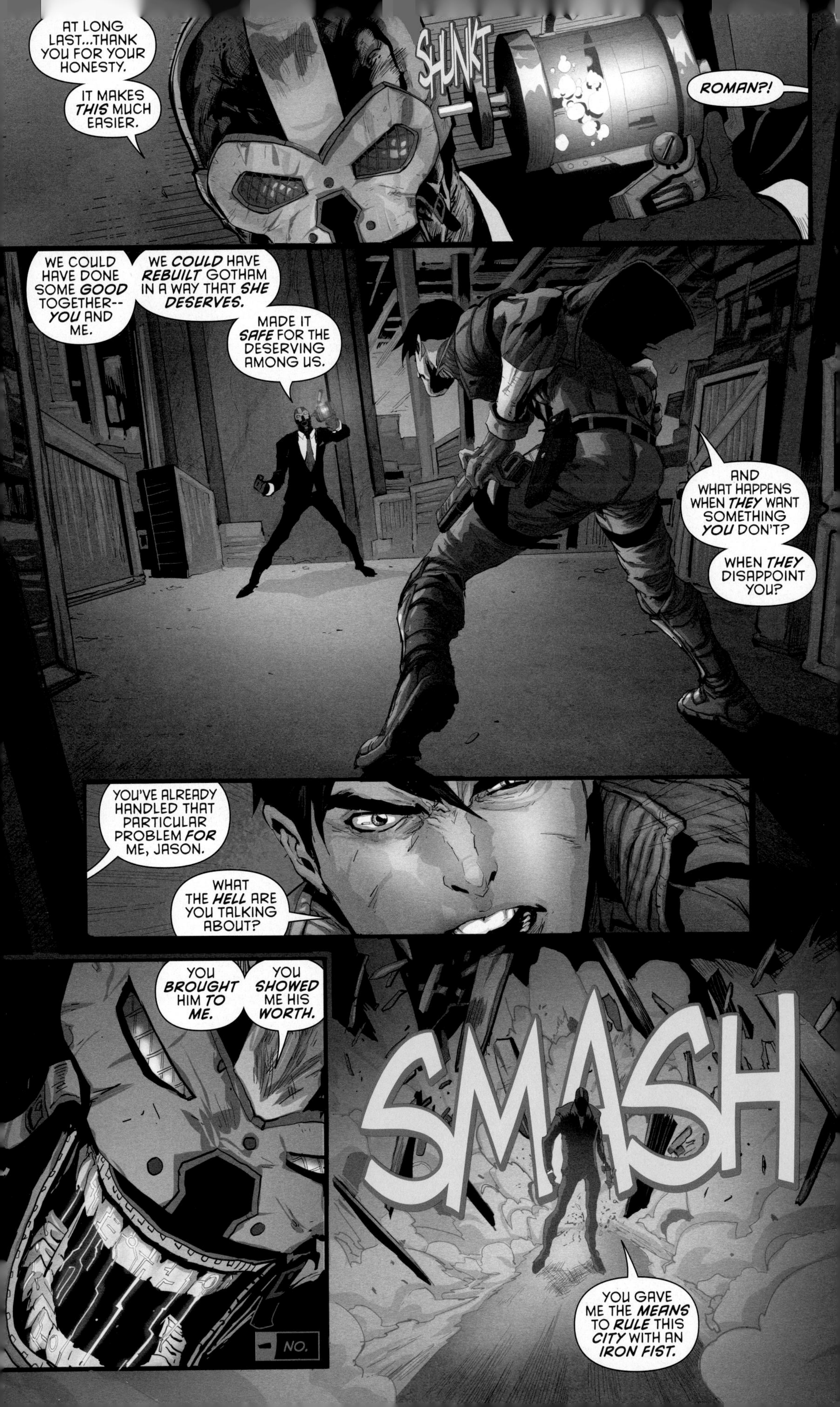
AT LONG LAST...THANK YOU FOR YOUR HONESTY.
IT MAKES THIS MUCH EASIER.
SHUNKT
ROMAN?!
WE COULD HAVE DONE SOME GOOD TOGETHER-- YOU AND ME.
WE COULD HAVE REBUILT GOTHAM IN A WAY THAT SHE DESERVES.
MADE IT SAFE FOR THE DESERVING AMONG US.
AND WHAT HAPPENS WHEN THEY WANT SOMETHING YOU DON'T?
WHEN THEY DISAPPOINT YOU?
YOU'VE ALREADY HANDLED THAT PARTICULAR PROBLEM FOR ME, JASON.
WHAT THE HELL ARE YOU TALKING ABOUT?
YOU BROUGHT HIM TO ME.
YOU SHOWED ME HIS WORTH.
NO.
SMASH
YOU GAVE ME THE MEANS TO RULE THIS CITY WITH AN IRON FIST.

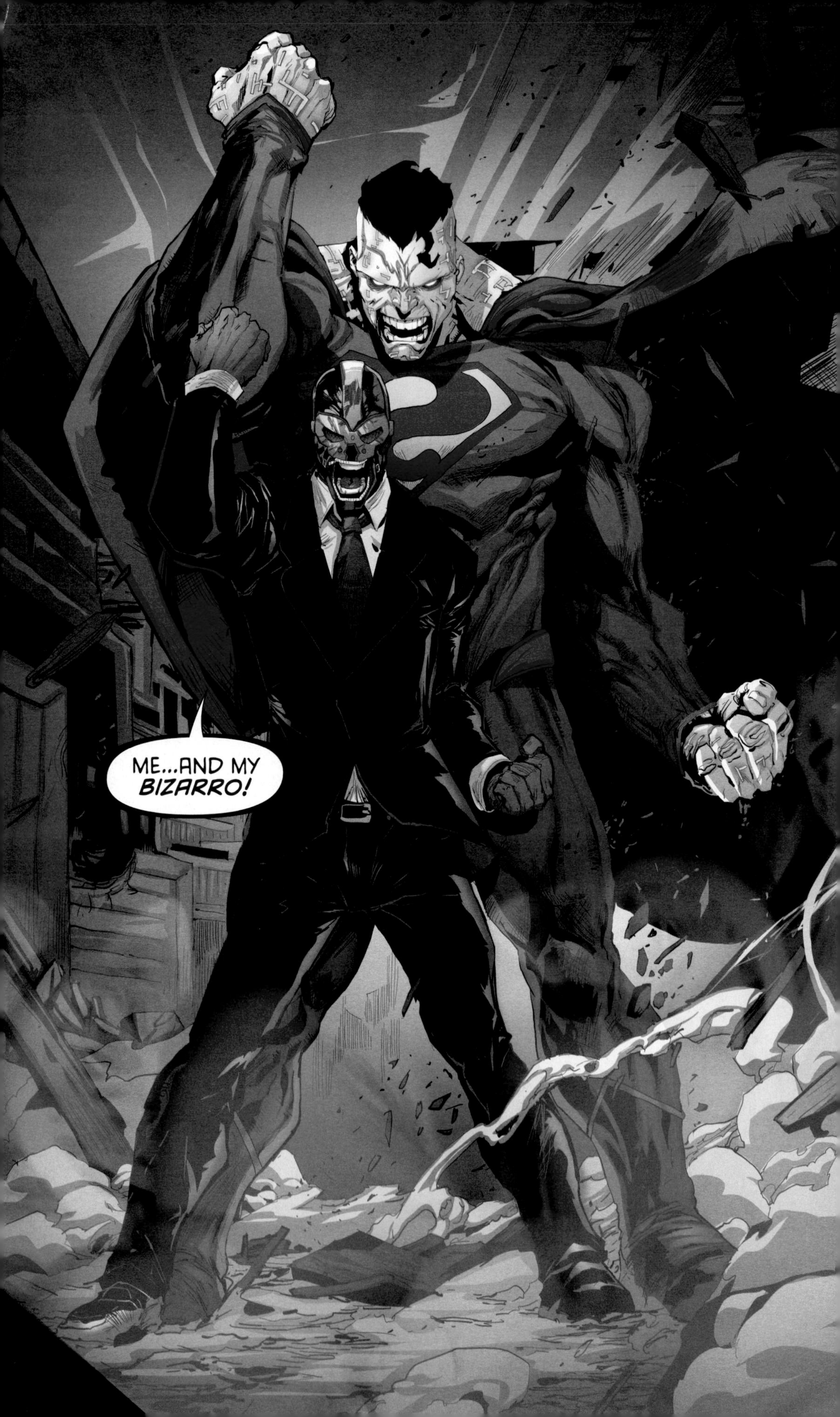
ME...AND MY BIZARRO!

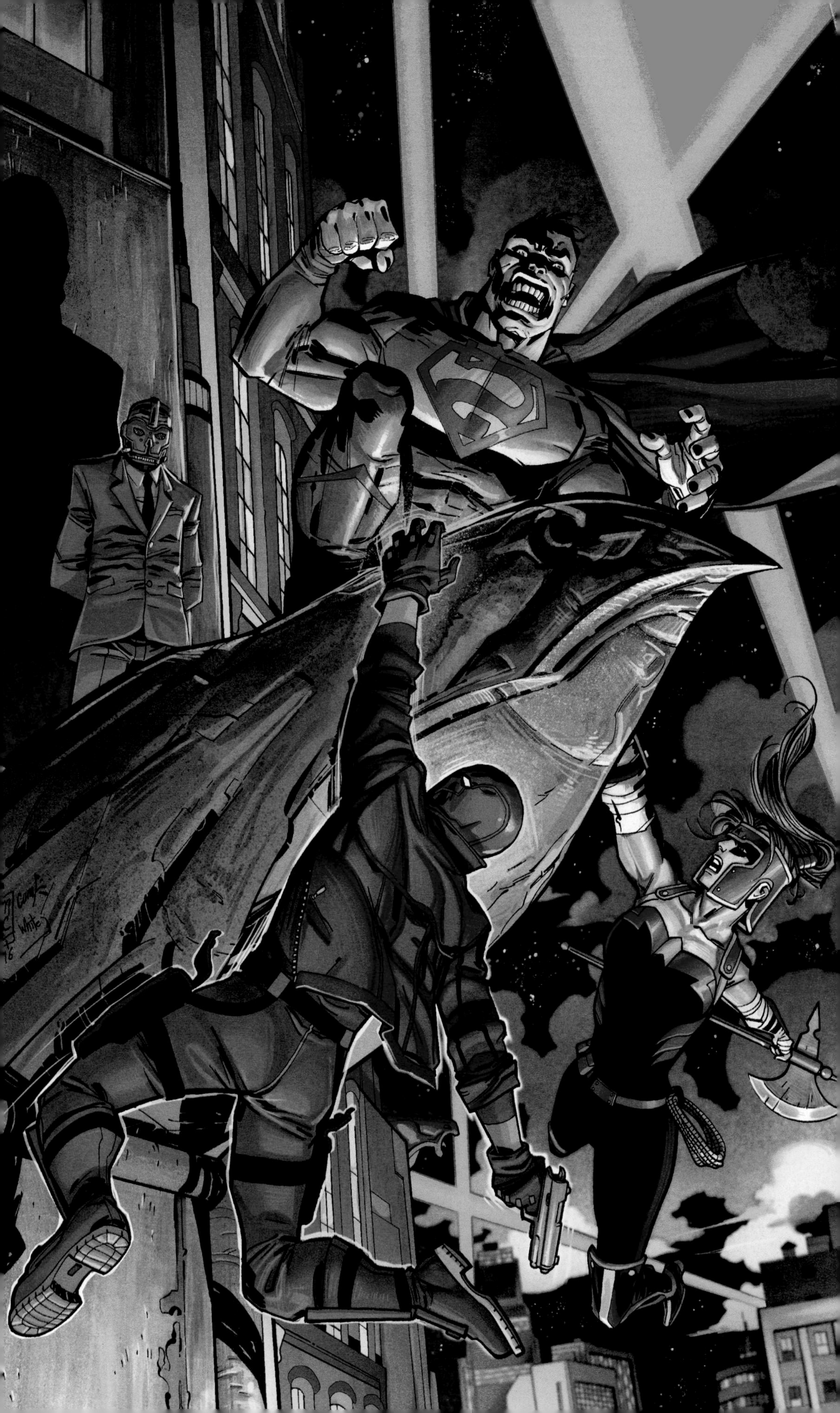

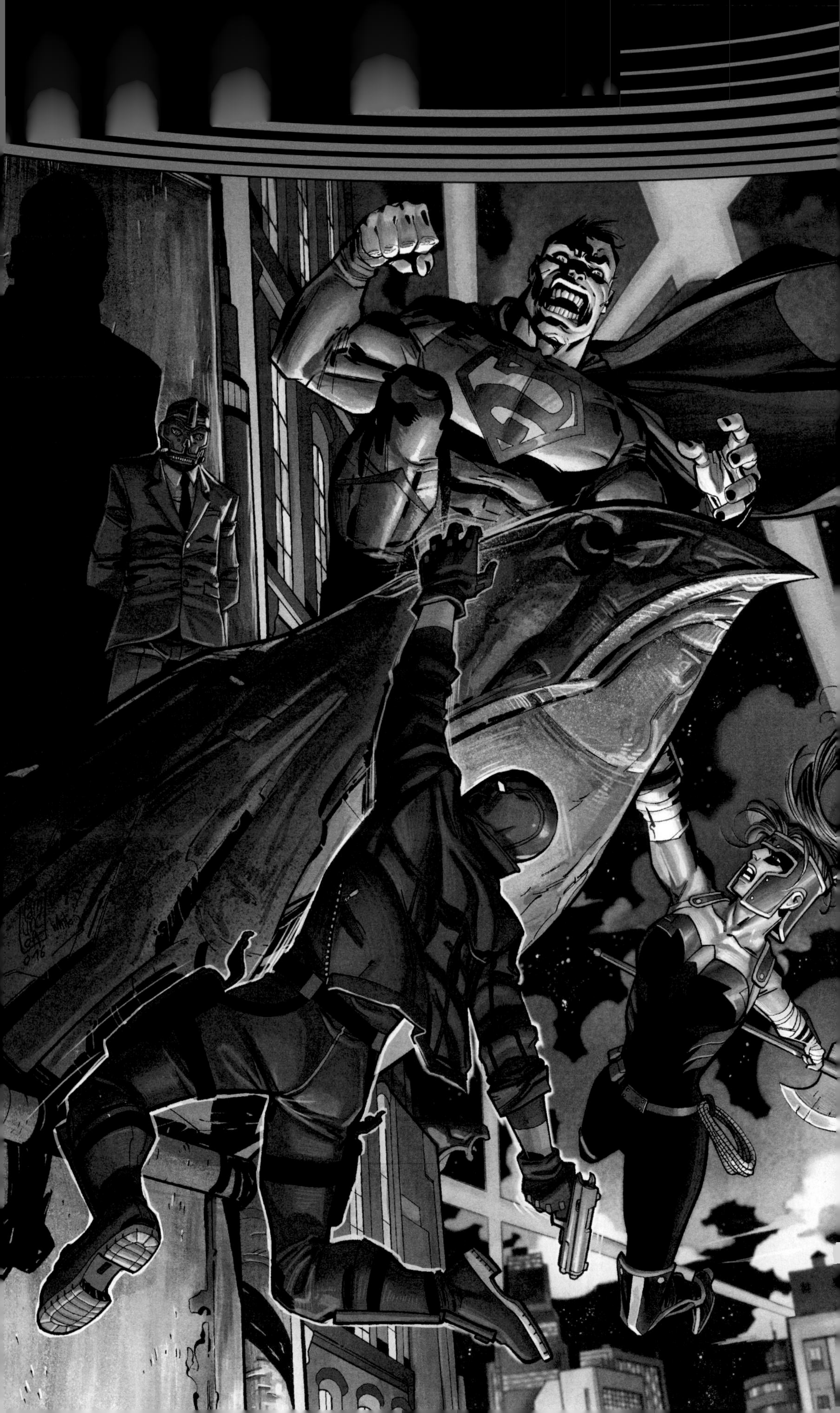

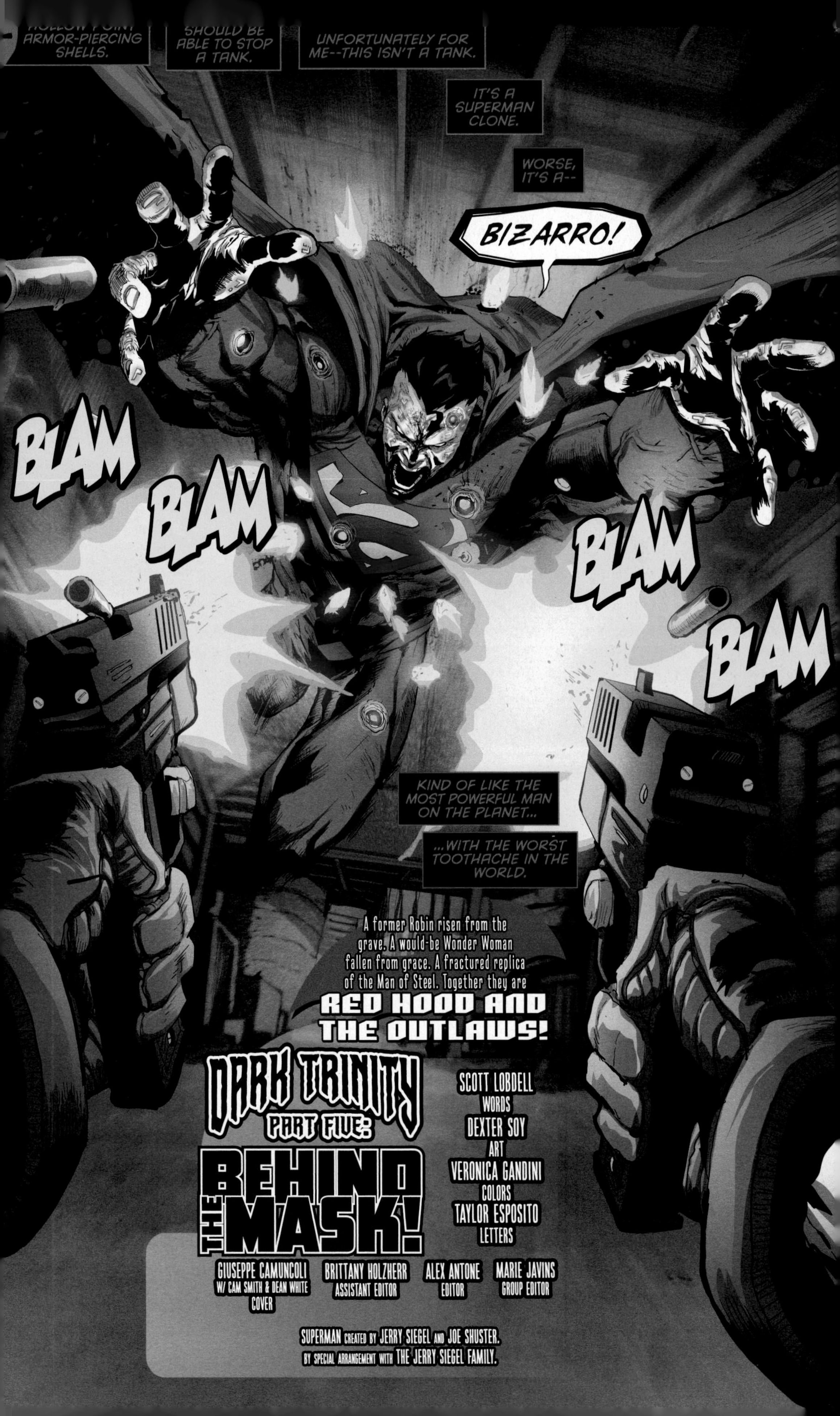

ARMOR-PIERCING SHELLS.
SHOULD BE ABLE TO STOP A TANK.
UNFORTUNATELY FOR ME--THIS ISN'T A TANK.
IT'S A SUPERMAN CLONE.
WORSE, IT'S A--
BIZARRO!
BLAM
BLAM
BLAM
BLAM
KIND OF LIKE THE MOST POWERFUL MAN ON THE PLANET...
...WITH THE WORST TOOTHACHE IN THE WORLD.
A former Robin risen from the grave. A would-be Wonder Woman fallen from grace. A fractured replica of the Man of Steel. Together they are
RED HOOD AND THE OUTLAWS!
DARK TRINITY PART FIVE:
BEHIND THE MASK!
SCOTT LOBDELL WORDS
DEXTER SOY ART
VERONICA GANDINI COLORS
TAYLOR ESPOSITO LETTERS
GIUSEPPE CAMUNCOLI W/ CAM SMITH & DEAN WHITE COVER
BRITTANY HOLZHERR ASSISTANT EDITOR
ALEX ANTONE EDITOR
MARIE JAVINS GROUP EDITOR
SUPERMAN CREATED BY JERRY SIEGEL AND JOE SHUSTER.
BY SPECIAL ARRANGEMENT WITH THE JERRY SIEGEL FAMILY.

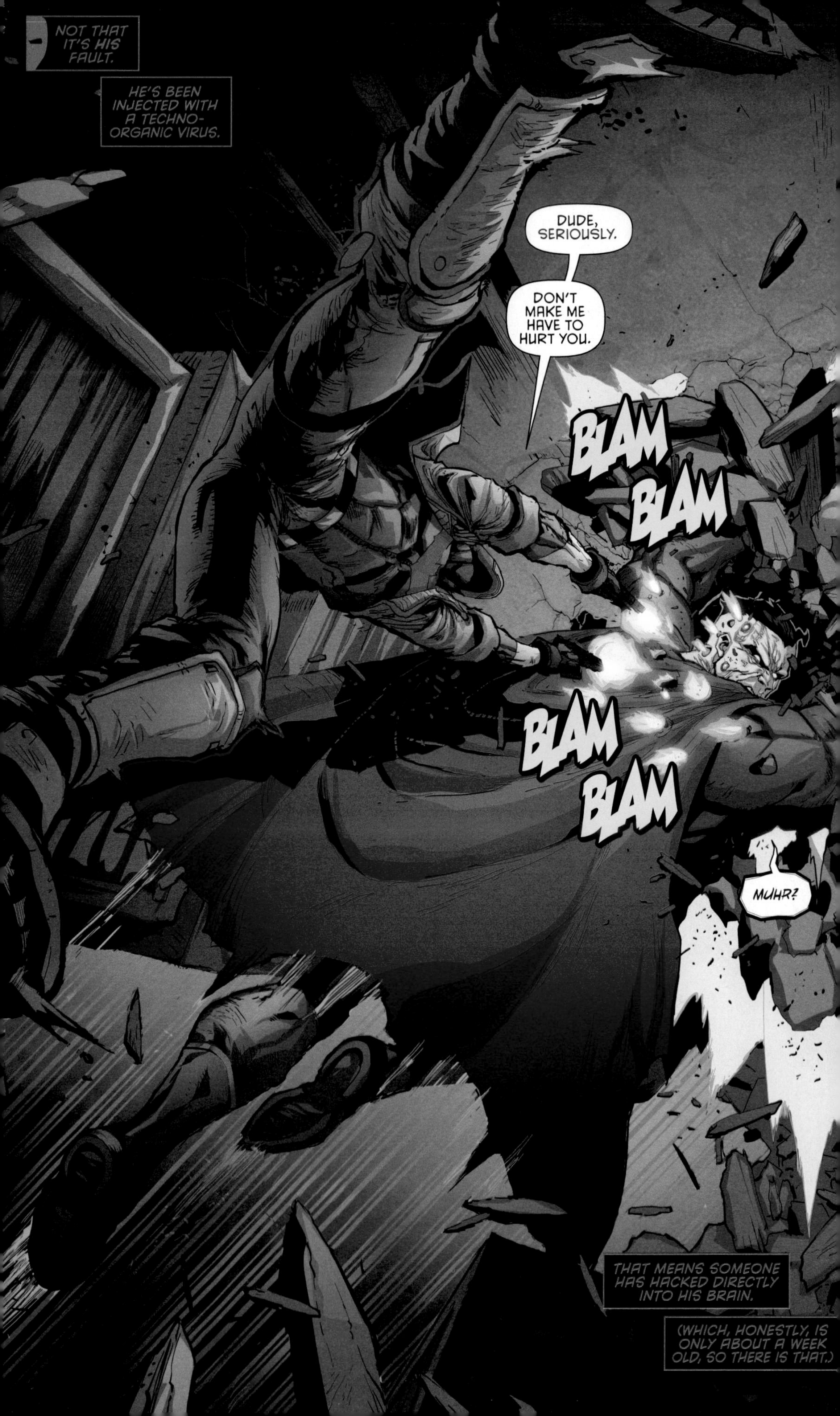

NOT THAT IT'S HIS FAULT.
HE'S BEEN INJECTED WITH A TECHNO-ORGANIC VIRUS.
DUDE, SERIOUSLY.
DON'T MAKE ME HAVE TO HURT YOU.
BLAM
BLAM
BLAM
BLAM
MUHR?
THAT MEANS SOMEONE HAS HACKED DIRECTLY INTO HIS BRAIN.
(WHICH, HONESTLY, IS ONLY ABOUT A WEEK OLD, SO THERE IS THAT.)

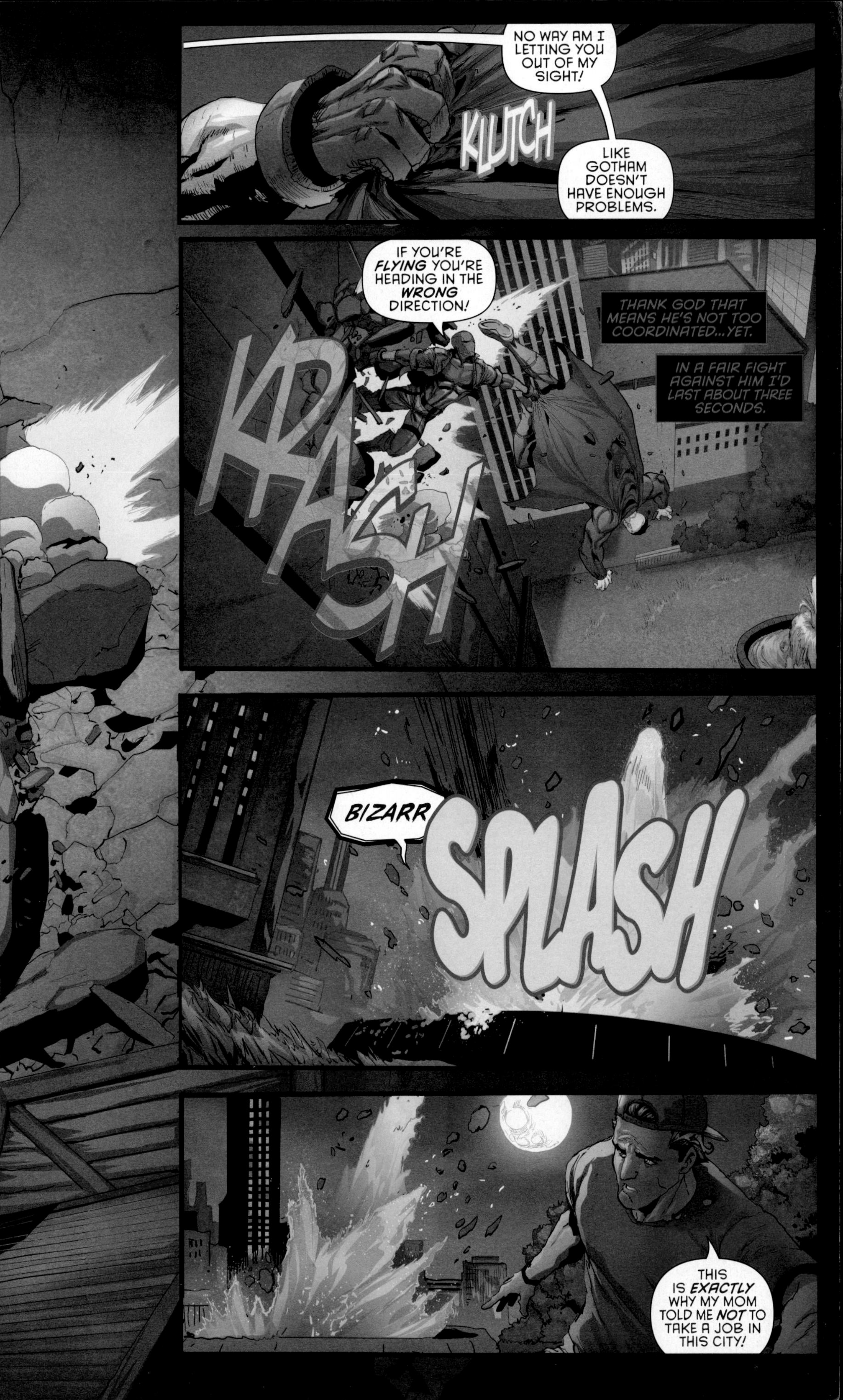
NO WAY AM I LETTING YOU OUT OF MY SIGHT!
KLUTCH
LIKE GOTHAM DOESN'T HAVE ENOUGH PROBLEMS.
IF YOU'RE *FLYING* YOU'RE HEADING IN THE *WRONG* DIRECTION!
KRASH
THANK GOD THAT MEANS HE'S NOT TOO COORDINATED...YET.
IN A FAIR FIGHT AGAINST HIM I'D LAST ABOUT THREE SECONDS.
BIZARR
SPLASH
THIS IS *EXACTLY* WHY MY MOM TOLD ME *NOT* TO TAKE A JOB IN THIS CITY!

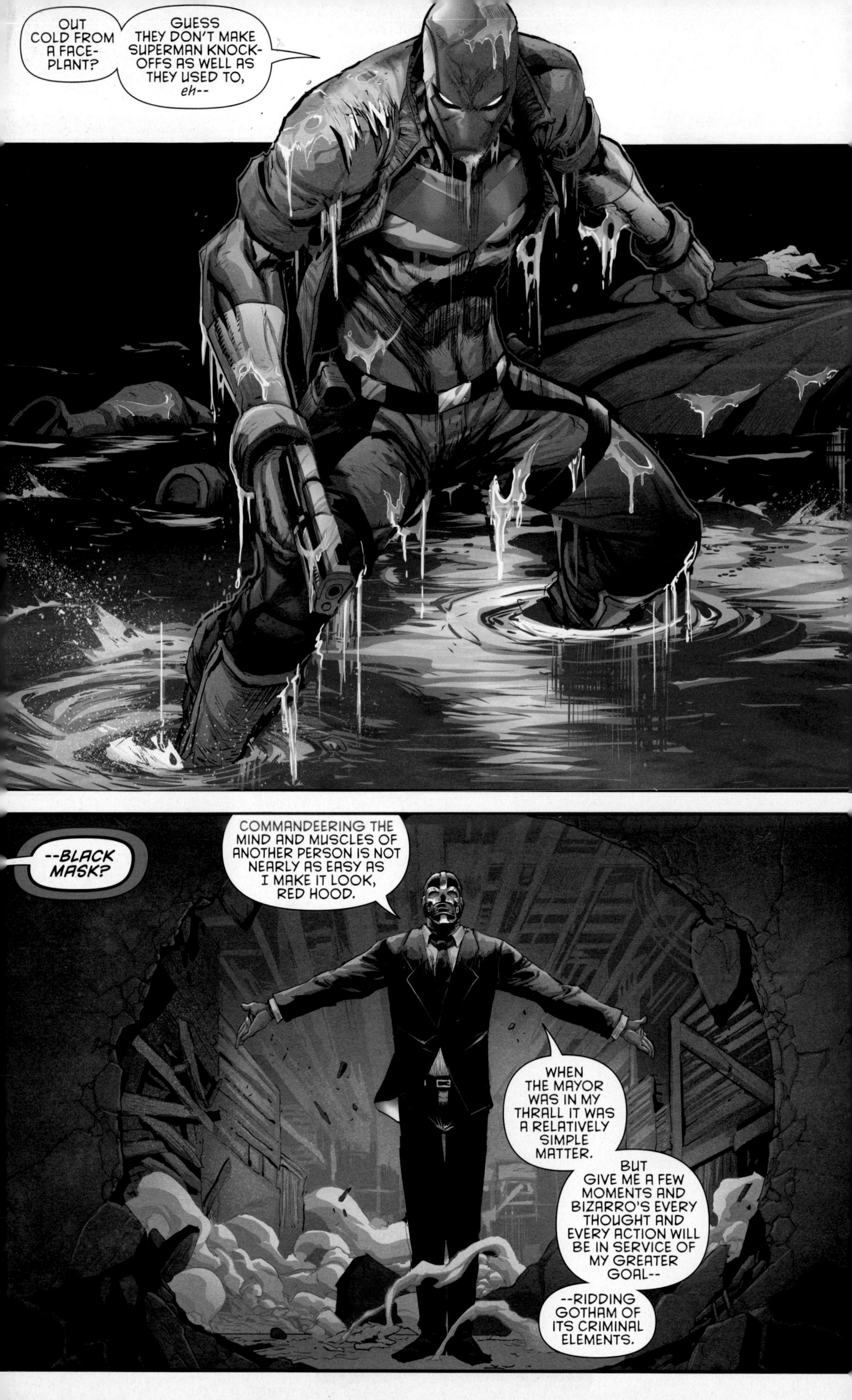
OUT COLD FROM A FACE-PLANT?
GUESS THEY DON'T MAKE SUPERMAN KNOCK-OFFS AS WELL AS THEY USED TO, *eh*--
--BLACK MASK?
COMMANDEERING THE MIND AND MUSCLES OF ANOTHER PERSON IS NOT NEARLY AS EASY AS I MAKE IT LOOK, RED HOOD.
WHEN THE MAYOR WAS IN MY THRALL IT WAS A RELATIVELY SIMPLE MATTER.
BUT GIVE ME A FEW MOMENTS AND BIZARRO'S EVERY THOUGHT AND EVERY ACTION WILL BE IN SERVICE OF MY GREATER GOAL--
--RIDDING GOTHAM OF ITS CRIMINAL ELEMENTS.

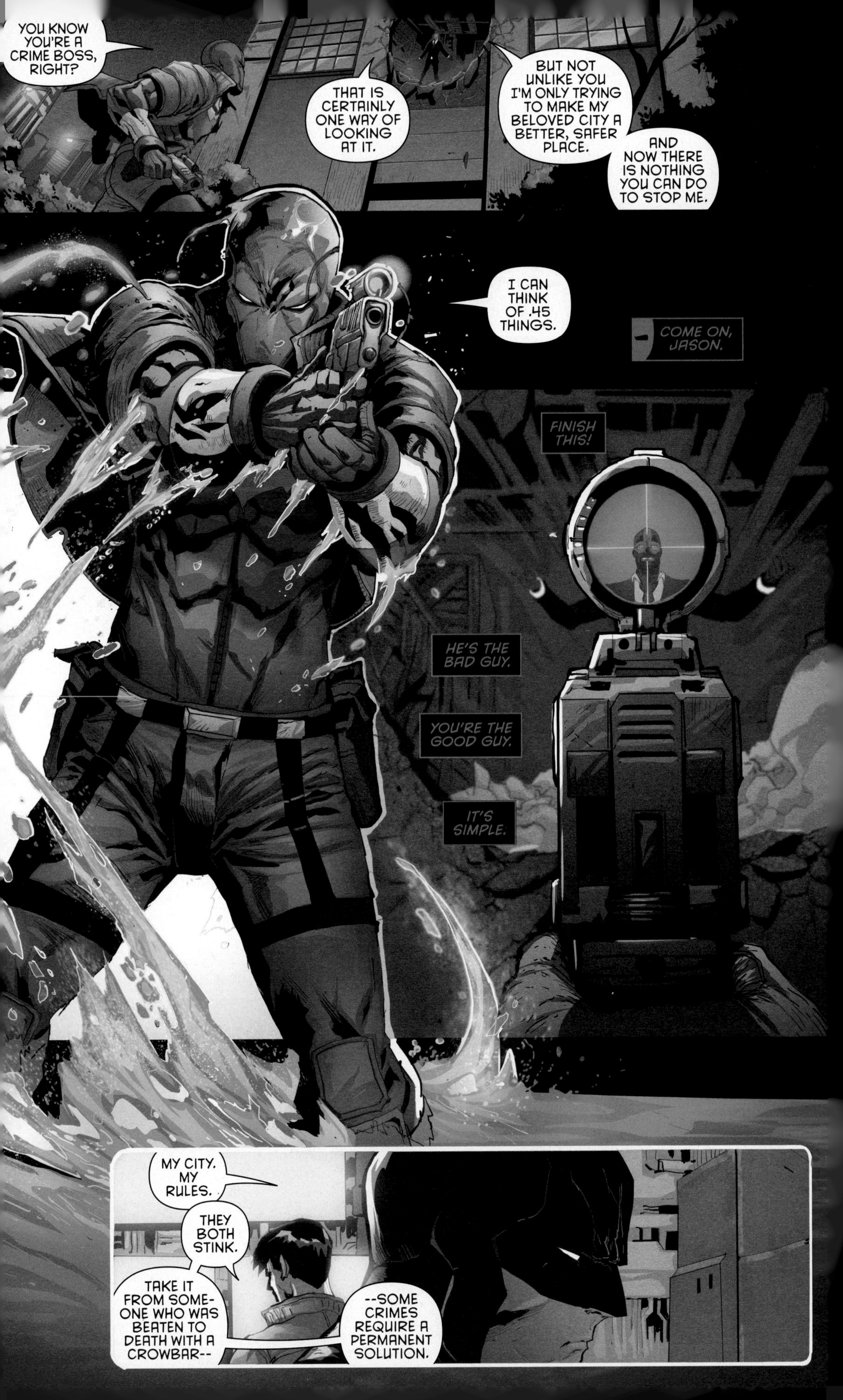
YOU KNOW YOU'RE A CRIME BOSS, RIGHT?
THAT IS CERTAINLY ONE WAY OF LOOKING AT IT.
BUT NOT UNLIKE YOU I'M ONLY TRYING TO MAKE MY BELOVED CITY A BETTER, SAFER PLACE.
AND NOW THERE IS NOTHING YOU CAN DO TO STOP ME.
I CAN THINK OF .45 THINGS.
COME ON, JASON.
FINISH THIS!
HE'S THE BAD GUY.
YOU'RE THE GOOD GUY.
IT'S SIMPLE.
MY CITY. MY RULES.
THEY BOTH STINK.
TAKE IT FROM SOME-ONE WHO WAS BEATEN TO DEATH WITH A CROWBAR--
--SOME CRIMES REQUIRE A PERMANENT SOLUTION.

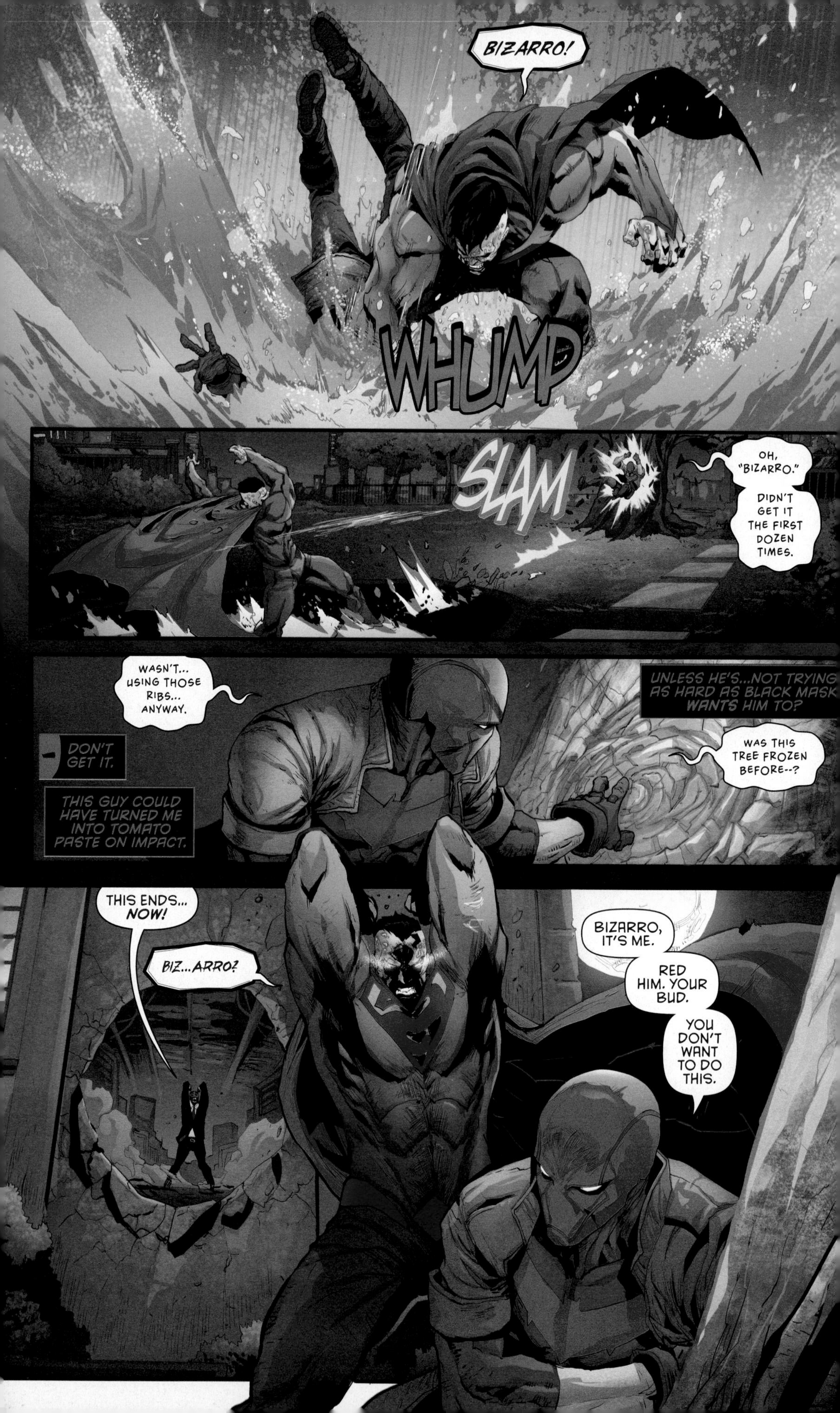
BIZARRO!
WHUMP
SLAM
OH, "BIZARRO."
DIDN'T GET IT THE FIRST DOZEN TIMES.
WASN'T... USING THOSE RIBS... ANYWAY.
UNLESS HE'S...NOT TRYING AS HARD AS BLACK MASK WANTS HIM TO?
DON'T GET IT.
THIS GUY COULD HAVE TURNED ME INTO TOMATO PASTE ON IMPACT.
WAS THIS TREE FROZEN BEFORE--?
THIS ENDS... NOW!
BIZ...ARRO?
BIZARRO, IT'S ME.
RED HIM. YOUR BUD.
YOU DON'T WANT TO DO THIS.

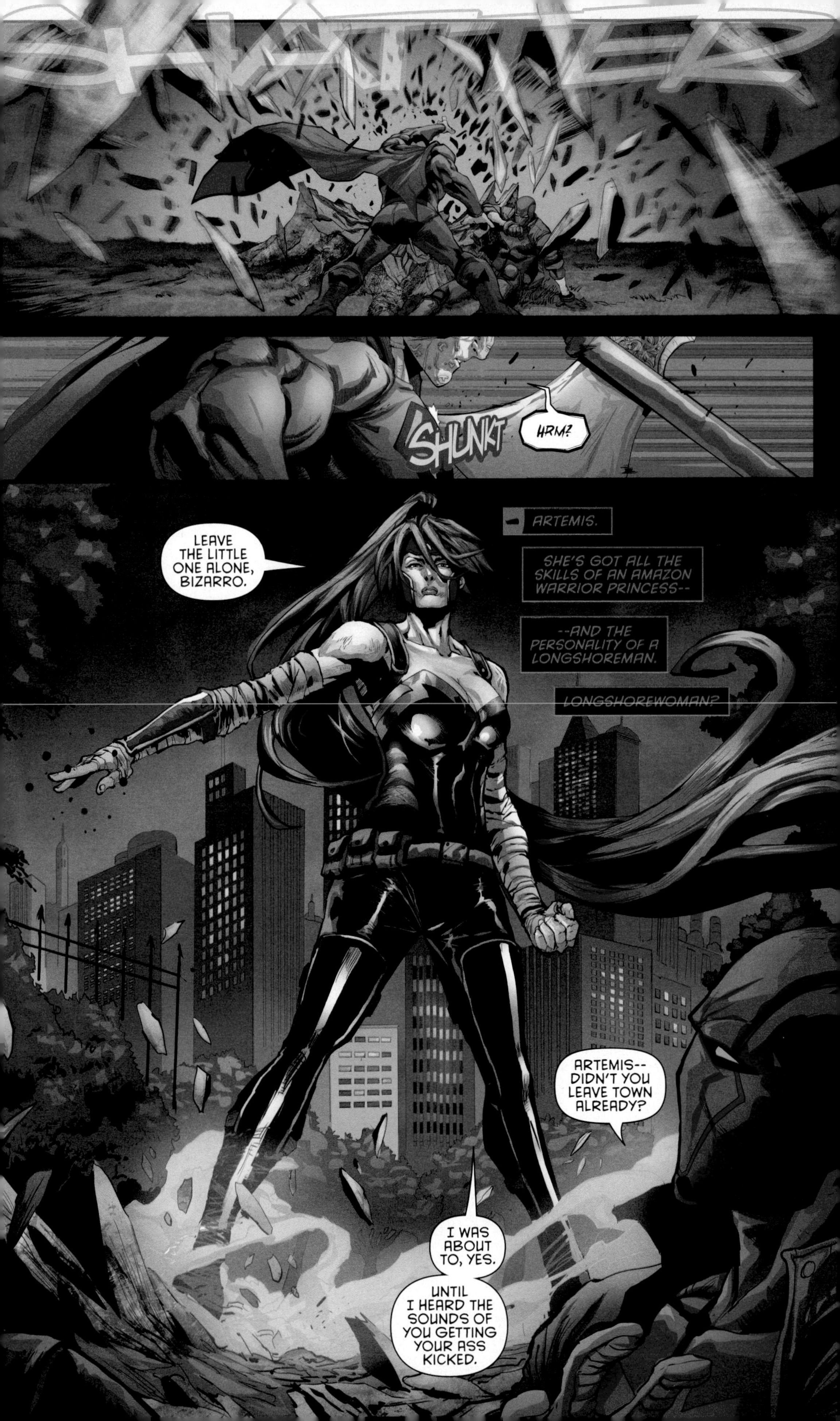
SHATTER
SHUNKT
HRM?
ARTEMIS.
LEAVE THE LITTLE ONE ALONE, BIZARRO.
SHE'S GOT ALL THE SKILLS OF AN AMAZON WARRIOR PRINCESS--
--AND THE PERSONALITY OF A LONGSHOREMAN.
LONGSHOREWOMAN?
ARTEMIS-- DIDN'T YOU LEAVE TOWN ALREADY?
I WAS ABOUT TO, YES.
UNTIL I HEARD THE SOUNDS OF YOU GETTING YOUR ASS KICKED.

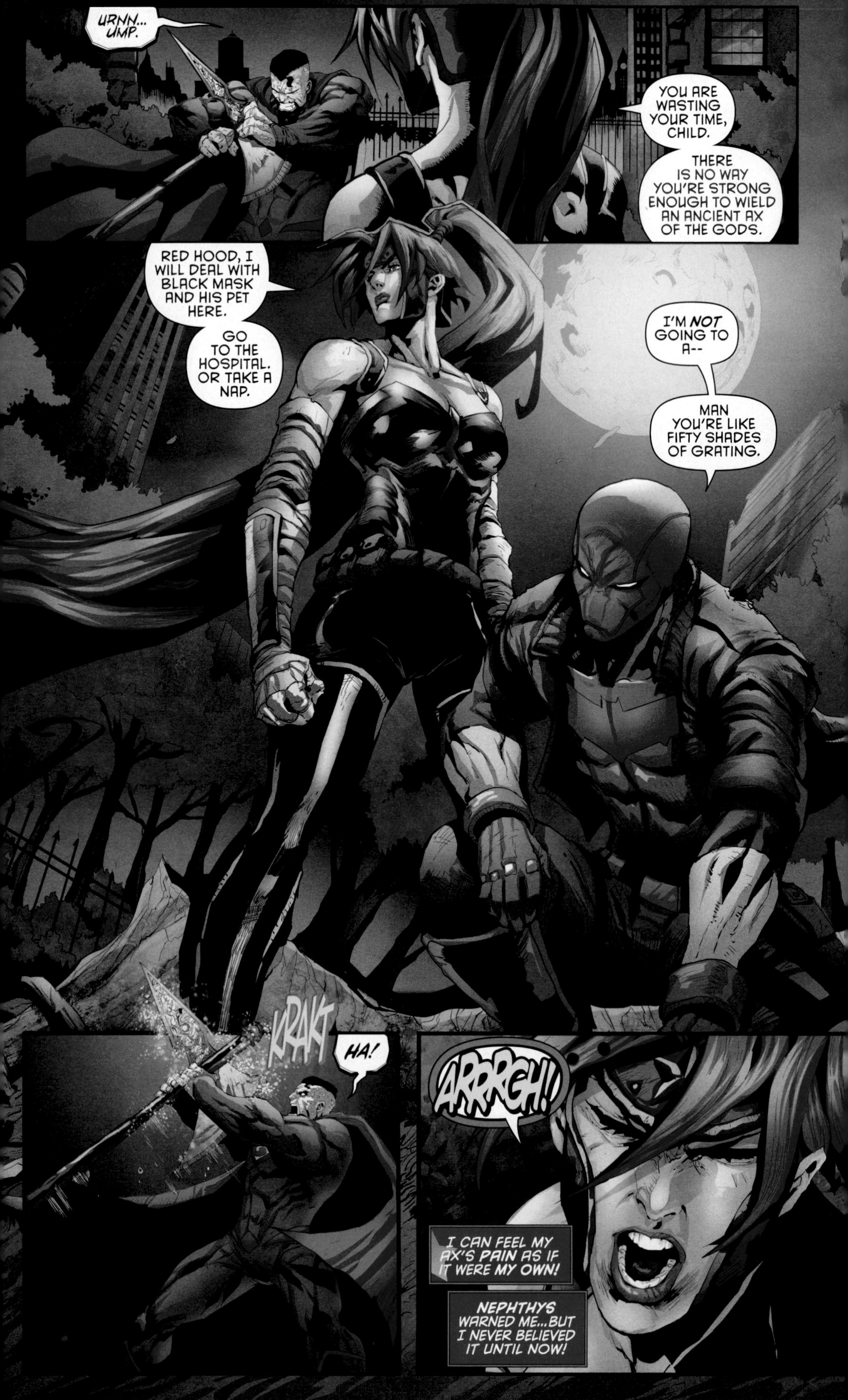
URNN... UMP.
YOU ARE WASTING YOUR TIME, CHILD.
THERE IS NO WAY YOU'RE STRONG ENOUGH TO WIELD AN ANCIENT AX OF THE GODS.
RED HOOD, I WILL DEAL WITH BLACK MASK AND HIS PET HERE.
GO TO THE HOSPITAL. OR TAKE A NAP.
I'M *NOT* GOING TO A--
MAN YOU'RE LIKE FIFTY SHADES OF GRATING.
KRAKT
HA!
ARRRGH!!
I CAN FEEL MY AX'S PAIN AS IF IT WERE MY OWN!
NEPHTHYS WARNED ME...BUT I NEVER BELIEVED IT UNTIL NOW!

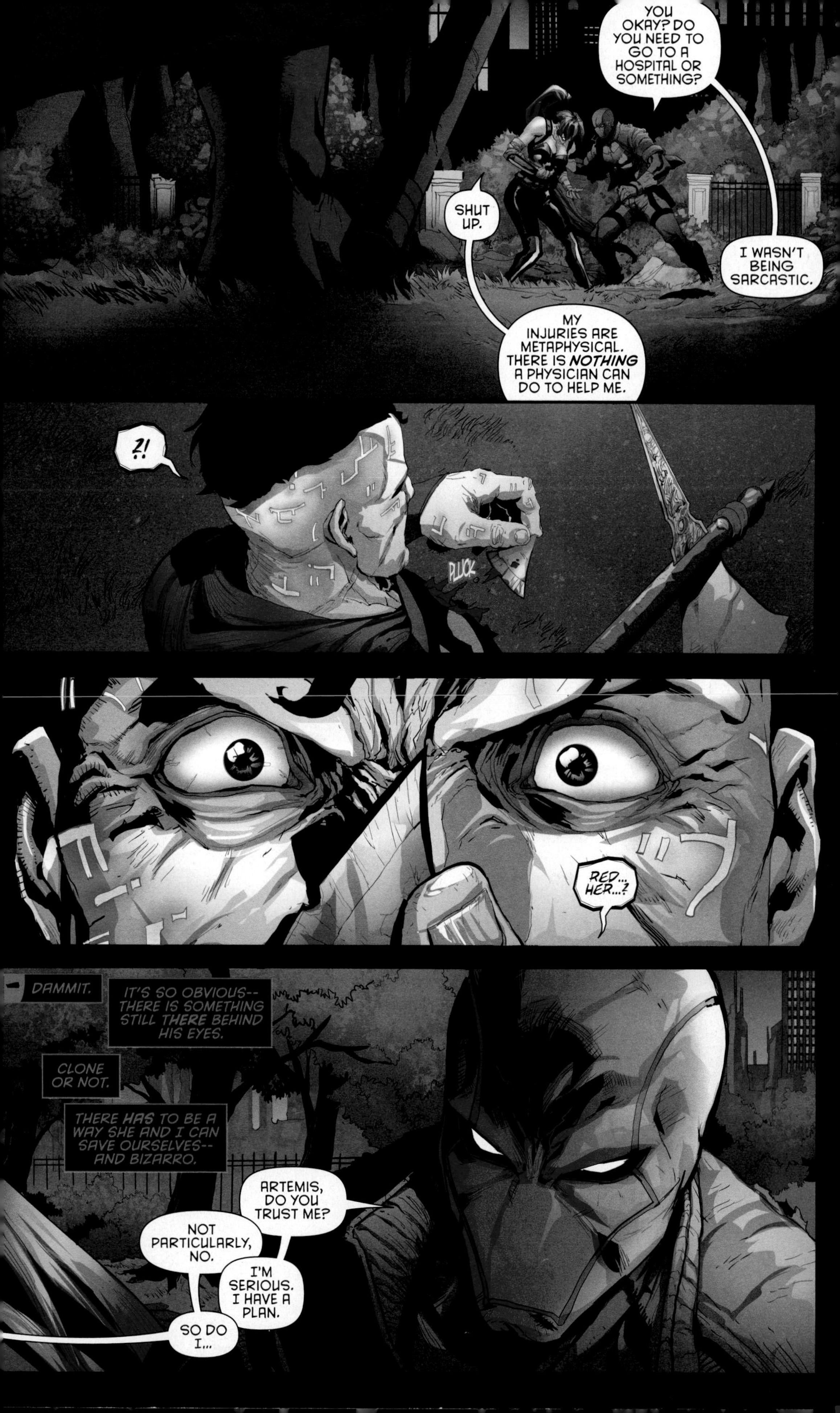
YOU OKAY? DO YOU NEED TO GO TO A HOSPITAL OR SOMETHING?
SHUT UP.
I WASN'T BEING SARCASTIC.
MY INJURIES ARE METAPHYSICAL. THERE IS ***NOTHING*** A PHYSICIAN CAN DO TO HELP ME.
?!
PLUCK
RED... HER...?
DAMMIT.
IT'S SO OBVIOUS-- THERE IS SOMETHING STILL ***THERE*** BEHIND HIS EYES.
CLONE OR NOT.
THERE ***HAS*** TO BE A WAY SHE AND I CAN SAVE OURSELVES-- AND BIZARRO.
ARTEMIS, DO YOU TRUST ME?
NOT PARTICULARLY, NO.
I'M SERIOUS. I HAVE A PLAN.
SO DO I...

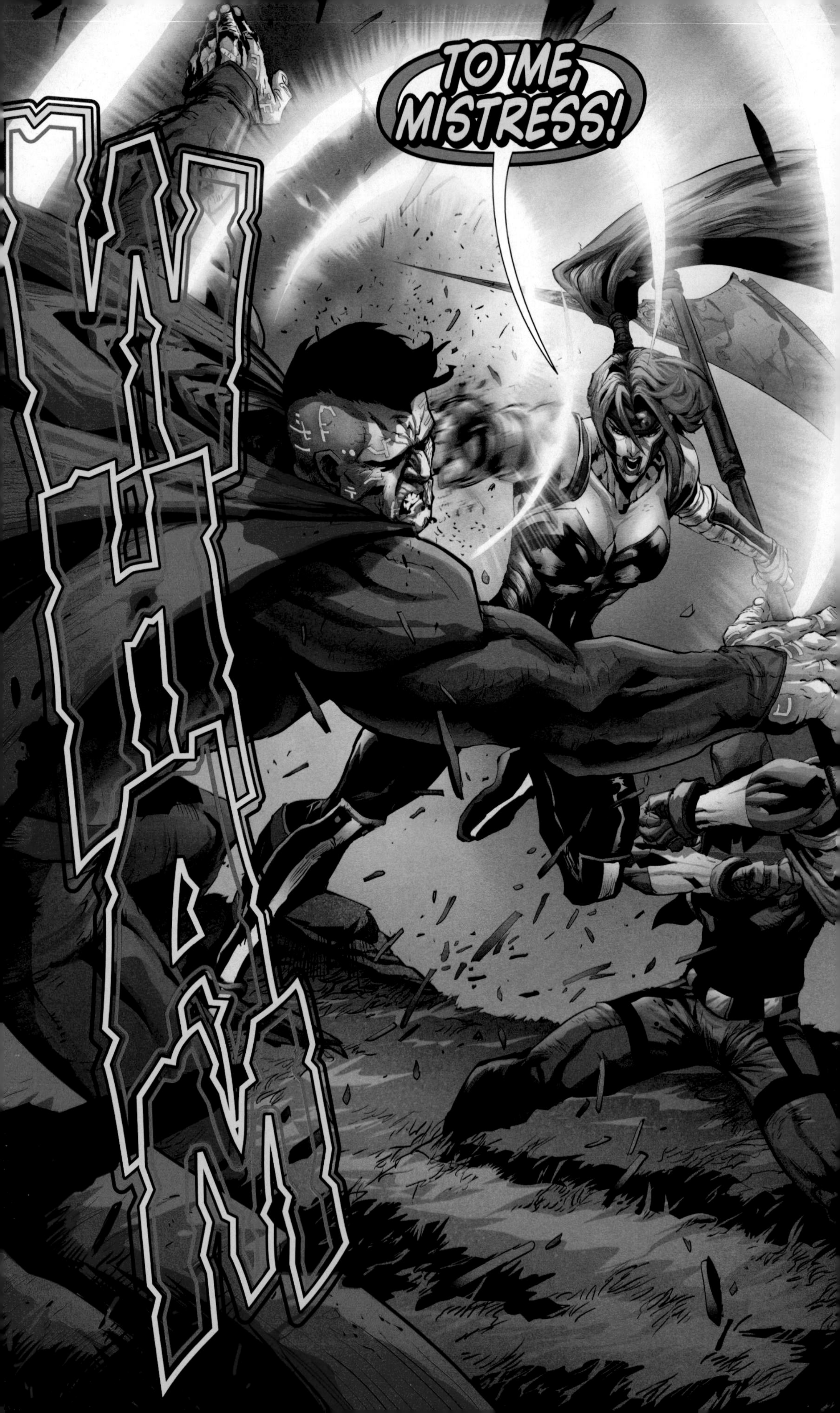
TO ME, MISTRESS!

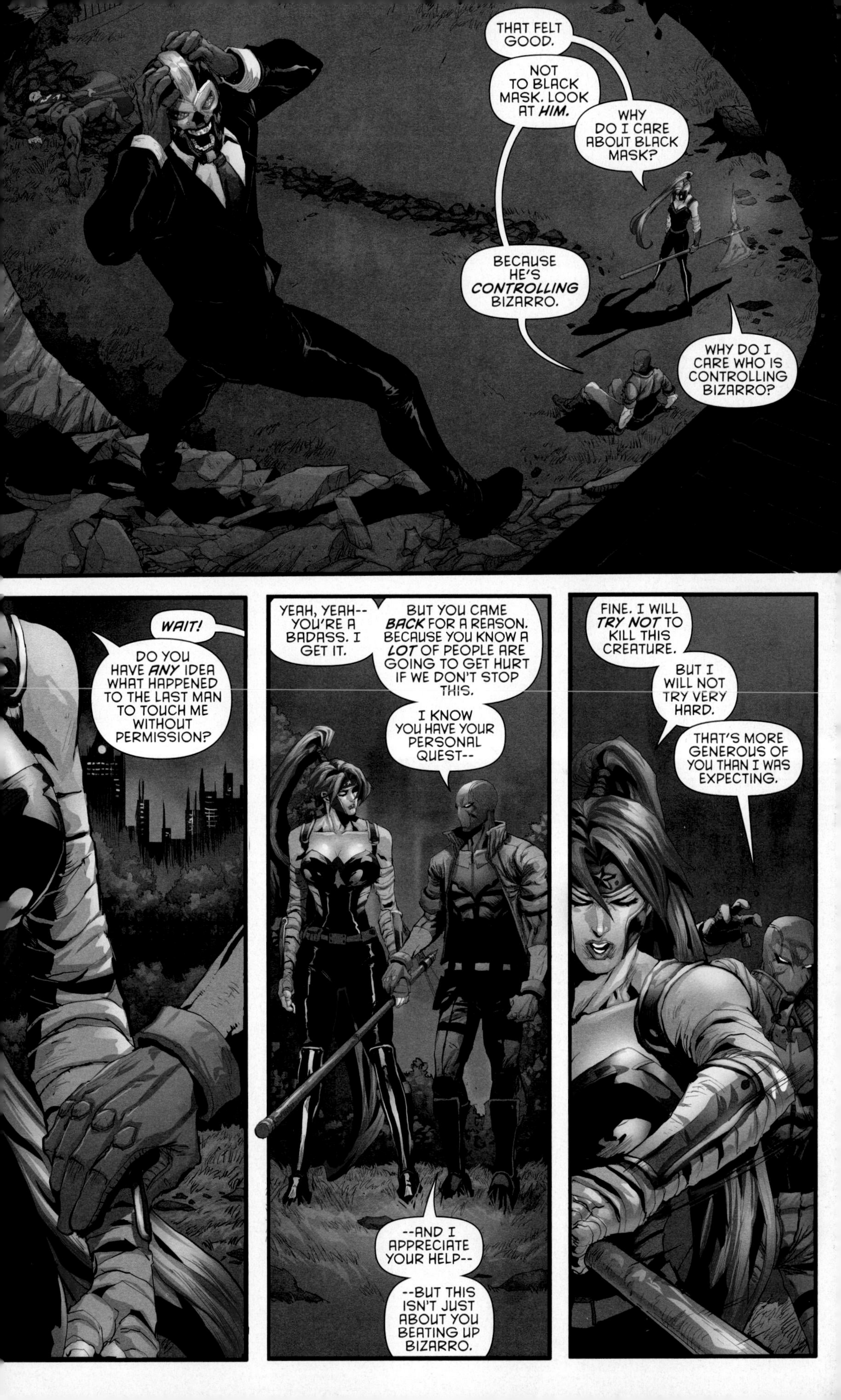
THAT FELT GOOD.
NOT TO BLACK MASK. LOOK AT *HIM.*
WHY DO I CARE ABOUT BLACK MASK?
BECAUSE HE'S *CONTROLLING* BIZARRO.
WHY DO I CARE WHO IS CONTROLLING BIZARRO?
WAIT!
DO YOU HAVE *ANY* IDEA WHAT HAPPENED TO THE LAST MAN TO TOUCH ME WITHOUT PERMISSION?
YEAH, YEAH-- YOU'RE A BADASS. I GET IT.
BUT YOU CAME *BACK* FOR A REASON. BECAUSE YOU KNOW A *LOT* OF PEOPLE ARE GOING TO GET HURT IF WE DON'T STOP THIS.
I KNOW YOU HAVE YOUR PERSONAL QUEST--
--AND I APPRECIATE YOUR HELP--
--BUT THIS ISN'T JUST ABOUT YOU BEATING UP BIZARRO.
FINE. I WILL *TRY NOT* TO KILL THIS CREATURE.
BUT I WILL NOT TRY VERY HARD.
THAT'S MORE GENEROUS OF YOU THAN I WAS EXPECTING.

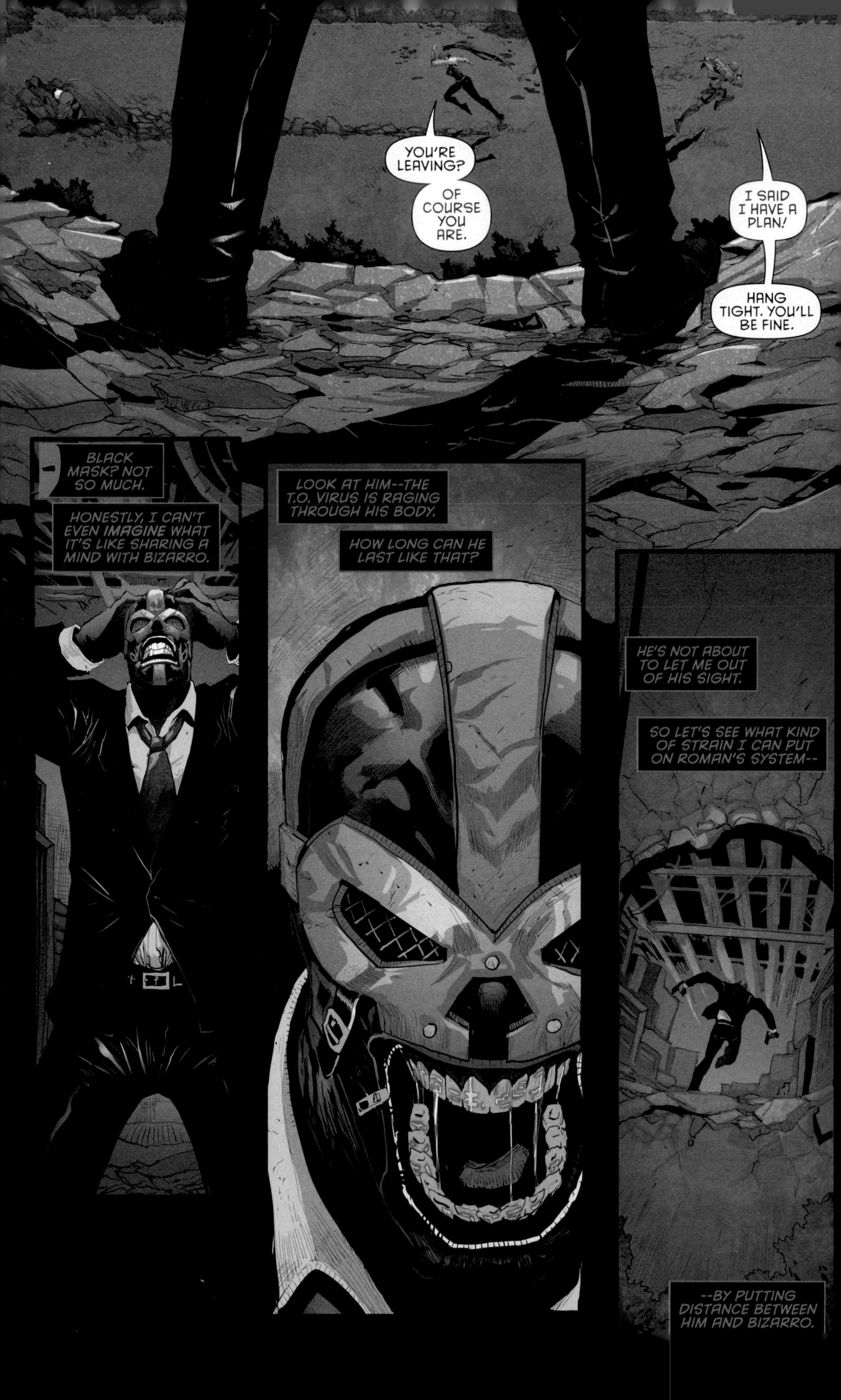

YOU'RE LEAVING?
OF COURSE YOU ARE.
I SAID I HAVE A PLAN!
HANG TIGHT. YOU'LL BE FINE.
BLACK MASK? NOT SO MUCH.
HONESTLY, I CAN'T EVEN IMAGINE WHAT IT'S LIKE SHARING A MIND WITH BIZARRO.
LOOK AT HIM--THE T.O. VIRUS IS RAGING THROUGH HIS BODY.
HOW LONG CAN HE LAST LIKE THAT?
HE'S NOT ABOUT TO LET ME OUT OF HIS SIGHT.
SO LET'S SEE WHAT KIND OF STRAIN I CAN PUT ON ROMAN'S SYSTEM--
--BY PUTTING DISTANCE BETWEEN HIM AND BIZARRO.

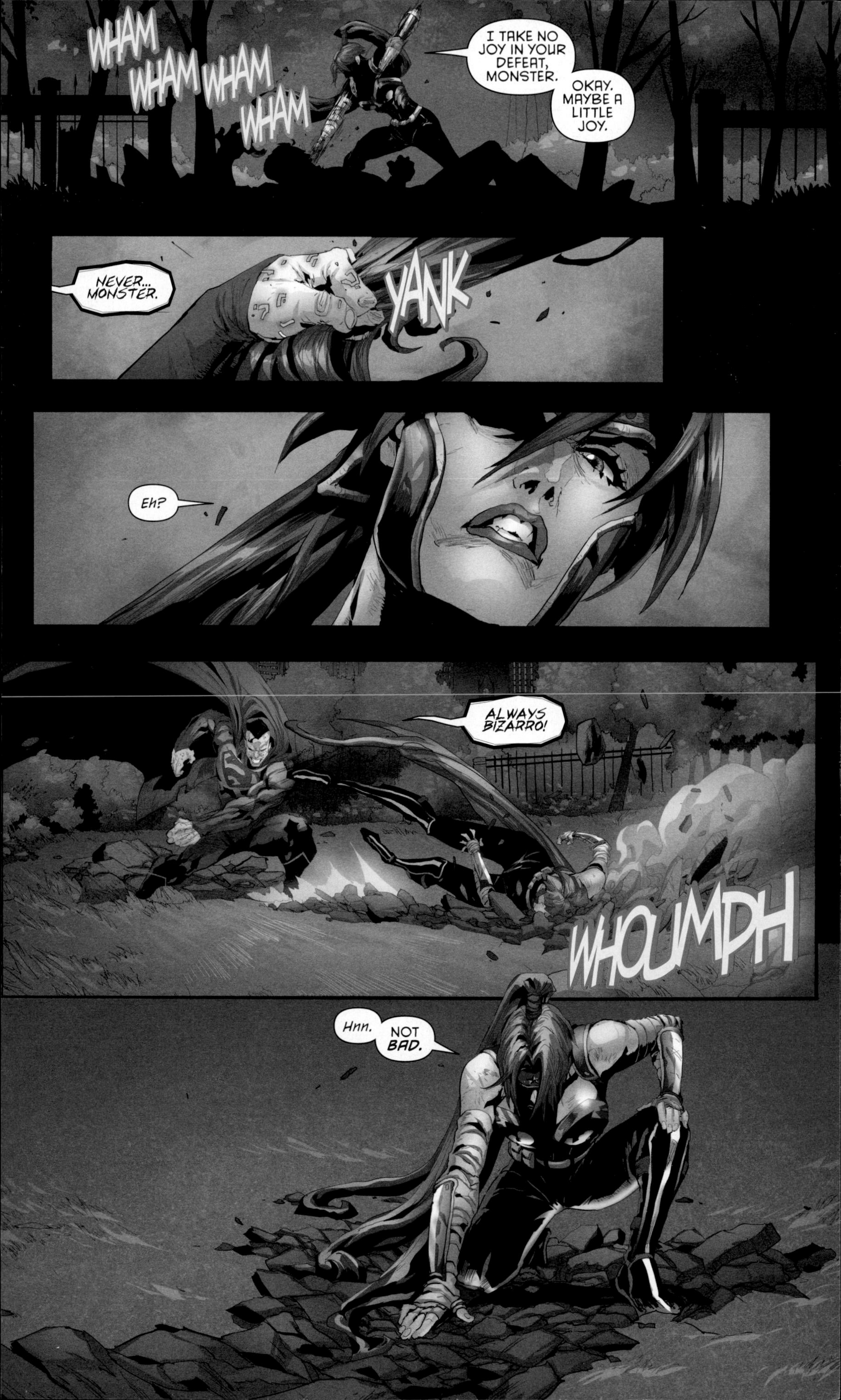
WHAM
WHAM WHAM
WHAM
I TAKE NO JOY IN YOUR DEFEAT, MONSTER.
OKAY. MAYBE A LITTLE JOY.
NEVER... MONSTER.
YANK
Eh?
ALWAYS BIZARRO!
WHOUMPH
Hnn.
NOT BAD.

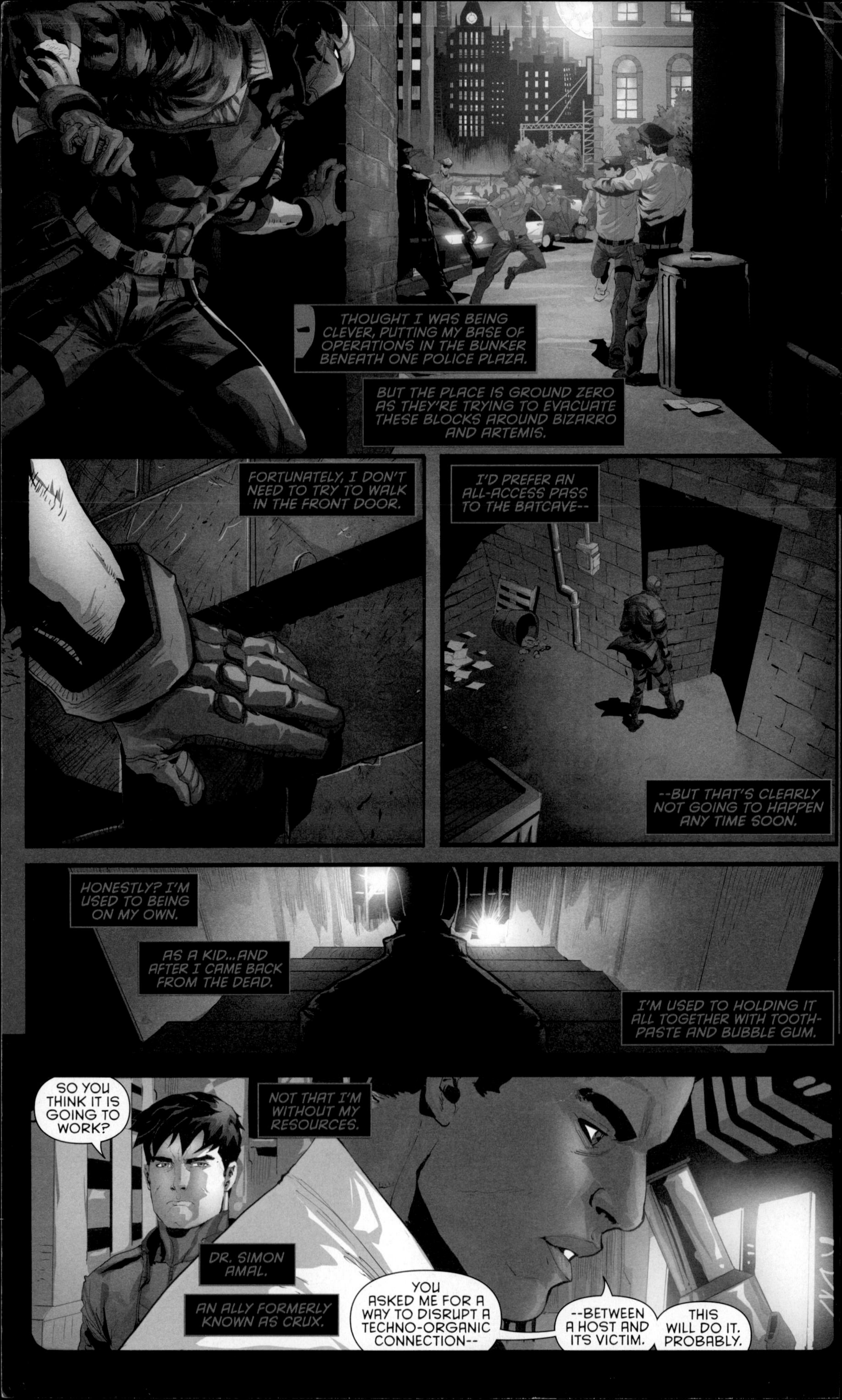
THOUGHT I WAS BEING CLEVER, PUTTING MY BASE OF OPERATIONS IN THE BUNKER BENEATH ONE POLICE PLAZA.
BUT THE PLACE IS GROUND ZERO AS THEY'RE TRYING TO EVACUATE THESE BLOCKS AROUND BIZARRO AND ARTEMIS.
FORTUNATELY, I DON'T NEED TO TRY TO WALK IN THE FRONT DOOR.
I'D PREFER AN ALL-ACCESS PASS TO THE BATCAVE--
--BUT THAT'S CLEARLY NOT GOING TO HAPPEN ANY TIME SOON.
HONESTLY? I'M USED TO BEING ON MY OWN.
AS A KID...AND AFTER I CAME BACK FROM THE DEAD.
I'M USED TO HOLDING IT ALL TOGETHER WITH TOOTH-PASTE AND BUBBLE GUM.
SO YOU THINK IT IS GOING TO WORK?
NOT THAT I'M WITHOUT MY RESOURCES.
DR. SIMON AMAL.
AN ALLY FORMERLY KNOWN AS CRUX.
YOU ASKED ME FOR A WAY TO DISRUPT A TECHNO-ORGANIC CONNECTION--
--BETWEEN A HOST AND ITS VICTIM.
THIS WILL DO IT. PROBABLY.

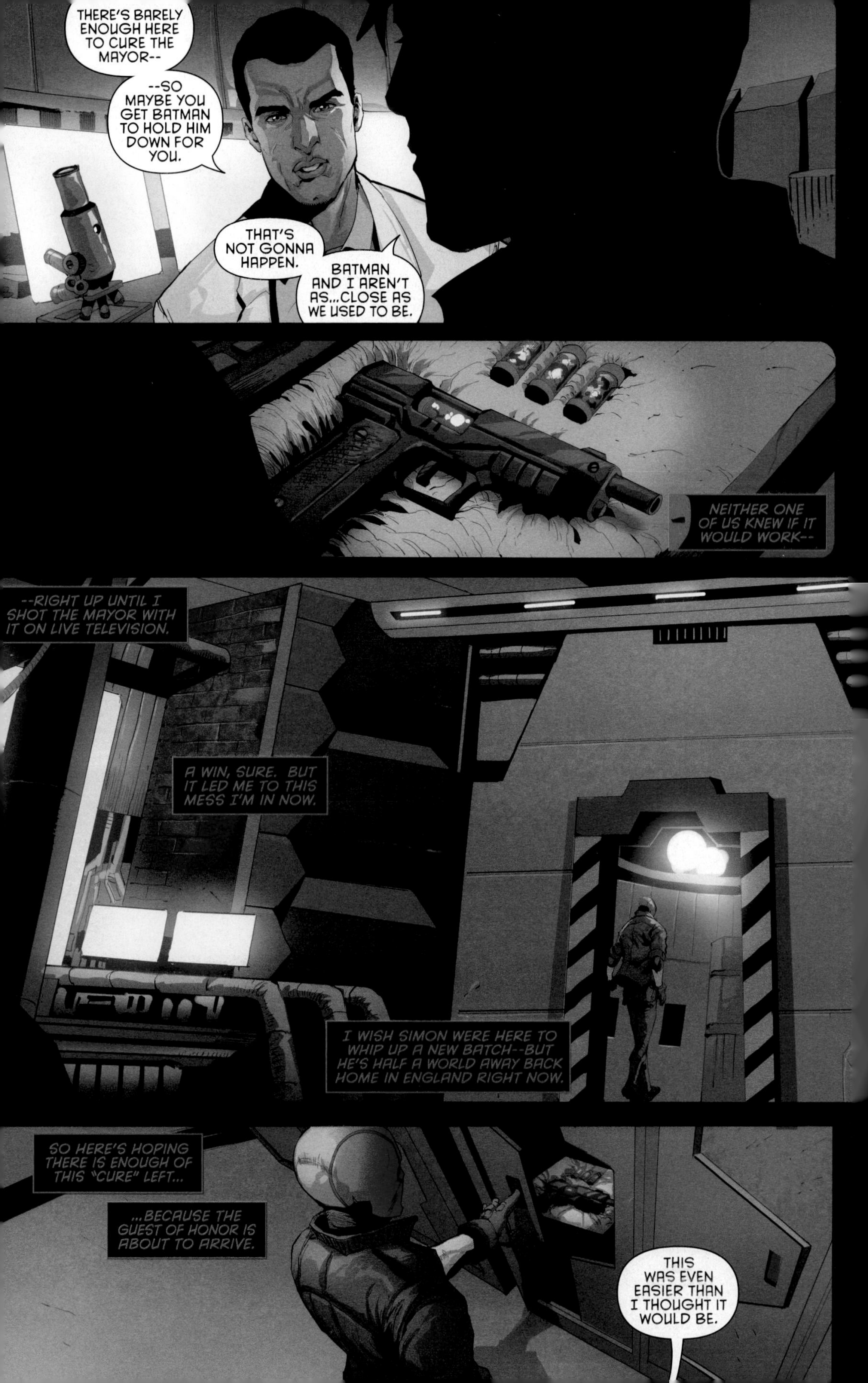
THERE'S BARELY ENOUGH HERE TO CURE THE MAYOR--
--SO MAYBE YOU GET BATMAN TO HOLD HIM DOWN FOR YOU.
THAT'S NOT GONNA HAPPEN.
BATMAN AND I AREN'T AS...CLOSE AS WE USED TO BE.
NEITHER ONE OF US KNEW IF IT WOULD WORK--
--RIGHT UP UNTIL I SHOT THE MAYOR WITH IT ON LIVE TELEVISION.
A WIN, SURE. BUT IT LED ME TO THIS MESS I'M IN NOW.
I WISH SIMON WERE HERE TO WHIP UP A NEW BATCH--BUT HE'S HALF A WORLD AWAY BACK HOME IN ENGLAND RIGHT NOW.
SO HERE'S HOPING THERE IS ENOUGH OF THIS "CURE" LEFT...
...BECAUSE THE GUEST OF HONOR IS ABOUT TO ARRIVE.
THIS WAS EVEN EASIER THAN I THOUGHT IT WOULD BE.

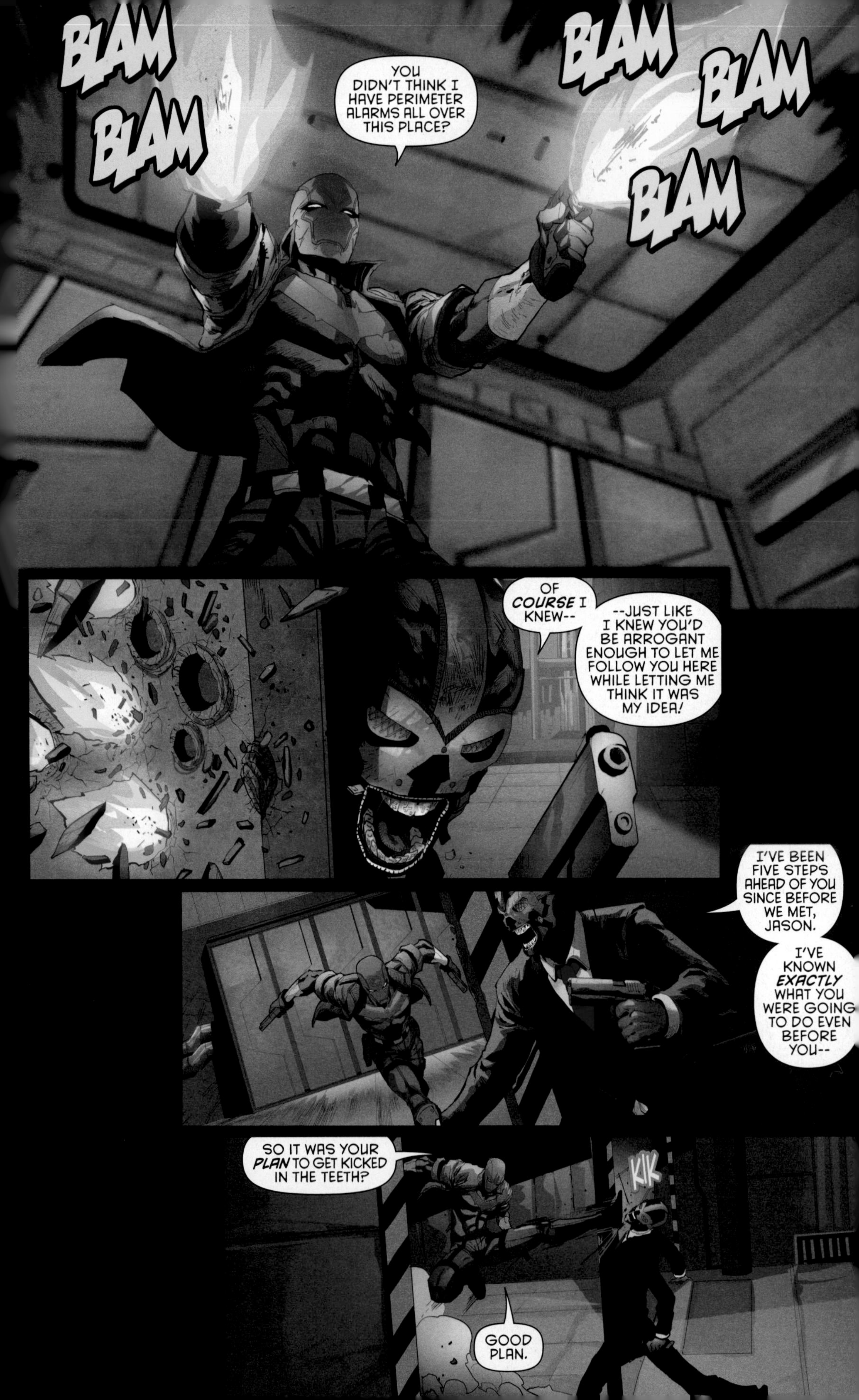
BLAM
BLAM
YOU DIDN'T THINK I HAVE PERIMETER ALARMS ALL OVER THIS PLACE?
BLAM
BLAM
BLAM
OF *COURSE* I KNEW--
--JUST LIKE I KNEW YOU'D BE ARROGANT ENOUGH TO LET ME FOLLOW YOU HERE WHILE LETTING ME THINK IT WAS MY IDEA!
I'VE BEEN FIVE STEPS AHEAD OF YOU SINCE BEFORE WE MET, JASON.
I'VE KNOWN *EXACTLY* WHAT YOU WERE GOING TO DO EVEN BEFORE YOU--
SO IT WAS YOUR *PLAN* TO GET KICKED IN THE TEETH?
KIK
GOOD PLAN.

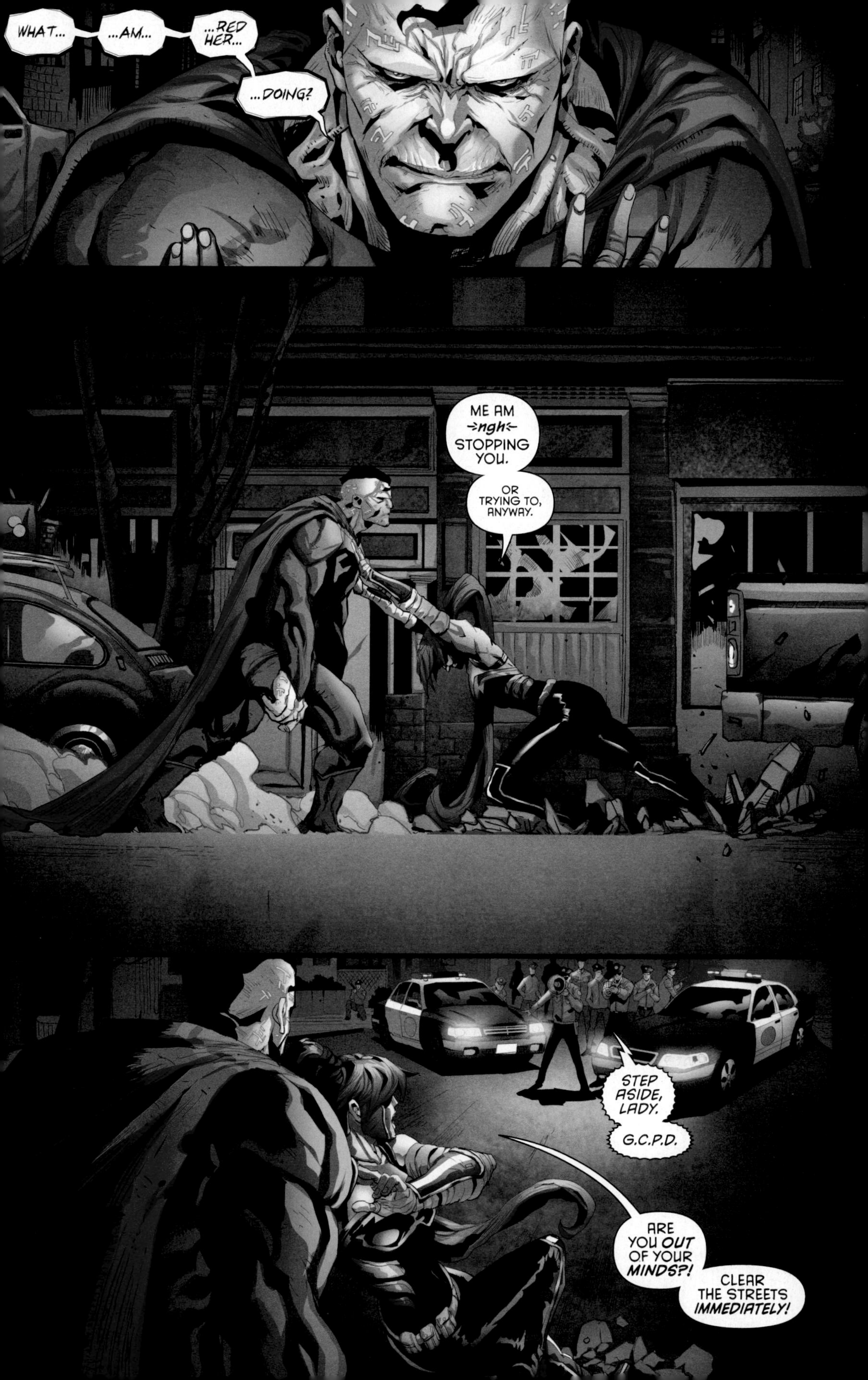
WHAT...
...AM...
...RED HER...
...DOING?
ME AM -ngh- STOPPING YOU.
OR TRYING TO, ANYWAY.
STEP ASIDE, LADY.
G.C.P.D.
ARE YOU OUT OF YOUR MINDS?!
CLEAR THE STREETS IMMEDIATELY!

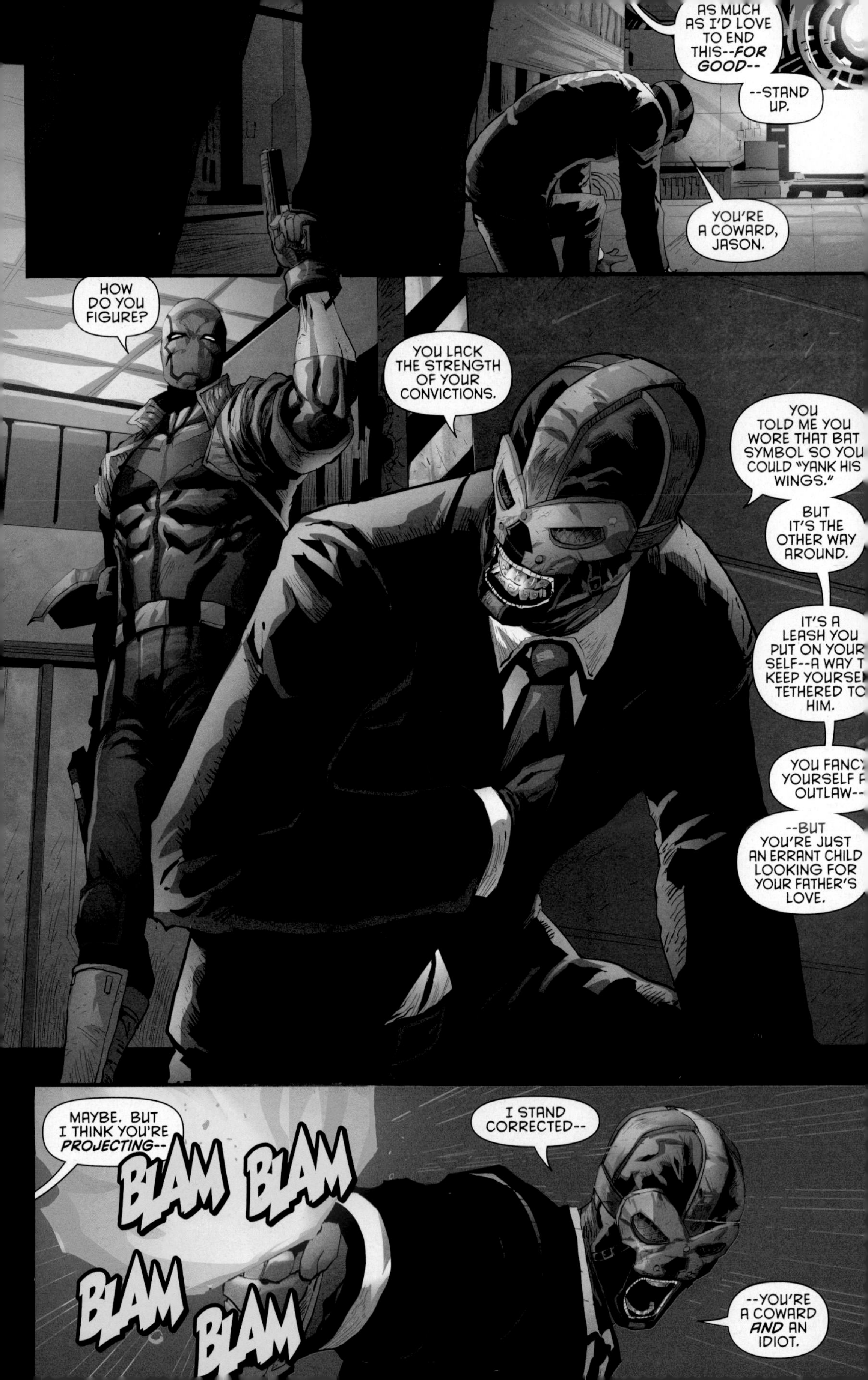
AS MUCH AS I'D LOVE TO END THIS--*FOR GOOD*--
--STAND UP.
YOU'RE A COWARD, JASON.
HOW DO YOU FIGURE?
YOU LACK THE STRENGTH OF YOUR CONVICTIONS.
YOU TOLD ME YOU WORE THAT BAT SYMBOL SO YOU COULD "YANK HIS WINGS."
BUT IT'S THE OTHER WAY AROUND.
IT'S A LEASH YOU PUT ON YOURSELF--A WAY TO KEEP YOURSELF TETHERED TO HIM.
YOU FANCY YOURSELF AN OUTLAW--
--BUT YOU'RE JUST AN ERRANT CHILD LOOKING FOR YOUR FATHER'S LOVE.
MAYBE. BUT I THINK YOU'RE *PROJECTING*--
BLAM BLAM
BLAM
BLAM
I STAND CORRECTED--
--YOU'RE A COWARD *AND* AN IDIOT.

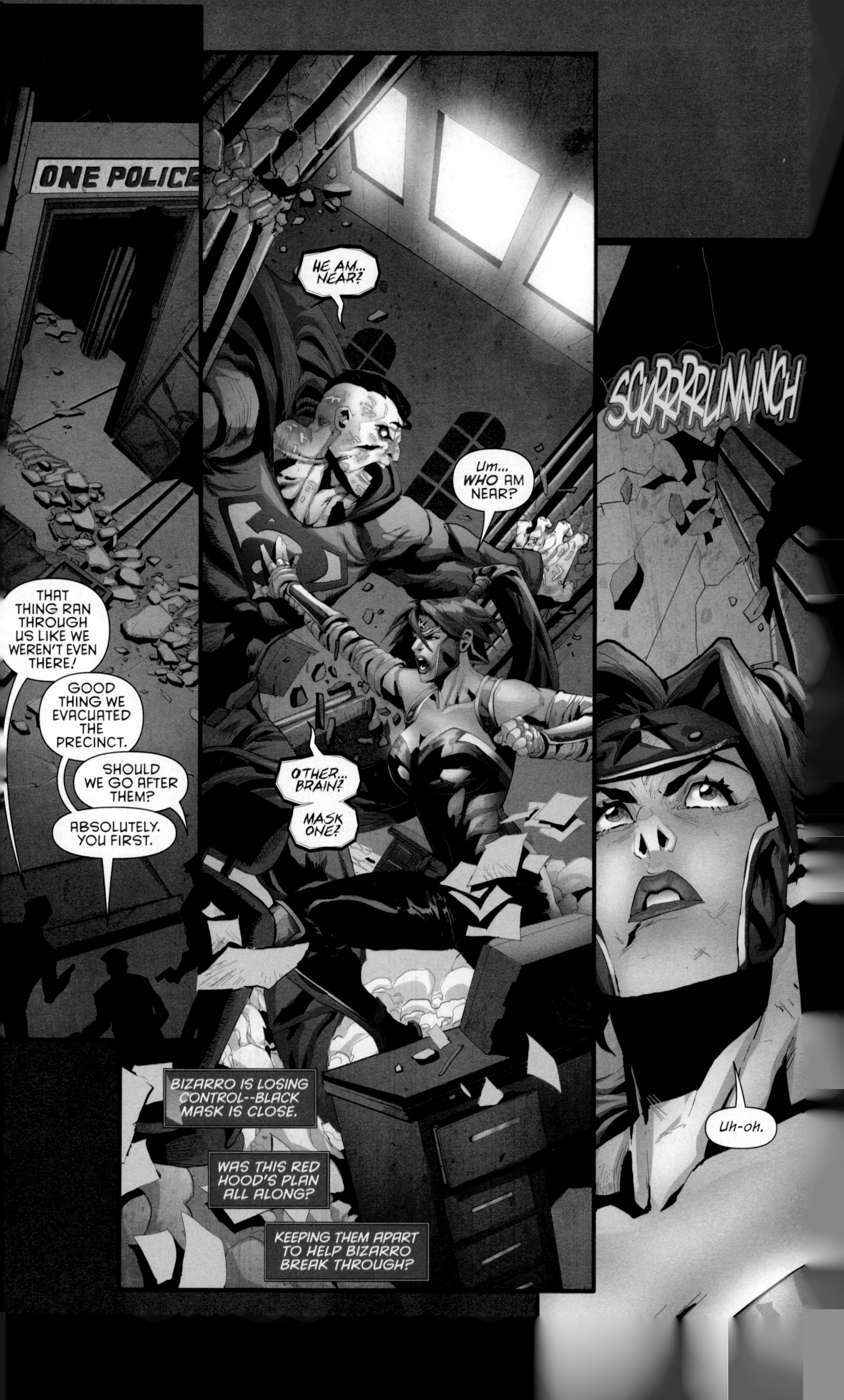
ONE POLICE
HE AM... NEAR?
SCKRRRUNNNCH
UM... WHO AM NEAR?
THAT THING RAN THROUGH US LIKE WE WEREN'T EVEN THERE!
GOOD THING WE EVACUATED THE PRECINCT.
SHOULD WE GO AFTER THEM?
ABSOLUTELY. YOU FIRST.
OTHER... BRAIN?
MASK ONE?
BIZARRO IS LOSING CONTROL--BLACK MASK IS CLOSE.
WAS THIS RED HOOD'S PLAN ALL ALONG?
KEEPING THEM APART TO HELP BIZARRO BREAK THROUGH?
Uh-oh.

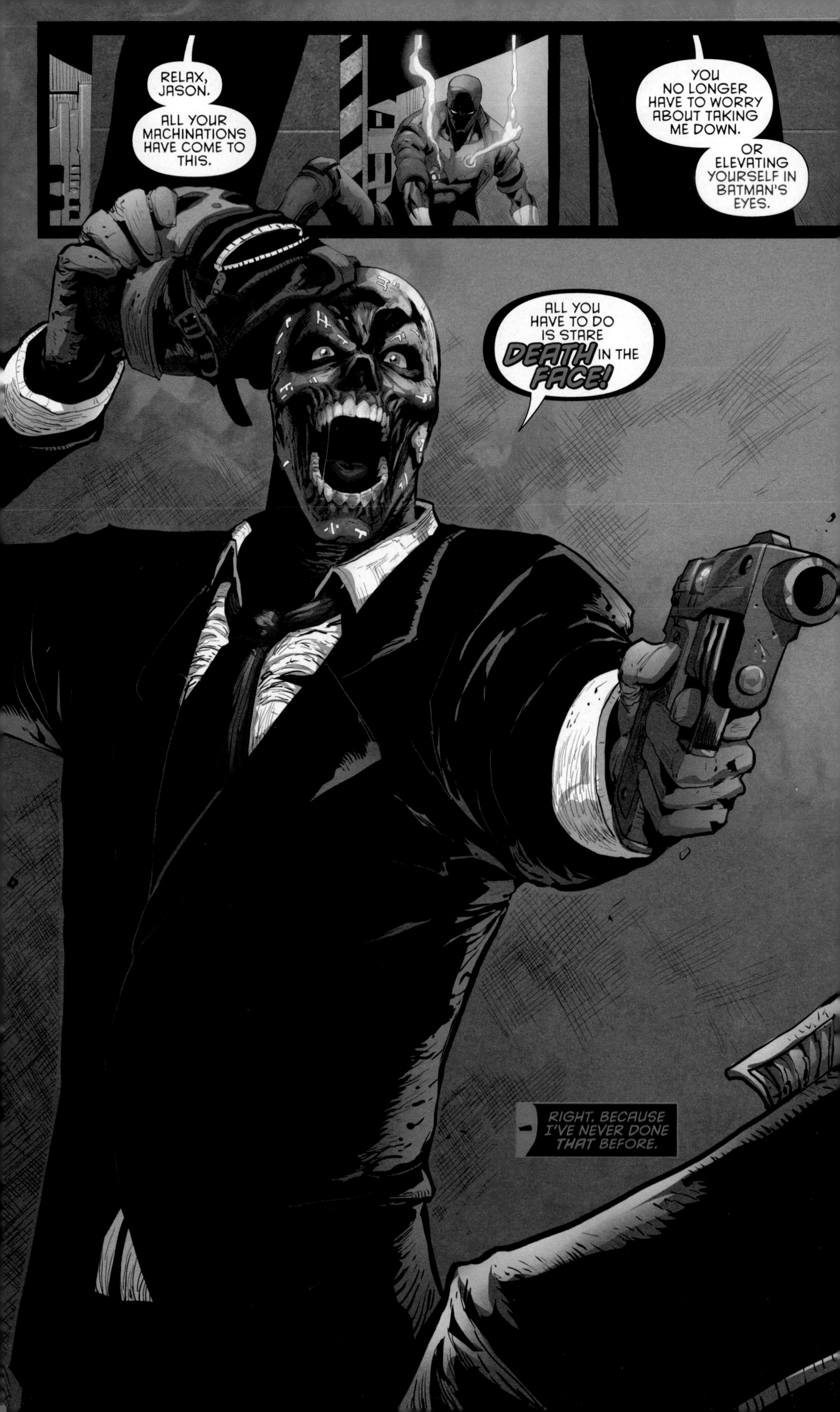
RELAX, JASON.
ALL YOUR MACHINATIONS HAVE COME TO THIS.
YOU NO LONGER HAVE TO WORRY ABOUT TAKING ME DOWN.
OR ELEVATING YOURSELF IN BATMAN'S EYES.
ALL YOU HAVE TO DO IS STARE DEATH IN THE FACE!
RIGHT. BECAUSE I'VE NEVER DONE THAT BEFORE.

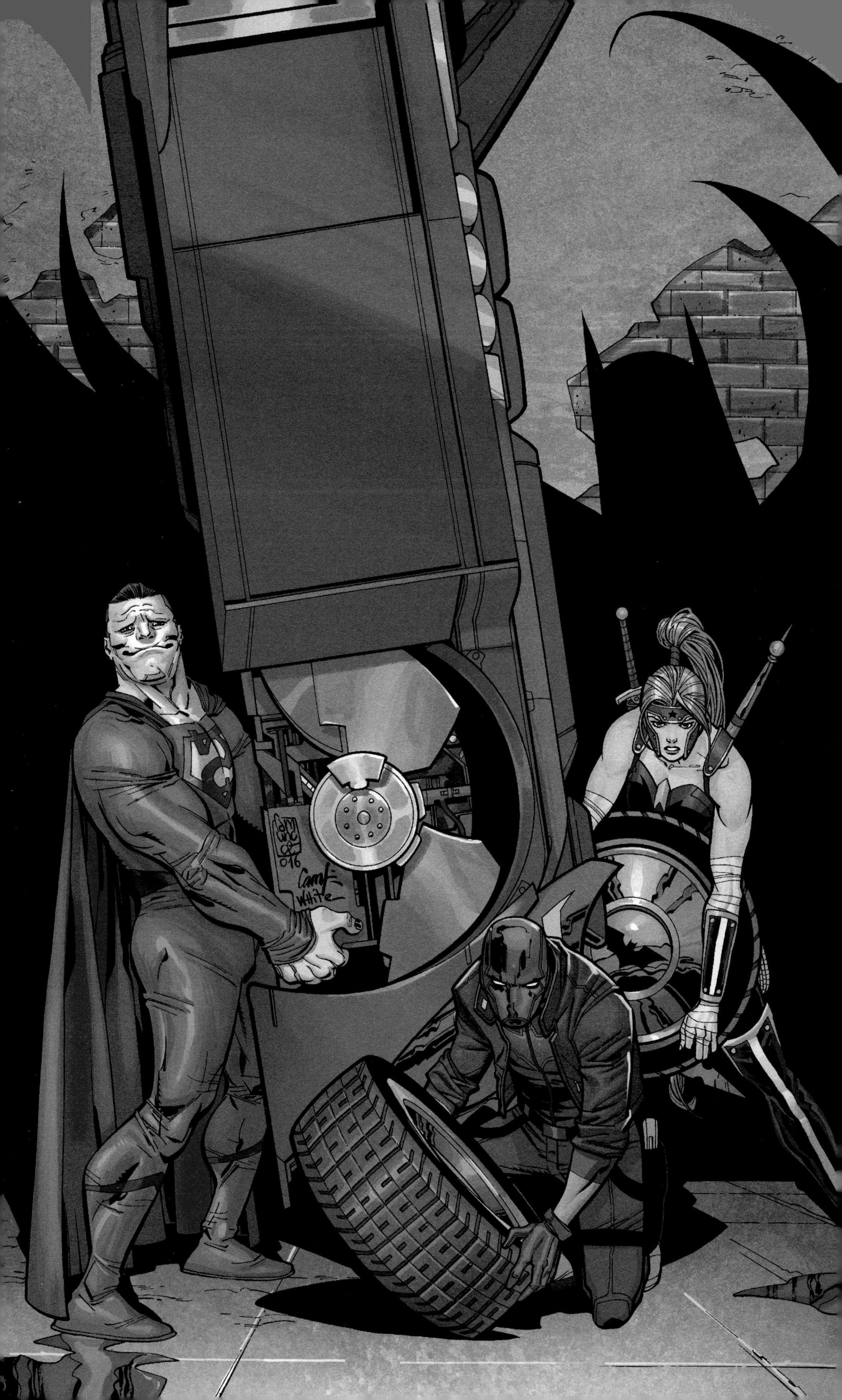

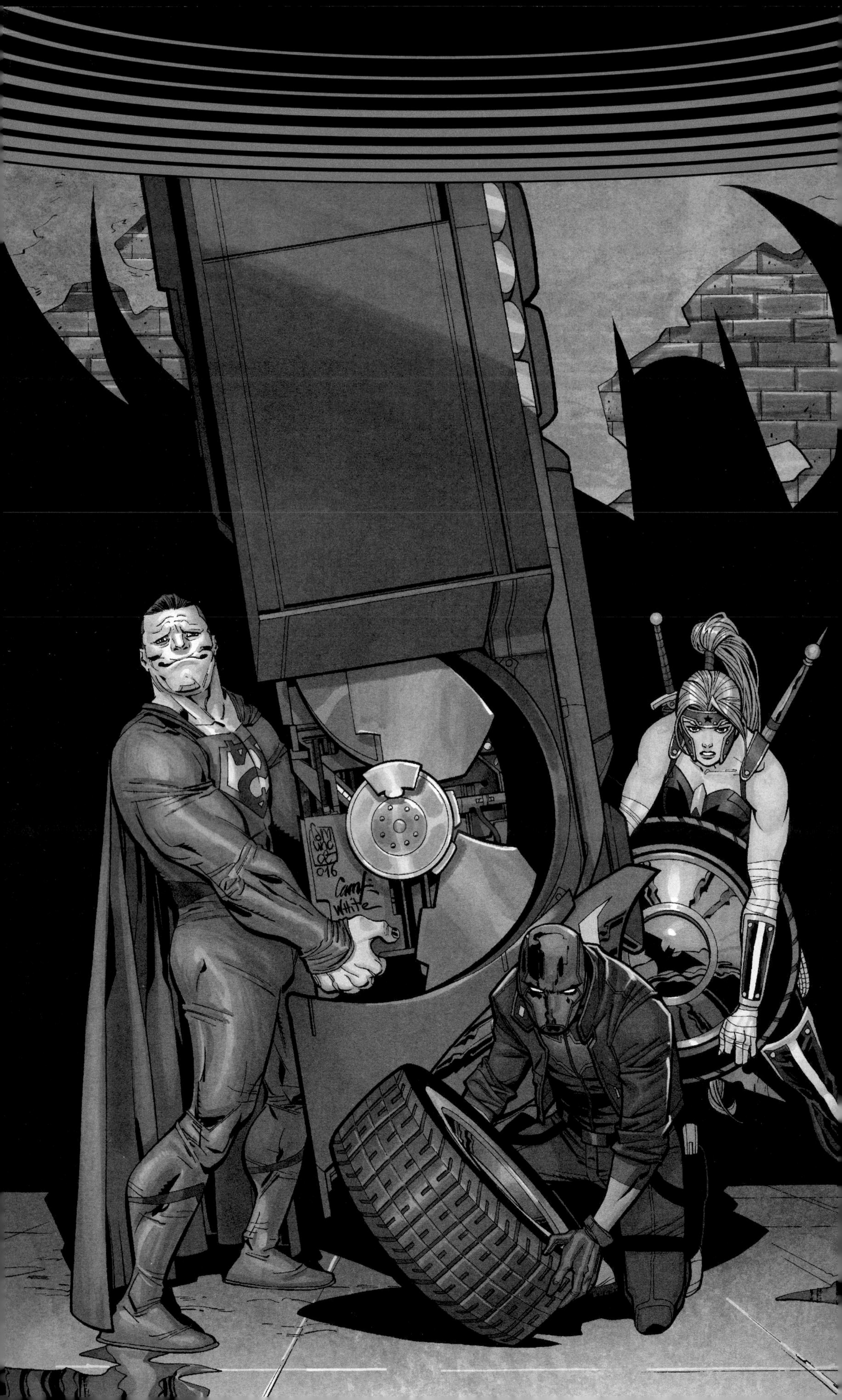

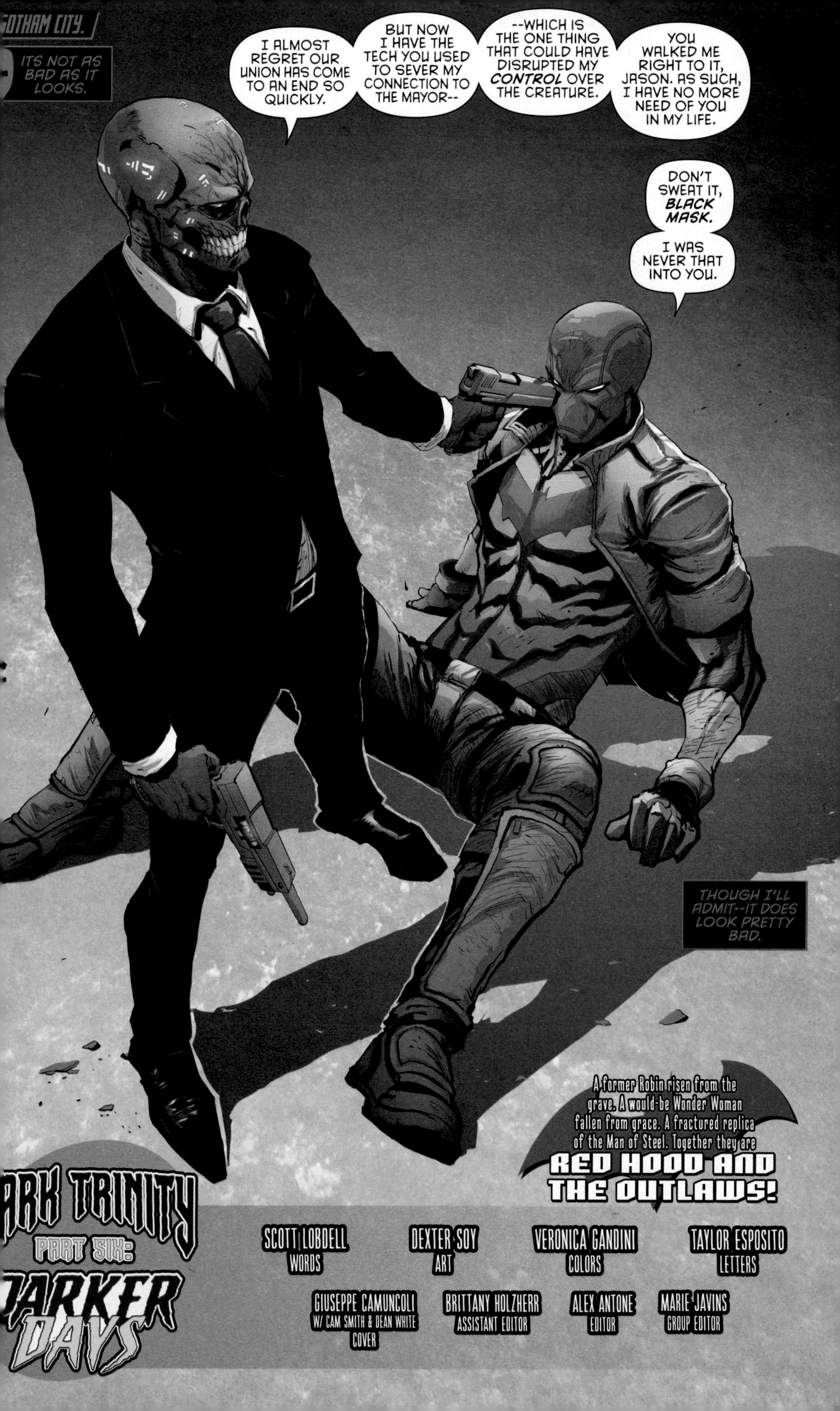

GOTHAM CITY.
ITS NOT AS BAD AS IT LOOKS.
I ALMOST REGRET OUR UNION HAS COME TO AN END SO QUICKLY.
BUT NOW I HAVE THE TECH YOU USED TO SEVER MY CONNECTION TO THE MAYOR--
--WHICH IS THE ONE THING THAT COULD HAVE DISRUPTED MY CONTROL OVER THE CREATURE.
YOU WALKED ME RIGHT TO IT, JASON. AS SUCH, I HAVE NO MORE NEED OF YOU IN MY LIFE.
DON'T SWEAT IT, BLACK MASK.
I WAS NEVER THAT INTO YOU.
THOUGH I'LL ADMIT--IT DOES LOOK PRETTY BAD.
A former Robin risen from the grave. A would-be Wonder Woman fallen from grace. A fractured replica of the Man of Steel. Together they are
RED HOOD AND THE OUTLAWS!
DARK TRINITY
PART SIX:
DARKER DAYS
SCOTT LOBDELL WORDS
DEXTER SOY ART
VERONICA GANDINI COLORS
TAYLOR ESPOSITO LETTERS
GIUSEPPE CAMUNCOLI W/ CAM SMITH & DEAN WHITE COVER
BRITTANY HOLZHERR ASSISTANT EDITOR
ALEX ANTONE EDITOR
MARIE JAVINS GROUP EDITOR

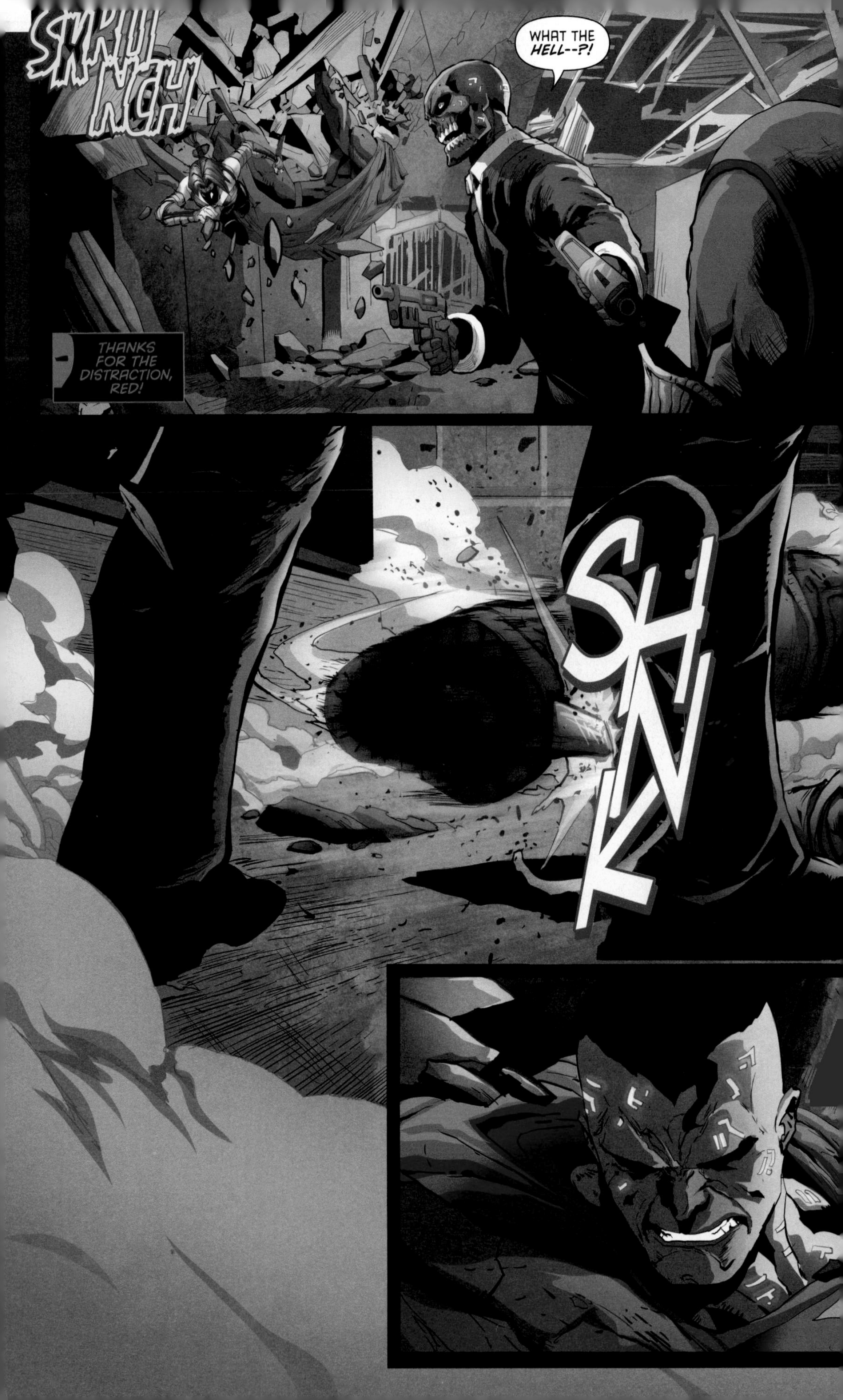
SKRUNCH
WHAT THE HELL--?!
THANKS FOR THE DISTRACTION, RED!
SHNK

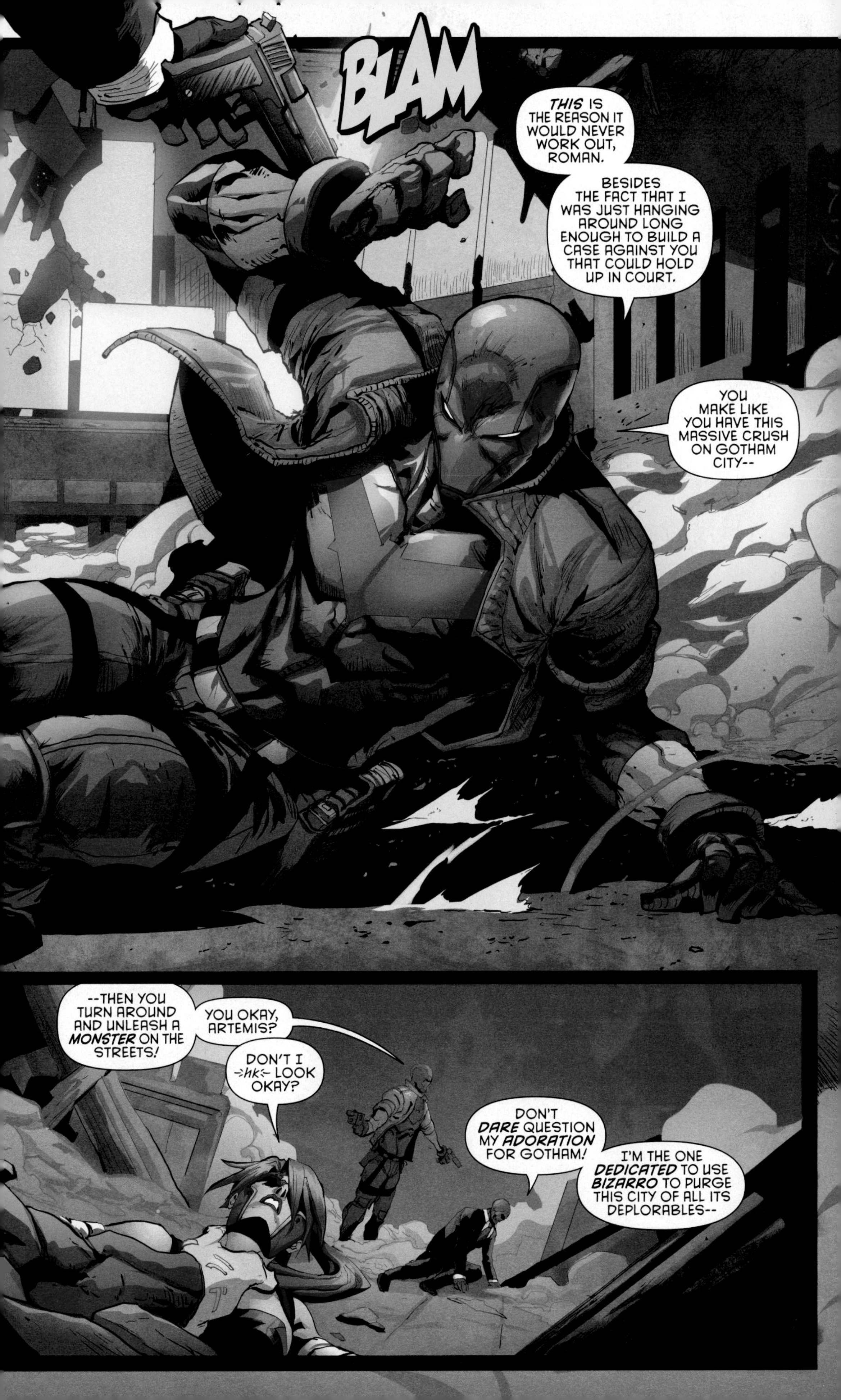

BLAM
THIS IS THE REASON IT WOULD NEVER WORK OUT, ROMAN.
BESIDES THE FACT THAT I WAS JUST HANGING AROUND LONG ENOUGH TO BUILD A CASE AGAINST YOU THAT COULD HOLD UP IN COURT.
YOU MAKE LIKE YOU HAVE THIS MASSIVE CRUSH ON GOTHAM CITY--
--THEN YOU TURN AROUND AND UNLEASH A MONSTER ON THE STREETS!
YOU OKAY, ARTEMIS?
DON'T I -hk- LOOK OKAY?
DON'T DARE QUESTION MY ADORATION FOR GOTHAM!
I'M THE ONE DEDICATED TO USE BIZARRO TO PURGE THIS CITY OF ALL ITS DEPLORABLES--

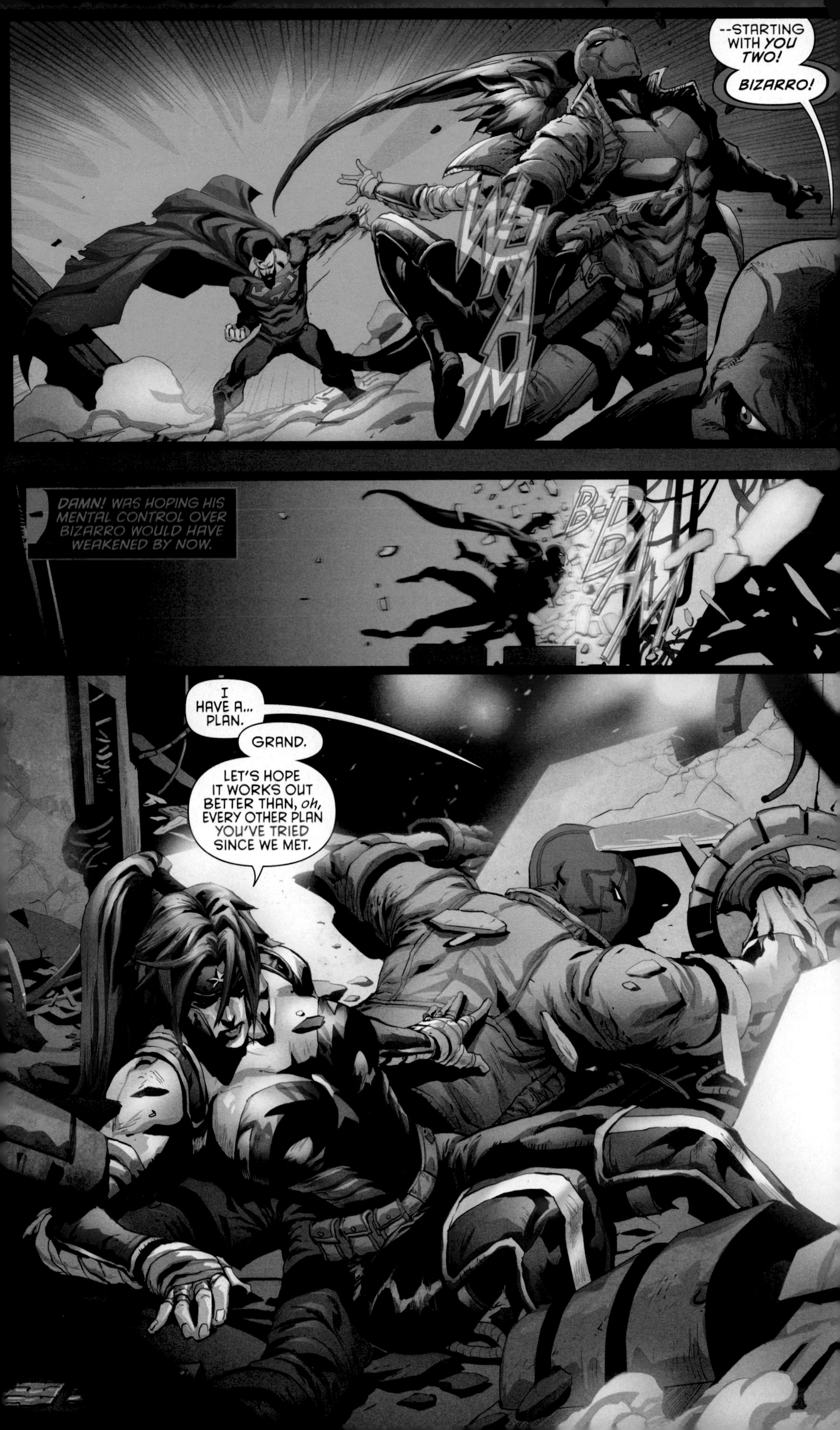
--STARTING WITH YOU TWO!
BIZARRO!
WHAM
DAMN! WAS HOPING HIS MENTAL CONTROL OVER BIZARRO WOULD HAVE WEAKENED BY NOW.
B-DAM
I HAVE A... PLAN.
GRAND.
LET'S HOPE IT WORKS OUT BETTER THAN, oh, EVERY OTHER PLAN YOU'VE TRIED SINCE WE MET.

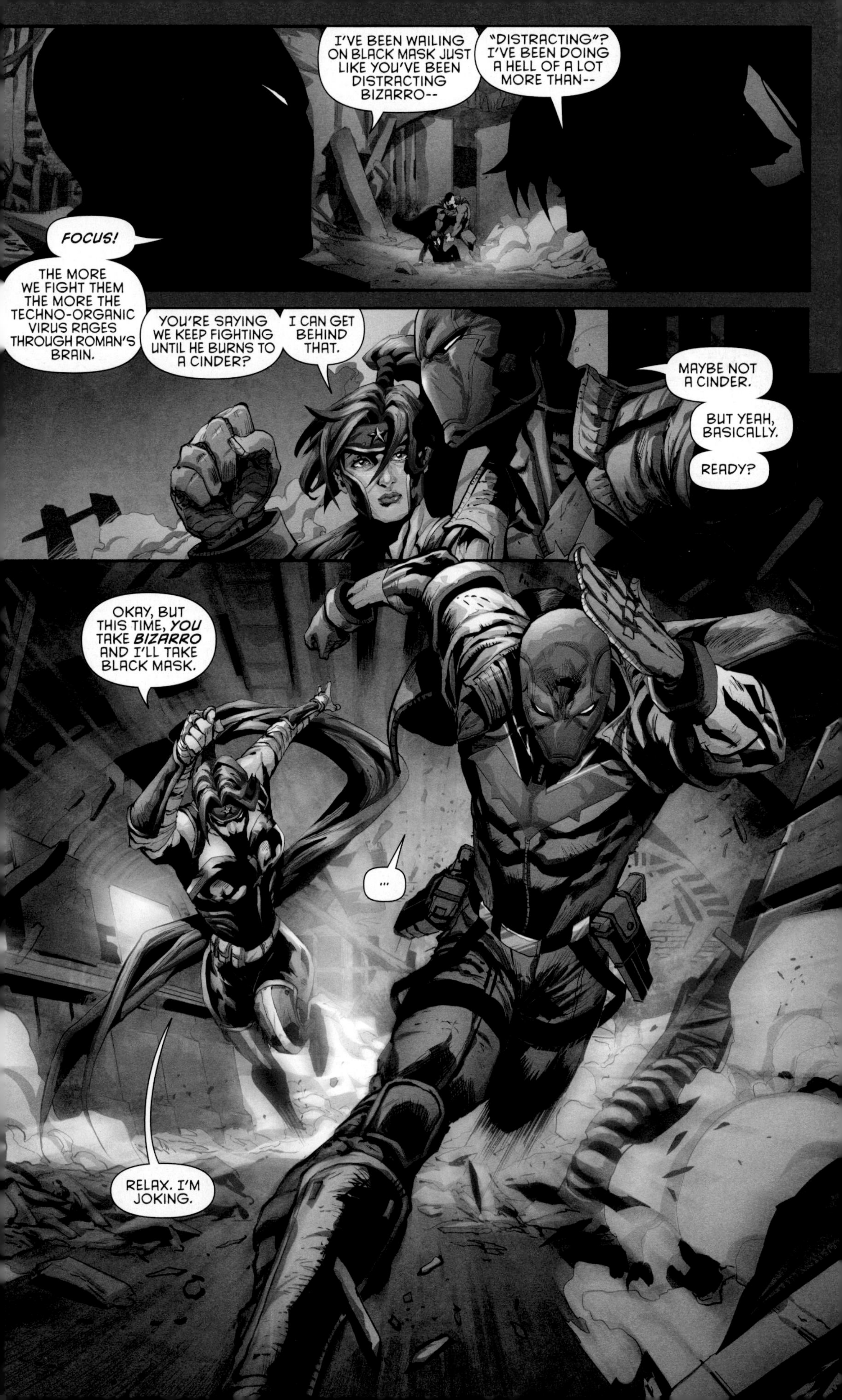
I'VE BEEN WAILING ON BLACK MASK JUST LIKE YOU'VE BEEN DISTRACTING BIZARRO--
"DISTRACTING"? I'VE BEEN DOING A HELL OF A LOT MORE THAN--
FOCUS!
THE MORE WE FIGHT THEM THE MORE THE TECHNO-ORGANIC VIRUS RAGES THROUGH ROMAN'S BRAIN.
YOU'RE SAYING WE KEEP FIGHTING UNTIL HE BURNS TO A CINDER?
I CAN GET BEHIND THAT.
MAYBE NOT A CINDER.
BUT YEAH, BASICALLY.
READY?
OKAY, BUT THIS TIME, YOU TAKE BIZARRO AND I'LL TAKE BLACK MASK.
...
RELAX. I'M JOKING.

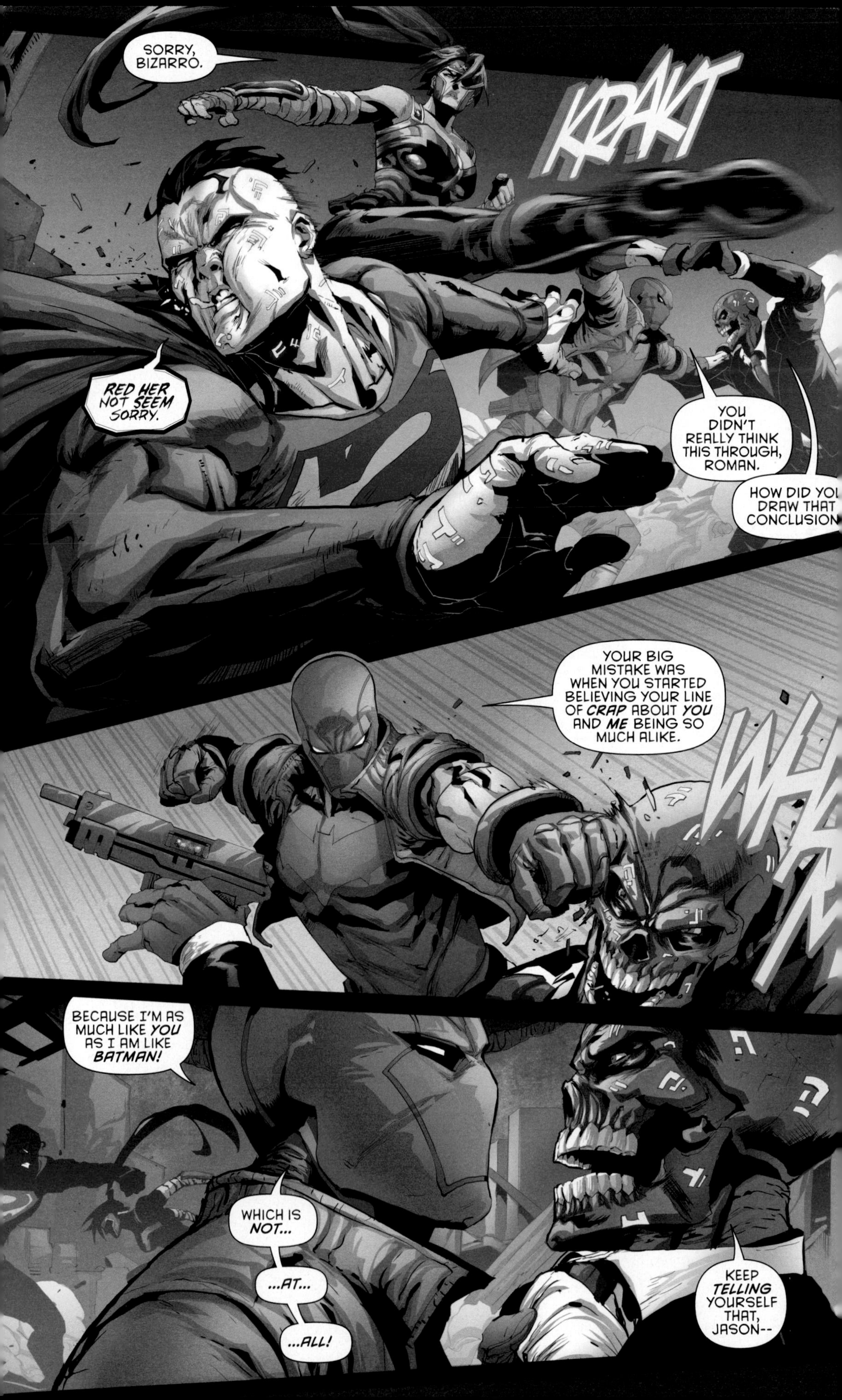
SORRY, BIZARRO.
KRAKT
RED HER NOT SEEM SORRY.
YOU DIDN'T REALLY THINK THIS THROUGH, ROMAN.
HOW DID YOU DRAW THAT CONCLUSION
YOUR BIG MISTAKE WAS WHEN YOU STARTED BELIEVING YOUR LINE OF CRAP ABOUT YOU AND ME BEING SO MUCH ALIKE.
BECAUSE I'M AS MUCH LIKE YOU AS I AM LIKE BATMAN!
WHICH IS NOT...
...AT...
...ALL!
KEEP TELLING YOURSELF THAT, JASON--

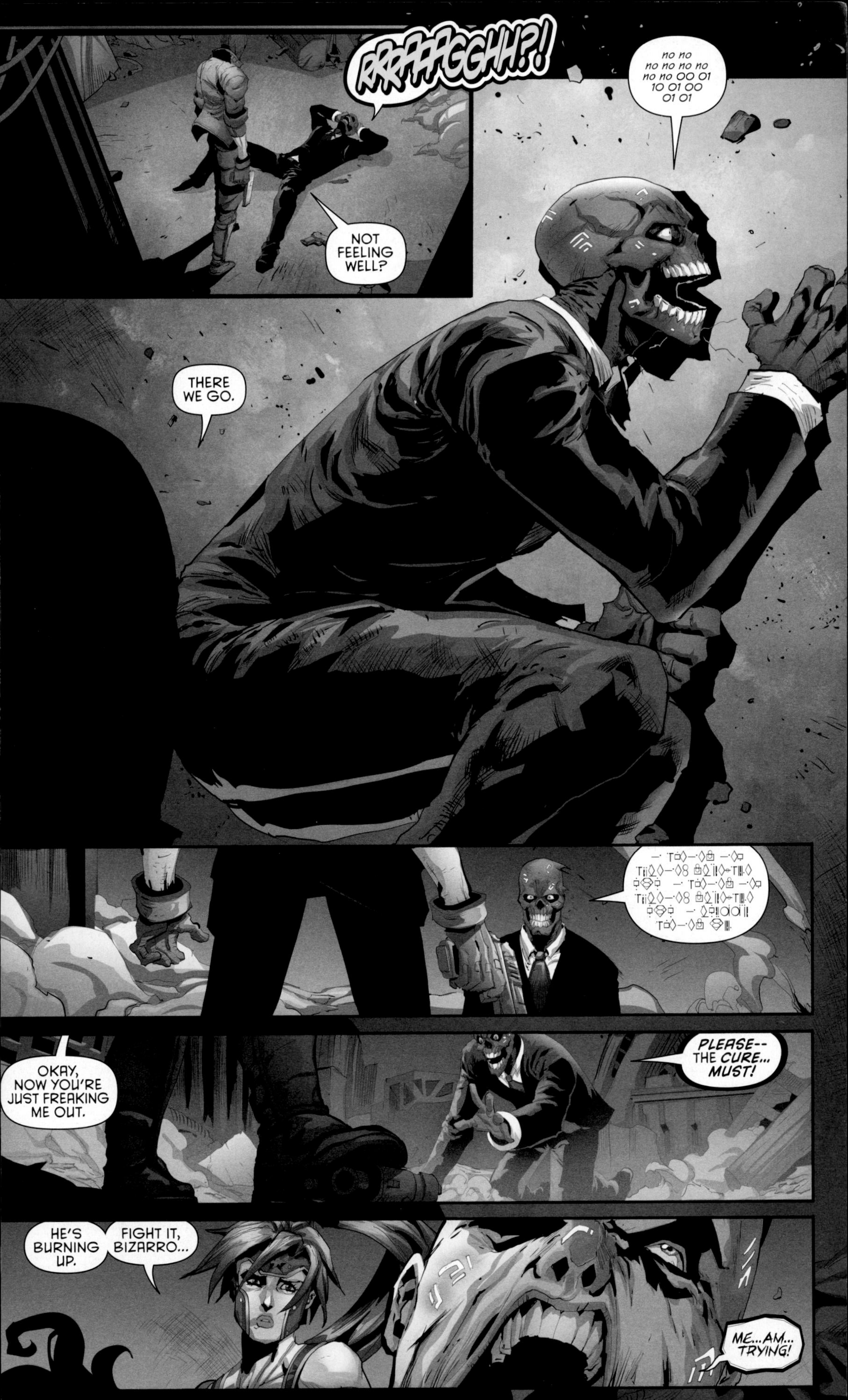
RRRAAAGGHH?!
NOT FEELING WELL?
no no no no no no no no OO 01 10 01 00 01 01
THERE WE GO.
OKAY, NOW YOU'RE JUST FREAKING ME OUT.
PLEASE-- THE CURE... MUST!
HE'S BURNING UP.
FIGHT IT, BIZARRO...
ME...AM... TRYING!

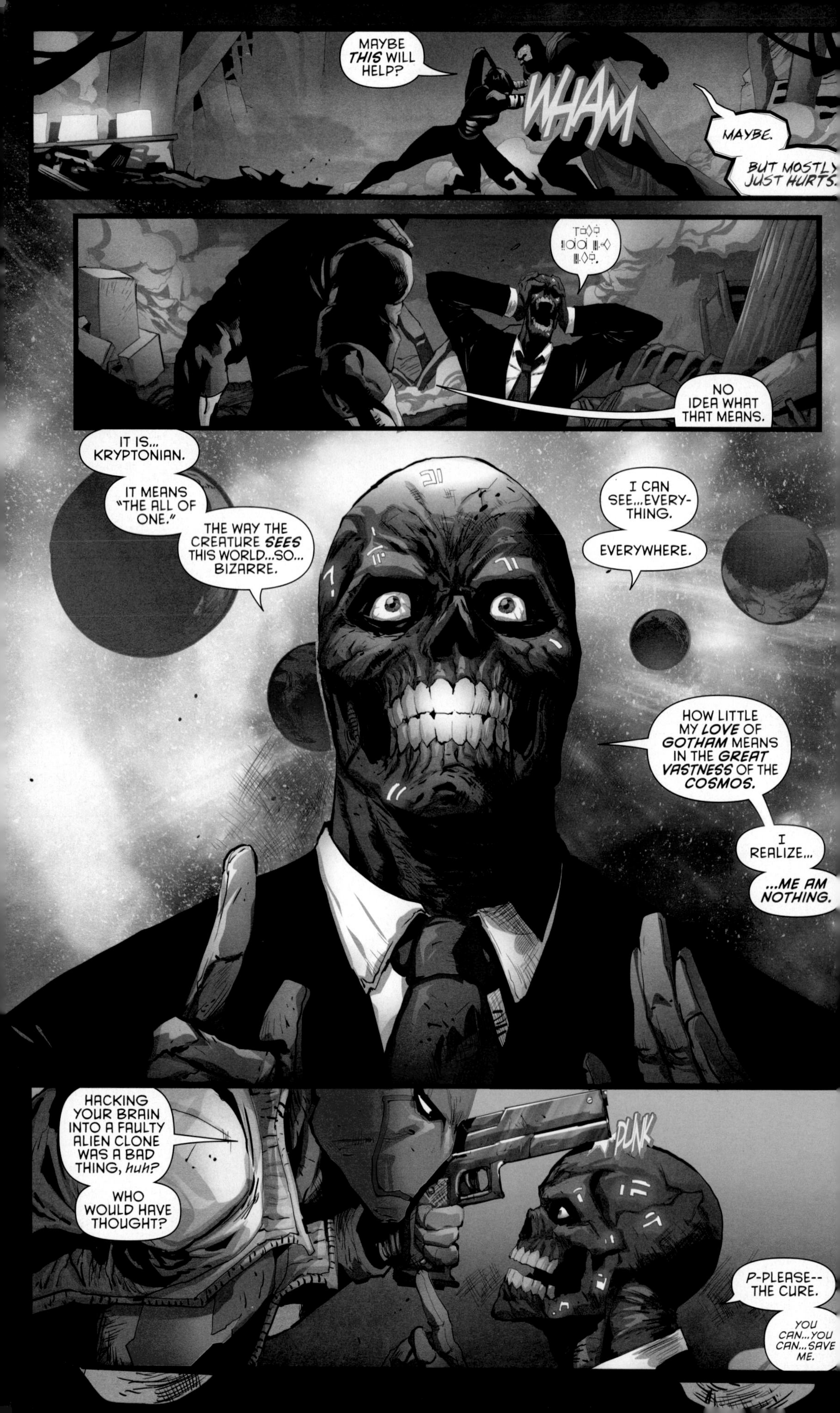
MAYBE *THIS* WILL HELP?
WHAM
MAYBE.
BUT MOSTLY JUST HURTS.
NO IDEA WHAT THAT MEANS.
IT IS... KRYPTONIAN.
IT MEANS "THE ALL OF ONE."
THE WAY THE CREATURE *SEES* THIS WORLD...SO... BIZARRE.
I CAN SEE...EVERY-THING.
EVERYWHERE.
HOW LITTLE MY *LOVE* OF *GOTHAM* MEANS IN THE *GREAT VASTNESS* OF THE *COSMOS.*
I REALIZE...
...ME AM NOTHING.
HACKING YOUR BRAIN INTO A FAULTY ALIEN CLONE WAS A BAD THING, *huh?*
WHO WOULD HAVE THOUGHT?
PUNK
P-PLEASE-- THE CURE.
YOU CAN...YOU CAN...SAVE ME.

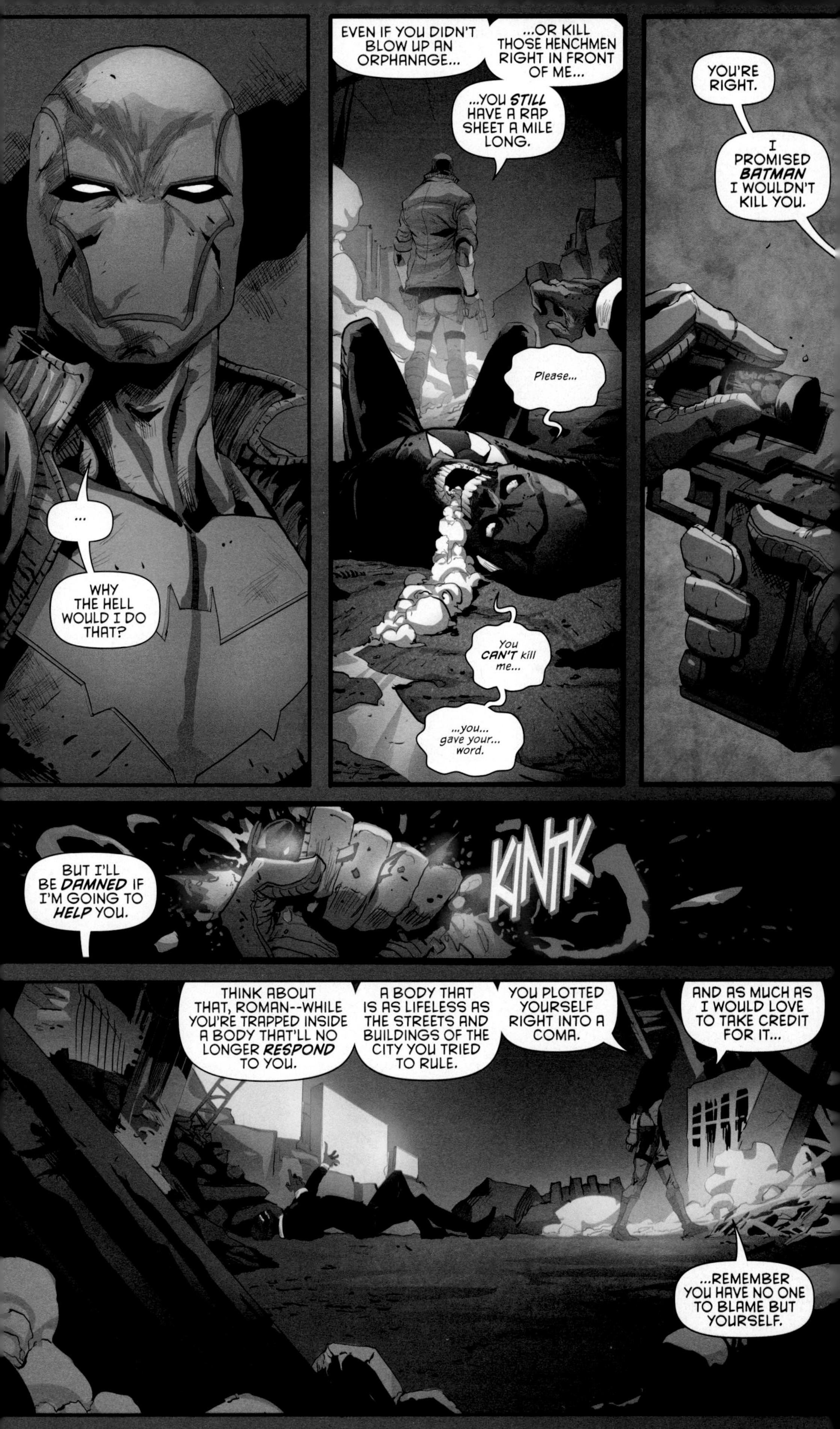
...
WHY THE HELL WOULD I DO THAT?
EVEN IF YOU DIDN'T BLOW UP AN ORPHANAGE...
...OR KILL THOSE HENCHMEN RIGHT IN FRONT OF ME...
...YOU STILL HAVE A RAP SHEET A MILE LONG.
Please...
You CAN'T kill me...
...you... gave your... word.
YOU'RE RIGHT.
I PROMISED BATMAN I WOULDN'T KILL YOU.
BUT I'LL BE DAMNED IF I'M GOING TO HELP YOU.
KINTK
THINK ABOUT THAT, ROMAN--WHILE YOU'RE TRAPPED INSIDE A BODY THAT'LL NO LONGER RESPOND TO YOU.
A BODY THAT IS AS LIFELESS AS THE STREETS AND BUILDINGS OF THE CITY YOU TRIED TO RULE.
YOU PLOTTED YOURSELF RIGHT INTO A COMA.
AND AS MUCH AS I WOULD LOVE TO TAKE CREDIT FOR IT...
...REMEMBER YOU HAVE NO ONE TO BLAME BUT YOURSELF.

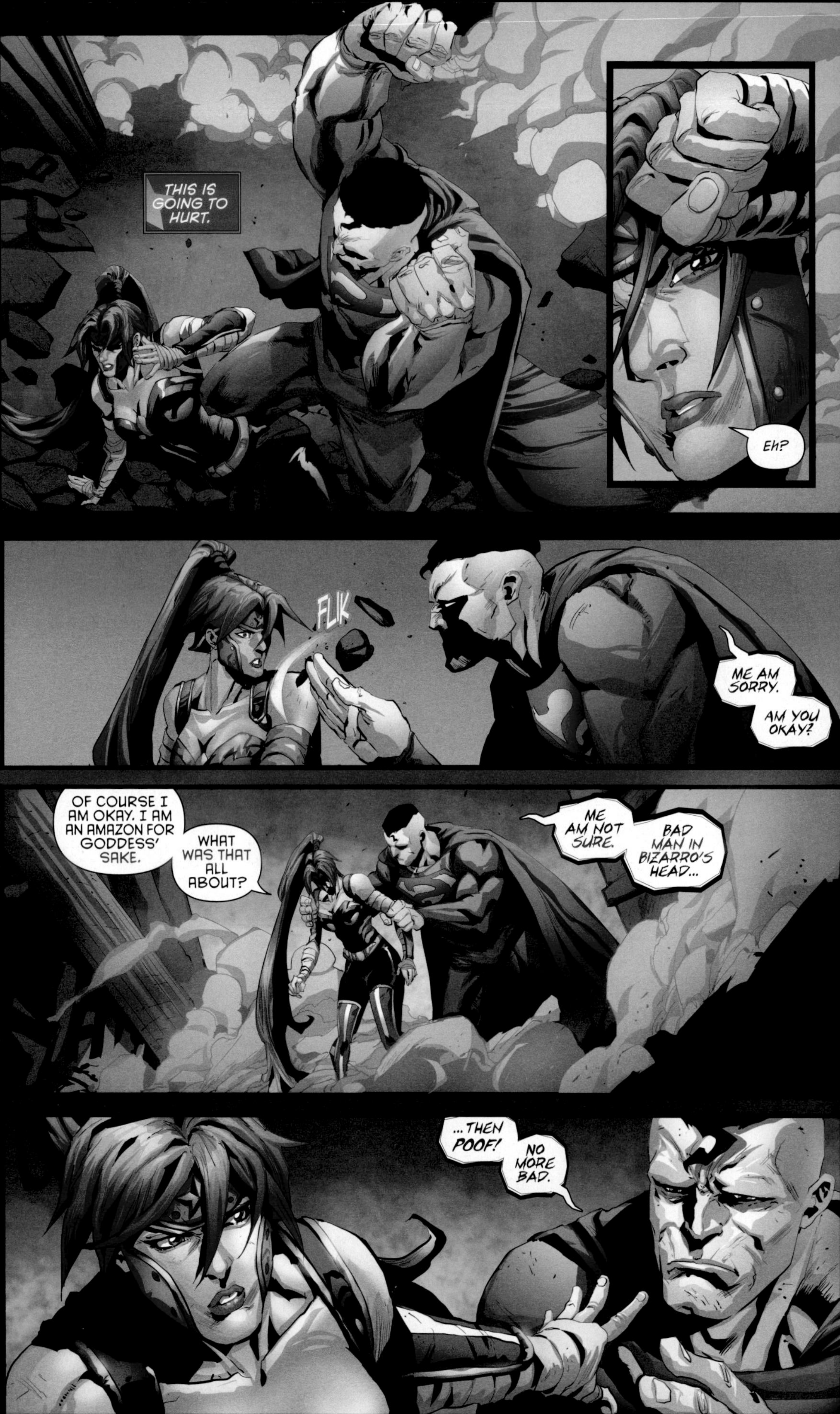
THIS IS GOING TO HURT.
Eh?
FLIK
ME AM SORRY.
AM YOU OKAY?
OF COURSE I AM OKAY. I AM AN AMAZON FOR GODDESS' SAKE.
WHAT WAS THAT ALL ABOUT?
ME AM NOT SURE.
BAD MAN IN BIZARRO'S HEAD...
...THEN POOF!
NO MORE BAD.

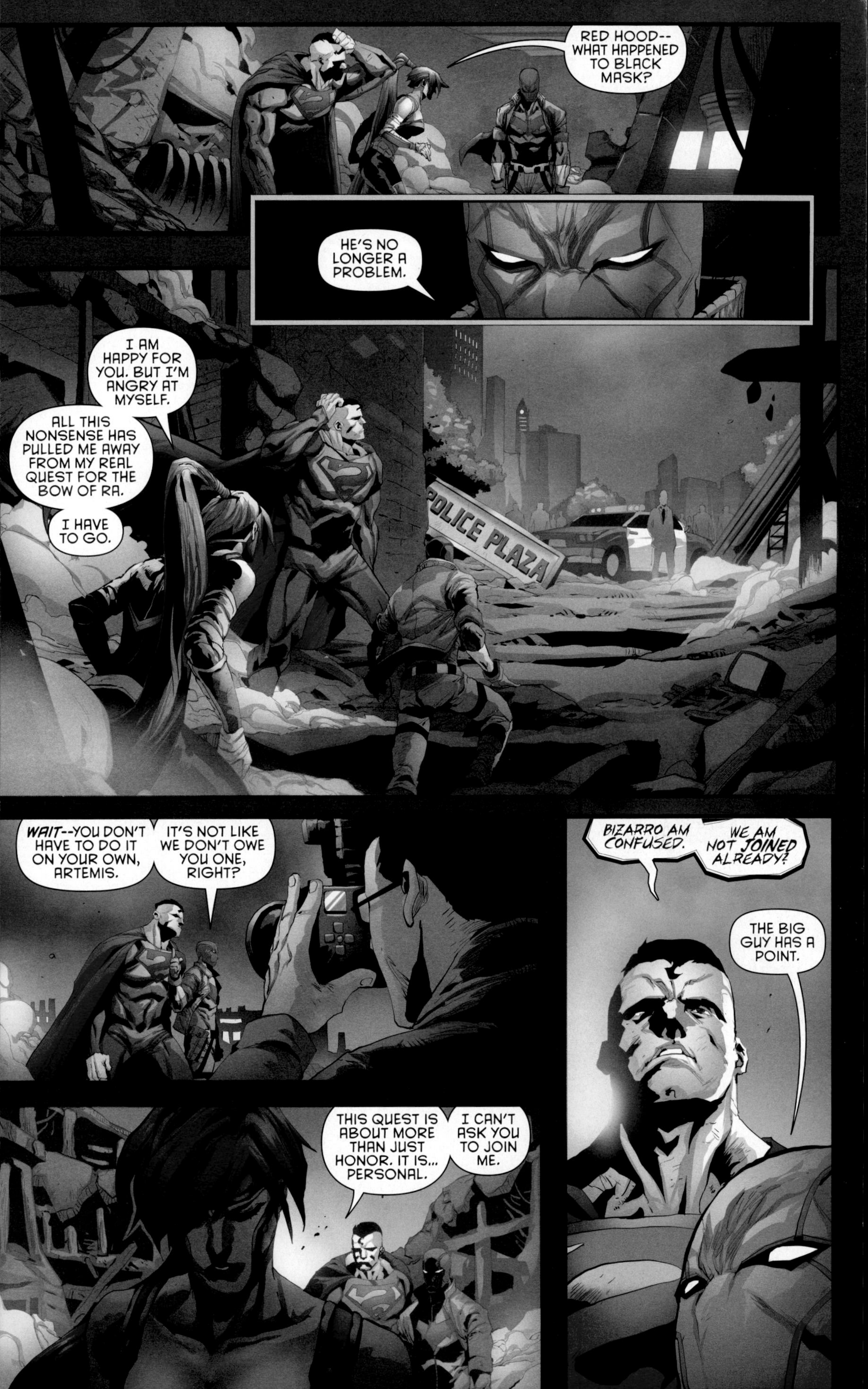
RED HOOD--WHAT HAPPENED TO BLACK MASK?
HE'S NO LONGER A PROBLEM.
I AM HAPPY FOR YOU. BUT I'M ANGRY AT MYSELF.
ALL THIS NONSENSE HAS PULLED ME AWAY FROM MY REAL QUEST FOR THE BOW OF RA.
I HAVE TO GO.
POLICE PLAZA
WAIT--YOU DON'T HAVE TO DO IT ON YOUR OWN, ARTEMIS.
IT'S NOT LIKE WE DON'T OWE YOU ONE, RIGHT?
THIS QUEST IS ABOUT MORE THAN JUST HONOR. IT IS... PERSONAL.
I CAN'T ASK YOU TO JOIN ME.
BIZARRO AM CONFUSED.
WE AM NOT JOINED ALREADY?
THE BIG GUY HAS A POINT.

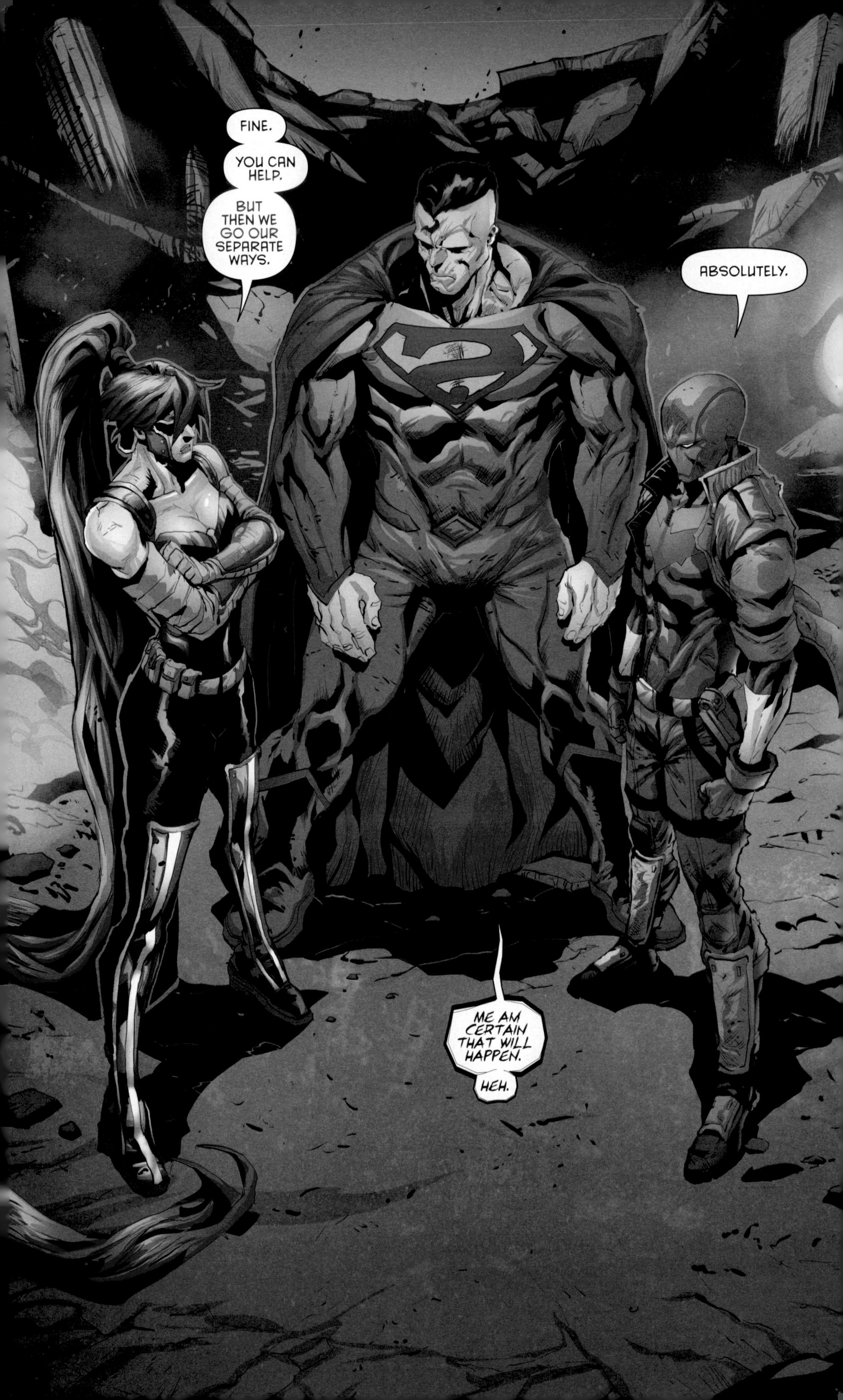
FINE.
YOU CAN HELP.
BUT THEN WE GO OUR SEPARATE WAYS.
ABSOLUTELY.
ME AM CERTAIN THAT WILL HAPPEN.
HEH.

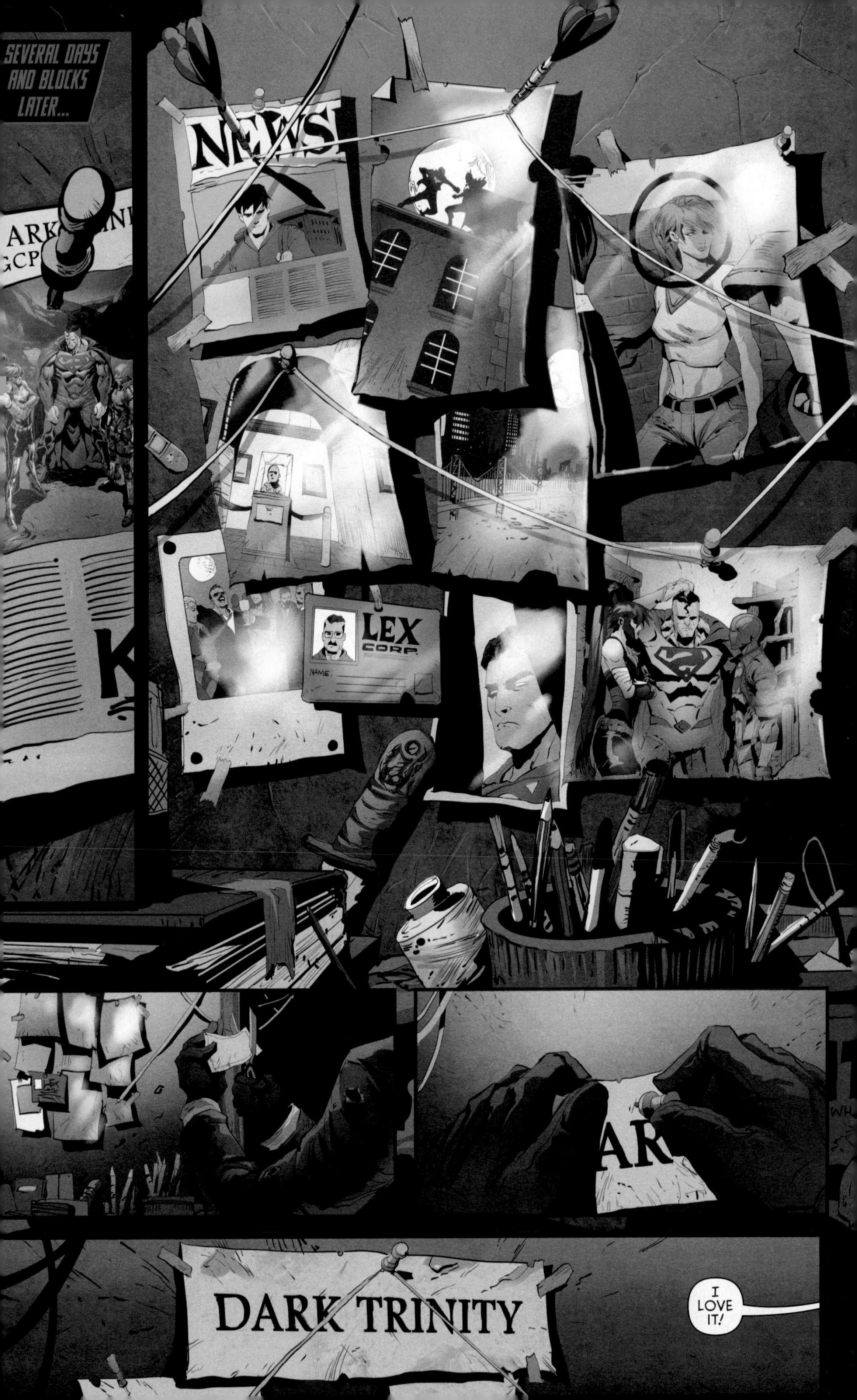
SEVERAL DAYS AND BLOCKS LATER...
NEWS
LEX CORP.
NAME
DARK TRINITY
I LOVE IT!

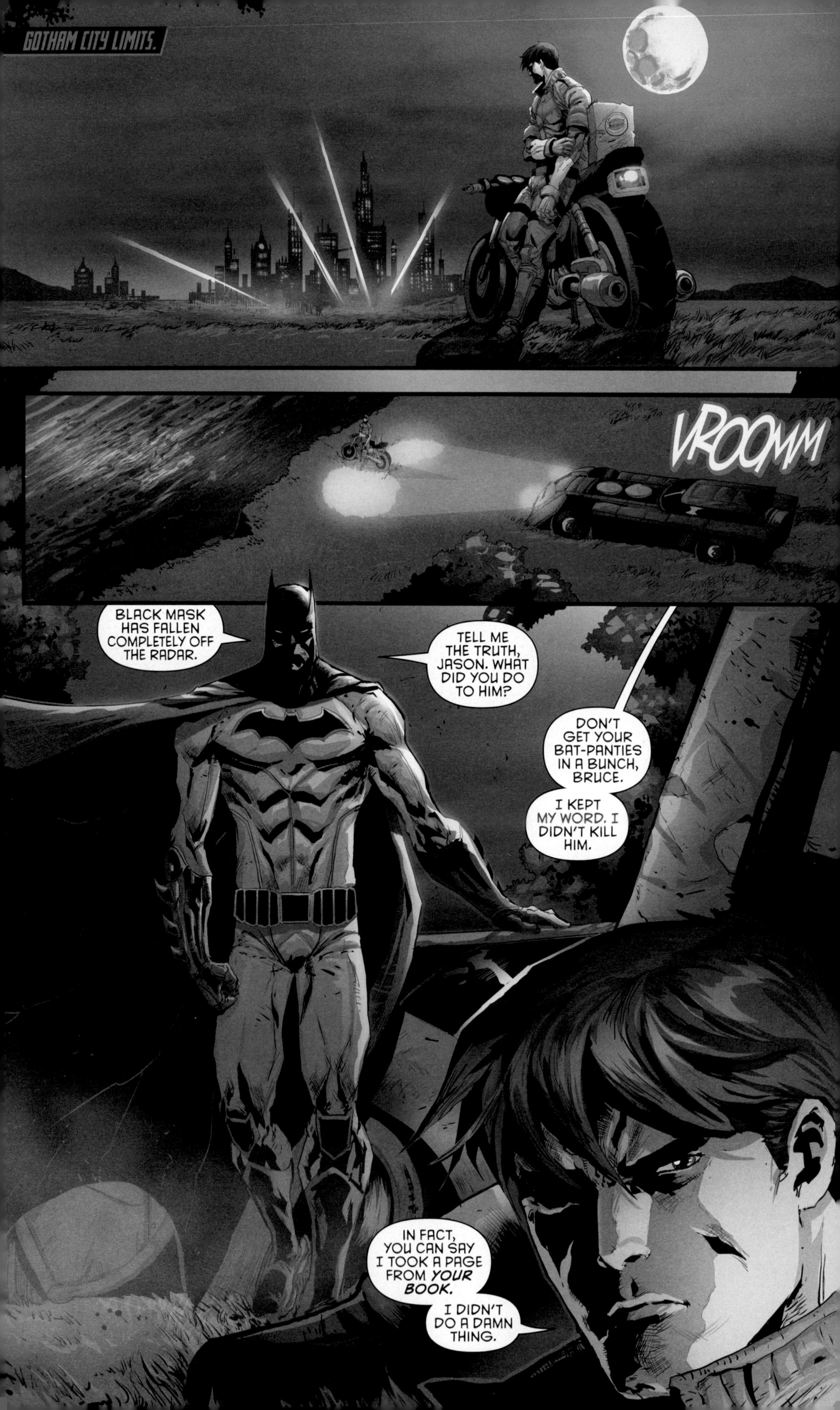
GOTHAM CITY LIMITS.
VROOMM
BLACK MASK HAS FALLEN COMPLETELY OFF THE RADAR.
TELL ME THE TRUTH, JASON. WHAT DID YOU DO TO HIM?
DON'T GET YOUR BAT-PANTIES IN A BUNCH, BRUCE.
I KEPT MY WORD. I DIDN'T KILL HIM.
IN FACT, YOU CAN SAY I TOOK A PAGE FROM YOUR BOOK.
I DIDN'T DO A DAMN THING.

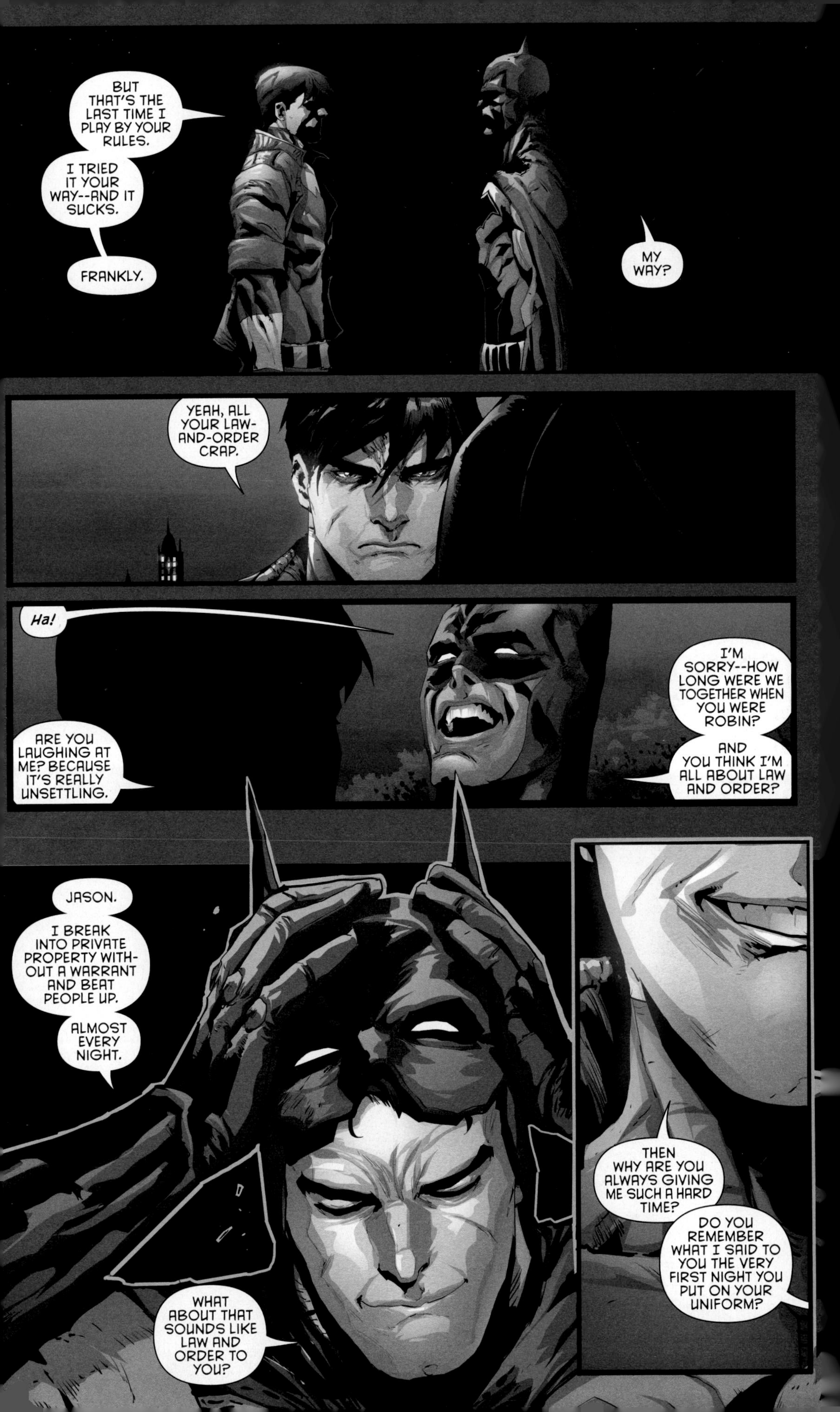

BUT THAT'S THE LAST TIME I PLAY BY YOUR RULES.
I TRIED IT YOUR WAY--AND IT SUCKS.
FRANKLY.
MY WAY?
YEAH, ALL YOUR LAW-AND-ORDER CRAP.
Ha!
ARE YOU LAUGHING AT ME? BECAUSE IT'S REALLY UNSETTLING.
I'M SORRY--HOW LONG WERE WE TOGETHER WHEN YOU WERE ROBIN?
AND YOU THINK I'M ALL ABOUT LAW AND ORDER?
JASON.
I BREAK INTO PRIVATE PROPERTY WITH-OUT A WARRANT AND BEAT PEOPLE UP.
ALMOST EVERY NIGHT.
WHAT ABOUT THAT SOUNDS LIKE LAW AND ORDER TO YOU?
THEN WHY ARE YOU ALWAYS GIVING ME SUCH A HARD TIME?
DO YOU REMEMBER WHAT I SAID TO YOU THE VERY FIRST NIGHT YOU PUT ON YOUR UNIFORM?

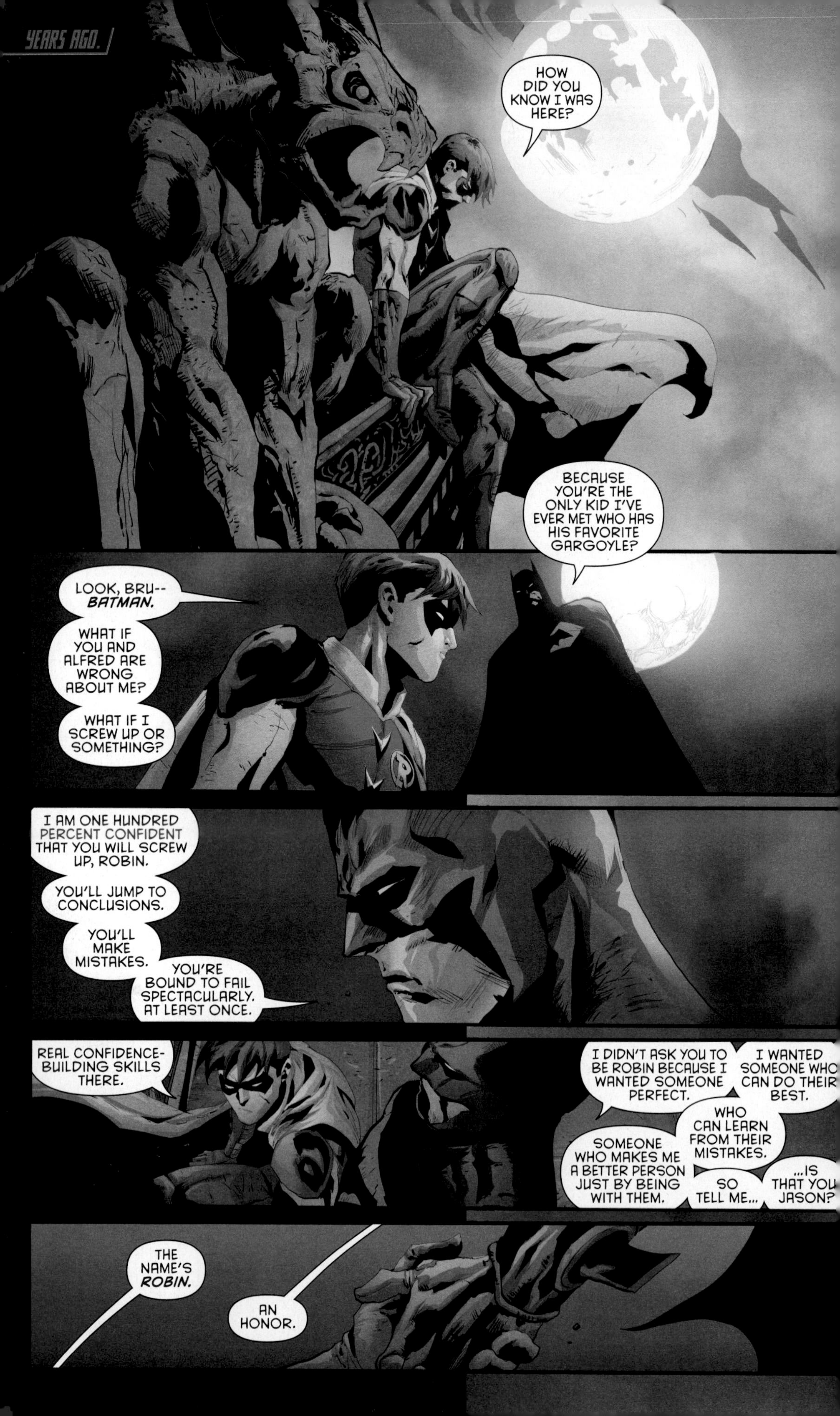
YEARS AGO.
HOW DID YOU KNOW I WAS HERE?
BECAUSE YOU'RE THE ONLY KID I'VE EVER MET WHO HAS HIS FAVORITE GARGOYLE?
LOOK, BRU-- BATMAN.
WHAT IF YOU AND ALFRED ARE WRONG ABOUT ME?
WHAT IF I SCREW UP OR SOMETHING?
I AM ONE HUNDRED PERCENT CONFIDENT THAT YOU WILL SCREW UP, ROBIN.
YOU'LL JUMP TO CONCLUSIONS.
YOU'LL MAKE MISTAKES.
YOU'RE BOUND TO FAIL SPECTACULARLY. AT LEAST ONCE.
REAL CONFIDENCE-BUILDING SKILLS THERE.
I DIDN'T ASK YOU TO BE ROBIN BECAUSE I WANTED SOMEONE PERFECT.
I WANTED SOMEONE WHO CAN DO THEIR BEST.
WHO CAN LEARN FROM THEIR MISTAKES.
SOMEONE WHO MAKES ME A BETTER PERSON JUST BY BEING WITH THEM.
SO TELL ME...
...IS THAT YOU JASON?
THE NAME'S ROBIN.
AN HONOR.

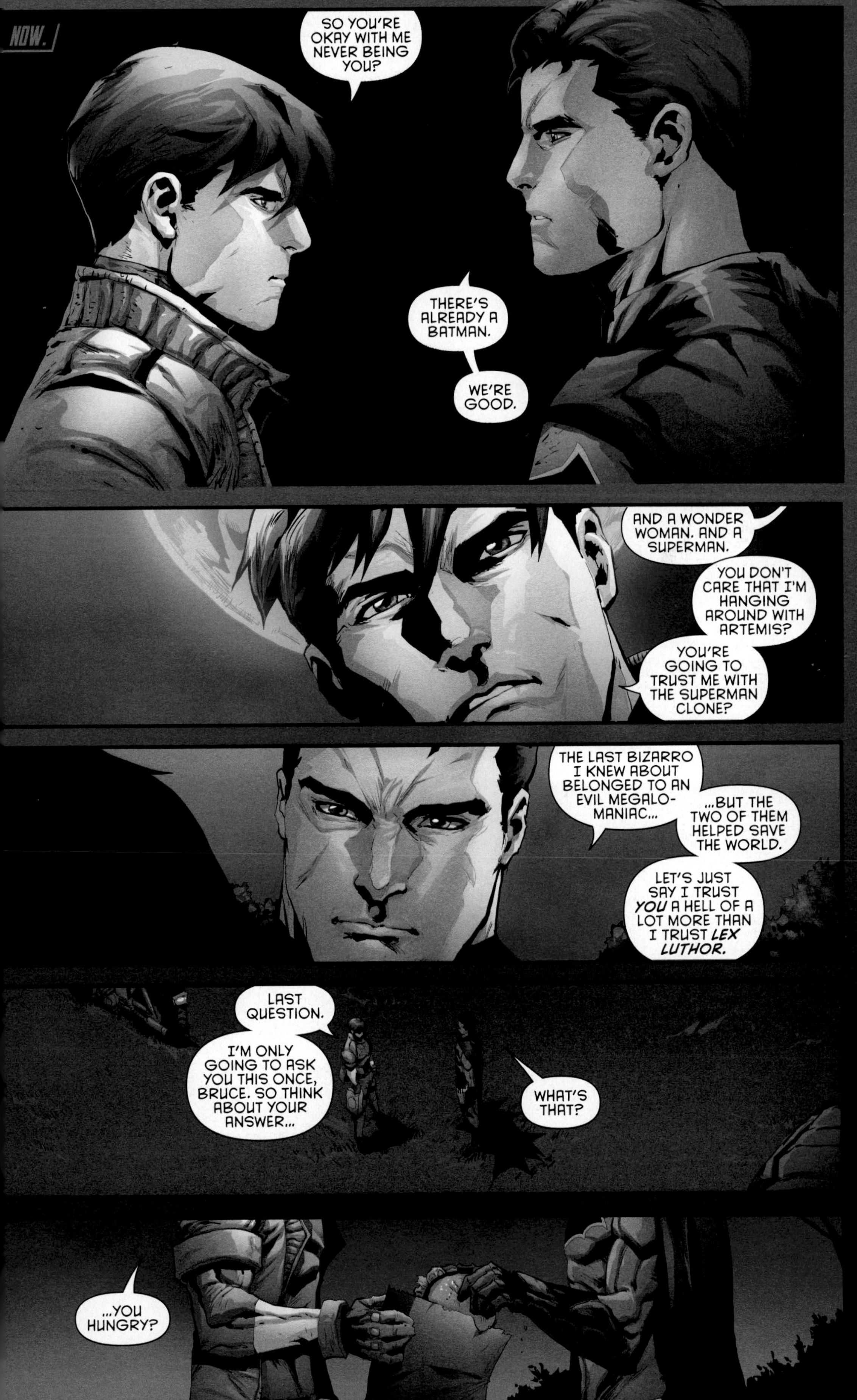
NOW.
SO YOU'RE OKAY WITH ME NEVER BEING YOU?
THERE'S ALREADY A BATMAN.
WE'RE GOOD.
AND A WONDER WOMAN. AND A SUPERMAN.
YOU DON'T CARE THAT I'M HANGING AROUND WITH ARTEMIS?
YOU'RE GOING TO TRUST ME WITH THE SUPERMAN CLONE?
THE LAST BIZARRO I KNEW ABOUT BELONGED TO AN EVIL MEGALO-MANIAC...
...BUT THE TWO OF THEM HELPED SAVE THE WORLD.
LET'S JUST SAY I TRUST *YOU* A HELL OF A LOT MORE THAN I TRUST *LEX LUTHOR.*
LAST QUESTION.
I'M ONLY GOING TO ASK YOU THIS ONCE, BRUCE. SO THINK ABOUT YOUR ANSWER...
WHAT'S THAT?
...YOU HUNGRY?

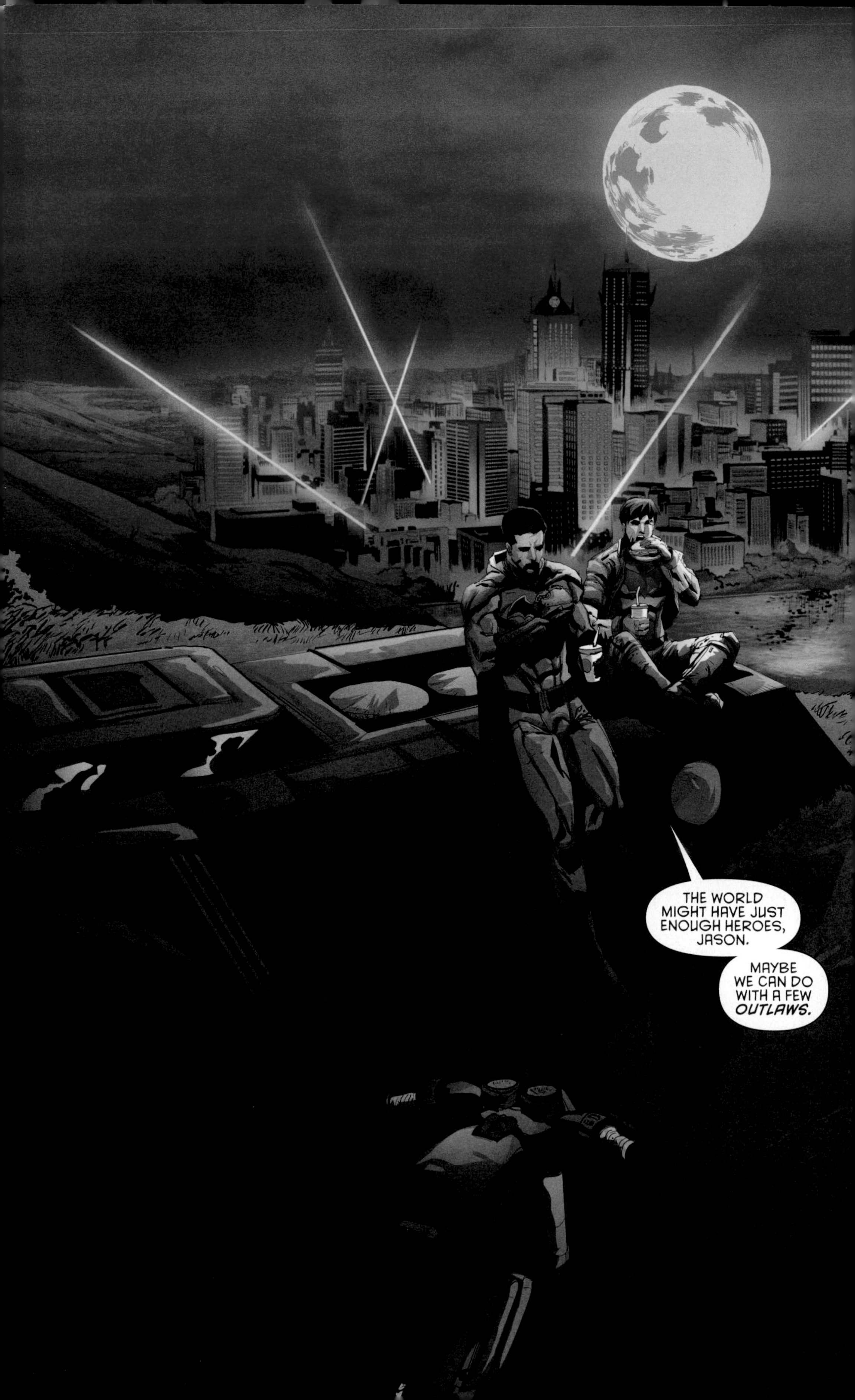
THE WORLD MIGHT HAVE JUST ENOUGH HEROES, JASON.
MAYBE WE CAN DO WITH A FEW *OUTLAWS.*

"BUT SERIOUSLY... WHERE *IS* ROMAN?"

MA GUNN'S HOME FOR THE CRIMINALLY IMPAIRED.

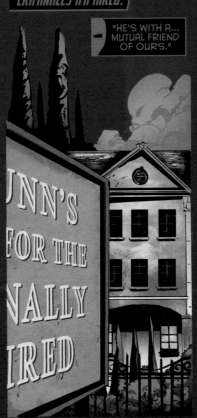
"HE'S WITH A... MUTUAL FRIEND OF OURS."

DOES MY LITTLE MAN WANT HIS *NOM NOMS?*

SO YUMMY.

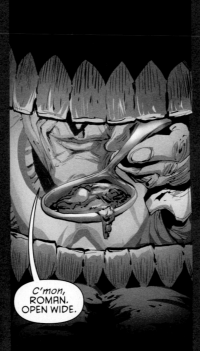
C'MON, ROMAN. OPEN WIDE.

THAT'S IT. THERE'S MY LITTLE MAN...

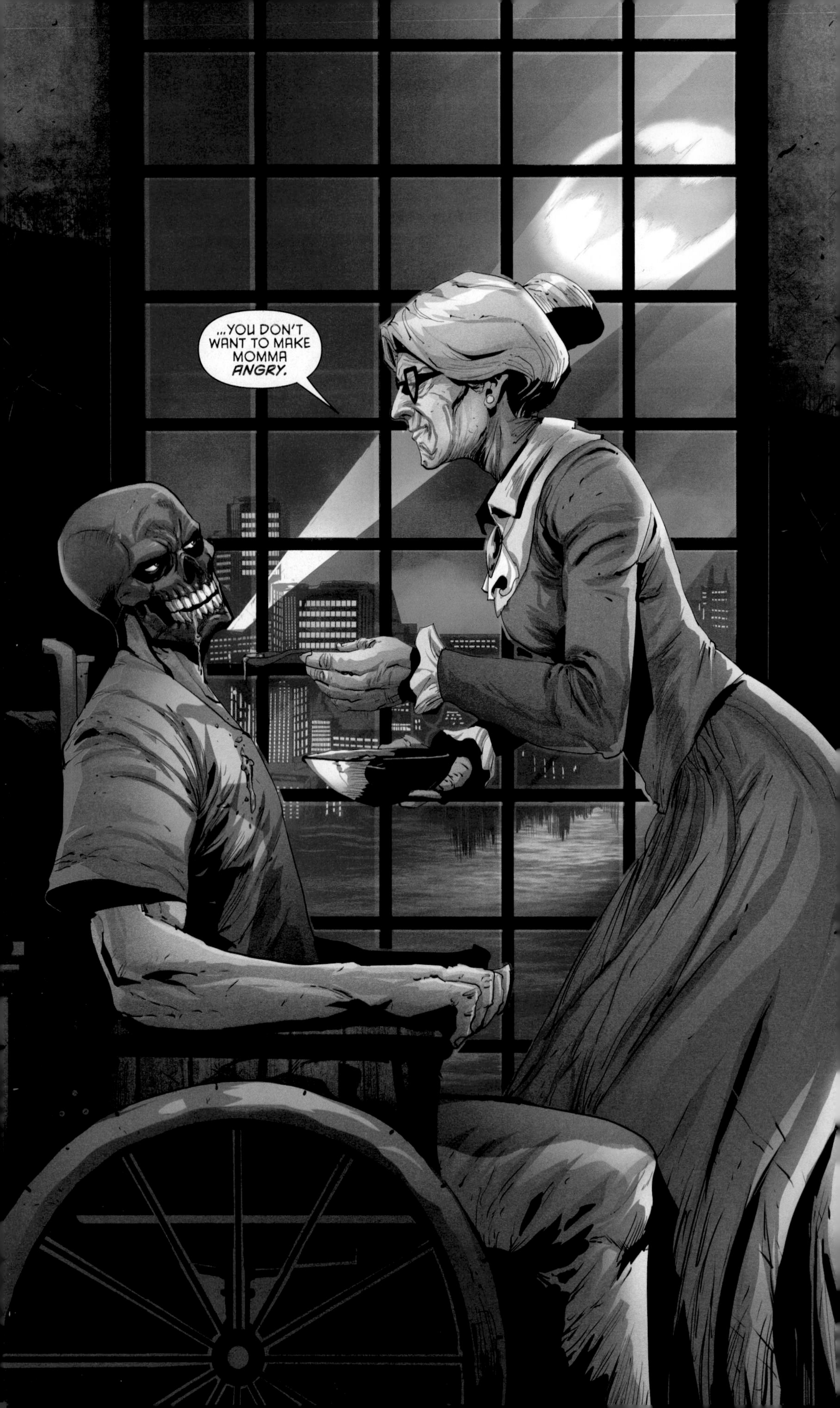
...YOU DON'T WANT TO MAKE MOMMA ANGRY.

RED HOOD AND THE OUTLAWS: REBIRTH #1 variant cover by BENGAL

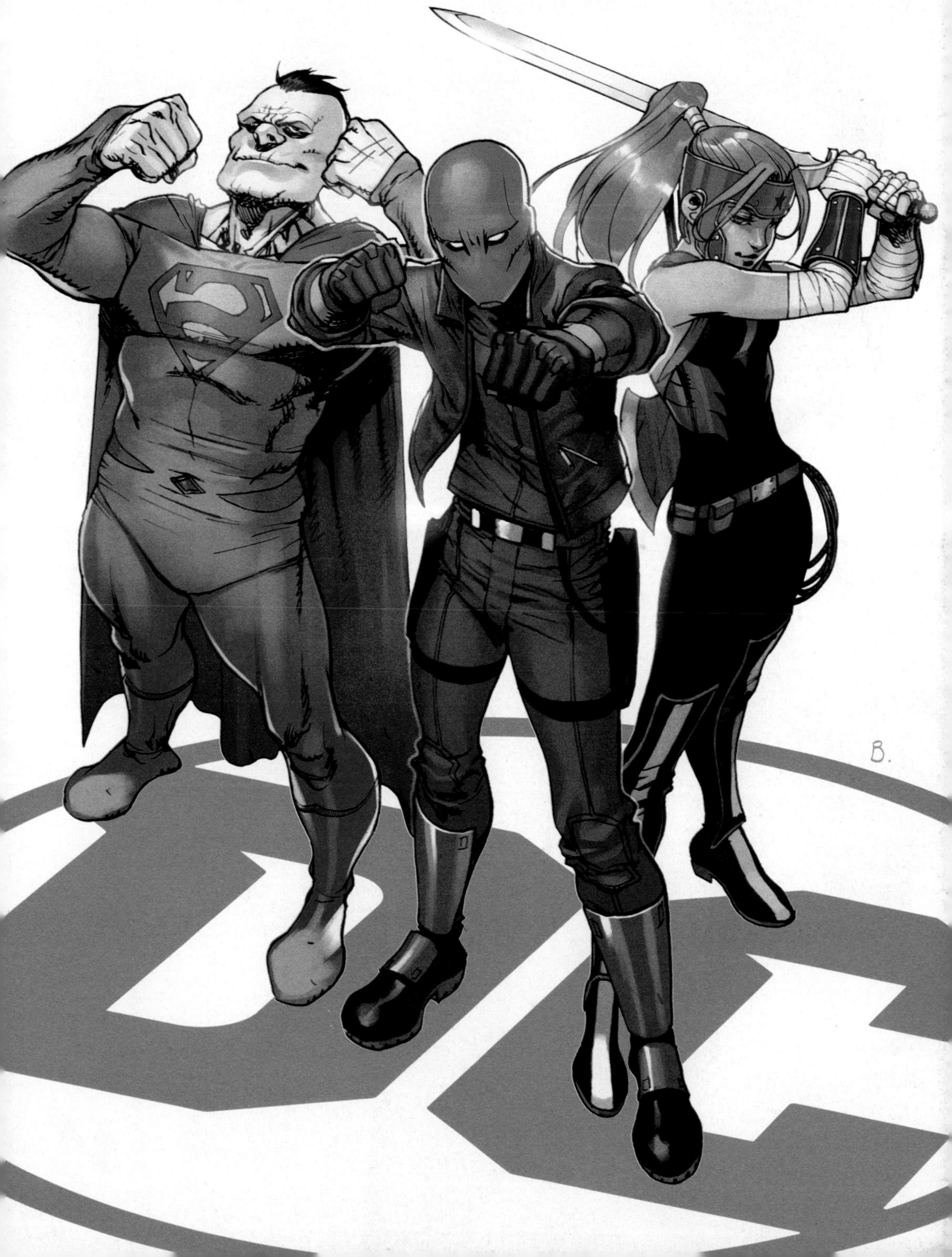
B.

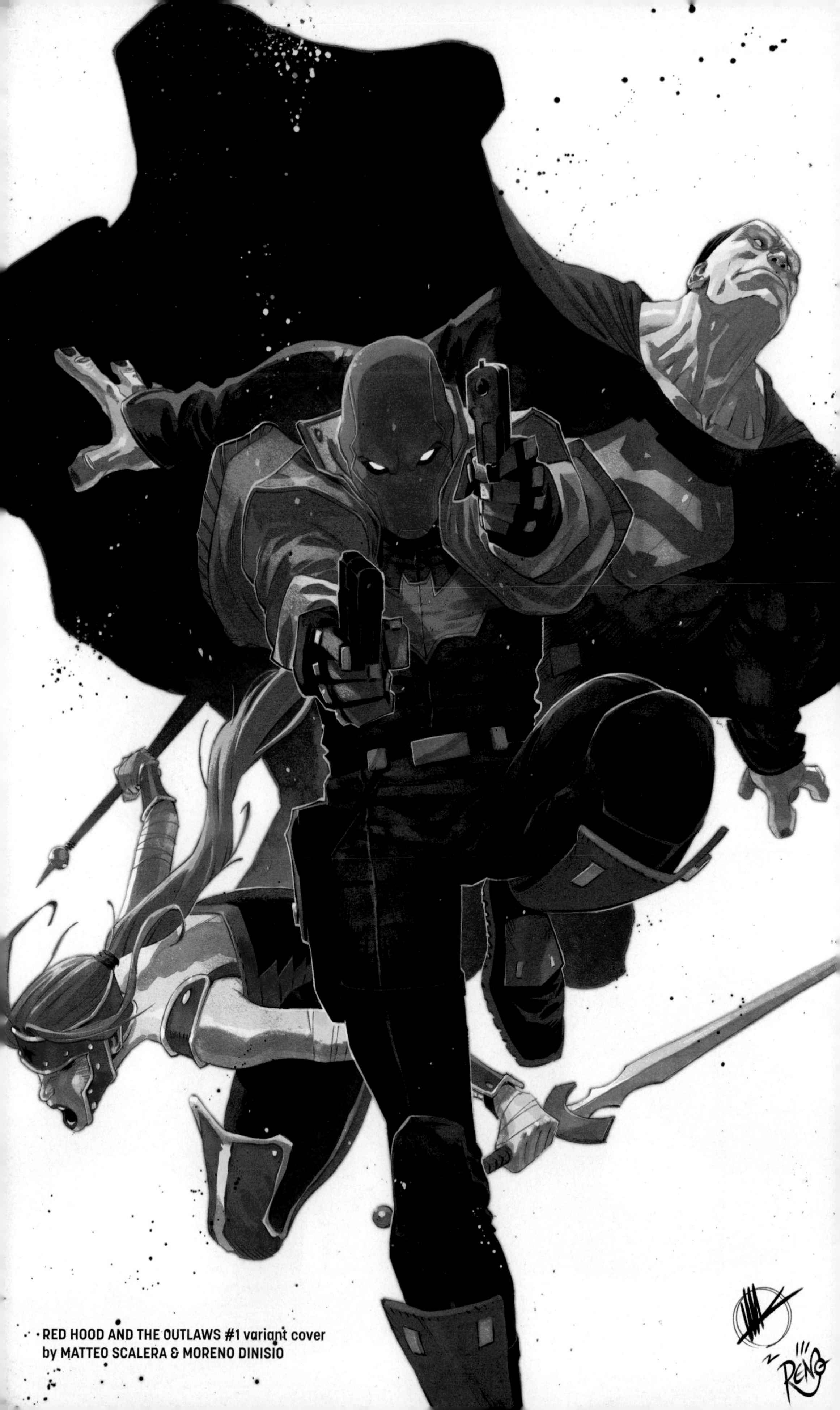

RED HOOD AND THE OUTLAWS #1 variant cover
by MATTEO SCALERA & MORENO DINISIO

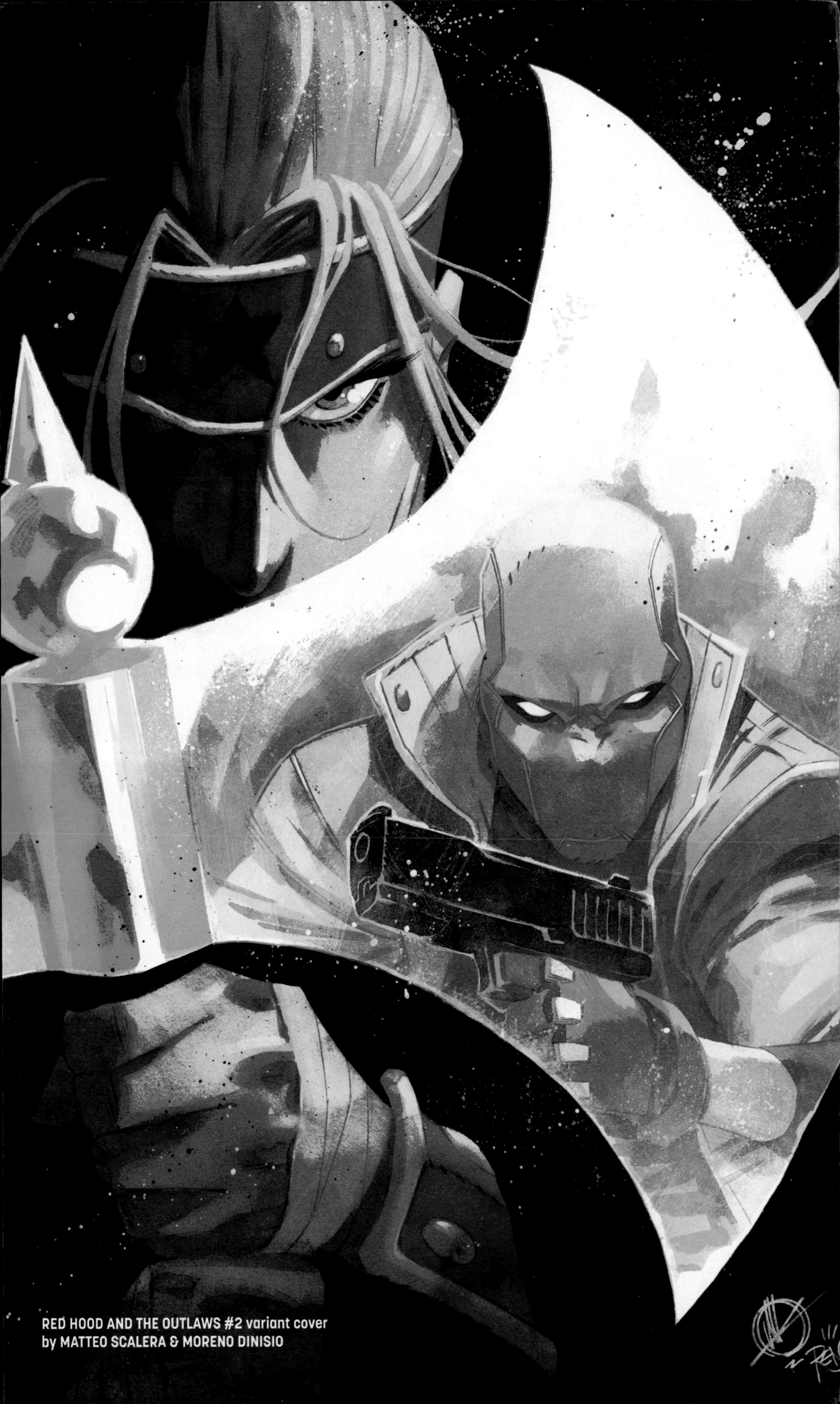

RED HOOD AND THE OUTLAWS #2 variant cover
by MATTEO SCALERA & MORENO DINISIO

RED HOOD AND THE OUTLAWS #3 variant cover
by MATTEO SCALERA & MORENO DINISIO

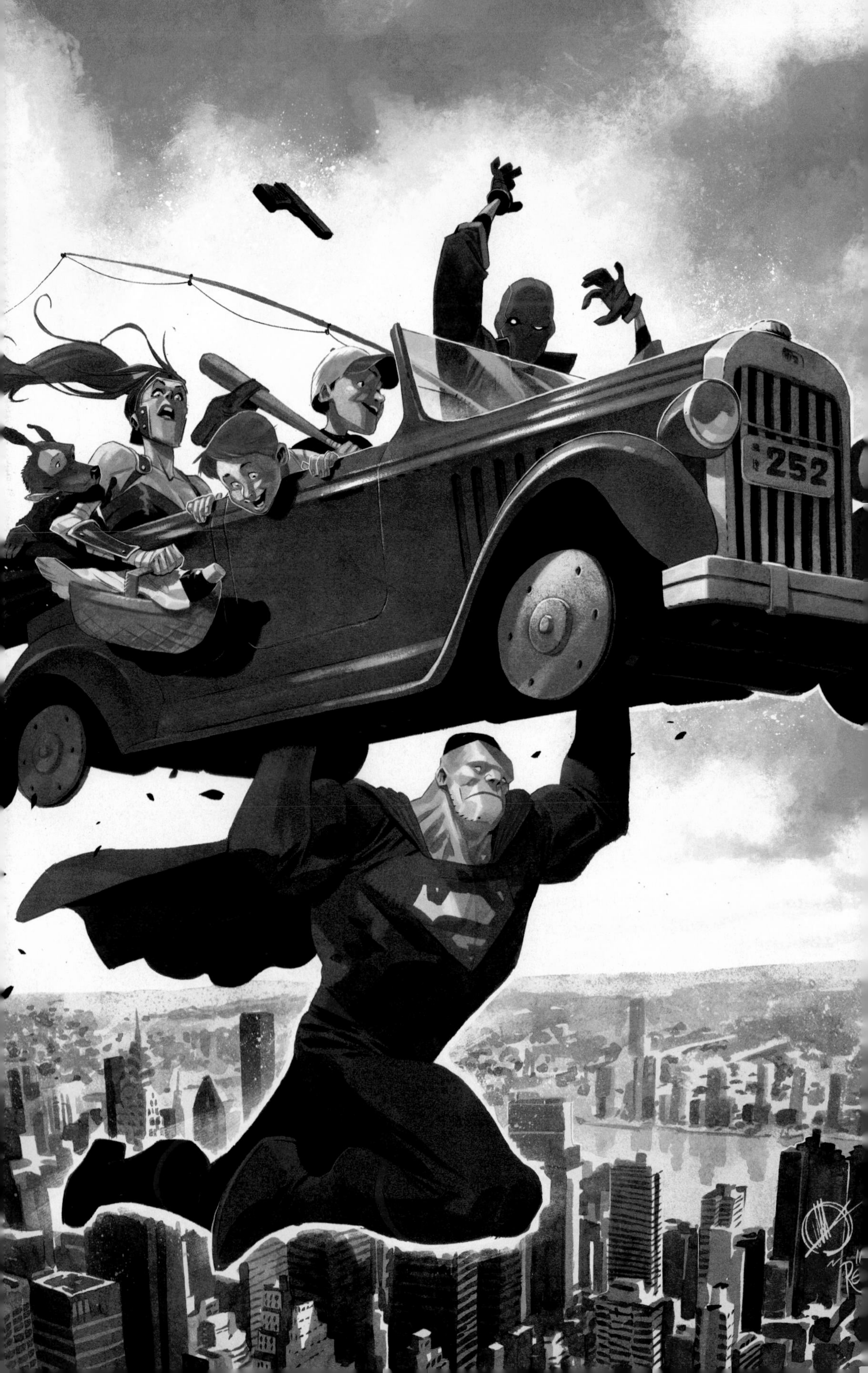
252

RED HOOD AND THE OUTLAWS #4 Variant Cover
by MATTEO SCALERA & MORENO DINISIO

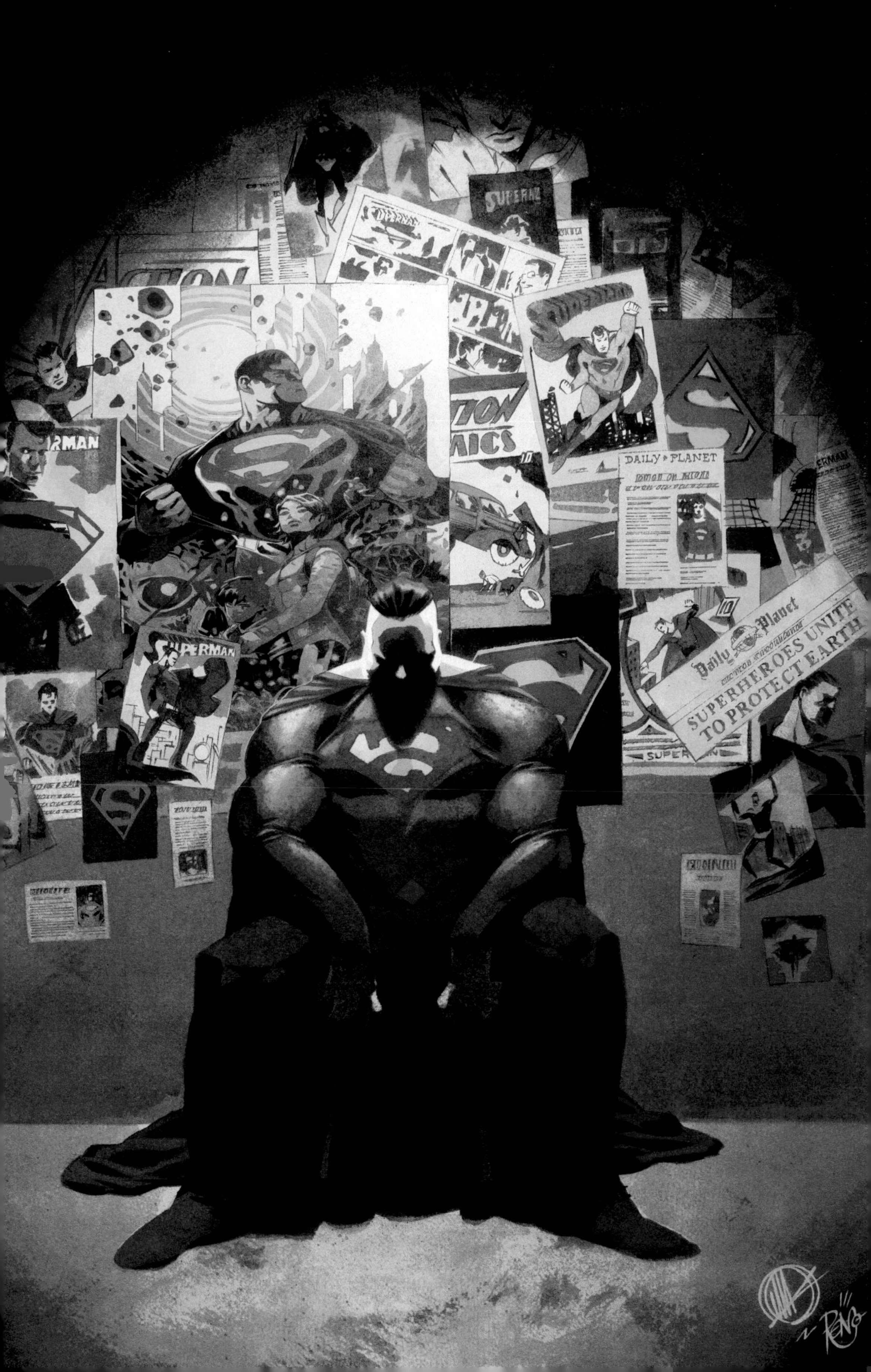
SUPERMAN
DAILY PLANET
Daily Planet
SUPERHEROES UNITE
TO PROTECT EARTH

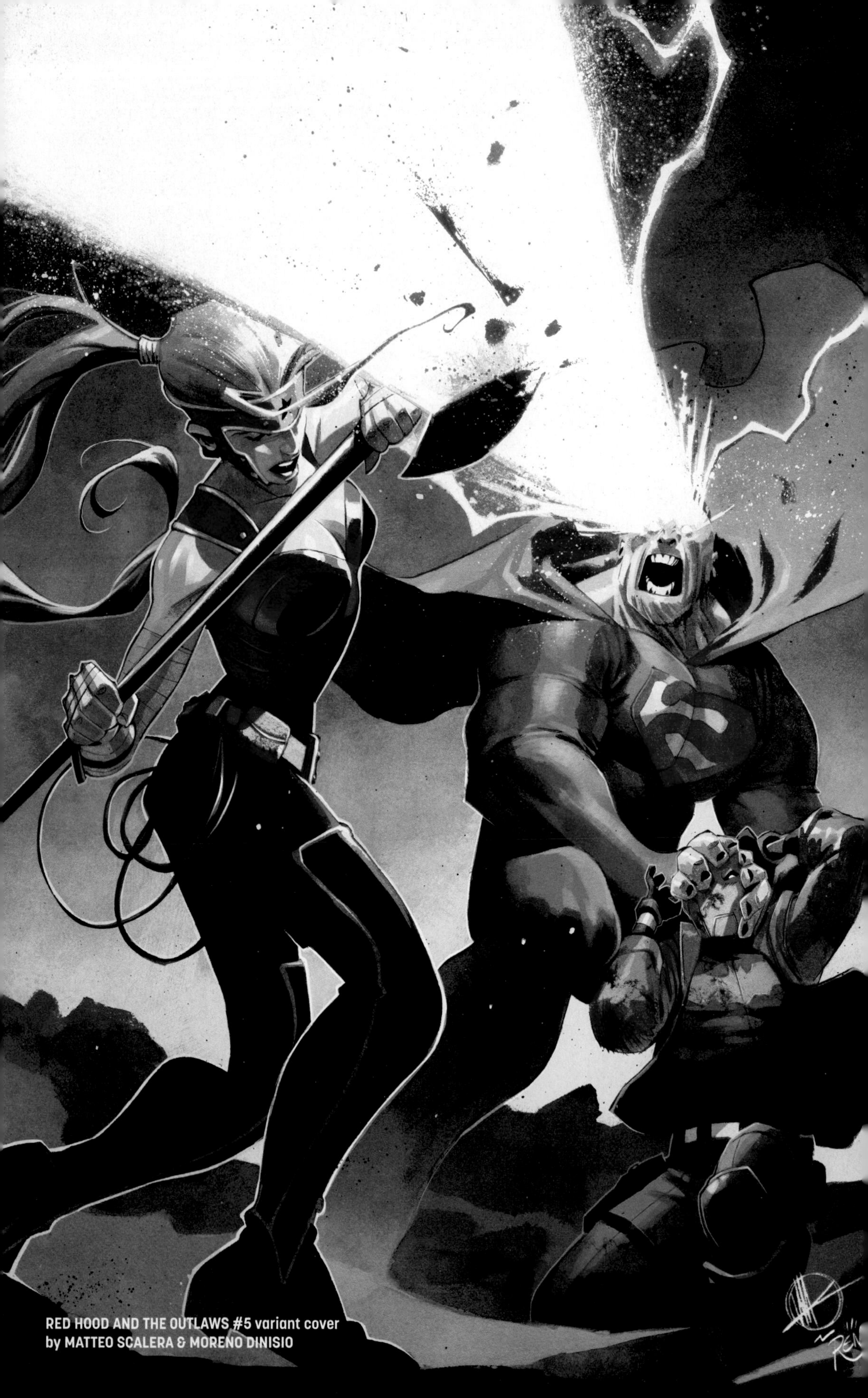

RED HOOD AND THE OUTLAWS #5 variant cover
by MATTEO SCALERA & MORENO DINISIO

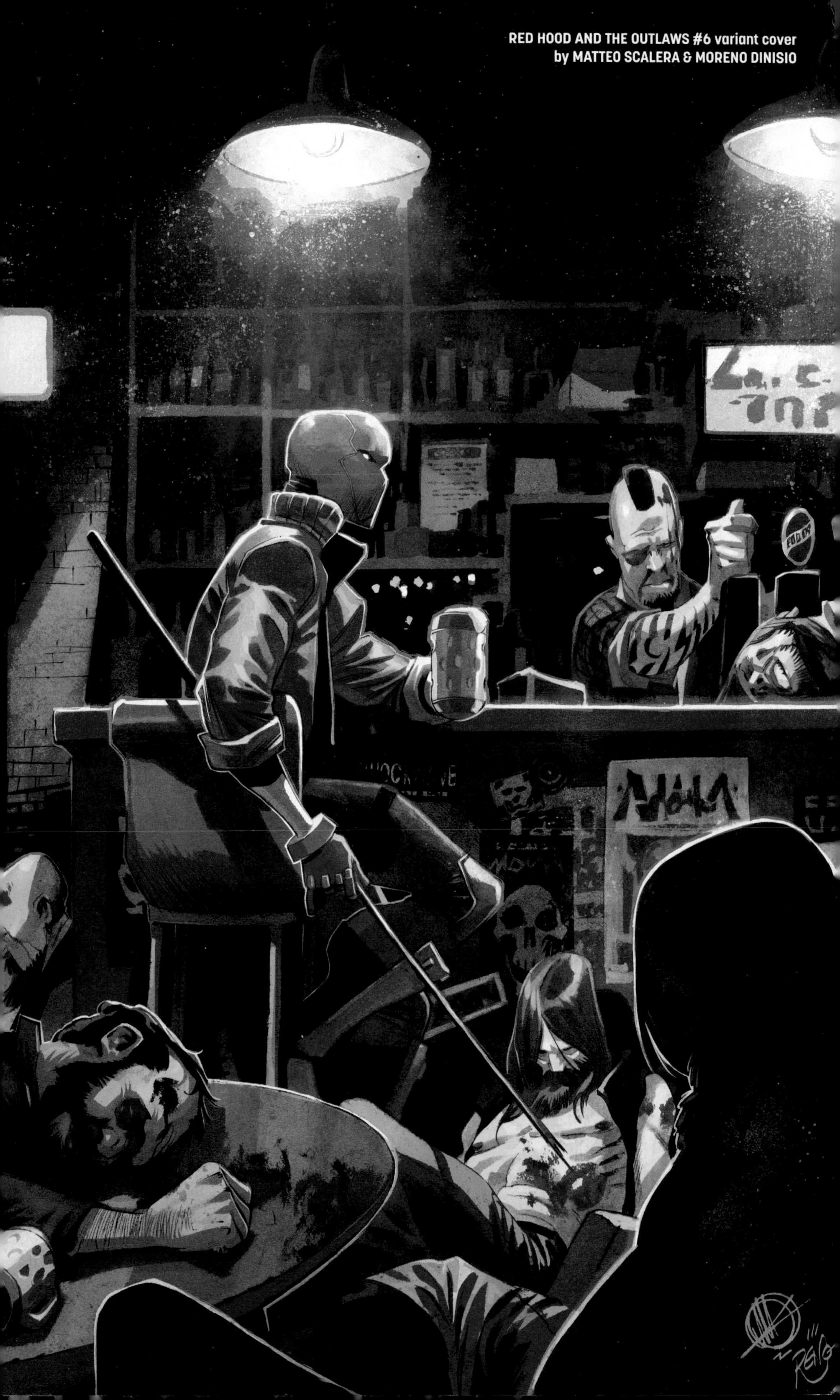

RED HOOD AND THE OUTLAWS #6 variant cover
by MATTEO SCALERA & MORENO DINISIO

"It's nice to see one of the best comics of the late '80s return so strongly."
– **Comic Book Resources**

"It's high energy from page one through to the last page." – **BATMAN NEWS**

DC UNIVERSE REBIRTH

SUICIDE SQUAD

VOL. 1: THE BLACK VAULT

ROB WILLIAMS
with JIM LEE and others

VOL.1 THE BLACK VAULT
ROB WILLIAMS • JIM LEE • PHILIP TAN • JASON FABOK • IVAN REIS • GARY FRANK

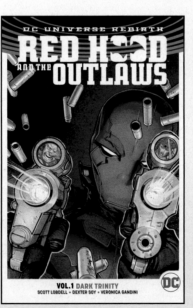

"A pretty irresistible hook..."
– THE ONION A.V. CLUB

"A CLEVERLY WRITTEN, OUTSTANDING READ FROM BEGINNING TO END." – USA TODAY
THE NEW 52!
SUICIDE SQUAD
VOLUME 1 KICKED IN THE TEETH
ADAM GLASS FEDERICO DALLOCCHIO CLAYTON HENRY

SUICIDE SQUAD

VOL. 1: KICKED IN THE TEETH

ADAM GLASS with
FEDERICO DALLOCCHIO

THE NEW 52!
SUICIDE SQUAD
VOLUME 2 BASILISK RISING
ADAM GLASS FERNANDO DAGNINO

SUICIDE SQUAD
VOL. 2: BASILISK RISING

THE NEW 52!
SUICIDE SQUAD
"A CLEVERLY WRITTEN, OUTSTANDING READ FROM BEGINNING TO END." – USA TODAY
VOLUME 3 DEATH IS FOR SUCKERS
DEADSHOT
ADAM GLASS HENRIK JONSSON SANDU FLOREA

SUICIDE SQUAD
VOL. 3: DEATH IS FOR SUCKERS

READ THE ENTIRE EPIC!

SUICIDE SQUAD VOL. 4:
DISCIPLINE AND PUNISH

SUICIDE SQUAD VOL. 5:
WALLED IN

"A cleverly written, outstanding read from beginning to end."
– USA TODAY

Get more DC graphic novels wherever comics and books are sold!

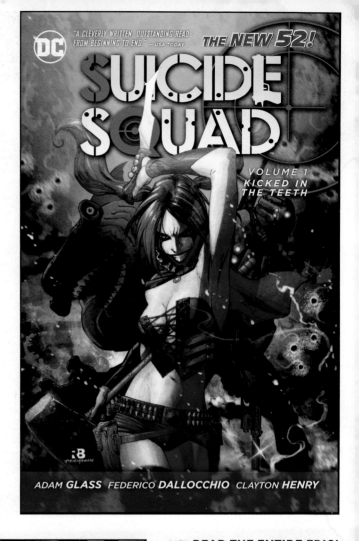

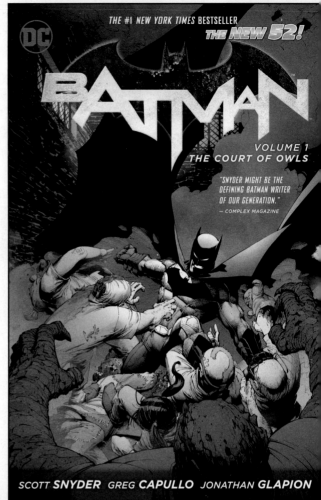
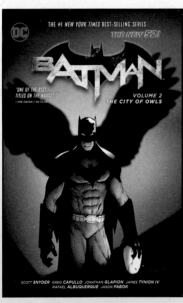
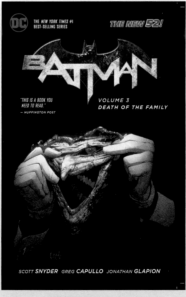